19世纪西方传教士编汉语方言词典

丛书主编　姚小平　姚喜明　　副主编　杨文波

英 粤 字 典

An English and Cantonese Dictionary

［英］湛约翰（John Chalmers）　编著

罗　琼　张晓芬　姚喜明　杨文波　校注

侯兴泉　审订

上海大学出版社

图书在版编目(CIP)数据

英粤字典/(英)湛约翰编著;姚喜明等校注.--上海:上海大学出版社,2019.1

(19世纪西方传教士编汉语方言词典/姚小平,姚喜明主编)

ISBN 978-7-5671-3380-8

I.①英… II.①湛… ②姚…III.①粤语-方言词典-广东-近代 IV.①H178-61

中国版本图书馆CIP数据核字(2018)第299810号

本书由上海文化发展基金会图书出版专项基金、上大社·锦珂优秀图书出版基金资助出版

书　　　名	英粤字典
编　　　著	[英]湛约翰(John Chalmers)编著
校　　　注	罗琼　张晓芬　姚喜明　杨文波
审　　　订	侯兴泉
责 任 编 辑	陈强
装 帧 设 计	柯国富
技 术 编 辑	金鑫　钱宇坤
出 版 发 行	上海大学出版社
社　　　址	上海市上大路99号
邮 政 编 码	200444
网　　　址	http://www.shupress.cn
发 行 热 线	021-66135112
出 版 人	戴骏豪
印　　　刷	江苏凤凰数码印务有限公司
经　　　销	各地新华书店
开　　　本	787mm×1092mm　1/16
印　　　张	20
字　　　数	400千
版　　　次	2019年2月第1版
印　　　次	2019年2月第1次
定　　　价	118.00元
书　　　号	ISBN 978-7-5671-3380-8/H·362

"19世纪西方传教士编汉语方言词典"

编委会

主　编　姚小平　姚喜明

副主编　杨文波

编　委　姚小平　游汝杰　薛才德
　　　　陶飞亚　姚喜明　杨文波

总　序

中西语言学传统各有所长：西方长于语法，中国长于辞书。公元前1世纪，希腊语文学者色雷克氏便撰成《语法术》，对本族语的语法体系做了分析，整理出名、动、代、介等八大词类。约在同一时期，中国人有了第一部语文词典《尔雅》，分19个义组及语类，收列词汇并作解释。《尔雅》被奉为十三经之一，足见古人对词典的看重。两汉有《方言》《急就篇》《说文解字》《释名》，或搜辑方言词语，或意在教人识字，或系统梳理文字，或以阐释词源为旨——这种以辞书服务于语文教学进而带动语言文字研究的繁荣景象，在同时期的罗马帝国是绝对看不到的。这些辞书当中，尤其值得一提的是《说文解字》，它是第一部严格意义上的字典，所发明的部首析字和检索法一直沿用至今。之后的发展不烦细述，总之辞书越出越多，到了明末传教士来华，一方面发现中国人没有语法书，觉得不可思议，以为是中国学术的一大缺憾；另一方面，看到中国辞书种类奇多，代代传承而编纂有方，则不能不大为叹服。

外国人学习和教授汉语，尤其需要了解它的语法体系，把握它的运作规则。由于没有现成的中国语法书可用，传教士必须自力更生，花大力气编写汉语语法书。此时，欧洲传统的语法学范畴、概念、分析方法等便开始发挥作用，颇能供传教士编撰汉语语法书借力。当然坏处也在这里，即常为今人诟病的套用。然而词典不同。词典中国人有的是，传教士虽然不能拿来就用而得自编，但因为有中国本土词典当作样本，从整体框架、编纂路数到字词条目的设立和释义，都可以参考利用，于是就能省力许多；甚至直接就拿本土词典（如明末清初畅行的《字汇》)当母本,把其上的字条悉数或者挑选一部分译成西文,便算是编成了一部西洋汉语词典,也就是汉欧双语词典。这样的汉欧词典,常见的编排方式有两种:一种采用中国传统的部首笔画法,一种采用音序法。后者又分中式的和西式的:中式的,即按中国韵书如《广韵》上所见的韵类编排;西式的,即根据拉丁注音,按字母的顺序排列。用作检索的方法,部首法和音序法各有便利与不便,所以,有些考虑周全的编纂者会为部首词典配上一个音序检索表;反过来也一样,音序词典的后面经常附有部首检字表。这说的是汉欧词典,以汉语字词立条,用欧语诠释意义。如果是欧汉词典,用欧语的词目立条,以带出汉语对应词,则一般就采用西式的音序法。

早期传教士来中国,都是走海路,从华南口岸入境。入华之初,逗留于广东、福建等地,有些人就在那里播教而终其一生;有些人得以继续北上,抵达江浙、华北以及中国西部。而正是在粤、闽两省,方言问题较之其他省份更加突出:官话主要通行于公务人员、学者书生中间,日常生活中传教士们仍不得不面对难以听懂的方言土语。所以,在早期的西洋汉语词典上,官话与方言混杂的现象十分普遍;即便是万济国所编的西班牙语—汉语词典,明确题作《官话词汇》(*Francisco Varo. Vocabulario de la Lengua Mandarina.* 1679),也夹杂着许多闽方言的语词,其中有些可能是无意间混入的,有些则可能明知属于方言,而仍予以收录,只是没有说明而已。后来的词典家更倾向于区分,虽然也常把明显不属于官话的词语收进词典,但会刻意说明来源。这种把方言与官话分开处理的意识逐渐增强,至19世纪中期应中西交往大增之需,便终于促成了各种方言词典的产生。收于本系列的《上海方言词汇集》(1869)、《英粤字典》(1891)、《宁波方言字语汇解》(1876)、《西蜀方言》(1900)、《客英词典》(1905),就是其中较重要的五种;细分之,前三种为欧汉型,后两种则属于汉欧型。

中国古代不是没有记录方言的著述。两千年前,西汉扬雄便辑有《方言》,可以划归辞书之属。可惜之后的十多个世纪里,再也没有出现堪与扬雄之著比肩的同类作品。直到明清,似乎才有了起色:与一批搜辑俚言俗语的著作一道,出现了一些考索某一特定地区方言词语的专书,如明末李实的《蜀语》,康熙时毛奇龄的《越语肯綮录》,乾隆年间茹敦和的《越言释》以及胡文英的《吴下方言考》。这些方言书上所见的词条，从百余到近千不等，均为编著者出于个人偏好而选收，或多或少显露出猎奇之趣，其诠释则经常带有溯源或考据的目的。

对比之后，我们会发现西方传教士所编的方言词典很不一样：

一是使用拉丁字母注音，较准确地记录了当时汉语方言的实际音值；

二是为日常交际服务，着眼于听和说，更全面地收集了一种方言的普通词汇，包括大量常用的词组和短句；

三是载录了19世纪我国各口岸及商埠洞开以后进入汉语的大批西洋物名、西学概念、西语表达及其汉译。

对于今人考察中国近代方言发展史以及中西语言文化交通史，这批西洋汉语方言词典独具价值，非中国本土的任何方言著作所能取代。唯其种类颇多，本次组织重印并予注释的仅为其中的一小部分，期盼未来能有更多同类的著作，以这种具有研究性质的重刊本形式面世。

姚小平

2016年2月22日

出版说明

《英粤字典》（第6版）（An English and Cantonese Dictionary）由来自英国的传教士湛约翰（John Chalmers, 1825—1899）所著。

湛约翰早年毕业于阿伯丁大学（又译鸭巴甸大学, University of Aberdeen），1852年加入伦敦传道会（the London Missionary Society）成为苏格兰新教传教士。同年6月抵达香港，在英华书院（Anglo-Chinese College, Ying Wa College）教书，并负责英华书院印刷所的工作。1859—1879年间，担任香港与广州的新教传道站负责人，居留广州20年。在此期间，他编撰了《初学粤音切要》（A Chinese Phonetic Vocabulary, 1855）、《英粤字典》（An English and Cantonese Dictionary, 1859）。此外，他还首次将老子的《道德经》译成英文。

《英粤字典》是其流传最广的一本书。1859年第1版时的《英粤字典》是一本袖珍词典，全书159页，收词只有9568条；到1891年的第6版扩充到296页，而1907年的第7版已经扩充到822页，收词11926条，俗语和例句近3万条。本词典按字母顺序编排。每个英文词目用粤语对译，对译词目时，列出粤语汉字及相应的罗马拼音字母注音。

本次再版，为保存原书全貌，只对有粤方言特色的疑难词句予以注释，并按顺序列于页面侧边。例如：

【作笑戏文】喜剧。

【噉样】这样。

《英粤字典》一书采用罗马拼音标注,笔者参照陈咏渝(2002)《十九世纪中期至二十世纪初期之粤语研究》(复旦大学硕士学位论文)一书,将罗马拼音与现代国际音标的音系对照转写如下:

(1)声调

原书符号	原书例字	调类
ˌ	边[pin]	平
ˈ	纸[ˈchi]	上
ˀ	棍[kwɑnˀ]	去
无①	勒[lak]	入

注:①原书未标入声符号,但有入声尾-p/-t/-k作为标志。

(2)声母

p[p]彼边别	p'[ph]批剖篇	m[m]迷亩灭	f[f]辉否废	
t[t]低斗跌	t'[th]梯天铁	n[n]你郎溺		l[l]吕龙厉
ts[ts]祭剪足	ts'[tsh]齐千切		s[s]西先序	
ch[tʃ]知展住	ch'[tʃh]迟处畜		sh[ʃ]世身舌	
k[k]鸡九洁	k'[kh]求穷曲	ng[ŋ]危银艺	h[h]气向学	
kw[kw]归君骨	kw'[kwh]葵困狂			
y[j]衣影益				
w[w]为云永				
Ø[Ø]矮盎恶				

(3)韵母

单韵母	复韵母		鼻音韵母			入声韵母		
	ei[ei]眉	o[ou]告	ng[ŋ]五		m[m]不			
	ai[ɐi]废	au[ɐu]偷	an[ɐn]亲	ang[ɐŋ]能	am[ɐm]暗	ap[ɐp]不	at[ɐt]实	ak[ɐk]特
a[a]下	aai[ai]埋	aau[au]胞	aan[an]产	aang[aŋ]横	aam[am]减	aap[ap]集	aat[at]发	aak[ak]逆
e[ɛ]遮			un[ɐn]问	eng[ɛŋ]腥	um[ɛm]金	up[ɐp]给	ut[ɛt]笔	ek[ɛk]石
i[i]尾		iu[iu]照	in[in]然	ing[iŋ]成	im[im]兼	ip[ip]叠	it[it]灭	ik[ik]识
ue[y]鱼			uen[yn]短				uet[yt]缺	
	ui[ɵy]嘴		uun[ɵn]纯	eung[ɵŋ]丈			uut[ɵt]栗	euk[ɵk]脚
oo[u]乌	ooi[ui]会		oon[un]盘	uung[uŋ]丰			oot[ut]活	uuk[uk]目
oh[ɔ]多	oi[ɔi]耐		ohn[ɔn]岸	ong[ɔŋ]东	om[ɔm]噉	op[ɔp]合	ot/oht[ɔt]割喝①	ok[ɔk]角
eu[œ]								
ze[ɿ]寺								

注：①《英粤字典》中"割"的韵母记为ot，"喝"的韵母记为oht，现代粤语中两者读音皆为[ot]。此韵母在《英粤字典》中或有分立，但具体音值无法确定，故只好暂将两者归并为同一韵母。

在本书的校注过程中，上海大学国际交流学院给予了大力支持和帮助。参与校勘整理工作的有姚喜明、杨文波、罗琼、张晓芬等。其中，姚喜明负责全书统稿及英译校对，罗琼、杨文波、张晓芬负责全书词条校注，此外杨文波另负责音系整理及音标转写，全书由暨南大学侯兴泉审订。

此次《英粤字典》的校注出版，对于粤语方言以及我国双语词典的研究具有一定的参考价值。但由于笔者时间和精力有限，疏漏之处再所难免，书中不足之处敬请诸位专家学者指正。

参考文献

[1] 白宛如.广州方言词典[M].南京：江苏教育出版社，2003.
[2] 陈咏渝.十九世纪中期至二十世纪初期之粤语研究[D].复旦大学硕士学位论文，2002
[3] 黄雪贞.梅县方言词典[M].南京：江苏教育出版社，1995.
[4] 李新魁.广州方言研究[M].韶关：广东人民出版社，1995.
[5] 吴开斌.简明香港方言词典[M].广州：花城出版社，1991.
[6] 詹伯慧，陈晓锦.东莞方言词典[M].南京：江苏教育出版社，1997.
[7] 郑定欧.香港粤语词典[M].南京：江苏教育出版社，1997.
[8] 饶秉才，欧阳觉臣，周无忌.广州话方言词典[M].香港：商务印书馆，1994.
[9] E.C.Bridgman. *A Chinese Chrestomathy in the Canton Dialect*[M]. Macao: S.Wells Williams, 1841.

典字粵英

AN
ENGLISH AND CANTONESE
DICTIONARY,
FOR THE
*USE OF THOSE WHO WISH TO LEARN THE SPOKEN
LANGUAGE OF CANTON PROVINCE.*

BY
JOHN CHALMERS, LL.D.

Sixth Edition.
With the Changing Tones marked.

———⋯⋙⋘⋯———

Hongkong:
KELLY & WALSH, LIMITED.
HONGKONG—SHANGHAI—YOKOHAMA—SINGAPORE.
—
1891.

Registered in accordance with the provisions of Ordinance No. 10 of 1888, at the Office of the Registrar General, Supreme Court House, Hongkong.

目 录

使用指南 / 1
正文 / 1-296

译文

使用指南

　　本字典采用的拼音系统根据卫三畏先生①的《英华分韵撮要》改编，为便于本词典的书写、印刷及使用，省去了变音符。其元音发音如下：

　　aa，及韵母a，发音与$father$中的a音相同。

　　a（非韵母），发音同于$company$中的a音。

　　e，同于单词$they$中的e音。

　　i，与$machine$中的i同音，但若出现在ng与k之前，则同于$king$中的k音。

　　o，在音节末尾时与no中的o音相同，不在音节末尾时与hop中的o同音。

　　oh，发音与单词$horn$相同。

　　$ö$，与$Göthe$中的$ö$音相同。

　　oo，与$school$中的oo同音。

　　u，与fun中的u同音（可与短音a替换）。

　　uu，近似于$bull$中的u音。

　　ue，发音与$Trübner$中的$ü$音相同。

　　ai，与fly中的y同音。

　　aai，在单词$far-reaching$中，与ea中的a同音。

　　au，与单词now中的ow同音。

　　aau，与单词$far ruling$中的a和u的共同

DIRECTIONS FOR USING THE ENGLISH AND CANTONESE DICTIONARY.

THE system of spelling here used is adapted from that of Dr. Williams' Tonic Dictionary, only dispensing with his diacritic marks for the sake of convenience in writing and printing, and, it is hoped, also in using the Dictionary. The vowels are to be pronounced as follows:—

　　aa, and *a* final, as in *father*.
　　a, not final, as in *company*.
　　e, as in *they*.
　　i, as in *machine*, but before *ng* and *k* as in *king*.
　　o, final as in *no*, and not final, as in *hop*.
　　oh, as in *horn*.
　　ŏ, as in *Göthe*.
　　oo, as in *school*.
　　u, as in *fun*, (interchanged with short *a*.)
　　uu, nearly as in *bull*.
　　ue, as *ü* in *Trübner*.
　　ai, as *y* in *fly*.
　　aai, as *a* with *ea* in *far-reaching*.
　　au, as *ow* in *now*.
　　aau, as *a* with *u* in *far ruling*.
　　eu, as *eyo* in *beyond*, or *ayo* in *crayon*.
　　iu, as *ee* with *ou* in *see you*.
　　oi, as *oy* in *boy*.
　　ui, nearly as in *Louis*.
　　ooi, as in *cooing*.
　　sze or *sz'* is a mere buzz, with scarcely any vowel sound.

IV   ENGLISH AND CANTONESE DICTIONARY.

The use of short *u* in many cases where the other Dictionaries have short *a* is to prevent a habit which English learners are very liable to get into of pronouncing, for example, 民 'mun,' people, exactly the same as the English word 'man'; 佛 'Fut,' Buddha, the same as the English word 'fat,' &c. The broader Scotch *a* is a little nearer the Cantonese, but 分 is in any case not 'fan' but 'fun.'

The double *u* is a little different from double *o*. 'Kau-loon' should be written Kau-luung, the second syllable being indeed quite different from the English 'lung,' yet not by any means the same as the Scotch 'loon.'

Words ending in *ue* (*ü*) often vary in Canton so as to be not distinguishable from words ending in *ui*; but it is an exaggeration to make 去 'hue rhyme with 水 'shui.

The only vowel used with a diacritical mark is *ö*; and it is of rare occurrence. I cannot accept, even on the authority of Mr. Parker, this vowel as a substitute for *eu* in *sheung, sheuk*, &c. There is some truth in the suggestion, but if *sheung* gives too much of a diphthong, *shöng* gives too little. Considering that 郎 *long* and 良 *leung* rhyme with each other in the universal language of China, it would seem almost better to write the Cantonese sounds *long* and *leong*, than to introduce the peculiar *ö*, which, after all, does not represent the Cantonese perfectly. However, students may take Mr. Ball's *shöng*, *löng*, &c. as a warning not to exaggerate the diphthong.

The 8 Tones.—There are only eight regular tones in the Chinese language, and even these are not all found in many dialects. The upper series of tones is printed in Italics, and the lower series in Roman letters. Syllables printed in Italics must always be pronounced on a higher key than the others. (1) Syllables without any tonal mark are in the 'even' tone.

译文

完全不像。试想在中国通用的语言里，"郎"（*long*）与"良"（*leung*）彼此谐音，与其采用特别的ö音，还不如将写为"*long*"和"*leong*"，毕竟，ö音无法完美诠释广东话音。然而，学生或可将鲍康宁③先生的 *shöng, löng* 等音看成一种警醒，提醒我们不可夸大双元音的作用。

八大声调汉语里只有八个常规声调，其中某些声调甚至并不存在于方言中。上层声调采用斜体表示，下层声调则用罗马字母表示。在发音上，用斜体表示音节的音调总是高于其他音节。(1) 无音调标记的音节为"平声"。(2) 左上角带（ʻ）标记的为"上声"。(3) 右上角带（ʼ）标记的为"去声"。(4) 汉字以k, p或t结尾则为"入声"；这类词以闭辅音结尾，不发声。在我看来，把第一声调视为"本调"、第三声调视为"平调"更为恰当；因为第三声调即"去声"，类似于一种持续同一音高的调子。其音高最开始比第一声调低，但之后一直保持这种状态，不继续减弱。

八个声调的示例见注④，它们被应用于汉语音节中（*t*只是对*n*的修正）。

附加声调：承蒙庄延龄先生的研究，我们得以知晓广东话除了以上八个声调外还存在其他声调。

首先，平声有三个，而非两个，最高平声近似一种叫声。典型的例子有：*maau*—猫，该名称即模拟了猫的叫声。此类最高平声在本字典中很容易进行区分，因为除了斜体印刷外，作者另在音节左下角进行了声调标记。对于此声调

DIRECTIONS. v

(2) Those with a tonal mark (ʻ) on the upper left corner are in the 'rising' tone. (3) Those with a tonal mark (ʼ) on the upper right corner are in the 'going' tone. (4) And words ending in *k*, *p*, or *t* are in the 'abrupt' tone; that is to say, they end in a close consonant which cannot be sung out. It seems to me that the first tone might more properly be called the 'natural' and the third the 'even' tone; for the third or 'going' tone resembles a note of music which continues at the same pitch. It begins rather lower than the first, but does not drop at all.

The following is an example of the eight tones applied to what the Chinese regard as one syllable (*t* being only a modification of *n*):—

		UPPER SERIES.		LOWER SERIES.	
			Williams.		*Williams.*
平	even	溫	*wun*	雲	wun ₍wan
上	rising	穩	ʻ*wun*	尹	ʻwun ʻwan
去	going	慍	*wun*ʼ	混	wunʼ wan²
入	abrupt	屈	*wut*	核	wut wat₂

Additional Tones:—We are indebted to Mr. E. H. Parker for first calling attention to other tones, besides the above eight, which occur in Canton Colloquial.

First, there are three even tones instead of two, the uppermost one being a sort of cry. A typical case is ₍*maau*, a cat, the name being an imitation of its cry. These *uppermost* even tones are distinguished in this Edition of the Cantonese Dictionary by a tonal mark on the lower left corner of the syllable in addition to its being printed in Italics. I have been guided entirely by a Cantonese Teacher in this and the following distinctions of tones.

Second, there are three abrupt tones instead of two, the middle one being about as much lower than the one above as the upper 'going' tone is lower than the upper 'even.' This

VI   ENGLISH AND CANTONESE DICTIONARY.

lowering of the upper fourth tone takes place almost invariably in connection with long or broad vowels. The first tonal exercise familiar to most beginners affords an example of it—

   Sin ʿSin Sinʾ Sitʾ.

The *i* being long (= *ee*) the fourth tone follows the cadence of the third; so that this middle fourth tone is appropriately marked like the third. What is probably the normal upper fourth tone is heard where the vowel is short, as in—

   Sing ʿSing Singʾ Sik.

Third, all the tones, except perhaps the upper even and the upper abrupt, are liable to be changed into an exaggerated rising tone; the initial letter always following the proper tone of the word, and the raising of the voice commencing from that pitch whatever it may be. This exaggerated rising tone is indicated by an asterisk on the upper left side of the syllable. For example, the character 近 (near) has three pronunciations according to the shades of meaning, kanʾ, ʿkʿan, and *kanʾ. The last is to commence like the first and has no aspirate (ʿ) but it rises even more than the second.

It is well to keep in mind that the lower even and the lower rising tones always take the aspirate after *ch*, *k*, *p*, *t*, and *ts*, while the lower 'going' tone never takes it, and the lower abrupt tone seldom. There is some little help in this to a foreigner in distinguishing so many tones.

More than nine-tenths of the characters given as equivalents of English words in this Dictionary will answer equally well for the general language of China; and I have thought it well with this in view to substitute authorized characters for 唔 'm, 嘅 keʾ, 有 ʿmo, 嚟 lai, &c. in many cases while retaining the colloquial sounds. It seems a little absurd to write 嚟 for 'lai,' to come, when the proper character 來 'loi' is pronounced

译文

字既可对应英文单词,也可对应中国的通用语言;就这一点,我认为可以用此类文字来替代某些官方文字,比如:唔（'m）,嘅（ke'）,冇（'mo）,嚟（lai）等字在许多情况下,既可解释意义,又保留了口语音。但若汉字"来"（loi）在其他方言里发音为"lai",此时将"lai"音写作"嚟",则似乎略显荒谬。

这种情况,就好比随着"浅文言"版《圣经》的不断增加,最终只会导致理解变得愈发困难。

本字典主要对象为英国初学者,而非中国学生。任何查阅此书的人,如果无法找到某个特殊英文单词,则用同义字替换;同时,如若个人想从所给材料中组织一段演讲,那么:

通过在名词及动词后加 ke',可以形成各种形容词。

通常,在形容词前加 $'ching$ 或 tso' 可变为动词,如:$'ching-paak$, 变白。

有时,音节括号里的发音,往往可与另一发音替换使用,甚至更为口语化。比如:就"毗连"一词,$foo'-kan'$ $('k'an)$ 是一种简化说法,即:$foo'-kan'$ 或 $foo'-'k'an$。

湛约翰
1891年3月28日于香港

'lai' in other dialects. This sort of thing, like the multiplication of 'easy wênli' versions of the Scriptures, will in the end only multiply difficulties.

This Dictionary was from the first intended for English people rather than Chinese, and those who consult it are requested, if they fail to find any particular English word, to look for a synonym or an approximate synonym; and to learn to form parts of speech themselves from the material given, thus:—

Adjectives may be formed at pleasure by adding *ke*' to nouns and verbs.

Verbs may often be formed by placing '*ching* or tso' before adjectives, as '*ching*-paak, to whiten.

Sometimes an alternative pronunciation of a syllable is given in parentheses which will generally be found equally or more colloquial. For example, under 'Adjoin,' foo'-kan' ('k'an), is an abbreviated way of saying, foo'-kan', *or* foo'-'k'an.

J. C.

HONGKONG, 28th March, 1891.

注释

①Samuel Wells Williams (1812—1884)，美国第一位研究中国问题的专家，被称为美国"汉学之父"，其名著《中国总论》把中国研究作为一种纯粹的文化来进行综合的研究，是标志美国汉学开端的里程碑，该书与他所编《汉英拼音字典》过去一直是外国人研究中国的必备之书。

②Parker，即Edward Harper Parker（1849—1926），英国人，中文名庄延龄。曾在上海、福州、广州等地领事馆任职，对中国有深入的研究。

③Baller，即Frederick William Baller（1852—1922），英国人，中文名鲍康宁，语言学家和汉学家，中国内地会（China Inland Mission）传教士，著有《汉英分解字典》(An Analytical Chinese-English Dictionary, 1900)、《官话初阶》(A Mandarin Primer, 1911)等。

④

		阴调类			阳调类	
			Williams			*Williams*
平	*even*	温 *wun*	*wan*	云 *wun*	≤*wan*
上	*rising*	稳 '*wun*	'*wan*	尹 '*wun*	≤*wan*
去	*going*	愠 *wun*'	*wan*'	混 *wun*'	*wan*≥
入	*abrupt*	屈 *wut*	*wat*,	核 *wut*	*wat*≥

注释

【减笔】汉字的一种修辞格，通过有意减少汉字的笔画来表意。
Abbreviation 现译为：缩写词、缩略语、缩写等。
Abet: 译为"帮助"不确切。编者没有注意到汉语"帮助"一词为褒义，而英文 *abet* 为贬义，应译为"教唆"。

AN
ENGLISH AND CANTONESE
DICTIONARY.

A

A, an, (one) 一 *yat*. [The numerals or classifiers are given after (a) or (an) under different nouns. The most common of all numerals is 個 *koh*ʾ, as 一個人 *yat-koh*ʾ-*yan*, "one man" or "a man," but where other numerals are given they must be used in connection with the classes of nouns to which they respectively belong, as 一隻獸 *yat-chek*ʾ-*shau*ʾ, "a beast," 一條魚 *yat-t'iu-*ue*, "a fish."]

Abacus, 算盤 *suen*ʾ-*p'oon*, (an), 一個算盤 *yat ko*ʾ-*suen*ʾ-*p'oon*.

Abaft, 向船尾 *heung*ʾ-*shuen-ʿmi*.

Abandon, 捨棄 ʿ*she-hi*ʾ.

Abate, 減少 ʿ*kaam-*ʿshiu*.

Abbey, (Bud.) 佛寺 *Fut-*tsze*ʾ, (an) 一間佛寺 *yat-kaan-Fut-*tsze*ʾ, (Tau.) 道觀 *To*ʾ-*koon*ʾ, (Rom.) 修道院 *sau-to*ʾ-*uen*ʾ.

Abbot, (Bud.) 方丈 *fong-cheung*ʾ, (an) 一位方丈 *yat-wai*ʾ-*fong-cheung*ʾ, (Tau) 道長 *To*ʾ-*cheung*ʾ.

Abbreviate, 減短 ʿ*kaam-*ʿtuen*.

Abbreviation, (in writing) 減筆 ʿ*kaam-put*.

Abet, 幫助 *pong-choh*ʾ.

Abhor, 憎懨 *tsang-im*ʾ.

英粤字典　1

ABO 2 ABU

Abide, 住實 chue²-shat, 住吓 chue²-ha, 耐 noi².
Ability, 才能 ts'oi-nang, 本領 ʻpoon-ling, 能幹 nang-kohn².
Abjure, 誓願絶 *shai² uen²-tsuet.
Able, 能 nang, 會 ʻooi.
Aboard, 在船上 tsoi²-shuen-sheung², 喺船處 ʻhai-shuen-shue².
Abolish, 廢除 fai²-ch'ue.
Abominable, 百家憎 paak-ka-tsang.
Abominate, 至憎 chi²-tsang.
Aborigines, 土人 ʻt'o-yan, (of China) 苗子 Miu-ʻtsze.
Abortion, 墮胎 toh²-t'oi 小產 ʻsiu-ʻch'aan.
Abound, 處處都多 ch'ue²-ch'ue²-too-toh, 豐盛 fuung-shing².
About, (round-) 周圍 chau-wai, (more or less) 上下 sheungʻ-*ha, 左右 tsoh-yau², (about to) 將近 tseung-*kan (concerning) 論 luun².

Above, 上 sheung².
Abreast, 並肩 ping²-kin, 一拍 yat-p'aak².
Abridge, 簡畧 ʻkaan-leuk, 整簡畧 ʻching-ʻkaan-leuk.
Abroad, 外 ngoi².
Abrogate, 廢 fai².
Abrupt, 突屹 tat-ngat.
Abruptly, 突然 tat-in.
Abscess, 膿瘡 nuung-ch'ong.
Abscond, 躱避 ʻtoh-pi², (with money) 起尾注 ʻhi-ʻmi-chue².
Absent, 不在 ʼm-tsoi².
Absolutely, 必定 pit-ting².
Absolve, 赦 she².
Absorb, 欵去 shok²-hue².
Abstain from, 戒 kaai².
Abstracted, 忘形 *mong-ying, 想入神 ʻseung-yup-shan.
Abstruse, 深奧 shum-o².
Absurd, 斷不合理 tuen²-ʼm-hop-ʻli, 混賬 wan²-cheung².
Abundant, 豐阜 fuung-fau².

注 释

【誓愿绝】发誓弃绝。
【喺船处】在船上。
【百家憎】所有人都讨厌的。
【起尾注】本是赌场骗财的一种手法，庄家一开始先输给某个赌徒，引诱或用激将法诱使其下重注，当赌徒倾囊而出时，庄家最后让他输个精光。现在指连本带利，被人席卷一空。与abscond一词词义上并不完全对应。前者突出"诱骗，骗光"之义，而后者突出"逃跑"。
【欵去】吸收。
【丰阜】同"丰富"。

注释

【同埋】在粤语中是连词：和。如：我钟意游水同埋跑步（我喜欢游泳和跑步）。
Accompany为动词，意为"陪伴"。
【相和】符合；一致。
【噉就】那就。
【是问】有责任的；可解释的。
【掌柜】会计师，会计人员。
【集埋】收集起来。
【惯熟】习惯的，惯常的。
Acorn：译为"石栗"有误，应为"橡果"。"石栗"英文为：candlenut。

ACC　　3　　ACQ

Abuse, (things) 亂用 luen⟩-yuung⟩, (people) 詈罵 li⟩-ma⟩, 殘害 ts'aan-hoi.
Abyss, 深淵 shum-uen.
Acacia, 金鳳 kum-fuung⟩, 聲息花 shing-sik-fa.
Accept, 收納 shau-naap.
Access, 走近路 ʿtsau-ʿk'an-lo⟩.
Accidental, 意外 i⟩-ngoi⟩, 偶然 ʿngau-in.
Acclamation, 齊聲喝彩 ts'ai-sheng-hoht-ts'oi.
Acclimated, 服水土 fuuk-ʿshui-ʿt'o.
Acclivity, 斜坡 ts'e-poh.
Accommodate, 從——便, ts'uung——*pin⟩, 依 i.
Accompany, 同埋 t'uung-maai, 陪 p'ooi.
Accomplice, 從犯 tsuung⟩-*faan⟩.
Accomplish, 成 shing.
Accord, 相和 seung-woh.
According to, 照依 chiu⟩-i.
Accordingly, 噉就 ʿkom-tsau⟩.

Account, (money) 數目 sho⟩-muuk, 賬目 cheung⟩-muuk, 單 taan.
Accountable, 是問 shi⟩-mun⟩.
Accountant, 掌匱 ʿcheung-*kwai⟩.
Accumulate, 集埋 tsaap-maai.
Accumulation, 重重疊疊 ch'uung-ch'uung-tip-tip.
Accurate, 無錯 ʿmo-ts'oh⟩.
Accusation, 告狀 ko⟩-*chong⟩.
Accuse, 告 ko⟩, (a superior) 攻訐 kuung-k'it⟩.
Accustomed, 慣熟 kwaan⟩-shuuk.
Ache, 痛 t'uung⟩.
Achieve, 成就 shing-tsau⟩.
Achievement, 成功 shing-kuung.
Acid, 酸 suen.
Acknowledge, 認 ying⟩.
Acorn, 石栗 shek-luut.
Acquaintance, 熟識 shuuk-shik, 相識 seung-shik.
Acquire, 得到 tak-ʿto, 獲 wok.

ADD	4	ADM

Acquit, 擬無罪 ‘i-‘mo-tsui, 審無罪 ‘shum-‘mo-tsui.
Acre, (Chinese) 畝 ‘mau (6½ = 1 Eng.).
Acrid, 辣 laat.
Across, 橫 waang, 過 kwoh⁾.
Act, 做 tso⁾, 行 hang, 做事幹 tso⁾-sze⁾-kohn⁾.
Acting officer, 署任 ‘ch‘ue-yum⁾.
Actions 行爲 hang-wai.
Action-at-law, 訟詞 tsuung⁾-ts‘ze.
Actionable, 可告發 ‘hoh-‘ko⁾-faat.
Active, 手快 ‘shau-faai⁾, 活動 oot-tuung⁾.
Actor, (play-) 戲子 hi⁾-‘tsze.
Acute, 尖銳 tsim-yui⁾, (clever) 伶俐 ling-li⁾.
Adam's apple, 喉欖 hau-‘laam.
Adapt, 合 hop.
Add, 加 ka, 添 t‘im.
Addict to, 專務 chuen-mo⁾.
Addition (the rule of), 加法 ka-faat.

Addled, 膶 ‘woh.
Address, (a person) 稱呼 ch‘ing-foo, (a letter) 寫信皮 ‘se-suun⁾-p‘i, (an) 信皮 suun⁾-p‘i.
Adept, 老手 ‘lo-‘shau.
Adequate, 够便 kau⁾-‘shai, 能够 nang-kau⁾.
Adhere, 黏緊 nim-‘kan, 依實 i-shat.
Adhesive, 黐 ch‘i.
Adieu, 好行 ‘ho-hang, 望你好咯 mong⁾-‘ni-‘ho-lok.
Adjoin, 附近 foo⁾-kan⁾ (‘k‘an).
Adjourn, 訂期 ting⁾-k‘i, 訂期再會 ting⁾-k‘i-tsoi-ooi⁾.
Adjust, 整齊 ‘ching-ts‘ai, 做歸一 tso⁾-kwai-yat.
Adjutant, 副將 foo⁾-tseung⁾, 協台 hip-t‘oi.
Administer, 總管 ‘tsuung-‘koon.
Admiral, 水師提督 ‘shui-sze-t‘ai-tuuk.

注 释

Action-at-law：译为"讼词"不确切，应为"诉讼"。
【专务】沉溺于，醉心于；癖好。
【膶】混乱的；腐烂的。
【好行】走好。
【订期】约定日期。
Adjourn：译为"订期"不确切，应为"延期""推迟"（会议或审批）暂停"。
【做归一】做整齐，整理。归一：一致，统一。

注 释

【赞羡】赞许。
【事做/事干】事情。
【契爷/契姆】干爹,干妈。
【贴街招】在街上贴公告。
【合势色】明智的,可取的。
【錛】锛子,扁斧。
【响弓】风弦琴。
【好相与】好相处。

ADU　　5　　AFF

Admire, 讚羨 tsaan²-sin².
Admit, 許進 ʻhue-tsuun², 俾入 ʻpi-yup, 允准 wan-ʻchuun.
Admonish, 勸誡 huen²-kaai².
Ado, 事做 sze²-tso², 事幹 sze²-kohn².
Adopt a son, 立義子 laap-i²-tsze, 立螟蛉 laap-ming-ling.
Adopted, (personally) 契 kʻai², (father, mother) 契爺, 契姆 kʻai²-ye, kʻai²-ʻna, (by a second marriage) 繼 kai².
Adore, 崇拜 shuung-paai².
Adorn, 文飾 mun-shik, 整飾 ʻching-shik.
Adrift, 漂流 pʻiu-lau.
Adroit, 善精 shin²-tsing.
Adult, 長大成人 ʻcheung-taai²-shing-yan, 大人 taai²-yan.
Adulterate, 摳雜假貨 kʻau-tsaap-ka-foh².
Adultery, 姦淫 kaan-yum.

Advance, 進 tsuun², (money) 預先交出 ue²-sin-kaau-chʻuut, 支 chi, (goods on credit) 賒 she.
Advantage, 贏 yeng, 益 yik.
Adventure, 行險 hang-ʻhim.
Adversary, 對頭 tui²-tʻau, 對敵 tui²-tik.
Adverse, 凶 huung, 不幸 pat-hang², 逆 yik, ngaak, 滯 chai².
Advert to, 提起 tʻai-ʻhi.
Advertise, 通報 tʻuung-po², 報告 po²-ko², (by posting bills) 貼街招 tip-ʻkaai-ʻchiu.
Advisable, 合勢色 hop-shai²-shik.
Advise, 勸 huen².
Advocate, to, 代訴 toi²-so².
Adze, 錛 poon.
Aeolian Harp, 响弓 ʻheung-kuung.
Aeolus, 風神 fuung-shan.
Affable, 好相與 ʻho-seung-ʻue.
Affair, 事幹 sze²-kohn².

AFT 6 AGO

Affect, 感 ˊkom, (concern) 關 kwaan°.
Affectation, 整腥詐靚 ˊching-seng-chaˋ-lengˊ.
Affectionate, 深情 shum-tsʻing.
Affiance, 定親 tingˋ-tsʻan.
Affinity, 姻親 yan-tsʻan.
Affirm, 話係 waˋ-haiˋ.
Afflict, 磨苦 moh-ˊfu.
Afflictions, 痛楚 tʻuungˋ-ˊchʻoh.
Affluent, 豐盛 fuung-shingˋ.
Afford, 供給 kuung-kʻup, (can) 買得起 ˊmaai-tak-ˊhi.
Affront, 相撞 chʻuung-chongˋ, 辱 yuuk.
Afloat, 浮 fau.
Afore-said, 個的前言 kohˋ-tik-tsʻin-in, 上文所講 sheungˋ-mun-ˊshoh-ˊkong.
Afraid, 恐怕 ˊhuung-pʻaˋ.
After, —— 後 —— hauˋ.
After-birth, 後人 hauˋ-*yan, 胎衣 tʻoi-i, 胞衣 paau-i.
Afternoon, 下午 haˋ-ˊng, 晏晝後 aanˋ-chauˋ-hauˋ.

Afterwards, 然後 in-hauˋ, 尾後 ˊmi-hauˋ, 後來 hauˋ-loi.
Again, 再復 tsoiˋ-fuuk, 又試 yauˋ-shi.
Against, 相反 seung-ˊfaan, 逆 yik, ngaak, (over-) 對面 tuiˋ-minˋ, (to rub—) 繽親 kʻwaang-tsʻan.
Agate, 瑪瑙 ˊma-ˊno.
Age, 年紀 nin-ˊki, (what is your?) 你有幾多歲 ˊni-ˊyau-ˊki-toh-suiˋ? (or politely) 貴庚呢 kwaiˋ-kang-ni?; (the) 世 shaiˋ.
Aged, 高壽 ko-shauˋ, 老大 ˊlo-*taaiˋ.
Agent, 代辦人 toiˋ-paanˋ-yan.
Aggravate, 整更關系 ˊching-kangˋ-kwaan-haiˋ, 整重 ˊching-chʻuungˋ.
Aggressor, 先下手 sin-haˋ-ˊshau, 先攻人 sin-kuung-yan.
Agitate, 郁動 yuuk-tuungˋ.
Agitated, 徬徨 pʻong-wong.
Ago, 前 tsʻin.

注 释

【整腥詐靚】矯揉造作。
【话系】主张，肯定，确认，断言。
【个的前言】上述。
【晏昼后】下午。
【整更关系】加重。
【郁动】骚动，活动，动静。

注释

【和合】同意。
【合心水】符合心意。
【啹船】搁浅的船。
Aide-de-camp: 应译为"副手，侍从"，译为"守备"不确切。"守备"是清朝武官名，指管理军队总务、军饷、军粮等的正五品官。
Air-plant: 气生植物。吊兰是其中一种。
Alert: 应译为"警告"。该词并无"关心"的意思。

AIR　7　ALL

Agony, 苦極 ʻfoo-kik.
Agree, 和合 woh-hop.
Agreeable, 温和 wan-woh, (willing) 歡喜 foon-ʻhi, (to one's liking) 合心水 hop-sum-ʻshui.
Agreement, 約 yeukˌ, 合同 hop-tʻuung, 契約 kʻai-yeukˌ.
Agriculture, 耕種 kang-chuungˌ, 農事 nuung-szeˌ.
Aground, 擱淺 kokˌ-tsʻin, 啹船 hong-shuen.
Ague, 發冷病 faat-ʻlaang-pengˌ.
Ah! 嚱 Haai! Ha!
Aha! 暇暇 Ha-ha!
Ahead, 在前頭 tsoi-tsʻin-tʻau (to go) 前去 tsʻin-hueˌ.
Ahoy! 喴 Wai!
Aid, 幫助 pong-chohˌ.
Aide-de-camp, 守備 ʻshau-piˌ.
Aim, 向准 heungˌ-ʻchuun.
Air, 氣 hiˌ.
Air, to, 晾 longˌ, 晾爽 longˌ-shong.

Air-plant, 吊蘭 tiuˌ-laan.
Airy, 涼爽 leung-ʻshong.
Alarm, 震驚 chanˌ-king, (arouse) 儆醒 ʻking-ʻsing.
Alarm-clock, 鬧鐘 naau-chuung.
Alas! 嗳呀 Aaiˌ-ya!
Ale-house, 酒店 ʻtsau-timˌ.
Alert, 關心 kwaan-sum.
Aleurites, nuts, 石栗 shek-luutˌ.
Alias, 別名 pitˌ-*meng.
Alien, 外國人 ngoi-kwokˌ-yan, 不相屬 'm-seung-shuukˌ, (他人的) 人哋嘅 yan-ti-ˌkeˌ.
Alight, 落 lok.
Alike, 相似 seungˌ-tsʻze 一樣 yat-*yeungˌ.
Alive, 生活 shaang-oot.
All, 皆 kaai, 攏總 ʻluung-ʻtsuung, hamˌ-pang-lang, (are) 都係 too-hai, (before nouns) 衆 chuungˌ, 萬 maanˌ, 百 paakˌ.
All-along, 一路 yat-loˌ.
Allay, 止 ʻchi.
Allegory, 寓言 ueˌ-in.

| ALO | 8 | AMB |

Alliance, 結親 kit'-ts'an, 聯盟 luen-mang.
Alligator, 鱷魚 ngok-ue.
Allot, 照分 chiu'-fun, 分派 fun-p'aai'.
Allow, 准 'chuun.
Alloy, (base metal) 金低 kum-tai, (to), 摳 k'au.
Allure, 引誘 'yan-'yan.
Allusion, 暗指 om'-'chi.
Almanac, 通書 t'uung-shue.
Almighty, 無所不能 mo-shoh-pat-nang.
Almond, 杏仁 hang'-yan.
Almost, 差不多 ch'a-pat-toh.
Alms, (to give) 施捨 shi-'she.
Aloes, 蘆薈 lo-ooi', 沈香 ch'um-,heung.
Alone, 獨一個 tuuk-yat-koh', 孤獨 koo-tuuk.
Along, (lengthwise) 掂 tim', 直 chik, (with) 同埋 t'uung-maai.
Alongside, 在傍 tsoi'-p'ong, (to go) 行埋 hang-maai.
Aloud, 大聲 taai'-sheng.

Already, 曾經 ts'ang-king, 已經 'i-king.
Also, 亦 yik, 都 too, 又 yau'.
Altar, 祭壇 tsai'-t'aan, 神臺 shan-t'oi.
Alter, 改 'koi.
Alternate, 互相替代 oo'-seung-t'ai'-toi'.
Alternately, (in succession) 輪流 luun-*lau, (every second one) 躏罅 laam'-la'.
Alternatives, 兩樣任揀 'leung-yeung'-yum-'kaan.
Although, 雖然 sui-in.
Altogether, 總共 'tsuung-kuung'.
Alum, 白礬 paak-faan.
Always, 時時 shi-shi, 常時 sheung-shi.
Am (I-), 我係 'ngoh-hai'.
Amaze, 驚着 king-cheuk.
Ambassador, 使臣 sze'-shan, (an) 一位使臣 yat-wai'-sze'-shan, (imperial) 欽差 yum-ch'aai'.
Amber, 琥珀 ,foo-paak'.
Ambitious, 志氣高 chi'-hi'-ko.

注 释

【照分】分配, 拨发, 分账。
【金低】合金。
【通书】也叫 "通胜", 指全书、年鉴、万年历等。
Aloes: 译文 "沈香" 应为 "沉香"。
【行埋】走在一起, 靠近。
【躏罅】缝隙。

注释

【唔着】出差错的，有缺陷的。
【情头】姘头，奸情。
【氹】哄（小孩）。
【鱼解】醢鱼酱。
【嬲】同"恼"，生气。
【耸起】惊动。
【脚眼骨】脚踝。

ANA 9 ANK

Ambush, 伏兵 fuuk-ping.
Amend, 改正 ʻkoi-ching'.
Amends, (to make) 賠補 pʻooi-ʻpo.
America, 亞美利加 Aʼ-ʻmi-liʼ-ka.
Amiable, 可愛 ʻhoh-oi'.
Amiss, 唔着 ʼm-cheuk.
Ammunition, 火藥銃子 ʻfoh-yeuk-chʻuung-tsze.
Among, 在——中 tsoiʼ—chuung.
Amorous, 多情 toh-tsʻing.
Amount, 共計 kuungʼ-kaiʼ.
Amour, 情頭 tsʻing-tʻau.
Amoy, 厦門 Haʼ-moon.
Ample, 廣大 ʻkwong-taaiʼ.
Amputate, 割去 kohtʼ-ʻhue.
Amuse, 開心 hoi-sum, 則劇 tsak-kʻek, (a child) 氹 tʻumʼ.
Amusement, 頑耍 waan-ʻsha.
Amusing, 趣 tsʻueʼ.
Analyze, 察實 chʻaatʼ-shat, 考究 ʻhaau-kau.
Anarchy, 大亂 taaiʼ-luenʼ.

Ancestor, 祖先 ʻtso-sin, 祖宗 ʻtso-tsuung, 太公 tʻaaiʼ-kuung.
Anchor, 鐵錨 tʻitʼ-naau, (to) 碇灣 tingʼ, waan.
Anchovy-sauce, 魚解 ue-ʻkaai.
Ancient, 古 ʻkoo.
And, 及 kʻaap, 兼 kim, 共 kuungʼ, 又 yau.
Anecdote, (an) 一段故事 yat-tuenʼ-ʻkoo-szeʼ.
Angel, 天使 tʻin-szeʼ.
Anger, 嬲 nau, 恨怒 hanʼ-noʼ.
Angle, 角頭 kokʼ-tʻau.
Angle, to 釣魚 tiuʼ-*ue.
Angry, 發怒 faatʼ-noʼ, 嬲怒 nau-noʼ.
Animals, 生靈 shang-ling, 禽獸 kʻum-shauʼ.
Animate, (to) 耸起 ʻsuung-ʻhi.
Animation, 精神 tsing-shan.
Animosity, 恨 hanʼ, 仇 shau.
Aniseed, 茴香 ooi-ʻheung.
Ankle, 腳眼骨 keukʼ-ʻngaan-kwut.

| ANT | 10 | APE |

Annex, 接續 tsip-tsuuk, 加 ka.

Annihilation, 歸無 kwai-moo.

Anniversary, 年期日子 nin-k'i-yat-'tze, (first) 對年 tui'-nin.

Annoy, 煩擾 faan-'iu.

Annual, 每年 'mooi-nin.

Anoint, 搽 ch'a, 搽油 ch'a-yau.

Anonymous placard, 白帖 paak-t'ip'.

Another, 別個 pit-koh', 第二 tai'-i', 他 t'a, aan'.

Answer, 答應 taap-ying', 回音 ooi-yum, (suit) 着使 cheuk-'shai.

Ant, 蟻 'ngai, (an) 一隻蟻 yat-chek'-'ngai.

Ante-, 先 sin, ——之先 —— chi-sin.

Antelope, 羚羊 ling-yeung.

Antennæ, 兩條鬚 'leung-t'iu-so.

Anti-, 逆 yik, 對面 tui'-min'.

Anticipate, 預料 ue'-liu'.

Antidote, 解毒 'kaai-tuuk.

Antiquities, 古事 'koo-sze'.

Antiquity, 上古 sheung'-'koo.

Antler, 丫角 a-kok'.

Anus, 肛門 kong-moon, (VULG.) 屎窟 'shi-fut.

Anvil, 鐵砧 t'it'-chum.

Anxious, 放心不下 fong'-sum-pat-ha', 掛心 kwa'-sum, (for) 嬲 nat.

Any, 無論邊個 mo-luun'-pin-koh', 乜野 mat-'ye, (some) 的 tik.

Anywhere 邊處 pin-ch'ue', 邊處都好 pin-ch'ue' too-'ho.

Apart, 離開的 li-hoi-tik, 疏 shoh.

Apartment, 房 *fong, (an) 一間房 yat-kaan-*fong.

Apathy, 無感動 'mo-'kom-tuung'.

Ape, 馬騮 'ma-lau.

Aperient, 輕瀉藥 hing-se'-yeuk.

Aperture, 空處 huung-ch'ue', 口 'hau, 籠 luung.

注 释

【归无】灭绝，消失。
【白帖】匿名帖。
【无论边个】无论哪一个。
【乜野】什么东西。
【边处】哪里。
【马骝】猴子。Ape的对应词应为"猿"。

注释

【背教】放弃信仰，变节。
【补违】附加物。
【英四月】四月。"英"意为英制，即现在所说的公历，以区别于当时流行的农历月份。
【莺哥鼻】鹰钩鼻。
【和头/中人】仲裁人。

APP　　　11　　　ARB

Apex, 巔頂 tin-῾ting, 尖處 tsim-ch῾ue᾿.
Apiece, 每一個 ῾mooi-yat-koh᾿.
Apologize, 觧說 ῾kaai-shuet, 說開 shuet-hoi, 賠禮 p῾ooi-῾lai.
Apoplexy, 腦血中風 ῾no-huet῾-chuung᾿-fuung, 腦水中風 ῾no-῾shui-chuung᾿-fuung.
Apostatize, 背教 pooi᾿-kaau᾿.
Apostle, 使徒 sze᾿-t῾o.
Apparatus, 傢伙 ka-῾foh, 器具 hi᾿-kue᾿, (complete set) 一副應當 yat-foo᾿-ying᾿-tong᾿.
Apparel, 衣服 i-fuuk.
Apparition, 顯迹 ῾hin-tsik, 怪物 kwaai᾿-mat.
Appeal, 控告 huung᾿-ko᾿, 上控 sheung᾿-huung᾿.
Appear, 出顯 ch῾uut-῾hin.
Appearance, 貌 maau᾿.
Appease, 息氣 sik-hi᾿.
Appeased, 平息 p῾ing-sik.
Appendix, 補違 ῾po-wai.
Appetite, 胃口 wai᾿-῾hau.

Applaud, 喝彩 hoht-῾ts῾oi.
Apple, 平菓 p῾ing-῾kwoh.
Apply, 着 cheuk, 用 yuung᾿, 哈 up, (ask, &c.) 求 k῾au, 向 heung᾿.
Appoint, 設立 ch῾it-laap.
Appraise, 估價 ῾koo-ka᾿.
Apprehend, (seize) 捉到 chuuk᾿-to, (mentally) 曉 ῾hiu, 估 ῾koo.
Apprentice, 徒弟 t῾o-*tai᾿.
Approach, 就近 tsau᾿-kan᾿, tsau᾿-*kan᾿, 將近 tseung-kan᾿.
Appropriate, (take) 擅取 shin᾿-ts῾ue᾿, (fit) 合使 hop-῾shai.
Approve, 中意 chuung-i᾿.
Apricot, 杏 *hang᾿.
April, 英四月 Ying-sze᾿-uet.
Apron, 圍裙 wai᾿-*k῾wan.
Apt to, 會 ῾ooi.
Aquiline nose, 鶯哥鼻 ang-koh-pi᾿.
Arbitrate, 公斷 kuung-tuen᾿.
Arbitrator, 和頭 woh-t῾au, 中人 chuung-yan.

| ARM | 12 | ART |

Arbute, 楊梅 yeung-mooi.
Arch, 拱 ʻkuung, 彎拱 waan-ʻkuung.
Archer, 箭手 tsin⁾-ʻshau.
Architect, 大匠 taai⁾-tseung⁾ [in Hongkong, waak-chik-keʼ].
Ardent, (hot) 熱 it.
Are, 係 hai⁾, (in) 喺 ʻhai.
Argue, 辯駁 pin-pokʼ.
Arise, 起 ʻhi.
Aristocracy, 世家 shai⁾-ka.
Arithmetic, 算法 suen⁾-faat⁾.
Arm, (upper-) 手臂 ʻshau-pi, (fore-) 手肘 ʻshau-ʻchau, 手瓜 ʻshau-kwa, (the whole) 肩膀 kin-ʻpong.
Arm-chair, 交椅 kaau-ʻi.
Armour, 盔甲 kʻwai-kaapʼ.
Armoury, 軍器局 kwan-hiʼ-*kuuk.
Arm-pits, 胳肋底 kaak-laak-ʻtai.
Arms, 兵器 ping-hiʼ.
Army, 三軍 saam-kwan, 六軍 luuk-kwan.

Aromatic, 香 heung.
Around, 周圍 chau-wai.
Arouse, 醒 ʻseng, 打醒 ʻta-ʻseng.
Arraign, 告 koʼ.
Arrange, 安排 ohn-pʻaai, 整齊 ching-tsʻai, 調停 tʻiu-tʻing.
Arrear, 拖欠 tʻoh-himʼ.
Arrest, 捉 chuukʼ.
Arrive, 到 toʼ.
Arrogant, 驕傲 kiu-ngoʼ.
Arrogate, 僭分 tʻsimʼ-funʼ.
Arrow, 箭 tsinʼ.
Arsenal, 軍器局 kwan-hiʼ-*kuuk.
Arsenic, 信石 suunʼ-shek, 人言 yan-in.
Arson, 放火 fongʼ-ʻfoh.
Art, 藝 ngaiʼ, 工藝 kuung-ngaiʼ.
Artemisia, 艾 ngaaiʼ.
Artery, 血脉管 huetʼ-mak-ʻkoon.
Artful, 乖巧 kwaai-ʻhaau.
Article, 件 kinʼ, *kinʼ.
Artifice, 詭計 ʻkwai-kai.

注 释

【大匠】建筑师。
【胳肋底】胳肢窝。
【僭分】超越本分。
【信石/人言】砒霜的别称。因砒霜原产信州（今江西上饶），故称信石。又因砒霜有剧毒，常用作谋杀的毒药，故拆"信"字为"人言"，作为隐语。

注释

【人手作】手工的，人工制作的。
【阿魏】又名臭阿魏、细叶阿魏，多年生一次结果草本植物，是新疆一种独特的药材。
【不灰木】石棉。
【收埋】收起来。
【天门冬/天冬】芦笋。
【讲坏】中伤。

Artificial, 人手作 yan⟩-shau-tsok⟩.
Artillery, 大炮 taai⟩-p'aau⟩, (-men) 砲手 p'aau⟩-shau.
Artisan, 匠人 tseung⟩-yan, 做工人 tso⟩-kuung-yan.
Artist, 巧匠 ʻhaau-tseung⟩, 妙手 miu⟩-ʻshau, (painter) 畫師 wa⟩-sze.
Artless, 魯鈍 ʻlo-tuun⟩, 純直 shuun-chik.
As, 好似 ʻho-ʻtsze, 即如 tsik-ue, 猶之乎 yau-chi-oo.
Asafœtida, 阿魏 oh-ngai⟩.
Asbestos, 不灰木 pat-fooi-muuk.
Ascend, 上 ʻsheung, 上去 ʻsheung-hue⟩, 升 shing, 登 tang.
Ascent, (way of) 上去之路 ʻsheung-hue⟩-chi-lo⟩, 上路 ʻsheung-lo⟩.
Ascertain, 查明 ch'a-ming, 查真 ch'a-chan.
Ascetic, 修鍊 sau-lin⟩.
Ascribe to, 歸于 kwai-ue.

Ashamed, 見羞恥 kin⟩-sau-ʻch'i, 怕醜 p'a⟩-ʻch'au.
Ashes, 火灰 ʻfoh-fooi.
Ashore, 喺岸上 ʻhai-ngohn-sheung⟩, (to go) 上岸 ʻsheung-ngohn⟩.
Aside, 在傍 tsoi⟩-p'ong, (to put) 收埋 shau-maai.
Ask, 問 mun⟩, (invite) 請 ʻts'eng, (beg for) 求 k'au.
Aslant, 斜 ts'e, t'se⟩.
Asleep, 瞓 ʻfun.
Asparagus, 天門冬 t'in-moon-tuung, 天冬 t'in-tuung, 龍鬚菜 luung-so-ts'oi⟩.
Aspect, 景色 ʻking-shik, 貌 maau⟩, 光景 kwong-ʻking.
Asperse, 講壞 ʻkong-waai⟩.
Aspirate, 噴氣 p'un⟩-hi⟩.
Aspire, 想上進 ʻseung-sheung⟩-tsuun⟩, 貪大 t'aam-taai⟩.
Ass, 驢 *lue, (an) 隻驢 chek⟩-lue, (a great) 大笨象 taai⟩-pun⟩-tseung⟩.
Assail, 攻 kuung.
Assassin, 刺客 ts'ze⟩-haak⟩.

| ASS | 14 | AT |

Assault, 攻打 kuung⸲-ta⸲, (as robbers) 打脚骨 ⸢ta-keuk⸲-kwut.

Assay, 考驗 ⸢haau-im⸲, 驗過 im⸲-kwo⸲.

Assemble, 聚集 tsue⸲-tsaap.

Assembly, 會 *ooi⸲.

Assent, 話肯 wa⸲-⸢hang, 允 ⸢wan.

Assert, 話係 wa⸲-hai⸲, 力言 lik-in.

Assess, 估稅 ⸢koo-shui⸲.

Assets, 遺業 wai-ip, 遺產 wai-ch'aan.

Assign, 立限 laap-haan⸲, 限定 haan⸲-ting⸲, (-to) 定歸 ting⸲-kwai.

Assist, 幫助 pong-choh⸲, 照顧 chiu⸲-koo⸲.

Assistant, 二手 i⸲-⸢shau, (in government) 副 foo⸲.

Assize, 官擬價 koon-⸢i-ka⸲.

Associate, to, 相與 seung-⸢ue, 往來 ⸢wong-loi, (an) 同伴 t'uung-poon⸲.

Association, 會 *ooi⸲.

Assort, 排列 p'aai-lit, 安排 ohn-p'aai.

Assuage, 解 ⸢kaai.

Assume, 以為 ⸢i-wai, 假借 ⸢ka-tse⸲, (a name) 冒名 mo⸲-*meng.

Assuming, 擅自 shin⸲-tsze⸲.

Assurance, (faith) 篤信 tuuk-suun⸲, (presumption) 膽 ⸢taam.

Assure, 擔保 taam-⸢po.

Assuredly, 果然 ⸢kwoh-in.

Asthma, 氣喘 hi⸲-ch'uen.

Astonish, 驚着 king-cheuk.

Astonishing, 出奇 ch'uut-k'i.

Astound, 驟嚇 tsau⸲-(chaau⸲)-haak.

Astray, 蕩失 tong⸲-shat.

Astringent, 收濕藥料 shau-shup-yeuk-liu⸲.

Astrology, 星學 sing-hok.

Astronomy, 天文 t'in-mun.

Asylum, 院 *uen⸲, (for children) 育嬰堂 yuuk-ying-*t'ong.

At, 在 tsoi⸲, 喺 ⸢hai, (-last) 卒之 tsuut-chi, 究竟 kau⸲-⸢king.

注 释

【话无上帝者】无神论者。
【做和头】做和事佬。
Attitude:译为"容""状貌"是误译。应译为"态度"。
【状师】律师。
【喊夜冷】冷，即"栏"。以前在广州把生意的地方称为"栏"，这里是指商贩在夜市中叫卖减价清货。
【考数司】总审计员。

Atheist, 話無上帝者 wa'-mo-sheung'tai'-che.
Atlas, 地圖書 ti'-t'o-shue.
Atmosphere, 天氣 t'in-hi'.
Atom, 微末 mi-moot.
At once, 卽時 tsik-shi.
Atone, 代贖 toi'-shuuk, 使敵和 'shai-tik-woh, 做和頭 tso'-woh-t'au.
Atrocity, 殘認之事 ts'aan-yan-chi-sze'.
Attach, 貼近 t'ip'-kan' ('k'an) 相連 seung-lin.
Attachment, 貼心 t'ip'-sum.
Attack, 攻打 kuung-'ta, 攻擊 kuung-kik.
Attain, 得到 tak-'to, 得至 tak-chi', 及至 k'aap-chi'.
Attempt, 試爲 shi'-wai, 試做下 shi'-tso'-'ha.
Attend to, 留心 lau-sum, (at) 在 tsoi', (upon) 侍奉 shi'-fuung', 服事 fuuk-sze', (manage) 打理 'ta-'li.
Attendants, 跟班 kan-paan.
Attentive, 檢點 'kim-'tim, 細心 sai'-sum.

Attest, 作証 tsok'-ching'.
Attire, 裝扮 chong-paan'.
Attitude, 容 yuung, 狀貌 chong'-maau'.
Attorney, 狀師 chong'-sze, 小狀師 'siu-chong'-sze, (to act as) 代辦 toi'-paan'.
Attorney General, 國家律政司 Kwok'-ka-luut-ching-sze.
Attract, 招引 chiu-'yan.
Auburn, 褐色 hoht'-shik.
Auction, (sell by) 投賣 t'au-maai', (sale) 喊夜冷 haam'-ye'-'laang.
Audacious, 果敢 'kwoh-'kom, 大膽 taai'-'taam.
Auditor General, 考數司 'Haau-sho'-sze.
Augment, 加增 ka-tsang, 添 t'im.
August, 英八月 Ying-paat'-uet.
Augúst, 皇 wong.
Aunt, (paternal) 姑母 koo-'moo, (maternal) 姨母 i-'moo.

| AWA | 16 | BAC |

Auspicious, 吉 *kat*.
Austere, 局肅 *kuuk-suuk*.
Author, 造主 tso'-*chue*, 著造之人 *chue*'-tso'-*chi*(*ke*')-yan, 作家 *tsok-ka*.
Authority, 權 k'uen, 權勢 k'uen-*shai*', 權柄 k'uen-*ping*'.
Autumn, 秋天 *ts'au-t'in*.
Avail one's self of, 趁 *ch'an*', 乘 shing, 趁勢 *ch'an*'-*shai*', (be of use) 有益 *yau-yik*.
Avarice, 貪財 *t'aam-ts'oi*, 貪婪 *t'aam-laam*.
Avenge, 報仇 po'-*ch'au*.
Average, 拉扯算 laai-*ch'e-suen*'.
Averse, 不中意 'm-chuung-i', 不耐煩 'm-noi'-faan.
Avoid, 脫免 *t'uet*-'min, 避 pi'.
Avouch, 認眞 ying'-*chan*.
Avow, 直話 chik-wa'.
Await, 等待 *tang-toi*'.
Awake, 瞓醒 fun'-'seng, 醒 'seng, (wide-) 醒定 'sing-ting'.

Aware, 知到 *chi-to*'.
Away, 去 'hue, 離 li.
Awe, 畏懼 wai'-kue'.
Awkward, 粗魯 *t'so*-'lo, 不(唔)入世 'm-yup-*shai*'.
Awl, 錐 chui, yui.
Awning, 遮帳 *che-cheung*', 布帳 po'-*cheung*'.
Awry, 歪 'me.
Axe, 斧頭 'foo-*t'au*.
Axle, 轉軸 'chuen-chuk.
Ay, 係咯 hai'-lok, 係 hai'.
Azalea, 杜鵑花 to'-*kuen-fa*.
Azure, 蒼色 *ts'ong-shik*.

B

Babble, 嘹嘈 lo-ts'o, 嘈吵 ts'o-*ch'aau*.
Babbler, 嘈吵之人 ts'o-*ch'aau-ke*'-yan.
Baby, 亞蘇仔 a'-so-*tsai*.
Bachelor, 未娶 mi'-*ts'ue*'.
Back, (the) 背 pooi', 背脊 pooi'-tsek, (turn-) 返 'faan, 回轉 ooi-'chuen, (behind one's) 背後邊 pooi'-hau'-*pin*.

注 釋

【局肅】严峻的。
【拉扯算】平均。
Avouch: 断言，保证。译为"认真"属误译。
【知到】意识到。
【苍色】蔚蓝色。
【亚苏仔】婴儿。

注释

【揩阻】困惑,使……受挫。
【无定埋手】没办法。
【保领】保释。
【一支野】"野"指是东西,编者在这里应该是用"野"指代歌曲、音乐。
【责载】压舱物。

BAI　　17　　BAM

Back-bite, 背後譖謗 pooi’-hau`-wai-p‘ong’.
Back-bone, 背脊骨 pooi’-tsek`-kwut.
Back-door, 後門 hau`-*moon.
Backslide, 背道 pooi’-to’.
Backstitch, 鉤 k‘au’.
Backward, 向後 heung’-hau`, 退後 t‘ui`-hau`, (to walk) 倒行 ’to-hang.
Bacon, 烟豬肉 in-chue-yuuk.
Bad, 惡 ok`, 不好 ’m-‘ho, 醜 `ch‘au, 滲 sum’, 呀 yai.
Badge, 記號 ki’-ho’.
Badger, 狗獾 `kau-foon.
Baffle, 揩阻 k‘ang’-choh, 擺佈倒 `paai-po’-to, (him) 奈佢何 noi’-k‘ue-hoh.
Baffled, 無定埋手 ‘mo-teng`-maai-`shau, 無計 ‘mo-kai’.
Bag, 袋 *toi, 囊 nong.
Baggage, 行李 hang-‘li.
Bail, 保領 ’po-‘ling.
Bait, 餌 ni’.

Baize, 粗大呢 ts‘o-taai’-ni.
Bake, 炕 hong’, 局 kuuk.
Balance, (a) 天平 t‘in-p‘ing, (steelyard) 把秤 ’pa-ch‘ing’, (small do.) 釐戥 li-*tang, (to) 抵相抵 tai’, seung-tai’, 平兌 p‘ing-tui’, (the) 剩銀 shing-*ngan.
Bald, 光 kwong, 禿 t‘uuk, (-head) 光頭 kwong-t‘au.
Bale, (a) 包 paau, (to, water) 戽水 foo’-shui’.
Ball, (a) 毬 k‘au, (cannon) 砲子 p‘aau’-tsze, 砲碼 p‘aau’-*ma.
Ballad, 曲 k‘uuk, huuk, (a) 一支野 yat-chi-`ye.
Ballast, 責載 chaak-*tsoi.
Balloon, 輕氣毬 hing-hi-k‘au.
Balsam, (flower) 指甲花 `chi-kaap’-fa, 鳳仙花 fuung’-sin-fa.
Bamboo, 竹 chuuk, (a) 條竹 t‘iu-chuuk.

| BAN | 18 | BAR |

Bamboo shoots, 竹笋 chuuk-꜀suun.
Banana, 蕉 ꜁tsiu.
Band, (tie) 帶 taai꜃, (company) 一隊 yat-tui꜃, 一班 yat-paan.
Bandage, (a) 纏帶 ch꜀in-taai꜃ (꜀taai), (to) 纏 ꜁chin.
Band-box, 紙盒 ꜂chi-*hop.
Banditti, 賊夥 ts꜀aak-foh, 匪黨 fi-꜁tong.
Bandy-legged, 曲脛 kuuk-king꜄, 八字腳 paat꜄-tsze꜄-keuk꜄, 蜂髀 paang꜁-꜂pi.
Bane, 毒 tuuk.
Bang, 碰 p꜀uung꜃, 蜂 p꜀aang꜃, ꜁paang.
Bangle, 鈪 aak꜄.
Banian, 榕樹 yuung-shue꜃.
Banish, 充軍 ch꜀uung-kwun, 問軍 mun꜃-kwun.
Bank, (of a river) 河岸 hoh-ngohn꜃, 海邊 ꜂hoi-pin, (for money) 銀行 ngan-*hong.
Bankrupt, 倒行 ꜂to-*hong, 倒灶 ꜂to-tso꜃.

Banner, 旗 k꜀i, (large) 大翻 taai꜃-t꜀o.
Bannermen, 旗下 k꜀i-*ha꜃.
Banquet, 酒席 tsau-tsek.
Banter, 詼諧 fooi-haai꜁, 激笑 kik-siu꜃.
Baptism, 洗禮 ꜂sai-꜂lai.
Baptize, 施洗 shi-꜂sai, (to be baptized) 受洗 shau꜃-꜂sai 領洗 ꜂ling-꜂sai.
Bar, (of a door) 門閂 moon-shaan, 橫遏 waang-aat꜄, (of a cage) 橫櫳 waang-luung, *waang.
Barbarous, 蠻 maan, 蠻夷 maan-i.
Barbel, 嘉魚 ka-ue.
Barber, 剃頭人 t꜀ai꜃-t꜀au-yan.
Bare, 裸 ꜂loh, 赤 ch꜀ik꜄, 光 kwong, (to) 剝 mok꜄, 袒 ꜂t꜀aan, 捋 luet꜄, (-faced) 無臉 ꜂mo-lim꜂.
Bargain, (to) 講價 ꜂kong-ka꜃, (settle a) 講定價錢 ꜂kong-ting꜃-ka꜃-ts꜀in.
Bark, (of a tree) 樹皮 shue꜃-p꜀i.

注释

【曲胫】膝向外弯曲的,罗圈腿的。
【鈪】手镯,脚镯。
【倒灶】倒霉,破产。在陕西关中、浙江台州等地方言中均有倒霉的意思。
【无脸】赤裸裸的,不要脸的。

注释

【苡米】又称"薏米""薏苡",英译为"Job' stears""pearlbarley",是研磨加工后的大麦粒。

【风雨针】气压计。

【怕丑】害羞。

【紫苏】罗勒,一种亚洲热带植物,药食两用,味似茴香,全株小巧,叶色翠绿,花色鲜艳,芳香四溢。

【野仔】私生子。

【飞鼠】蝙蝠。

BAS　19　BE

Bark, (to) 吠 fai⁾.
Barley, 大麥 taai⁾-maak, (pearl) 苡米 ⸌i-⸌mai.
Barn, 田庄 t'in-⸌chong.
Barometer, 風雨針 fuung-⸌uc-chum.
Baron, 男爵 naam-tseuk⸌.
Barque, 兩枝半桅船 ⸌leung-chi-⸌poon⸌-*wai-shuen.
Barracks, 兵房 ping-fong.
Barrel, 洋酒桶 yeung-⸌tsau-⸌t'uung.
Barren, (womb) 石胎 shek-t'oi (land) 瘠土 tsik⸌-⸌t'o.
Barricade, 栅欄 ch'aak-laan.
Barrier, 閘 chaap, 保障 ⸌po-cheung⸌, 阻碍 choh-ngoi⸌.
Barrister, 大狀師 taai-chong⸌-sze.
Barrow, 手車 ⸌shau-ch'e.
Barter, 兌換 tui⸌-oon⸌.
Base, (bottom) 底 ⸌tai, 墩 ⸌tun, 基 ki, 腳 keuk⸌.
Base, (mean) 鄙陋 ⸌p'i-lau⸌, (bad) 歹 ⸌taai.
Basement, 地牢 ti⸌-loo, 墩 ⸌tun.
Bashful, 怕醜 p'a⸌-ch'au.

Basil, (sweet) 紫蘇 ⸌tsze-soo.
Basin, 盆 p'oon, (small) 碗 ⸌oon.
Basket, 籃 *laam, 籮 loh, 筐 hong, k'waang, 笠 lap, 籬 li.
Bastard, 野仔 ⸌ye-⸌tsai, (in abusive language) 龜仔 kwai-⸌tsai.
Baste clothes, 攤衣服 naan⸌-i-fuuk.
Bastinado, 打板子 ⸌ta-⸌paan-⸌tsze.
Bat, 飛鼠 fi-⸌shue, (a) 一隻飛鼠 yat-chek-fi-⸌shue.
Bathe, 洗身 ⸌sai-shan.
Battery, 炮臺 p'aau⸌-*t'oi.
Battle, (a) 打仗一陣 ⸌ta-cheung⸌-yat-chan⸌.
Bawdy-house, 娼寮 ch'eung-*liu, cheung-*liu.
Bawl, 呼喊 foo-haam⸌.
Bay, (of the sea) 灣 waan, 澳 o⸌.
Bayonet, 鎗頭劍 ⸌ts'eung-t'au-kim⸌.
Be, 係 hai⸌, (be in) 喺 ⸌hai, 在 tsoi⸌.

Beach, 海邊 ʻhoi-pin.
Beacon, 烟墩 in-tuun.
Bead, 珠 chue, (a string of beads) 一串珠 yat-chʻuenʼ-chue, (a bead) 一粒珠 yat-nup-chue.
Beak, 嘴 ʻtsui.
Beam, (a) 梁木 leung-muuk, 條陳 tʻiu-chanʼ.
Beam, (to) 發光 faatʼ-kwong.
Bean, 豆 *tauʼ, (French) 豆角 tauʼ-kokʼ, 邊豆 pin tauʼ, 面豆 minʼ-*tau (sprouts), 芽菜 nga-tsʻoi.
Bean-curd, 豆腐 tauʼ-fooʼ.
Bear, (carry on the shoulder) 擔 taam, (between two) 擡 tʻoi, (on the back) 狽 me, (endure) 抵住 ʻtai-chueʼ, 受 shanʼ, (a child) 生 shang.
Bear, (a) 一隻熊人 yat-chekʼ-huung-*yan.
Beard, 鬚 so, 下爬鬚 haʼ-pʻa-so.
Bearer, (chair-) 擡夫 tʻoi-foo, (letter-) 拈信人 nim-suunʼ-yan.

Beast, 獸 shauʼ, (a) 一隻獸 yat-chekʼ-shauʼ.
Beat, 打 ʻta, (up eggs, &c.) 拂 faakʼ, (defeat) 打敗 ʻta-paaiʼ.
Beau, 大亞官 taaiʼ-aʼ-koon.
Beautiful, 美 ʻmi, 好睇 ʻho-ʻtʻai, 好樣 ʻho-*yeungʼ, 標緻 piu-chiʼ, 威 wai.
Beauty, female, 色 shik.
Beaver, 海驟 ʻhoi-*loh.
Becalmed, 無風駛 mo-fuung-ʻshai, 聽風 tʻingʼ-fuung.
Because, 因爲 yan-wai.
Beche-de-mer, 海參 ʻhoi-shum.
Beckon, 手招 ʻshau-chiu, 噏 ngup.
Become, 成 shing, 爲 wai, 做 tsoʼ, (to grow) 生成 shaang-shing.
Becoming, (fit) 合式 hop-shik.
Bed, 牀 chʻong, (a) 一張床 yat-cheung-chʻong.

【烟墩】灯塔。
【抬夫】搬运工人，轿夫。
【大亚官】大官人。
【无风驶】因无风而停止不能前进，平静的。
【手招】召唤，手势。

注 释

【蜜笼】蜂房。
Beet:现译为"甜菜",与苋菜(amaranth)不是同一种植物。
【初造】开始,首先。
【扯咯】走了。
【打嗳气】打嗝。

BEG　　21　　BEL

Bed-chamber, 臥房 ngoh⸴-fong, 瞓房 fun⸴-fong, *fong.
Bedding, 床鋪 ch'ong-p'oo, 鋪蓋 p'oo-k'oi⸴, 被 p'i.
Bee, 蜂 fuung, 蜜蜂 mat-fuung.
Bee-hive, 蜜籠 mat-*luung.
Beef, 牛肉 ngau-yuuk.
Beef-steak, 牛肉耙 ngau-yuuk-*p'a.
Beer, 卑酒 pe-⸌tsau.
Beet, 莧菜 in⸴-ts'oi⸴.
Beet-root, 紅菜頭 huung-ts'oi⸴-*t'au.
Beetle, 甲蟲 kaap⸴-ch'uung.
Before, 先 sin, 前 ts'in, (formerly) 從前 ts'uung-ts'in, 先時 sin-shi.
Beforehand, 預先 ue⸴-sin.
Befriend, 照顧 chiu⸴-koo⸴, 體恤 ⸌t'ai-suut.
Beg, 乞 hat, 乞求 hat-k'au.
Beget, 生 shaang.
Beggar, 乞兒 hat-i, 花子 fa-⸌tsze.

Begin, 初造 ch'oh-tso⸴, 開手 hoi-⸌shau, 埋手 maai-⸌shau, 起首 ⸌hi-⸌shau, 興工 hing-kuung.
Beginning, 始初 ⸌ch'i-ch'oh, 首 ⸌shau.
Begone, 扯咯 ⸌ch'e-lok.
Begonia, 春海棠 ch'uun-⸌hoi-t'ong.
Beguile, 欺 hi, 欺惑 hi-waak.
Behalf, (in) 替代 t'ai⸴-toi⸴.
Behave, 行 hang, (towards) 待 toi⸴.
Behaviour, 品行 ⸌pun-hang⸴.
Behead, 斬頭 ⸌chaam-*t'au, 殺頭 shaat-*t'au.
Behind, 後 hau⸴, (to be) 喺後頭 ⸌hai-hau⸴-t'au.
Behold, 顧住 koo⸴-chue⸴, 睇 ⸌t'ai, (lo !) 睇嗱 ⸌t'ai-na !
Behoof, 利益 li⸴-yik.
Behove, 應該 ying-koi.
Being, (existence) 有 ⸌yau, 有者 ⸌yau-che.
Belch, 打嗳氣 ⸌ta-⸌oi-hi, (COL.) yeuk-⸌hi-lai, yeuk.

BEN　22　BES

Believe, 信 *suun*'.
Bell, 鐘 *chuung*, 鈴 ˌ*ling*.
Bell-flower, 吊鐘花 *tiu*'-*chuung-fa*.
Belladonna, 巔茄 *tin*-*k'e*.
Bellows, 風箱 *fuung-seung*, 皮排 *p'i-p'aai*.
Belly, 肚 ˌ*t'o*, 腹 *fuuk*.
Belong, 屬 *shuuk*, 關屬 *kwaan-shuuk*.
Beloved, 愛 *oi*', 所愛 ˌ*shoh-oi*'.
Below, 下 *ha*', 底下 ˌ*tai-ha*', 下底 *ha*'-*tai* (*tai*)
Belt, 腰帶 *iu-taai*', 帶圍 *taai*'-*wai*.
Bemoan, 悲哀 *pi-oi*.
Bench, 板凳 ˌ*paan-tang*', (magistrate's) 公案 *kuung-ohn*'.
Bend, (to) 屈曲 *wat-huuk* (*k'uuk*), 整曲 ˌ*ching-huuk*, 嚟 ˌ*lai*, (a) 彎曲 *waan-huuk*.
Beneath, 在下 *tsoi*'-*ha*', 喺下邊 ˌ*hai-ha*'-*pin* (*pin*').
Benefactor, 恩主 *yan*-ˌ*chue*.

Beneficent, 肯䦧恤 ˌ*hang-chau-suut*.
Benefit, 益 *yik*, (grace) 恩澤 *yan-chaak*, (to) 滋益 *tsze-yik*.
Benevolence, 仁愛 *yan-oi*', 仁 *yan*, 仁德 *yan-tak*.
Benighted, 居黑暗中 *kue-hak-om*'-*chuung*.
Bent, 曲 *k'uuk*, *huuk*, 拗了 ˌ*aau*-ˌ*liu* (*hiu*).
Bent of mind, 志氣 *chi*'-*hi* 志向 *chi*'-*heung*'.
Bequeath, 留落 *lau-lok*, 遺囑 *wai-chuuk*.
Bereaved of, 喪失 *song*' *shat*.
Berth, 房位 *fong*-*wai*'.
Beseech, 懇求 ˌ*han-k'au*.
Beset, 圍住 *wai-chue*'.
Beside, 側邊 *chak-pin*.
Besides, 另外 *ling*'-*ngoi*'.
Besiege, 圍困 *wai-k'wun*'.
Besotted, 昏迷 *fun-mai*.
Bespeak, 定 *ting*', 講定 ˌ*kong-ting*'.
Best, 第一好 *tai*'-*yat*-ˌ*ho*, 至好 *chi*'-ˌ*ho*, 頂好 ˌ*ting*-ˌ*ho*.

注　释

【皮排】风箱,古称"橐籥",是古代一种用皮革制作的鼓风器具。
【恩主】恩人,施主。
【肯䦧恤】慈善的。
【留落】遗赠,把……传下去。
【房位】卧铺。

注释

【卖付】出卖。
【口水肩】围嘴。
【张单】清单，账单。
【揽载纸】提货单。
【波楼】台球馆。

Bestow, 施賜 shi-ts'ze', 給 k'up.
Bet, 輸賭 shue-'to.
Betelnut, 檳榔 pun-long.
Betel-pepper-leaf, 荖葉 lau-ip.
Betray, 賣付 maai'-foo', 欺陷 hi-haam'.
Betroth, (of men) 定親 ting'-ts'an, (of women) 許聘 'hue-p'ing'.
Better, 更好 kang'-ho, (a little) 好的 'ho-tik, (quite) 好嘥 'ho-saai.
Between, 中間 chuung-,kaan, —之間 —chi ,kaan.
Bewail, 哀哭 oi-huuk.
Beware, 提防 t'ai-fong, 關顧 kwaan-koo'.
Bewildered, 心亂 sum-luen', 入迷路 yup-mai-lo', 恍惚 'fong-fut.
Bewitched, 鬼迷 'kwai-mai.
Beyond, —之外 —chi-ngoi', —外 —ngoi', (to go) 過 kwoh'.
Bezoar, 牛黃 ngau-wong.

Bias, 偏 p'in.
Bib, 口水肩 ,hau-'shui-kin, ,hau-'shui-lau.
Bible, 聖經 shing'-king.
Bid, (order) 囑咐 chuuk-foo, (invite) 請 'ts'ing, (offer) 出 ch'uut.
Bide, 等 'tang, 耐 noi'.
Bier, 運柩架 wun'-kau'-ka'.
Big, 大 taai'.
Bignonia, 凌霄花 ling-siu-fa.
Bigoted, 固執 koo'-chup, 泥 ni', 泥住本教 ni'-chue'-'poon-,kaau'.
Bile, 膽汁 'taam-chup.
Bill, (beak) 嘴 'tsui, (paper) 張單 ,cheung-,taan.
Bill of exchange, 匯單 ooi'-,taan.
Bill of lading, 攬載紙 laam'-tsoi'-'chi.
Billiard, 波 poh, (to play) 打波 'ta-poh, (room) 波樓 poh-*lau.
Billows, 波浪 poh-long'.

| BIT | 24 | BLA |

Bind, 札 chaat`, 綁 ‵pong, 綁住 ‵pong-chue‵ (agree) 約 yeuk` (books) 釘 teng, 釘裝 teng-chong`.
Binding, (of clothes) 綑邊 ‵k'wun-pin, 綑條 ‵k'wun-*t'iu, 緣 nen`.
Biography, 行狀 hang-chong`.
Birch, 樺木 wa-muuk.
Bird, 鳥 ‵niu, 雀鳥 tseuk`-‵niu, (small) 雀仔 tseuk`-‵tsai, (a) 一隻鳥 yat-chek`-‵niu, (and beast) 禽獸 k'um-shau`.
Bird-lime, 黐膠 c‵hi-kaau.
Bird's-nest, (edible) 燕窩 in`-woh.
Birth, 生 shaang.
Birth-day, 生日 shaang-yat.
Biscuit, 餅乾 ‵peng-kohn.
Bit, (of a bridle) 馬口鉗 ‵ma-‵hau-k'im, (piece) 塊 faai`.
Bitch, 狗母 ‵kau-‵moo, 狗姆 ‵kau-‵na.
Bite, 咬 ngaau, (a) 一啖 yat-taam`.

Bitter, 苦 ‵foo.
Bittern, 朱鷺 chue-lo`.
Bitumen, 瀝青 lik-ts‵ing.
Bivalve, 蜆殼 ‵hin-hok`.
Black, 黑 hak, 黑色 hak-shik.
Blackguard, 光棍 kwong-kwun`, 爛仔 laan`-‵tsai, 爛口 laan`-‵hau.
Blacking, (shoe-) 鞋墨 haai-maak.
Blackleg, 摘家仔 lo-ka-‵tsai.
Black-smith, 打鐵匠 ‵ta-t'it`-*tseung`.
Bladder, 尿胞 niu`-paau, (animal's) 小肚 ‵siu-t'o.
Blade, (of grass) 草葉 ‵ts'o-ip, (of a knife) 刀肉 to-*yuuk, (shoulder-) 飯匙骨 faan`-shi-kwut.
Bladed knife, three, 三開刀 saam-hoi-to.
Blain, 血旺色 huet`-wong`-shik.
Blame, 罪 tsui`, (to) 彈 t'aan, 怪 kwaai`, 責 chaak`.
Blameless, 無罪 ‵mo-tsui`.

注 释

Bittern:应译为"麻鳽"。"朱鷺"的英文是ibis或flinthead。
【光棍】流氓,无赖。
【烂仔】小混混,恶棍。
【尿胞】膀胱。
【血旺色】水疱,痘。

注 释

【牛乳冻】一种家常的甜品。
【摸盲】捉迷藏。
【律罗】阻止，阻塞。
【吟佬】木头人，笨蛋，傻子。

BLI　　25　　BLU

Blanc-mange, 牛乳凍 ngau-ʻue-tuung'.
Blank, 空白 huung'-paak.
Blanket, 白氈 paak-chin.
Blaspheme, 褻瀆 sit'-tuuk, 謗讟 pʻong'-tuuk.
Blast rocks, 打石炮 ʻta-shek-pʻaau'.
Blaze, 火焰 ʻfoh-im', 火光 ʻfoh-kwong, 火氣 ʻfoh-hi', 火猛 ʻfoh-maang.
Bleach, 漂白 pʻiu'-paak.
Bleat, 咩 me, 咩聲 me-sheng.
Bleed, 流血 lau-huet'.
Blemish, 汚點 oo-ʻtim, 病 peng', 毛病 mo-peng', 瑕疵 ha-tsʻze.
Blend, 和匀 woh'-wan, 摳匀 kʻau-wan.
Bless, 祝 chuuk, 祝福 chuuk-fuuk.
Blight, 殘 tsʻaan, 弊 pai'.
Blind, 盲眼 maang-ʻngaan.
Blind-man's-buff, 捉迷蒙 chuuk'-mi-*muung, 摸盲 ʻmoh-maang.
Blinds, 簾 *lim, (venetian-) 百葉窗 paakʻ-ip-chʻeung.

Blink, 閃 ʻshim, (the eyes) 喵 ngup, (elude sight) 閃過眼 ʻshim-kwoh'-ngaan.
Bliss, 福 fuuk.
Blister, 水泡 ʻshui-pʻaau, (pʻok), (to) 發水泡 faat'-shui-pʻaau.
Bloated, 浮腫 fau-ʻchuung.
Block, (of wood, &c.) 頭 tʻau, 俗 kau', (for printing) 板 ʻpaan, (pulley) 律羅 luut-*loh.
Blockade, 阻塞港口 ʻchoh-sak-ʻkong-ʻhau, 阻塞津要 ʻchoh-sak-tsuun-iu'.
Blockhead, 木偶人 muuk-ngau-yan, 吟佬 yai-ʻlo.
Blood, 血 huet'.
Bloom, (to) 開花 hoi-fa.
Blot, 塗污 tʻo-oo, (out) 塗抹 tʻo-moot', 搽 chʻa.
Blotch, 酒𤴪 tsau-cha.
Blow, (strike) 打 ʻta, (a) 打一下 ʻta-yat-ha, (as wind) 吹 chʻui, (the nose) 擤鼻 sang'-piʻ, (out) 吹滅 chʻui-mit'.
Blue, 藍色 laam-shik, 靛 tin'.

| BOD | 26 | BOM |

Blunder, 錯誤 ts'oh'-'ng'.
Blunt, 鈍 tuun', tuen', 痴呆 ch'i-ngoi.
Blur, 矇 muung, 模糊 moo-oo.
Blush, 發紅變面 faat-huung-'nin-min', 含羞 hom-sau.
Bluster, 躁暴 ts'o'-po'.
Boa-constrictor, 蟒蛇 mong-she.
Boar, 猪郎 chue-long.
Board, (wood) 木板 muuk-'paan, (a) 一塊板 yat-faai-'paan, (department) 部 po'.
Board, (to eat with) 同食 t'uung-shik, 搭食 taap'-shik, (one's self) 食自己 shik-tsze'-'ki, (ship) 上船 'sheung-shuen.
Boast, 矜誇 king-k'wa, 誇 k'wa.
Boat, 艇 't'eng, 三舨 saam-'paan, 船 shuen.
Bob, 奀 ngan'.
Bodice, 押胸 moon-huung.

Bodkin, 串帶針 ch'uen'-taai'-chum.
Body, 身 shan, 身體 shan-'t'ai, 體 't'ai.
Bog, 洴池 paan'-ch'i.
Bohea-tea, 武彞茶 'moo-i-ch'a.
Boil, (to) 煲 po, 煠 shaap.
Boiled, 熟 shuuk.
Boiling, 滾 'kwan, (with rage) 心滾 sum-'kwan.
Boils, 瘡 ch'ong.
Boiler, 鑊 wok, 塔 tap, 煲 po.
Boisterous, 暴 po', 猛 'maang.
Bold, 大膽 taai'-'taam, 剛毅 kong-ngai'.
Bolster, 大牀枕 taai'-ch'ong-'chum.
Bolt, 釘 teng, 楔 suut, 鐵貫 t'it'-koon', (of a door) 門閂 moon-shaan, (to) 閂 shaan.
Bomb, 開花炮 hoi-fa-p'aau', (COL.) 'pom-p'aau'.
Bombay ducks, 肚魚乾 't'o-*ue-kohn'.

注 释

【同食】搭伙,包饭。
【矜夸】自夸,自吹自擂。
【奀】(人)瘦弱。
【扪胸】妇女紧身内衣,抹胸。
【串带针】大眼粗针。
【洴池】沼泽。
Bombay ducks:龙头鱼。

注 释

【约单】约定，债券。
【大头虾】粗心的人。
【蛮村佬】乡下佬（含贬义），粗鄙无礼的人。
【弊家伙】糟糕。
【打恭】鞠躬，弯腰。
【船头拔】船头的斜桅。

Bond, 約單 yeuk`-taan, (money-) 借單 tse`-taan, (band) 帶 taai`.
Bond-servant, 奴僕 no-puuk.
Bone, 骨 kwut.
Bonnet, 女帽 nue-*mo`.
Booby, 戇人 ngong`-yan, 大頭蝦 taai`-t'au-ha.
Book, 書 shue, (a) 一部書 yat-po`-shue, 部 *po`.
Book case, 書櫃 shue-*kwai`.
Bookbinder, 釘書人 teng-shue-yan.
Book-worm, 蠹魚 to`-ue.
Boom, 帆杠 faan-kong`.
Boor, 蠻村佬 maan-ts'uen-`lo.
Boot, 靴 hö.
Booth, 茅屋 maau-uuk, 棚 p'aang.
Bo-peep, 覗睒 ͺchong-ͺngaau.
Borax, 硼砂 p'ang-sha.
Border, 邊 pin, 界 kaai`, 邊境 pin-`king.
Bore, 鑽 tsuen`, 穿 ch'uen.
Born, 生 shang, 出世 ch'uut-shai`.

Borrow, 借來 tse`-loi, 假借 ͺka-tse`.
Bosom, 胸懷 huung-waai.
Botany, 草木學 `ts'o-muuk-hok.
Botch, 弊家伙 pai`-ka-foh.
Both, 兩個 `leung-koh`.
Bother, 煩擾 faan-`iu, 撈 lo.
Bothered, 厭悶 im-moon`.
Bottle, 罇 tsuun.
Bottle-gourd, 葫蘆 oo-*loo.
Bottom, 底 `tai.
Bound, }
Bounce, } 跳 t'iu`.
Boundary, 變界 kaau-kaai`.
Boundless, 無限 `mo-haan`.
Bountiful, 厚重 hau`-chuung`.
Bow, (to) 打恭 `ta-kuung, 作揖 tsok`-yup.
Bow, (a) 弓 kuung, 一把弓 yat-`pa-kuung.
Bowels, 腸 ch'eung, 肚 `t'o.
Bowl, 碗 `oon.
Bowsprit, 船頭拔 shuen-t'au-pat.

BRA 28 BRE

Box, 箱 *seung*, (to) 拳打 *k'uen-ta*, 打拳頭 *ta-k'uen-t'au*.
Boy, 男仔 *naam-tsai*, (servant-) 事仔 *sze-tsai*, (waiting-) 侍仔 *shi-tsai*.
Bracelet, 手鈪 *shau-aak*.
Braces, 褲帶 *foo-taai*.
Brag, 誇大 *k'wa-taai*.
Braggart, 誇口 *k'wa-hau*.
Braid, 欄杆 *laan-kohn*, (to) 編織 *pin-chik*, 搒 *pin*.
Brain, 腦漿 *no-tseung*.
Bramble, 荊棘 *king-kik*, 笏 *lak*.
Bran, 麥糠 *mak-hong*.
Branch, 枝 *chi*.
Brand, (a) 火把 *foh-pa*, 鐵烙 *t'it-lok*, (to) 烙印 *lok-yan*.
Brandish, 舞 *moo*, 手舞 *shau-moo*.
Brandy, 罷欄地酒 *pa-laan-ti-tsau*.
Brass, 銅 *t'uung*, 黃銅 *wong-t'uung*.
Brassica, 白菜 *paak-ts'oi*.
Brave, 勇敢 *yuung-kom*.

Bravo: 好 *ho*!
Brawl, 鬧交 *naau-kaau*.
Bray, 驢鳴 *lue-ming*.
Brazen-faced, 無臉 *moo-lim*.
Brazier, 打銅人 *ta-t'uung-yan*, *tup-t'uung-yan*.
Breach-loader, 後堂（炮）*hau-t'ong (p'aau)*.
Bread, 麵包 *min-paau*, 麵頭 *min-t'au*.
Breadth, 闊度 *foot-to*.
Break, 打爛 *ta-laan*, 整爛 *ching-laan*, 破 *p'oh*, 折 *chit*, (off) 斷 *t'uen*, (out) 發 *faat*, (the law) 犯法 *faan-faat*, (bread) 擘餅 *maak-peng*, (wind) 放屁 *fong-p'i*.
Breakfast, 早飯 *tso-faan*, 朝餐 *chiu-ts'aam*.
Bream, 扁魚 *pin-*ue*, 魴魚 *fong-*ue*.
Breast, 胸前 *huung-ts'in*. -
Breastplate, 護心鏡 *oo-sum-keng*.
Breasts, 奶 *naai*.
Breath, 口氣 *hau-hi*, 氣息 *hi-sik*.

注 释

Braid:该词并无"栏杆"的意思。
Brandy:现译为"白兰地"。
Brassica:芸苔属植物，包括白菜、芥蓝、甘蓝等。
【鬧交】吵架。
【闊度】宽度，幅度。

注 释

【气都绝】上气不接下气。
【风仔】微风。
【光朗】明亮的，闪亮的。
【脆】脆。

BRI　　29　　BRO

Breathe, 抖氣 ʻtʻau-hi’, 呼吸 foo-kʻup.
Breathless, 氣都絕 hi-too-tsuet.
Breech, the, 臀 tʻuen, (VULG.) 屄 tuuk, ʻshi-fut-ʻtun.
Breeches, 褲 foo’.
Breed, (to), 生產 shaang-ʻchʻaan, 生 shaang, 畜養 chʻuuk-ʻyeung.
Breeze, (a light) 風仔 fuung ʻtsai.
Brethren, 兄弟 hing-tai’.
Brew, 釀 yeung’.
Bribe, 賄賂 ʻfooi-lo’, 買囑 ʻmaai-chuuk.
Bribery, 錢神用事 tsʻin-shan-yuung’-sze’.
Brick, 磚 chuen, (common) 青磚 tsʻing-chuen.
Brick-layer, 坭水匠 nai-ʻshui-*tseung’ (ʻlo).
Bride, 新娘 san-*neung, 新抱 san-ʻpʻo, sum-ʻpʻo.
Bridegroom, 新郎 san-*long.
Bridge, 橋 kʻiu, (a) 一道橋 yat-to’-kʻiu, (of the nose) 鼻梁 pi’-*leung.
Bridle, 韁 keung, 籠絡 luung-lok’.
Brief, 短 ʻtuen.
Brig, 兩枝桅船 ʻleung-chi-*wai-shuen.
Bright, 光明 kwong-ming.
Brilliant, 光朗 kwong-ʻlong.
Brim, 墘 kʻeng.
Brimful, 滿到墘 ʻmoon-to’-kʻeng.
Brimstone, 硫磺 lau-wong.
Brine, 鹹汁 haam-chup, 鹹水 haam-ʻshui.
Bring, 撐——來 ning——lai, 拈——來 nim lai, 帶——來 taai’——lai.
Brinjal, 茄 *kʻe, 矮瓜 ʻai-kwa.
Brink, 邊 pin, 変界 kaau-kaai’, (on the) 將近 tseung-*kan 呡 mun’.
Brisket, 脢肉 mooi-yuuk.
Bristles, 豬鬃毛 chue-tsuung-mo, 箭毛 tsin’ mo.
Brittle, 脆 tsʻui’.
Broad, 闊 foot, 廣闊 ʻkwong-foot’.

| BRO | 30 | BUC |

Broad-cloth, 大呢 taai²-ni, 大絨 taai²-yuung.
Brocade, 花緞 fa-*tuen², 局緞 kuuk-*tuen².
Broccoli, 白菜 paak-ts'oi².
Brogue, 土談 't'o-t'aam.
Broil, 燒炙 shiu-chek².
Broker, 經紀 king-'ki.
Bronchocele, 鵝喉 ngoh-hau.
Bronze, 古銅色 'koo-t'uung-shik.
Brooch, (a) 襟頭針 k'um-t'au-chum, 心口針 sum-'hau-chum.
Brood, 伏卵 fuuk-'luun, 菢蛋 po²-*taan².
Brook, 溪 k'ai, 溪澗 k'ai-kaan², 山水坑 shaan-'shui-haang.
Broom, 把掃 'pa-so², 掃把 so²-pa.
Brothel, 老舉寨 'lo-'kue-*chaai², 媚寮 ch'eung-*liu, 妓館 ki²-'koon.
Brother, (elder) 兄 hing, 哥 koh, 大佬 taai²-'lo, (younger) 弟 tai², 細佬 sai²-'lo.

Brother-in-law, (a husband's) 妻舅 ts'ai-k'au, (a wife's) 大伯 taai²-paak², 細叔 sai²-shuuk, (brother's or sister's) 姐夫 'tse-foo, 妹夫 mooi²-foo.
Brow, 額 ngaak.
Brow-beat, 尅薄 haak²-pok.
Brown, 棕色 tsuung-shik, 豬肝色 chue-kohn-shik.
Bruise, (to powder) 研爛 ngaan-laan², (with the foot) 躂 'ch'aai, 'naai, (hurt) 瘀傷 'ue-sheung, 'ue-choh.
Brush, 擦 's'aat², 刷 shaat², (a) 一個刷 yat-koh-shaat.
Brute, 禽獸 k'um-shau².
Brutish, 獸心 shau²-sum.
Bubble, 浮泡 fau-'p'o, (up) 濆上 p'un²-sheung.
Bubo, 魚口 ue-'hau.
Buck, 鹿公 luuk-kuung.
Bucket, 桶 't'uung, 吊桶 tiu²-'tuung.
Buckle, 扣帶環 k'au²-taai²-*waan, 帶扣 taai²-k'au.
Buckwheat, 三角麥 saam-kok²-mak.

注 释

Broccoli: 应译为"西兰花"。
【土谈】土音,方言口音。
【伏卵】孵蛋。
【把扫】扫帚。
【老举寨】妓院。老举,指妓女。
【三角麦】荞麦。

注释

【杂脚】滑稽；打诨。
Bumptious:傲慢的。译为"抗排"原因不明，粤语中似无此用法。
【劣工人】笨拙者。
【锚漂】浮标。
【担头】负担，责任。
【缅甸】"Burmah"应为"Burma"。

BUL　　31　　BUR

Bud,, 芽 nga, 咪 muuk (flower) 啉 lum, (to) 發芽 faat-nga, 爆咪 paau-muuk, 出啉 ch'uut-lum.
Buddhism, 佛教 Fut-kaau'.
Buffalo, 水牛 ‵shui-*ngau.
Buffoon, (male) 男丑 naam-‵ch'au, (female) 女丑 ‵nue-‵ch'au.
Buffoonery, 雜脚 tsaap-keuk'.
Bug, 木虱 muuk-shat.
Build, 起 ‵hi, 建造 kin-tso', 築 chuuk.
Bulb, 頭 t'au.
Bulk, (to break) 開艙 hoi-ts'ong.
Bulky, 太大 t'aai'-taai', 大個 taai-koh'.
Bull, 牛公 ngau-kuung.
Bullet, 彈子 taan'-'tsze, 碼 *‵ma.
Bullock, 騸牛 shin'-ngau.
Bullock's brains, 牛腦 ngau-‵no.
Bully, 嚇 ha.
Bulwarks, 欄檻 laan-laam', 欄圍 laan-wai, (of a city or fort) 城垣 sheng-oon.

Bum, 臀 t'uen, 臀墩 t'uen-tun, 屁股 p'i-‵koo, 尾启 ‵mi-tuuk.
Bum-boat, 雜貨艇 tsaap-foh'-t'eng.
Bump, (to) 揰着 p'uung-cheuk, (down) 墩 tun', tuun'.
Bumptious, 抗排 k'ong-p'aai.
Bunch, (a) 一把 yat-‵pa, 一匰 yat-k'uung, 一球 yat-k'au, yat-kau'.
Bundle, 包 paau, 札 chaat', 束 ch'uuk.
Bung, 樸 suut, 枳 chat.
Bungler, 劣工人 luet'-kuung-yan.
Buoy, 錨漂 naau-p'iu, 錨桶 naau-‵t'uung, (to) 浮起 fau-‵hi, 泡起 p'o-‵hi.
Burden, 擔頭 taam'-*t'au, 負任 foo-yum'.
Burglary, 夜竊 ye-sit'.
Burmah, 緬甸 ‵Min-tin'.
Burn, (to) 燒 shiu, 燒壞 shiu-waai', (with an iron) 鈉 naat'.

BUS 32 BUT

Burnish, 磨光 moh-kwong.
Burrow, 爬地窿 p'a-ti-luung.
Burst, 爆 paau', 炸 cha'.
Bursting. (to eat to) 喫到肚爆 yaak-to'-t'o-paau', (with rage) 揸頸 cha-ʻkeng.
Bury, 埋葬 maai-tsong', 葬山 tsong'-shaan.
Bush, 小樹 ʻsiu-shue', 密叢 mat-ts'uung, 枝葉 chi-ip.
Bushel, or peck, 斗 ʻtau, (English) 七斗 ts'at-ʻtau.
Business, 事幹 sze'-kohn', (trade) 生意 shang-i', (calling) 事業 sze'-ip, 頭路 t'au-lo'.
Business-like, 合事例 hop-sze'-lai'.
Bustle, 忙速 mong-ch'uuk, 頻嶙 p'un-lun.
Busy, 未閒 mi'-haan, 事忙 sze'-mong, 有事 ʻyau-sze', (diligent) 勤力 k'an-lik.

Busy-body, 好事之人 ho'-sze'-ke'-yan.
But, 但 taan', 但係 taan'-hai', 惟係 wai-hai', (except) 除曉 ch'ue-hiu.
Butcher, 屠夫 t'o-foo, 屠戶 t'o-*oo, (to) 劏 t'ong.
Butcher-bird, 伯鷯 paak-liu.
Butler, 管家 ʻkoon-ka.
Butt, (to) 觸撞 chuuk-chong', 抵觸 tai-chuuk.
Butter, 牛乳油 ngau-ʻue-yau.
Butter-fly, 蝴蝶 oo-*tip, 崩紗 pang-sha.
Buttock, 臀脽 t'nen-chue, 尾后 ʻmi-tuuk.
Button, 鈕 *nau, (a) 一粒鈕 yat-nup-*nau, (officer's) 粒頂 nup-ʻteng, 頂帶 ʻteng-taai', (1st & 2nd) 紅頂 huung-ʻteng, (3rd & 4th) 藍頂 laam-ʻteng, (5th & 6th) 白頂 paak-ʻteng, (7th, &c.) 金頂 kum-ʻteng.
Button-hole, 鈕口 *nau ʻhau.

注 釋

【爬地窿】爬地洞，爬地道。
【事干/头路】生意。
【忙速】忙乱。
【频嶙】喧闹。

注 释

【朋党】阴谋集团。
【房仔】小屋。
【霸王】即"霸王花",又名"剑花",仙人掌科植物。
【挪然】以甜言蜜语勾引。
【算度】计算。
【月份牌】月历,日历。

CAB   33   CAL

Buttress, 柱墩 ‵ch‛ue-‵tun, 棨 ‵toh.
Buy, 買 ‵maai, 買入 ‵maai-yup, 買來 ‵maai-loi, 買到 ‵maai-to’, 收買 shau-‵maai.
Buzz, 微響 mi-‵heung, 孜孜聲 tsze-tsze-sheng, 轟轟 kwang-kwang.
Buzzing, ears, 耳鳴 ‵i-ming.
By, (with) 用 yuung’, (an agent) 被 pi’, (through) 打 ‵ta, 由 yau, (buy by the catty) 斷斤買 tuen’-kan-‵maai, (by himself) 另自 ling’-tsze’, (near) 近 kan’.
By-, (secluded) 背 pooi’.
By and bye, 慢慢 maan’-*maan’, 等一陣 ‵tang-yat-chan’.
By-word, 俗語 tsuuk-‵ue.

C

Cabal, 黨 ‵tong, 朋黨 p‛ang-‵tong.
Cabbage, 椰菜 ye-ts‛oi’.
Cabin, 房仔 fong-‵tsai, (ship's) 船房 shuen-*fong (‵ts‛ong).
Cabinet, 匣 haap, (council) 內閣 noi’-kok’.
Cable, 纜 laam’.
Cackle, 㗎㗎 kuuk-kuuk, 朗託 kat-t‛ok, kok-tok.
Cactus, 霸王 pa’-wong.
Caddy, 箱仔 seung-‵tsai.
Cage, 籠 luung.
Caitiff, 奴才 no-ts‛oi, 小人 ‵siu-yan.
Cajole, 挪然 noh-‵nan.
Cake, 餅 ‵peng, 糕 ko.
Calabash, 瓢 p‛iu, 葫蘆 oo-*loo.
Caladium, 茨菇 ts‛ze-koo.
Calamity, 禍患 woh’-waan’, 災害 tsoi-hoi’.
Calculate, 算度 suen’-tok, 推測 ch‛ui-ch‛aak.
Calculus, (stone) 石淋 shek-lum.
Calendar, 月份牌 uet-fun’-p‛aai.
Calender, 碾 shin’.

英粤字典   33

CAM　34　CAN

Calends, 月朔 uet-*shok*ʼ, 朔日 *shok*ʼ-yat.
Calf, 牛仔 ngau-ʻ*tsai*.
Calico, (white) 白洋布 paak-yeung-poʼ, (print) 印花布 yanʼ-fa-poʼ.
Calk, (to) 打挣 ʻ*ta*-chaangʼ.
Call, 叫 *kiu*ʼ, 呼 *foo*, 喊 *haam*ʼ, 嚶 *iu*, (name) 稱 chʻing, (invite) 請 ʻ*tsʻeng*, (on) 探 *tʻaam*ʼ.
Called, (named) 叫做 *kiu*ʼ-tsoʼ.
Calling, 事業 szeʻ-ip.
Callous, 硬 ngaangʼ, 不仁 *pat*-yan, 腍 ʻ*chum*.
Calm, 安靜 ohn-tsingʼ, 靜靜 tsing-ʻ*tsing*ʼ, 無風無浪 ʻmo-*fuung* ʻmo-long.
Calomel, 輕粉 hing-ʻfun.
Calumniate, 講壞 ʻkong-waaiʼ.
Calumny, 讒言 tsʻaam-in.
Calyx, 花托 fa-*tʻok*ʼ.
Cambric, 袈裟布 ka-sha-poʼ.
Camel, 駱駝 *lok*-tʻoh, 雙峰駝 sheung-*fuung*-tʻoh.

Cameleon, 螗蜓 ʻin-tʻing.
Camellia, 茶花 chʻa-*fa*.
Camlet, 羽紗 ʻue-*sha*, 羽緞 ʻue-*tuen*ʼ.
Camomile, 甘菊 kom-*kuuk*.
Camp, 營盤 ying-pʻoon.
Campaign, 塲 chʻeung.
Camp-stool, 馬极 ʻma-chaap.
Camphor, (tree) 樟木 cheung-muuk, (gum) 樟腦 cheung-ʻno.
Campoi-tea, 揀焙茶 ʻkaan-pooiʼ-chʻa.
Can, 得 *tak*, 做得 tsoʼ-*tak*.
Can, (a) 罐 koonʼ.
Canal, (the Great) 運河 wanʼ-hoh, (a) 水涌 ʻshui-chʻuung.
Canary, 時辰雀 shi-shan-tseuk, 白燕 paak-ʻin.
Cancel, 删去 shaan-hueʼ.
Cancer, 癰疽 yuung-tsue, 巖疽 ngaam-tsue.
Candareen, 分 fun.
Candid, 明白 ming-paak, 正直 chingʼ-chik.
Candidate, 候選 hauʼ-suenʼ, 候缺 hauʼ-kʻuetʼ.

注释

【月朔】（罗马古历的）每月第一天。
【打挣】打马蹄铁。
【花托】花萼。
【时辰雀】应为"布谷鸟"。Canary: 指金丝雀。

注释

【嬲嫩】不怀好意的；腐烂的。
【上盖】天篷，遮篷。
【水瓜钮】水瓜柳，又名水挂榴、酸豆，原产于地中海沿岸及西班牙等地，为蔷薇科长绿灌木，其果实酸而涩，可用于调味。
【鐉鸡】阉鸡。
【无定心】反复无常的，任性。

Candle, 燭 *chuuk*, (wax) 蠟燭 *laap-chuuk*.
Candle-stick, 燭臺 *chuuk-ˈt'oi*.
Candy, (to) 結冰 *kit'-ping*, (sugar) 冰糖 *ping-t'ong*.
Cane, (a) 枝鞭竿 *chi-pin-kohn*, (rattan) 籐 *t'ang*.
Cangue, 枷 *ka*, 木風領 *muuk-fuung-ˈleng*.
Canister, 鑵 *koonˈ*.
Canker, 熱毒 *it-tuuk*.
Cankered, 嬲嫩 *nau-nat*.
Cannibals, 食人國 *shik-yan-kwokˈ*.
Cannon, 大炮 *taaiˈ-p'aau*, 銃炮 *ch'uung-p'aau*, (-ball) 炮碼 *p'aau-ˈma*.
Cannot, 不能 *pat-nang*, 'm-nang, 不得 *pat-tak*, 'm-tak.
Canon, 典 *ˈtin*.
Canopy, 上蓋 *sheungˈ-k'oi*, 拱篷 *ˈkuung-ˈp'uung*.
Canton, (province) 廣東 *ˈKwong-tuung*, (city) 羊城 *Yeung-sheng*, 省城 *ˈshaang-sheng*, *sheng*.

Canvas, 帆布 *faan-poˈ*.
Canvass, (to make interest for) 吹噓 *ch'ui-hue*.
Cap, (a) 頂帽 *ˈting-ˈmo*, 冠 *koon*.
Capable, 能 *nang*, 會 *ˈooi*.
Capacity, 才質 *ts'oi-chat*, (containing) 度量 *toˈ-leungˈ*.
Cape, (of land) 山角 *shaan-kokˈ*.
Capers, 水瓜鈕 *ˈshui-kwa-ˈnau*.
Capital, (city) 京都 *king-too*, 京城 *king-shing*, (money) 本錢 *ˈpoon-ts'in*, (excellent) 妙 *miuˈ*.
Capon, 鐉雞 *sinˈ-kai*.
Capricious, 無定心 *ˈmo-tingˈ-sum*, 多心 *toh-sum*, 花花唪 *fa-fa-fik*.
Capsize, 覆轉 *fuukˈ-ˈchuen*, *p'uukˈ-ˈchuen*.
Capstan, 絞盆 *ˈkaau-p'oon*.
Captain, (ship-) 船主 *shuen-ˈchue*, (of a company) 把總 *ˈpa-ˈtsuung*.

| CAR | 36 | CAR |

Captain Superintendent of Police, 巡捕官 ts'uun-po⁾-koon.
Captive, (led-) 被虜 pi⁻-⸜lo
Capture, 拿獲 na-wok.
Carambola, 楊桃 yeung-*t'o.
Caraway, 細茴香 sai⁻-ooi-heung, 芫荽 uen-sai.
Carbuncle, (on the back) 發背 faat-pooi⁾, 背癰 pooi⁻-yuung.
Carcass, 遺骸 wai-hoi, 死屍 ⸜sze-shi, (abusively) 死佬乾 ⸜sze-⸜lo-kohn.
Card, (visiting) 拜帖 paai⁻-t'ip⁾, 名帖 ming-*t'ip⁾ (playing) 紙牌 ⸜chi-*p'aai.
Card-case, 帖套 t'ip⁾-t'o.
Cardamom, 白荳蔻 paak-tau⁾-k'au⸜.
Cardinal points, 四方 ⸜sze-fong.
Care, 掛慮 kwa⁾-lue⁾, 蔽翳 pai⁻-ai⁻, (to) 料理 liu⁻-⸜li, (don't) 不理 pat-⸜li.
Careful, 小心 ⸜siu-sum.

Carefully, look 睇仔細 ⸜t'ai-⸜tsze-sai⁻, 好聲 ⸜ho-sheng.
Careless, 無小心 ⸜mo-⸜siu-sum, 無睇顧 ⸜mo-⸜t'ai-koo⁻, 苟且 ⸜kau-ch'e.
Caress, 攬抱 ⸜laam-⸜p'o.
Cargo, 船貨 shuen-foh⁾.
Cargo-boat, 駁艇 pok⁻-⸜t'eng.
Carnation, (colour) 桃紅色 t'o-huung-shik.
Carnelian, 瑪瑙石 ⸜ma-⸜no-shek.
Carouse, 大飲一番 taai⁻-⸜yum-yat-faan 鬧酒 naau⁻-⸜tsau.
Carp, (a fish) 鯉魚 ⸜li-*ue.
Carp, (to) 捉字失 chuuk⁻-tsze⁻-shat.
Carpenter, 木匠 muuk-*tseung⁻.
Carpet, 地氈 ti⁻-⸜chin.
Carriage, (a) 車 ch'e, 馬車 ⸜ma-ch'e.
Carrot, 紅蘿蔔 huung-loh-paak, 黃蘿蔔 wong-loh-paak, 金笋 kum-⸜suun.

注 释

【四方】罗盘上的方位基点。
【挂虑】关心，顾虑。
【驳艇】接驳船。
【捉字失】咬文嚼字。

注 释

【九龙袋】子弹盒。
Castellated: 应译为"城堡状的"。
【割势】阉割。
【号单】目录。
【月水】月经。

Carry, (on a pole) 擔 taam, (resting on one) 托 t'ok⁾, (between two) 抬 t'oi, (about the person) 帶 taai⁾, (on the back) 狽 me, (in the arms) 抱 ‵p'o, (as a ship, &c.) 載 tsoi⁾.
Cart, 車 ch'e, (ox-) 牛車 ngau-ch'e.
Cartridge, 火藥筒 ‵foh-yeuk-*t'uung, 㘑碼 kip⁾-‵ma.
Cartridge-box, 九龍袋 ‵kau-luung-*toi⁾.
Carve, 雕刻 tiu-haak⁾, (ornament) 雕花 tiu-fa, (meat) 切 ts'it⁾.
Case, (holder) 套 t'o⁾, 套匣 t'o⁾-haap, (at law) 案件 ohn⁾-kin⁾.
Cash, 錢 *ts'in, 文錢 mun-ts'in, (ready) 現銀 in⁾-*ngan.
Cash-book, 進支簿 tsuun⁾-chi-‵po.
Cask, 桶 ‵t'uung, 琵琶桶 p'i-p'a-‵t'uung.

Casket, 小匣 ‵siu-haap, 寶匣 ‵po-haap.
Cassia, 桂 kwai⁾, (lignia) 桂皮 kwai⁾-p'i, (buds) 桂子 kwai⁾-‵tsze.
Cast, (throw) 投 t'au, 丟 tiu, (to found) 鑄 chue⁾.
Cast-iron, 生鐵 sheung-t'it⁾.
Castanets, 拍板 p'aak⁾-‵paan.
Castellated, 有城人 ‵yau-sheng-*yan.
Castle, 城樓 sheng-*lau.
Castor oil, 瀉油 se⁾-yau, 萆麻油 pi-ma-yau.
Castrate, 割勢 koht⁾-shai⁾, 閹 im, 鐌 sin⁾.
Casual, 無意中 mo-i⁾-chuung.
Casuistry, 是非 shi⁾-fi.
Cat, 貓 ‵maau, (a) 一隻貓 yat-chek⁾-‵maau.
Cat fish, 赤魚 ch'ik⁾-*ue.
Catalogue, 號單 ho⁾-taan, 目錄 muuk-luuk.
Catamenia, 月水 uet-‵shui.

| CAU | 38 | CEL |

Cataract, (water) 瀑布水 puuk-po`-`shui, (in the eye) 販睛 p`aan-tsing, 睛珠變質不明 tsing-chue-pin`-chat-pat-ming.

Catch, 捉到 chuuk`-`to, 捉獲 chuuk`-wok (fasten) k`ek`.

Catechism, 問答書 mun`-taap`-shue.

Catechu, 兒茶 i-ch`a.

Caterpillar, 螟蛉 ming-ling, 狗毛蟲 `kau-mo-*ch`uung, (silk-worm) 蠶蟲 ts`aam-*ch`uung.

Caterwaul, 拗烏聲 aau-oo-sheng.

Cattle, 畜生 ch`uuk-shaang.

Catty, 斤 kan.

Caul, 大腸網膜 taai`-ch`eung-`mong-mok.

Cauliflower, 花椰菜 fa-ye-ts`oi`.

Cause, 緣故 uen-koo`, 緣由 uen-yau, (to) 使 `shai, 令 ling`, 致 chi`.

Causeway, 逼石地 pik-shek-ti`, 鵝卵石地 ngoh-`luun-shek-ti`.

Cauterize, 灸 kau`.

Cautious, 謹慎 `kan-shan`, 小心 `siu-sum.

Cavalry, 馬兵 `ma-ping.

Cave, 山窿 shaan-luung, 巖穴 ngaam-uet.

Cavil, 捉字失 chuuk`-tsze-shat, 駁嘴 pok`-tsui.

Cayenne, 辣椒 laat-tsiu.

Cease, 停息 t`ing-sik, 止 `chi, 歇 hit`.

Cedar, 柏香木 paak`-heung-muuk.

Ceiling, 天花板 t`in-fa-`paan.

Celandine, 知母 chi-`mo.

Celebrate, (a day) 造 tso`, (midwinter) 造冬 tso`-tuung.

Celebrity, 名聲 ming-shing, 出名 ch`uut-*meng.

Celery, 旱芹菜 `hohn-k`an-ts`oi`, 塘蒿 t`ong-ho.

Cell, 房仔 *fong-`tsai.

注　释

【拗乌声】动物叫春的声音。
【驳嘴】顶嘴。
【造冬】过冬至。

注 释

【灰胶】水泥。
【阴山】阴间,指墓地。
【惹敌】挑战。
【学台】校长,总理,大法官。
【找钱人】货币兑换商。

Cellar, 地窖 ti²-kaau², (wine) 酒房 ʻtsau-*fong.
Cement, 灰膠 fooi-kaau.
Cemetery, 陰山 yum-shaan.
Censer, 香爐 heung-lo.
Censor, 諫官 kaan²-koon, 御史 ue²-sze.
Censure, 彈 tʻaan, 責 chaak².
Census, 民籍 mun-tsik, 口冊 ʻhau-chʻaak².
Centipede, 百足 paak²-tsuuk.
Centre, 正中間 ching²-chuung-kaan, 心 sum.
Centurion, 把總 ʻpa-ʻtsuung.
Century, 百年 paak²-nin.
Ceremony, 禮儀 ʻlai-i.
Certain, 的確 tik-kʻok², 定 ting², ʻting.
Certainly, 斷斷 tuen²-tuen², 定然 ting²-in, 定喇 ʻting-la.
Certificate, (of character) 薦書 tsin²-shue, (of goods) 驗單 im²-ʻtaan.
Certify, 實證 shat-ching².
Cess, 抽稅 chʻau-shui².
Cess-pool, 水氹 ʻshui-tʻum, 糞坑 fun²-haang.

Chafe, 擦壞 tsʻaat-waai², (a person) 激氣 kik-hi².
Chafer, 沙蟬 sha-shin.
Chaff, 秕糠 pʻi-hong, 糠 hong.
Chagrin, 鬱氣 wut-hi².
Chain, 鍊 *lin², 鏈 lin, (a) 條鏈 tʻiu-*lin.
Chair, (a) 張椅 cheung-ʻi, sedan, 頂轎 ʻting-*kiu, coolie, 轎夫 *kiu-foo.
Chalk, 火石粉 ʻfoh-shek-ʻfun.
Challenge, 惹敵 ʻye-tik.
Chamber, 房 *fong.
Chamber-pot, 便壺 pin²-*oo.
Chamois, 羚羊 ling-yeung.
Champion, 豪傑 ho-kit.
Chance, 偶然 ʻngau-in.
Chancellor, literary, 學台 hok-tʻoi.
Change, 改 ʻkoi, 更改 kang-ʻkoi, 更換 kang-oon², 換過 oon²-kwoh², 改變 ʻkoi pin².
Changer, (money-) 找錢人 ʻchaau-*tsʻin-yan.

| CHA | 40 | CHE |

Channel, 條水 t'iu-ˊshui, 水路 ˊshui-loˋ.
Chant prayers, 念經 nimˋ-king.
Chaos, 混沌 wunˋ-tuunˋ.
Chapel, 禮拜堂 ˊlai-paui-t'ong, 福音堂 fuuk-yum-t'ong.
Chapped, 坼口 ch'aakˋ-ˊhau.
Chapter, 章 cheung.
Char, 燒黑 shiu-hak.
Character, 品行 ˊpan-hangˋ, (or class) 脚色 keukˋ-shik, (a letter) 字 tszeˋ.
Charcoal, 柴炭 ch'aai-t'aanˋ.
Charge, (to give-) 付託 fooˋ-t'ok, (demand) 要取 iuˋ-ts'ue, (blame) 責罪 chaakˋ-tsuiˋ.
Chariot, 馬車 ˊma-ch'e.
Charity, 慈心 ts'ze-sum, (alms) 施舍 shi-ˊshe, 布施 poˋ-shi.
Charm, (a) 符籙 foo-luuk.
Charming, 悅意 uet-iˋ.
Chart, 海沙圖 ˊhoi-sha-t'o.
Charter-party, 合同 hop-t'uung.

Chase, (to) 追趕 chui-ˊkohn.
Chasm, 缺陷 huetˋ-haamˋ.
Chaste, 清節 ts'ing-tsitˋ, 貞節 ching-tsitˋ.
Chastise, 責罰 chaakˋ-faat, 打 ˊta.
Chat, 談談 t'aam-t'aam.
Chattels, 什物 shap-mat.
Chatter, (to) 嘶嘶聲 si-si-sheng, 嘓嘓聲 wak-wak-sheng.
Chatter-box, 多嘴 toh-ˊtsui.
Cheap, 平 p'eng, 價錢低 kaˋ-ts'in-tai.
Cheat, 阨騙 ngaak-p'inˋ, 欺騙 hi-p'inˋ.
Check, 壓止 aatˋ-ˊchi, (in chess) 將軍 tseung-kwun.
Check-mate, 全勝局 ts'uen-shingˊ-kuuk, 贏棋 yengˋ-ˊk'i.
Check, 面脥 minˋ-ˊchue, 腮 soi.
Cheek-bones, 兩顴 ˊleung-k'uen.
Cheer (to) 喝采 hohtˋ-ˊts'oi.
Cheerful, 快活 faaiˋ-oot.
Cheese, 牛奶餅 ngau-ˊnaai-ˊpeng.

注 释

【坼口】裂開的。
【脚色】角色。
Charter-party:应为"租船契约（合同）"。
【什物】动产；杂物。
【牛奶饼】奶酪。

注释

【银单】支票。
【夹万】柜子,特指保险箱柜。
【生萝卜】长冻疮。
【细蚊仔】小孩子。
Chill:风寒。译为"伤寒"属误译。
【烟通】烟囱。
【斧口柴】木头屑,柴屑。

CHI   41   CHI

Chemise, 近身衣 kan⟩-shan-i.
Chemistry, 化學 fa⟩-hok.
Cheque, (a) 銀單 ngan-⸌taan.
Cherish, 懷 waai.
Cherry, 李仔 ⸌li-⸌tsai, 櫻 ying.
Chess, 象棋 tseung⟩-k'i, (-board) 棋盤 k'i-p'oon, (-men) 棋子 k'i-⸌tsze.
Chest, 箱 seung, 槓 luung, (strong) 夾萬 kaap⟩-maan⟩.
Chestnut, 風栗 fuung-*luut.
Chevaux-de-frise, 鹿角寨 luuk-kok⟩-*chaai⟩.
Chew, 咬 ⸌ngaau, 嚼 tseuk⟩.
Chicken, 鷄仔 kai-⸌tsai.
Chicken-pox, 水痘 ⸌shui-*tau⟩.
Chicken-hearted, 小心小膽 ⸌siu-sum-⸌siu-⸌taam.
Chief, 頭一個 t'au-yat-koh⟩, (man) 頭目 t'au-muuk, 頭人 t'au-yan, 主 ⸌chue.
Chief Justice, 按察司 ohn⟩-ch'aat⟩-sze.

Chiefly, 大約 taai⟩-yeuk⟩, (most of all) 至緊要 chi⟩-kan-iu⟩.
Chilblains, 生蘿蔔 shang-loh-paak, 寒瘡 hohn-ch'ong.
Child, 細蚊仔 sai⟩-mun-⸌tsai.
Child-bed, 分娩 fun-⸌min.
Chill, 傷寒 sheung-hohn.
Chillies, 花椒 fa-tsiu.
Chimney, 烟通 in-t'uung.
Chin, 下頷 ha⟩-⸌hom, 下爬 ha⟩-p'a.
China, 中國 Chuung-kwok⟩, 唐山 T'ong-shaan.
China-aster, 菊花 kuuk-fa.
China-root, 茯苓 fuuk-ling.
Chinese, (a) 唐人 T'ong-yan (language) 唐話 T'ong-*wa⟩.
Chink, (a) 罅 la⟩, 條罅 t'iu-la⟩.
Chintz, 印花布 yan⟩-fa-po⟩.
Chip, (to) 斲 teuk⟩, 削 seuk⟩.
Chips, 斧口柴 foo-⸌hau-ch'aai, p'ek⟩-⸌hau-ch'aai.

Chirp, 吱喞 *chi-chaau*, 喞喞 *chaau-chaau*.	Chops, (meat) 脾骨 p'aai²-kwut.
Chisel, 鑿 *tsok, 鑿刀 ‚tsaam²-to.	CHRIST, 基督 KI-TUUK.
Chit (a), 一塊字紙 yat-faai²-tsze²-‚chi.	Christian, 信耶穌人 suun²-YE-SOO-yan.
Chit-book, 信部 suun²-*po².	Christianity, 耶穌敎 YE-SOO-kaau².
Chloroform, 痲藥 ma-yeuk.	Christmas, 耶穌生日 YE-SOO-shang-yat.
Choice ⎫ Chosen ⎭ 揀擇的 ‚kaan-chaak-ke².	Chronic, 舊病 kau²-peng².
Choke, 骾 ‚k'ang, 壅塞 ‚yuung-sak, tsuuk.	Chrysalis, 繭虫 ‚kaan-ch'uung, 蛹 ‚yuung, 蟭 p'iu.
Cholera, 攪腸沙 ‚kaau-ch'eung-sha, 霍亂吐瀉 fok²-luen²-t'o²-se².	Chrysanthemum, 菊花 kuuk-fa.
	Chub, (a fish) 鰱魚 lin-*ue.
Choose, 揀選 ‚kaan-‚suen.	Chunam, (to) 打灰沙 ‚ta-fooi-sha.
Chop, (a mark), 字號 tsze²-ho².	Church, 敎會 kaau²-ooi².
Chop (to) 切 ts'it².	Churlish 古毒 ‚koo-tuuk.
Chop-boat, 西瓜扁 sai-‚kwa-‚pin, (floating-house) 樓船 lau-*shuen.	Churn, (to) 扯 ‚ch'e, 攪 ‚kaau.
	Cicada, 秋蟬 ts'au-*shin.
Chopping block, 砧板 chum-‚paan.	Cigar, 呂宋烟 ‛Lue-suung²-‚in, (-ette) 孖姑烟 ‚ma-koo-‚in.
Chopping-knife, 切菜刀 ts'it²-ts'oi²-to.	
Chop-sticks 快子 faai²-‚tsze.	Cinders, 燒剩 shiu-shing².

注 釋

【一块字纸】便条。
【信部】回单簿。
【旧病】慢性病。
【打灰沙】批荡,即"抹灰",指用石灰砂浆、水泥砂浆等抹在建筑物的表面,使表面平整,同时也起到保护墙体、防水、隔热、隔声等作用。
【古毒】脾气坏的,粗野的。
【烧剩】灰烬。

> **注 释**
>
> 【圈界】周长。
> 【扭计】陷害，现指闹别扭。
> 【扭倒计】陷害，包围。
> 【剔达声】噼噼啪啪的声音。
> 【码住】固定住。

CIT　　43　　CLA

Cinnabar, 銀硃種 ngan-chue-ˇchuung, 硃砂 chue-sha.
Cinnamon, 肉桂 yuuk-kwaiˋ.
Circle, 圈 huen.
Circuit, 週 chau.
Circular, (a) 告白 koˋ-paak, 傳字 chʻuen-*tszeˋ.
Circulate, 循圜 tsʻuun-waan.
Circumcision, 割禮 kohtˋ-ˇlai.
Circumference, 圈界 huen-kaaiˋ.
Circumstance, 事勢 szeˋ-shaiˋ, 境遇 ˇking-ueˋ, 際遇 tsaiˋ-ueˋ.
Circumvent, 扭計 ˇnau-*kaiˋ.
Circumvented, 扭倒計 ˇnau-ˇto-(to)-kaiˋ.
Circus, 圓戲塲 uen-hiˋ-chʻeung.
Cistern, 蓄水缸 chʻuuk-ˇshui-kong, 石井 shek-ˇtseng.
Citron, 香櫞 heung-*uen, 佛手 futˋ-ˇshau.

City, 邑 yup, (walled) 城 sheng, *sheng.
Civet, 香狸 heung-*li.
Civil and military, 文武 mun-ˇmoo.
Civility, 禮 ˇlai, 禮數 ˇlai-shoˋ, (outward) 禮貌 ˇlai-maauˋ.
Civilize, 教化 kaauˋ-faˋ.
Clack, 剔撻聲 tʻik-tʻatˋ-sheng.
Claim, 討 ˇtʻo, 問要 munˋ-iuˋ.
Clam, 沙蜆 sha-ˇhin.
Clammy, 黐泥 chʻi-niˋ.
Clamour, 喧嘩 huen-wa, 巴嚹 pa-paiˋ.
Clamp, (to) 碼住 ˇma-chueˋ.
Clan, 族 tsuuk, 姓 singˋ.
Clap, 拍 pʻaak.
Claret, 紅酒 huung-ˇtsau.
Clash, 相撞 seung-chongˋ, 抵迕 ˇtai-ˇng.
Clasp, (a) 扣 kʻauˋ, (hands) 叉手 chʻa-ˇshau, (to mend) 碼 ma.
Clasp-knife, 摺刀 chipˋ-ˇto.

CLE 44 CLO

Class, (a) 等 ‘tang, (in school) 班 paan, (profession) 脚色 keuk’-shik.
Classic, 經 king.
Clatter, 摑摑聲 kwaak-kwaak-sheng.
Clause, 句 kue’, (of a treaty) 欵 ‘foon, 條 t‘iu.
Claw, 爪 ‘chaau.
Clay, 泥 nai.
Clean, 潔淨 kit’-tseng’, 乾淨 kohn-tseng’, ‘k‘i-‘li.
Cleanse, 做乾淨 tso’-kohn-tseng’.
Clear, 清 ts‘ing, 明 ming, (sky) 晴 ts‘ing.
Clearance, (port-) 紅牌 huung-*p‘aai.
Cleave, (split) 破開 p‘oh-hoi.
Clench, (the fist) 揸埋拳頭 cha-maai-k‘uen-t‘au.
Clepsydra, 滴漏 tik-lau’.
Clerk, 書辦 shue-*paan’, 寫字人 ‘se-tsze’-yan.
Clerodendrum, 龍船花 luung-shuen-fa.

Clever, 有本事 ‘yau-‘poon-sze’, 聰明 ts‘uung-ming, 精 tseng.
Click, 迪特聲 tik-tak-sheng.
Cliff, 企坡 ‘k‘i-poh, 巖 ngaam.
Climate, 水土 ‘shui-‘t‘o.
Climb, 攀上 p‘aan-‘sheung, 躝上 laan-‘sheung.
Clinch, (nails) 打開釘尾 ‘ta-hoi-‘teng-‘mi, 轉釘尾 ‘chuen-teng-‘mi.
Cling to, 膠漆 kaau-ts‘at.
Clip, 剪 ‘tsin, 裁剪 ts‘oi-‘tsin.
Cloak, 大褸 taai’-‘lau.
Clock, 時辰鐘 shi-shan-chuung, (o'clock) 點鐘 ‘tim-chuung.
Clock-tower (the), 大鐘樓 Taai’ chuung-*lau.
Clod, 僑坭 kau’-nai.
Clog, (to) 阻滯 ‘choh-chai’.
Clogs, 木屐 muuk-k‘ek.
Close, (to) 閂埋 shaan-maai, 闔埋 hop-maai, (finish) 完結 uen-kit’.

注释

【摑摑声】哗啦的声音。
【揸埋拳头】紧握拳头。
【书办】记账员，书记。
【迪特声】滴答的声音。
【企坡】悬崖峭壁。
【大褸】大衣。

注释

【手指密】吝啬的，一毛不拔的。
【白鼻哥】小丑。
【胎生脚】畸足的。
【灌谷道法】灌肠法。
【生埋】合并。
【破基峡】眼镜蛇。
【牙兰米】胭脂虫。

CLU　　45　　COC

Close, (ADJ.) 密 mat, (near) 近 kan', 'k'an.
Close-fisted, 手指密 'shau-'chi-mat.
Clot, (to) 結 kit', 擎 k'ing.
Cloth, 布 po', (woollen) 絨 *yuung.
Clothe, 着衣服 cheuk'-i-fuuk, 衣 i'.
Clothes, 衣服 i-fuuk, 衣裳 i-sheung.
Clothes-brush, 衣擦 i-ts'aat'.
Clothes-horse, 衣架 i-'ka.
Cloud, 雲 wan.
Cloudy, 矇矓 muung-luung.
Clove, 丁香 ting-heung.
Clown, (actor) 白鼻哥 paak-pi'-koh, (rustic) 鄉下佬 heung-ha'-'lo.
Club, (stick) 棍 kwan', 椎 *ch'ui.
Club-footed, 胎生脚 t'oi-'shang-keuk'.
Club-house, 會館 ooi'-'koon.
Cluck, 咯咯 kuuk-kuuk.
Clue, 毬線 k'au-sin', kau-sin', (winding of) 絮 'sue, 頭緒 t'au-sue.

Clumsy, 粗俗 ts'o-tsuuk.
Cluster, 球 k'au, kau'.
Clyster, 灌谷道法 chok-kuuk-to'-faat'.
Coach, 馬車 'ma-ch'e.
Coachman, 車夫 ch'e-foo.
Coagulate, 凝結 ying-kit', 結埋 kit'-maai.
Coal, 煤炭 mooi-t'aan', (burning) 着炭 cheuk'-t'aan'.
Coalesce, 生埋 shaang-maai.
Coarse, 粗 ts'o.
Coast, 海邊 'hoi-'pin.
Coat, 大衫 taai'-shaam, (of paint) 浸 chum'.
Coax, 引誘 'yan-'yau.
Cob-web, 蜘蛛網 'chi-'chue-'mong.
Cobra, 破基峡 p'oh'-ki-haap', 扁頭蜂 'pin-t'au-fuung.
Cochineal, 牙蘭米 nga-'laan-'mai.
Cock, 鷄公 'kai-'kuung.
Cock up, 竅起 hiu'-'hi.

COL 46 COL

Cock, (of a gun) 䪝鷄 ₍kat-₍kai, (to) 擸䪝鷄 ₍maan-kat-₍kai.
Cockatoo, 白鸚鵡 paak-ying-₍moo.
Cockles, 蠣蚶 ₍sze-₍om.
Cockroach, 曱甲 kaat-tsaat.
Cocoa-nut, 椰子 ye-₍tsze, (juice) 椰水 ye-₍shui.
Cocoon, 繭 ₍kaan, 蠶繭 ₍ts'aam-₍kaan.
Cod-fish, 鰵魚 ₍mun-ue.
Coerce, 強逼 ₍k'eung-ρik.
Coffin, 棺材 ₍koon-ts'oi.
Cog-wheel, 齒輪 ₍ch'i-luun.
Cohabit, 狎居 haap-₍kue.
Cohere, 黐埋 ch'i-₍maai.
Coil, (to) 盤埋 ₍p'oon-₍maai.
Coin, 錢 *ts'in.
Coincide, 符合 ₍foo-hop, 啱 ₍ngaam.
Coir, 椰衣 *ye-i, 椶 ₍suung.
Cold, 冷 ₍laang, 凍 tuung', (indifferent) 薄情 pok-ts'ing, 冷面 ₍laang-min', 冷淡 ₍laang-taam', (a cold) 傷風 ₍sheung-₍fuung, 感冒 ₍kom-mo'.

Colcopterous, 甲蟲類 kaap'-ch'uung-lui'.
Colewort, 黃牙白 ₍wong-₍nga-paak.
Colic, 肚痛 ₍t'o-t'uung'.
Collapse, 崩敗 ₍pang-paai', 凹嘵 nup-niu, 冚嘵 nip-hiu.
Collar, 風領 ₍fuung-₍leng.
Collar-bone, 鎖匙骨 ₍soh-₍shi-kwut.
Collate, 對過 tui'-kwoh'.
Collect, 聚埋 tsue'-₍maai.
Collision, 相撞 ₍seung-p'uung', 抵牾 ₍tai-₍ng.
Colloquial, 俗話 tsuuk-*wa.
Collusion, 同謀 ₍t'uung-₍mau.
Colonel, 參將 ₍ts'aam-tseung'.
Colonial Secretary, 輔政司 ₍foo'-ching'-₍sze.
Colonial Treasurer, 庫務司 foo'-moo'-₍sze.
Colony, 新疆 ₍san-₍keung, 屬國 shuuk-kwok'.
Colour, 色 shik, 顏色 ₍ngaan-shik, 色澤 shik chaak.

注 释

【忘魂】昏迷的，麻木的。
【作笑戏文】喜剧。
【擸搭星】彗星。
【糖弹】糖果。
【开手】开始，着手。

Column, (of letters) 行 hong, (pillar) 柱 ʽchʽue.
Coma, 昏睡病 fun-shuiʼ-peng.
Comatose, 忘魂 mong-wan.
Comb, 梳 shoh, (a) 隻梳 chekʼ-ʽshoh, (fine) 篦 *pi.
Combative, 鬥氣 tauʼ-hiʼ.
Combine, 和合 woh-hop.
Come, 來 loi, (COL.) 嚟 lai.
Comedy, 作笑戲文 tsokʼ-siuʼ-hiʼ-mun 劇 kʽek.
Comet, 掃把星 soʼ-ʽpa-sing, 擸搭星 laap-chʽa-ʽsing.
Comfits, 糖彈 tʽong-*taanʼ.
Comfort, 安慰 ohn-waiʼ, 勸解 huenʼ-ʽkaai.
Comfortable, 安樂 ohn-lok.
Comic, 好笑 ʽho-siuʼ.
Command, 吩咐 fun-fooʼ.
Commander, 兵頭 ping-*tʽau, 頭人 tʽau-yan.
Commandment, 誡命 kaaiʼ-mingʼ.
Commemorate, 表記 ʽpiu-kiʼ.
Commence, 開手 hoi-ʽshau, 埋手 maai-ʽshau, 開工 hoi-kuung, 起首 ʽhi-ʽshau.

Commencement, 起初 ʽhi-chʽoh, 興工 hing-kuung, 始初 ʽchʽi-chʽoh.
Commend, 褒獎 po-ʽtseung, 舉薦 ʽkue-tsinʼ.
Comment, 註解 chueʼ-ʽkaai.
Commerce, 貿易 mauʼ-yik, 交易 kaau-yik, 買賣 ʽmaai-maaiʼ, 生意 shang-iʼ.
Commiserate, 可憐 ʽhoh-lin.
Commission, (to) 差委 chʽaaiʼ-ʽwai 委托 ʽwai-tʽokʼ.
Commissioner, 欽差 yum-chʽaai.
Commit, (crime) 犯 faanʼ.
Committee, 值理人 chik-ʽli-yan.
Commode, 尿櫃 niuʼ-*kwaiʼ.
Common, (public) 公 kuung, (vulgar) 俗 tsuuk, (usual) 平常 pʽing-sheung.
Communicate, 交給 kaau-kʽup, (tell) 通知 tʽuung-chi.
Communion, 交通 kaau-tʽuung, (spiritual) 心交 sum-kaau.
Community, 人民 yan-manʼ, 百姓 paakʼ-singʼ.

| COM | 48 | COM |

Compact, 密實 mat-shat, (a) 合同 hop-t'uung.
Companion, 同班輩 t'uung-paan-pooi 同伴 t'uung-poon.
Company, (mercantile) 公司 kuung-sze.
Compare, 比較 ʻpi-kaau, 對過 tui-kwoh.
Compartment, 間房 kaan-*fong.
Compass, 羅經 loh-kaang, 羅盤 loh-pʻoon.
Compasses, 規 kʻwai.
Compassion, 慈悲 tsʻze-pi.
Compel, 強 kʻeung, 監 kaam.
Compendious, 簡畧 ʻkaan-leuk.
Compensate, 補償 ʻpo-sheung, 賠補 pʻooi ʻpo.
Compete, 鬥 tau.
Competent, 足用 tsuuk-yuung, (man) 能事 nang-sze, 稱職 chʻing-chik.
Complain, 訴寃 so-uen, 出怨言 chʻuut-uen-in.
Complaisant, 婉轉 ʻuen-ʻchuen.

Complete, 周全 chau-tsʻuen, 十全 shap-tsʻuen, (to) 成 shing.
Completely, 嗮 saai.
Complexion, 面色 min-shik.
Complicated } 深 shum, 深
Complex } 奧 shum-o, 多故 toh-koo.
Complication, 多事整埋 toh-sze-ʻching-maai.
Compliments, 問候 mun-hau, (congratulations) 恭喜 kuung-ʻhi.
Comply, 依從 i-tsʻuung, 聽從 tʻeng-tsʻuung, 順從 shuun-tsʻuung.
Compose, 安埋 ohn-maai, 砌埋 tsʻai-maai, (write) 作 tsok.
Compositor, 執字人 chup-tsze-yan 排活板人 pʻaai-oot-ʻpaan-yan.
Compound, 攪勻 ʻkaau-wan, 摳勻 kʻau-wan.
Compound interest, 利上利 li-sheung-ʻli.
Comprador, 買辦 ʻmaai-*paan.

注　釋

【密实】合同，契约。
【同班辈】同伴，朋友。
【足用】有能力，胜任。
【嗮】全部，完全。

注释

【相饶省事】妥协，折中。
【事干】涉及。
【拍和】调和，安抚。
【结埋】浓缩，凝结。
【景地】境地。

Comprehend, 曉透 ʻhiu-tʻauʾ, (comprise) 包括 paau-kʻootʾ.
Compress, 壓 aatʾ, 責住 chaakʾ-chue, 挾 kip, 夾 kaapʾ, 撿 kumʾ, 擸 maan.
Comprise, 包括 paau-kʻootʾ.
Compromise, 相饒省事 seung-iu-ʻshaang-szeʾ, (involve) 拖累 tʻoh-lui.
Compute, 算度 suenʾ-tok.
Comrade, 夥計 ʻfoh-kiʾ.
Concave, 中間凹 chuung-ʻkaan-nup.
Conceal, 藏匿 tsʻong-nik, (one's self) 躲匿 ʻtoh-nik, 避 piʾ, 匿埋 nik-maai, ni-maai.
Concede, 許准 ʻhue-ʻchuun.
Conceited, 自高 tszeʾ-ko, 自大 tszeʾ-taaiʾ.
Conceive, 懷胎 waai-tʻoi, 有六甲 ʻyau-luuk-kaapʾ, (think) 想 ʻseung.
Concern, (to) 關涉 kwaan-shipʾ, 關屬 kwaan-shuuk, (a) 事幹 szeʾ-kohnʾ.

Concert, (in) 和諧 woh-haai, (a) 和奏樂音 woh-tsauʾ-ngok-yum.
Conciliate, 拍和 pʻaakʾ-woh, 和 woh, 勸和 huenʾ-woh, 勸息 huenʾ-sik.
Concise, 簡畧 ʻkaan-leuk, 簡捷 ʻkaan-tsit.
Conclude, 完了 uen-ʻliu, uen-hiu, (decide) 定意 tingʾ-iʾ.
Concord, 和 woh.
Concubine, 妾 tsʻipʾ, 妾氏 tsʻipʾ-shiʾ.
Concur, 同意 tʻuung-iʾ, 同致 tʻuung-chiʾ.
Condemn, 定罪 tingʾ-tsuiʾ.
Condense, 收縮 shau-shuuk, 結埋 kitʾ-maai.
Condescend, 下顧 haʾ-kooʾ, 垂念 shui-nimʾ, 臨下 lum-haʾ.
Condiments, 醬料 tseungʾ-*liuʾ, 送 suungʾ.
Condition, 情勢 tsʻing-shaiʾ, 景地 ʻking-tiʾ, (terms) 章程 cheung-chʻing.

Condole, 弔慰 tiu'-wai'.	Confounded, 混賬 wan'-cheung'.
Conduct, 行爲 hang-wai.	Confront, 對面企 tui'-'min'-'k'i, 質訊 chat-suun'.
Conduct, 帶引 taai'-'yan.	
Cone, 筍子樣 'suun-'tsze-*yeung', 尖形 tsim-ying.	Confucius, 孔夫子 'Huung-foo-'tsze.
Confederate, 同盟 t'uung-mang.	Confute, 駁倒 pok'-'to.
Confer, (give) 賜 ts'ze', (consult) 斟酌 chum-cheuk'.	Confused, 亂 luen'.
	Congeal, 凝凍 k'ing-tuung'.
Confess, 認 ying', 招認 chiu-ying', (a mistake) 賠不是 p'ooi-pat-shi'.	Congee, 粥 chuuk.
	Congenial, 合心水 hop-sum-'shui.
Confide, 信托 suun'-t'ok'.	Congenital, 胎生 t'oi-shang.
Confident, 確信 k'ok'-suun'.	Congestion, 內熱成積 noi'-it-shing-tsik.
Confine, (to) 收禁 shau-kum', 押住 aap'-chue'.	
	Congo, 工夫茶 kuung-foo-ch'a.
Confirm, 堅定 kin-ting', 批實 p'ai-shat.	Congratulate, 恭喜 kuung-'hi, 賀喜 hoh'-'hi.
Confiscate, 歸官 kwai-koon.	
Conflict, 相撞 seung-chong', 反拗 'faan-aau'.	Congregate, 聚會 tsue'-ooi'.
	Congregation, 會眾 ooi'-'chuung'.
Conform, 照依 chiu'-i, 按 ohn', 按准 ohn'-'chuun.	Congruous, 符合 foo-hop, 啱 ngaam.
Confound, 打混 'ta-wan', (by fear) 驚亂 king-luen', (mix) 混雜 wan'-tsaap, 搯亂 lo-luen', lo-lo-*luen'.	Conical, 筍子樣 'suun-'tsze-*yeung', (COL.) 揆' tuet'.

注 釋

【信托】即托付給可信任之人。
【收禁】限制，禁閉。
【归官】充公。
【胎生】天生的。
【会众】聚会，人群。
【笋子样】圆锥的。

注释

【诈不见】默许，装作看不见。
【守经】保守的。
【特出】突出。
【凑埋来】凑在一起。
【地保】捕快。

Conjecture, 猜想 ch'aai-⸌seung, 猜摸 ch'aai-⸍moh, 估摸 ⸌koo-mok⸍.
Conjunction, 會合 ooi⸍-hop.
Connect, 接續 tsip⸍-tsuuk.
Connive, 詐不見 cha⸍-pat-kin⸍, cha⸍-⸌m-kin⸍.
Conquer, 勝敵 shing⸍-tik, 贏 yeng.
Consanguinity, 骨肉親 kwut-yuuk-ts'an.
Conscience, 良心 leung-sum.
Conscious, 自覺 tsze⸍-kok, 自知 tsze⸍-chi.
Consent, 允准 ⸌wun-⸌chuun, 允肯 ⸌wun-⸌hang.
Consequence, 關系 kwaan-hai⸍.
Consequently, 所以 ⸌shoh-⸌i.
Conservative, 守經 ⸌shau-king.
Consider, 思想吓 sze-⸌seung-⸌ha.
Considerably, 稍 ⸌shaau, 畧畧 leuk-*leuk.
Considerate, 有細心 ⸌yau-sai⸍-sum, 通情理 t'uung-ts'ing-⸌li.

Consignee, 承辦人 shing-paan⸍-yan.
Consist of, 內有 noi⸍-⸌yau.
Consistent, 前後相對 ts'in-hau⸍-seung-tui⸍, (with) 合 hop.
Console, 安慰 ohn-wai⸍.
Consipicuous, 特出 tak-ch'uut.
Conspire, 結盟 kit⸍-mang. (things) 湊埋來 ts'au-maai-lai.
Constable, (local _ protector) 地保 ti⸍-⸌po, (police) 捕役 po⸍-yik.
Constant, 耐久無變 noi⸍-⸌kau-mo-pin⸍, 不歇 pat-hit⸍.
Constipation, 痞滿 ⸌p'i-⸌moon, 大便不通 taai⸍-pin⸍-pat-t'uung, 結恭 kit⸍-kuung.
Constitute, 立 laap, 成 shing.
Constitution, 質地 chat-*ti⸍, 資質 tsze-chat.
Constrain, 勉強 min-⸌k'eung, 強使 ⸌k'eung-⸌shai.

Construct, 建造 kin²-tso².
Consul, 領事官 ʿling-sze-koon.
Consult, 斟酌 chum-cheuk² 商量 sheung-leung.
Consume, (spend) 費 ˳fai.
Consummate, 完全 uen-tsʻuen, (to) 成 shing.
Consummately, 十分 shap-fun.
Consumption, (disease) 肺勞症 faiʾ-lo-chingʾ.
Contact, 鬥合 tauʾ-hop, 湊合 tsʻauʾ-hop.
Contagious, 傳染 chʻuen-ʿim, 會傳染 ʿooi-chʻuen-ʿim.
Contain, 裝載 chong-tsoiʾ, 包涵 paau-haam.
Contemn, 鄙慢 ʿpʻi-maanʾ, 輕慊 hing-imʾ, 鄙薄 ʿpʻi-pok.
Contemplate, 默想 mak-ʿseung.
Contemptible, 可鄙 ʿhok-ʿpʻi.
Contend,
Contest, } 爭 chaang.

Content, 安分 ohn-funʾ, 見夠 kinʾ-kauʾ, 知足 chi-tsuuk, 自得 tszeʾ-tak.
Context, 上下文 sheungʾ-haʾ-mun.
Continent, 大洲 taaiʾ-chau.
Continually, 屢屢 luiʾ-luiʾ, 一流 yat-*lau, 不留 pat-*lau, 不歇 pat-hitʾ.
Continue, 耐久 noiʾ-ʿkau.
Continuous, 相連 seung-lin.
Contraband goods, 私貨 sze-fohʾ.
Contract, (a) 合同 hop-tʻunng, (to) 立約 laap-yeukʾ, (for work) 拌工 ʿpoonʾ kuung, (lessen) 縮短 shuuk-ʿtuen, 縮細 shuuk-saiʾ.
Contradict, 辯駁 pinʾ-pokʾ, 話不是 waʾ-pat-shiʾ, waʾ-ʾm-haiʾ, 翻轉話 faan-ʿchuen-waʾ.
Contrary, 相反 seung-ʿfaan, 逆 yik, ngaak.
Contribute, (money) 捐銀 kuen-*ngan.

注 释

【斗合】接触，联系。
【见够】满足。
【私货】违禁品，走私品。
【话不是】否定。

注释

【计算】设计，图谋。
【五爪龙】又称"五爪金龙"，是管花目旋花科番薯属多年生草本植物，俗名番仔藤，可药用。
【火头】厨师。
【整冻】使……冷却。
【管店】苦力。

Contrive, 計算 kai'-suen', 想像 ʻseung-tseung.
Control, 制 chai'.
Contumely, 凌辱 ling-yuuk.
Convalescent, 病將近好 peng' tseung-*kan'-ho.
Convenient, 便當 pin'-tong', 方便 fong-pin', 便 pin'.
Convent, 庵堂 om-t'ong.
Converse, 談論 t'aam-luun', 談談 t'aam-t'aam, 相交 seung-kaau.
Convert, (to) 感化 ʻkom-fa', 變轉 pin'-chuen.
Convert, (a) 進教 tsuun'-kaau'.
Convex, 中間凸 ʻchuung-kaan-tut.
Convey, 搬運 poon-wan', 搬帶 poon-taai', 載 tsoi'.
Convict, (to) 定罪 ting'-tsui'.
Convict, (a) 犯人 faan'-yan.
Convince, 辯倒 pin'-ʻto, 令——知 ling'——chi.
Convolvulus, 纏籐花 ch'in-t'ang-fa, (the lilac) 五爪龍 ʻng-chaau-*luung.
Convoy, 送行 suung'-hang.

Convulsions, 抽搐病 ch'au-ch'uuk-peng'.
Cook, 火頭 ʻfoh-*t'au, 廚人 ch'ue-yan, (female) 煮飯媽 ʻchue-faan'-ma (ma), (to) 煮 ʻchue, 煮熟 ʻchue-shuuk.
Cooked, 熟 shuuk, 煮熟 ʻchue-shuuk.
Cool, 凉 leung, (to) 整凍 ʻching-tuung', 凉過 leung-kwoh'.
Coolie, 管店 ʻkoon-tim', (strect-) 挑夫 t'iu-foo.
Coolly, 坦然 ʻt'aan-in.
Cooper, 箍桶匠 foo-ʻt'uung-tseung', foo-ʻt'uung-ʻlo.
Co-operate, 協力 hip-lik.
Copper, 銅 t'uung, 紅銅 huung-t'uung, 熟銅 shuuk-t'uung.
Copperas, 青礬 ts'ing-faan.
Coppersmith, 銅匠 t'uung-*tseung', ta-t'uung-ke'.
Copulate, 交媾 kaau-kau', 行房 hang-fong, 交合 kaau-hop, (said of animals) 打種 ʻta-ʻchuung.

| COR | 54 | COT |

Copy, (a) 稿 ʻko, (to) 抄寫 chʻaau-ʻse, (slips) 印字格 yanʼ-tszeʼ-*kaakʼ.
Coral, 珊瑚 shaan-*oo.
Cord, 繩 tʻiu-*shing, 繩仔 shing-ʻtsai.
Cordially, 熱中 it-chuung, 甘心 kom-sum.
Core, 心 sum.
Coriander, 芫荽 uen-ʻsai.
Cork, (a) 枳 chat, (to) 枳住 chat-chueʼ, 塞口 sakʼ-ʻhau.
Cork-screw, 酒鑽 ʻtsau-tsuenʼ.
Cormorant, 鸕鶿 lo-*tsʻze.
Corn, 禾 woh, 穀 kuuk, (on the toe) 鷄眼 kai-ngaan.
Cornelian, 瑪瑙 ʻma-ʻno.
Corner, 角 kok, 角頭 kokʼ-*tʻau, (of a room) 角洛頭 kokʼ-lok-*tʻau.
Cornice, 墻頭線 tsʻeung-tʻau-*sinʼ.
Coroner, 驗屍官 imʼ-shi-koon.
Corpse, 死屍 ʻsze-shi, 屍首 shi-ʻshau.

Corpulent, 肥大 fi-taaiʼ.
Correct, 無錯 ʻmo-tsʻohʼ, 着 cheuk, 端正 tuen-chingʼ, 端方 tuen-fong, (to) 改削 ʻkoi-seuk, 改正 ʻkoi-chingʼ.
Correspond, 相應 seung-yingʼ, (by letter) 通信 tʻuung-suunʼ.
Corridor, 廊 long.
Corroborate, 證實 chingʼ-shat.
Corrode, 銹壞 sauʼ-waaiʼ, 銹蝕 sauʼ-shik.
Corrupt, (morally) 邪 tsʻe, (putrid) 腐爛 fooʼ-laanʼ, (to) 滾壞 ʻkwun-waaiʼ.
Cosey, (tea) 茶唅 chʻa-ʻkʻam (see Cozy).
Cost, (the) 買價 ʻmaai-kaʼ, (to) 抵 ʻtai.
Costiveness, 大便不通 taaiʼ-pinʼ-pat-tʻuung.
Costly, 貴 kwaiʼ.
Costume, 粧扮 chong-paanʼ.
Cottage, 小屋 ʻsiu-uuk, 屋仔 uuk-ʻtsai.

注 释

【热中】热情的,诚恳的。
【枳】软木塞。
【角头】角落。
【茶唅】杯垫。

注释

【状师】律师,法律顾问。
【柜围】柜台。
【假做】假装,伪造。
【被面】被单。
【老举】花魁,妓女,交际花。
【礼文】礼貌,礼节。

Cotton, (raw) 棉花 min-fa, (yarn) 棉紗 min-sha, (cloth) 布 po`.
Couch, 睡椅 shui`-`i, 匡床 k`ong`-ch`ong.
Cough, 咳嗽 k`at-sau`.
Council, 會 `ooi`.
Counsel, 勸 huen`.
Counsellor, (legal) 狀師 chong`-sze.
Count, (to) 算數 suen`-sho`, 數 `sho.
Countenance, 面貌 min`-maau`, (to) 照顧 chiu`-koo`.
Counter, (a shop-) 櫃圍 kwai`-*wai.
Counter-balance, 對抵 tui`-`tai.
Counteract, 禁制 kum`-chai`, 擋住 `tong-chue`, 抵住 `tai-chue`.
Counterfeit, 假做 `ka-tso`.
Counterpane, 被面 p`i-*min`.
Country, 國 kwok`, (the) 鄉下 heung-*ha`.
Couple, 偶 `ngau, 對 tui`.

Couplet, 對聯 `tui-*luen, 對 `tui.
Courage, 膽量 `taam-leung`, 勇氣 `yuung-hi`, (keep up) 揚起心肝 tik-`hi-sum-kohn.
Courageous, 大膽 taai`-`taam.
Course, 道路 to`-lo`, (of course) 自然 tsze`-in, (at a meal) 一度 yat-to` 一味送 yat-*mi-sung`.
Court, (the Imperial) 朝廷 ch`iu-t`ing, (of justice) 衙門 nga-*moon, (Supreme) 臬署 nip-`shue, (Police) 巡理府 ts`uun-`li-foo, (to) 逑 k`au.
Court-yard, 天井 t`in-`tseng.
Courtesan, 老舉 `lo-`kue.
Courtesy, 禮文 `lai-mun, 禮體 `lai-`t`ai, 禮數 `lai-sho`.
Cousin, 堂兄弟 t`ong-hing-tai`, (of another surname) 表兄弟 `piu-hing-tai`.
Covenant, 約 yeuk`, 盟約 mang-yeuk`.

Cover, 遮蓋 che-k'oi', 唥住 ‵k'um-chue', 笠蓋 k'up, k'oi', 掩 ‵im, ‵um, (to put a covering on) 捫 moon.
Coverlet, 被面 ‵p'i-*min'.
Covet, 貪 t'aam.
Covetous, 貪心 t'aam-sum.
Cow, 牛母 ngau-‵moo, 牛姆 ngau-‵na.
Coward, 無膽 ‵mo-‵taam, 膽怯 ‵taam-hip', 泵堆 tum'-tui.
Coxcomb, (flower) 雞冠花 kai-koon-fa, (a fop) 貪威 t'aam-wai.
Cozy, 安煖 ohn-‵nuen (see Cosey).
Crab, 蟹 ‵haai, (small) 蟚蜞 p'aang-*k'i.
Crack, 坼裂 ch'aak'-lit, (to) 裂開 lit-hoi, 整裂 ‵ching-lit, (the fingers) 整手卟 ‵ching-‵shau-puuk.
Cracked voice, 坼坼聲 ch'aak-ch'aak-sheng.
Crackers, 爆竹 p'aau'-chuuk, 爆像 p'aau-*tseung'.

Cracking, 逼迫聲 pik-paak'-sheng, p'lik-p'lak.
Craft, 藝業 ngai'-ip.
Crafty, 乖巧 kwaai-‵haau.
Cram, 插實 ch'aap'-shat, 插滿 ch'aap'-moon.
Cramp, 筋縮埋 kan-shuuk-maai.
Cramped, 困逼 k'wan'-pik.
Crane, 鶴 hok, 天鵝 t'in-ngoh, 鶬鴰 ts'ong-k'oot', (a machine) 千斤絞架 ts'in-kan-‵kaau-‵ka.
Crank, (a) 絞柄 ‵kaau-peng'.
Crape, 縐綢 tsau'-ch'au, 縐紗 tsau'-sha.
Crash, 彭聲 p'aang-shing, 砰磅 ping-‵pong.
Crave, 求 k'au.
Craving, (an artificial) 癮 ‵yan, (natural) 欲 yuuk.
Craw-fish, (sea) 龍蝦 luung-ha.
Crawl, 躝 laan, 爬行 p'a-hang, (as a worm) 縮吓 shuuk-‵ha, 吵吵吓 ‵miu-‵miu-*ha'.

注　释

【牛母】母牛。
【逼迫声】破裂声。
【筋缩埋】抽筋，痉挛。
【千斤绞架】起重机。
【彭声】"嘭"的一声。

注 释

【躝】滚，爬。
【躝藤】①.匍匐植；②.爬行的人（含贬义，骂人的话）。
【拐带佬】拐卖贩子（拐卖人到船上做水手或去当兵）。
【脱衣换锦】岭南盆景的一种制作方法。为了使树木盆景的叶片更细小、更翠绿，往往将叶片全部摘除（如同脱掉旧衣服），不久会重新长出嫩绿的叶子（好像换上了锦衣）。Crinum指的是"文珠兰"，一种观赏植物。
Crockery:陶器，瓦器。

Crazy, 戇 ngong², 瘋癲 fuung-tin.
Creak, 嚦聲 nget-sheng, kwit-sheng.
Cream, 牛奶皮 ngau-ʻnaai-pʻi.
Crease, 縐 chʻaau, 整縐 ʻching-chʻaau, 挪縐 noh-chʻaau.
Create, 創造 chʻong²-tso².
Creator, 做化主 tso²-fa²-ʻchue, 創造主 chʻong²-tso²-ʻchue.
Credit, 信 suun², (buy or sell on) 賒 she, (give me) 過信 kwoh²-suun².
Creditor, 債主 chaai²-ʻchue.
Credulous, 輕信 hing-suun².
Creed, 信經 suun²-king.
Creek, 涌 chʻuung, 涌滘 chʻuung-kʻaau².
Creep, 躝 laan.
Creeper, 躝籐 laan-tʻang.
Creeping sensation, 麻麻痹 ma-ma-pi².
Crescent, 新月形 san-uet-ying.

Cress, 水芹菜 ʻshui-kʻan-tsʻoi².
Crest, (of a cock) 鷄冠 ˳kai-˳koon, ˳kai-˳kwaan, (of other birds) 鬐 ˳kai², ʻkai.
Crevice, 罅隙 la²-kwik.
Crib, 欄 laan; (a book for "cribbing") ʻlam.
Cricket, 蟋蟀 sik-tsuut, 促織 tsʻuuk-chik, tsuuk-tsit.
Crime, 罪 tsui².
Criminal, 罪人 tsui²-yan.
Crimp, (a) 拐帶佬 ʻkwaai-taai²-ʻlo.
Crimp, (to) 縐埋 tsau²-maai, chʻaau-maai.
Crimson, 大紅色 taai²-huung-shik.
Crinum, 脱衣換錦 tʻuet-i-oon²-ʻkum.
Cripple, 跛脚 pai-keuk².
Crisis, (come to a) 至極地 chi-kik-*tiʻ, 事到頭來 sze²-to²-tʻau-loi (lai).
Crisp, 脆 tsʻui².
Criticise, 批評 pʻai-pʻing.
Crockery, 磁器 tsʻze-hiʻ.

| CRO | 58 | CRU |

Crocodile, 鱷魚 ngok-ue.
Crooked, 彎曲 waan-k'uuk, 攣曲 luen-k'uuk.
Crop, 收獲 shau-wok, 造 tso', (a bird's) 穊胞 sui'-paau, 穊窩 sui'-woh.
Cross, (a) 十字架 shap-tsze'-ka, (-wise) 橫 waang, (make a) 交加 kaau-ka, (irritate) 激嬲 kik-nau.
Cross, (peevish) 蠻 maan, 嬲燷 nau-nat.
Cross-bar, 橫壓 wang-aat', 橫櫳 waang-*luung.
Cross-examine, 橫詰 waang-k'it, 橫間 waang-mun'.
Cross-grained, 橫紋 waang-*mun, 乖張 kwaai-cheung.
Crotchety, 奇橫 k'i-waang.
Crouch, 踎伏 ts'uen-fuuk, 屈氣 wut-hi', 瞪低 mau-tai.
Croup, 哮喘 haau-ch'uen, 哮病 haau-peng'.
Crow, 老鴉 'lo-a, 烏鵲 wo-tseuk', (to) 啼 t'ai.
Crowbar, 咸鍫 tuung'-ts'iu.

Crowd, 擁集 'yuung-tsaap, (to) 擠擁 tsai-'yuung, 偪 pik.
Crown, (top) 頂 'ting, (ornamental) 冠冕 koon-'min.
Crucify, 釘——十字架 teng——shap-tsze'-ka, 釘死 teng-sze'.
Cruel, 殘忍 ts'aan-'yan.
Cruet-stand, 五味架 'ng-mi'-ka.
Cruiser, 巡船 ts'uun-*shuen.
Crumb, 屑碎 sit'-sui, 呷碎 sap-'sui.
Crumble, 擣碎 'to-sui'.
Crumple, 縐搖搖 ch'aau-mang-mang.
Crush, 壓壞 aat'-waai', 壓爛 aat'-laan', 搾 cha', (with the hand) 揸爛 cha-laan', 搾 cha'.
Crust, 殼 hok', 硬皮 ngaang'-*p'i.
Crusty, 惡 ok'.
Crutch, 杈杖 ch'a-cheung'. 杈枴 ch'a-'kwaai, 枴杖 'kwaai-*cheung'.

注 释

【激嬲】惹怒。
【踎伏】蜷伏，蹲屈。
【咸鍫】撬棍。
【五味架】调味架。
【皺搖搖】皱巴巴。

注释

【嗌】喊。

【龟公】妓院中打杂的男人。Cuckold指的是妻子与人通奸的男人。

【催耕雀】布谷鸟。

【可责】有罪的；该责备的。

【挛埋】卷曲。

CUP　59　CUR

Cry, 喊 haam', 叫聲 kiu-sheng, 嗌 aai, 嘄 iu.
Crystal, 水晶 'shui-tsing.
Cube, 立方 laap-fong, 立方形 laap-fong-ying, 色子樣 shik-'tsze-*yeung.
Cubit, 尺 ch'ek'.
Cuckold, 龜公 kwai-kuung.
Cuckoo, (Chinese) 催耕雀 ts'ui-kang-tseuk', 杜鵑 to'-,kuen.
Cucumber, 王瓜 wong-kwa.
Cud, (to chew) 翻草 faan-ts'o.
Cudgel, 木棒 muuk-'p'aang.
Cue, 辮 pin, 條辮 t'iu-,pin.
Cuff, 𧙕口 tsau'-,hau, (to) 拳打 k'uen-ta.
Culpable, 可責 'hoh-chaak'.
Cultivate, 耕種 kang-chuung', (plants) 恁 ,nun.
Cumber, 阻滯 'choh-chai', 滯 chai'.
Cumbersome, 累贅 lui'-chui'.
Cunning, 多計 toh-*kai', 詭譎 'kwai-kwut.
Cup, 盃 pooi.
Cup-board, 碗櫃 'oon-*kwai.
Curb, 勒住 lak-chue', 管束 'koon-ch'iuk'.
Curd, 乳結 'ue-kit', (bean-) 荳腐 tau'-foo.
Curdle, 凝結 ying-kit'.
Cure, 醫好 i-'ho.
Curiosity, (of mind) 練見識 lin'-,kin'-shik, 查查察察 ch'a-ch'a-ch'aat'-ch'aat'.
Curiosities, 古董 'koo-'tuung, 奇珍 k'i-,chan.
Curl, 攣埋 luen-maai.
Curly hair, 捲髮 'kuen-faat'.
Currants, 珠菩提 chue-po-t'ai.
Current, (a) 水流 'shui-lau.
Current money, 通寶 t'uung-'po.
Current price, 時價 shi-ka'.
Curry-powder, 黃薑粉 wong-,keung-'fun, (-stuff) 架厘材料 ka'-li-ts'oi-liu'.
Curse, 咒咀 chau'-choh', (to vow) 賭呪 'to-chau'.
Curtain, 布簾 po'-*lim, (mosquito-) 蚊帳 mun-*cheung'.

Curve, 彎曲 waan-huuk.
Cushion, 褥仔 yuuk-ʿtsai, 椅墊 ʿi-tinʾ (tsinʾ).
Cuspidor, 痰罐 tʻaam-koonʾ.
Custard-apple, 番荔枝 faan-laiʾ-ʿchi.
Custom, (common) 規矩 kʻwai-ʿkue, 世俗 shai-tsuuk, 風俗 fuung-tsuuk, (tribute) 稅 shuiʾ, (house) 關口 kwaan-ʿhau, 稅館 shuiʾ-ʿkoon.
Customer, 買客 ʿmaai-haak.
Cut, 割 kohtʾ, 切 tsʻitʾ, (off) 斬 ʿchaam, (acquaintance) 不偢彩 ʾm-tsʻau-ʿtsʻoi.
Cuttlefish, 張魚 cheung-ue, 墨魚 mak-ue.
Cycle of sixty, 花甲 fa-kaapʾ.
Cyclone, 旋風 suen-fuung, 風颶 fuung-kauʾ.
Cymbals, 鐃鈸 naau-poot, 鈔 ʿchʻaau.
Cynical, 鼓氣 ʿkoo-hiʾ.
Cypress, 扁柏 ʿpin-paakʾ.

D

Dab, 搭 tap, 呾 tat, (to wet) 搭濕 tap-shup, tat-shup.
Dab, fish, 沙孟魚 sha-ʿmangʾ-*ue.
Dabble in, 弄 luungʾ.
Dace, fish, 黃尾鱗 wong-ʿmi-luun.
Daddy, 爹爹 te-te.
Dagger, 短劍 ʿtuen-kimʾ.
Daggle, 拖悷 tʻoh-ʿnun.
Dahlia, 芍藥 cheukʾ-yeuk.
Daily, 日日 yat-yat, 每日 ʿmooi-yat, (use) 日用 yat-yuungʾ.
Dainties, 味 *miʾ.
Dainty, 嬌貴 kiu-kwaiʾ.
Dam, (mother) 嫲 ʿna.
Dam, (a water-) 基圍 ki-wai, 陂 pi, (to) 塞陂 sak-pi, 壅 ʿyuung.
Damage, 損壞 ʿsuen-waaiʾ.
Damask, 大花緞 taaiʾ-fa-*tuenʾ.
Damn, (to curse) 咒詛 chauʾ-choh.

注释

【褥仔】坐墊，靠墊。
【鼓气】愤世嫉俗的；态度冷酷的。
【拖悷】拖拽。
【基围】水坝。

注释

【折堕】缺德,没良心;因做了缺德事而受报应。
【小梅】西洋李子(一种果子)。
【头坭】头皮屑。
【调调佷】摇晃地悬挂着。
【袖箭】镖,标枪。
【天仅光】黎明,破晓。

Damned, to be, 折堕 chit'-toh', 墮落雞 toh'-lok-kai.
Damp, 濕 shap, (and soft) 腍 num, (to become) 潮濕 ch'iu-shup, (to) 整濕 ‵ching-shup.
Damson, 小梅 ‵siu-mooi.
Dance, 跳舞 t'iu'-‵moo.
Dandelion, 蒲公英 p'oo-‵kuung-ying.
Dandle, 搖吓 iu-‵ha, 㨄吓 lau'-‵ha.
Dandruff, 頭坭 t'au-nai.
Dandy, 裝腔 chong-‵hong, 紈褲子弟 uen-foo' ‵tsze-tai.
Danger, 危險 ngai-‵him.
Dangerous, 險 ‵him.
Dangle, 調調佷 tiu'-*tiu'-fing'.
Dare, 敢 ‵kom, 膽敢 ‵taam-‵kom.
Daring, 大膽 taai'-‵taam.
Dark, 黑 hak, 黑暗 hak-om'.
Darling, 痛愛 t'uung'-oi', 掌上珠 ‵cheung-sheung-‵chue.

Darn, 織補 chik-‵po.
Dart, (to) 閃 ‵shim, (an arrow) 袖箭 tsau'-tsin', 標 piu.
Dash, (to) 冲撞 ch'uung-chong'.
Date, (time) 年月號 nin-uet-ho'.
Dates, (dried) 蜜棗 mat-‵tso, (jujube-tree) 棗樹 ‵tso-shue, (palm) 波斯棗 poh-sze-‵tso, 洋棗 yeung-‵tso.
Datura, 鬧羊花 naau'-yeung-fa, 曼陀羅 maan'-t'oh-loh.
Daub, 塗污 t'o-oo, 搽 ch'a.
Daubed, 抹得粗 maat-tak-t'so.
Daughter, 女 ‵nue, (your) 千金 ts'in-‵kum, (-in-law) 媳婦 sik-‵foo.
Daunted, 喪氣 song-hi'.
Davits, 朔枴 kat-‵kai.
Dawn, 天僅光 t'in-‵kan-kwong, 懞亮 muung-leung'.
Day, 日 yat, 日子 yat-‵tsze.

Day-light, 白晝 paak-chau, 白日 paak-yat, (morning) 天光 t'in-kwong.
Dazzle, 瞠花眼 ch'aang-fa-ngaan, 瞠 ch'aang.
Deacon, 執事 chap-sze.
Dead, 死咗 sze-choh, sze-hiu, 身故 shan-koo, 過身 kwoh-shan.
Deaf, 聾 luung, 耳聾 i-luung, (dull) 耳背 i-pooi.
Deal, (to) 變易 kaau-yik, (a good-) 好多 ho-toh.
Deal, (wood) 杉木 ch'aam-muuk.
Dear, 貴 kwai, (loved) 切愛 ts'it-oi.
Death, 死 sze, 死亡 sze-mong.
Death-rattle, 扯氣 ch'e-hi.
Debase, 傾低銀水 k'ing-tai-ngan-shui.
Debate, 鬥口角 tau-hau-kok, 爭論 chaang-luun.
Debauch, (to) 點污 tim-oo, 玷污 tim-oo.
Debauchee, 酒色之徒 tsau-shik-chi-t'o.
Debauchery, 蹭脚 sang-keuk.
Debilitate, 損元氣 suen-uen-hi, 壞氣力 waai-hi-lik, 壞身 waai-shan.
Debility, 軟弱 uen-yeuk, 元氣傷 uen-hi-sheung, 虛 hue.
Debit note 揭單 k'it-taan.
Debt, 欠債 him-chaai, 欠負 him-foo, (debts) 欠項 him-hong.
Debtor, 債仔 chaai-tsai, 欠債人 him-chaai-yan.
Decade, 旬 ts'uun.
Decalogue, 十誡 shap-kaai.
Decamp, 退避 t'ui-pi.
Decant, 揀 pi.
Decapitate, 殺頭 shaat-t'au.
Decapitation, 正法 ching-faat.
Decayed, 衰壞 shui-waai, 霉爛 mooi-laan, 枯槁 foo-ko.
Deceit, 詭譎 kwai-kwut.
Deceitful, 詐假 cha-ka.
Deceive, 瞞騙 moon-p'in, 呃 ngaak, 𧩙 t'um.

注释

【合礼/合式】合乎礼仪，体面。
【装雀】媒鸟，媒头，诱骗猎物上当的诱饵。
【老迈】衰老的，破旧的。
【短欠】缺陷，缺点。

DEC 63 DEF

December, 英十二月 Ying-shap-i'-uet.
Decency, 合禮 hop-'lai, 合式 hop-shik.
Decide, 決斷 k'uet'-tuen', 定 ting'.
Decision, 主意 ‘chue-i'.
Deck, (the) 艙板 ts'ong-‘paan, (to) 裝整 chong-‘ching.
Declare, 話實 wa'-shat, (shew) 表明 ‘piu-ming.
Decline, (downwards) 墜落去 chui'-lok-hue', 向低去 heung'-tai-hue', (refuse) 辭謝 ts'ze-tse', 推辭 t'ui-ts'ze, (seeing) 免見 ‘min-kin', 擋駕 ‘tong-ka'.
Declivity, 斜坂 ts'e'-‘paan, 斜落 ts'e-*ts'e-lok, 坡 poh.
Decoct, 煎 tsin.
Decorate, 裝整 chong-‘ching.
Decorum, 禮所當然 ‘lai-‘shoh-tong-in, 容儀 yuung-i, 儀注 i-chue'.
Decoy, (to) 引誘 ‘yan-‘yau, (birds) 裝雀 chong-*tseuk', (to) 做媒 tso'-*mooi.

Decrease, 減少 ‘kaam-‘shiu, 縮減 shuuk-‘kaam.
Decree, 命令 ming'-ling'.
Decrepit, 老邁 ‘lo-maai'.
Dedicate, 供奉 kuung-fuung'.
Deduct, 減 ‘kaam, 扣除去 k'au'-ch'ue-‘hue.
Deed, 行為 hang-wai, 事 sze', (bond) 契 k'ai', (stamped-) 印契 yan'-k'ai'.
Deep, 深 shum.
Deer, 鹿 *luuk, (moschus) 黃麖 wong-‘keng, 麞 cheung.
Deer's horn, 鹿茸 luuk-yuung.
Defame, 壞—名聲 waai'——ming-shing.
Defeat, 敗 paai', 打敗 ‘ta-paai', 打贏 ‘ta-yeng.
Defect, 虧缺 fai-k'uet'.
Defend, 保護 ‘po-oo'.
Defendant, 被告 pi'-ko'.
Defer, 改期 ‘koi-k'i, 展緩 ‘chin-oon', (yield) 推讓 t'ui-yeung', 寬限 foon-haan'.
Deficiency, 短欠 ‘tuen-him', 欠缺 him'-k'uet'.

DEL 64 DEM

Defile, 染汚 ʽim-oo, 玷汚 tim⁾-oo, (a) 山峽 shaan-haap.
Definite, 定 ting⁾, 定然 ting⁾-in.
Deflect, 轉邪 ʽchuen-tsʽe.
Deformed, 醜怪 ʽchʽau-kwaai⁾.
Defraud, 陀騙 ngaak-pʽin⁾.
Defy, 激鬥 kik-tau⁾, 惹敵 ʽye-tik, 輕敵 ʽhing-tik, 撩打 ʽliu-ʽta.
Degenerate, 下流 ha⁾-lau, 入下流 yup-ha⁾-lau, 不肖 pat-tsʽiu⁾.
Degrade, (in rank) 降級 kong⁾-kʽup, 參革 tsʽaam-kaak⁾, (one's self) 丟面 tiu-*min⁾.
Degree, 等 ʽtang, 層 tsʽang, 級 kʽup, (measure) 度 to⁾.
Deign, 垂顧 shui-koo⁾.
Dejected, 愁默默 shau-mak-mak, 悶沉沉 moon⁾-chʽum-chʽum.
Delay, 擔擱 taam-kok⁾, 遲緩 chʽi-oon⁾.

Delegate, (to) 委托 kaau-tok⁾, (a) 委托之人 ʽwai-tʽok⁾-ke⁾-yan.
Deliberate, 斟酌 chum-cheuk⁾, 商量 sheung-leung⁾, (ADJ.) 澹定 taam⁾-ting⁾.
Delicate, 嬌嫩 kiu-nuen⁾, 柔弱 yau-yeuk, 幼細 yau⁾-sai⁾.
Delicacy, (a) 珍饈 chan-sau.
Delicious, 佳味 kaai-mi⁾, 美味 ʽmi-mi⁾.
Delight, 歡喜 foon-ʽhi.
Delineate, 畫出 waak-chʽuut.
Delirious, 發狂 faat⁾-kʽwong.
Delirium, 狂 kʽwong.
Deliver, (save) 救 kau⁾, (up) 交 kaau, 遞 tai⁾, (over to) 解 kaai.
Delude, 迷惑 mai-waak, 蠱惑 ʽhoo-waak.
Deluge, 洪水 huung-ʽshui.
Demand, (in) 時興 shi-ʽhing.
Demand, (to) 問取 mun⁾-tsʽue, 要取 iu⁾-tsʽue, 必要 pit iu⁾, (with violence) 逼取 pik-ʽtsʽue.

注 释

【转邪】使转向,使偏斜。
【垂顾】屈尊,降低身份。
【时兴】所需要的,受欢迎的。

注 释

【溃】指士气低落。
【指实】指示。
【该管】部门。
【当头】指在当铺借钱时所用的抵押品。

DEP　　65　　DEP

Demolish, 拆嘥 ch'aak'-saai'.
Demon, 鬼 'kwai.
Demonstrate, 指明証據 'chi-ming-ching'-kue.
Demoralized, (as troops) 潰 'fui, 盡覆 tsuun'-fuuk, (the mind) 壞心術 waai'-sum-shuut.
Demur, 不肯 pat-'hang, 'm-'hang, 推 t'ui, 推延 t'ui-in.
Den, 籠 ,luung, 穴 uet, 竇口 tau'-'hau.
Denomination, 名字 ming-tsze', 字號 tsze'-ho'.
Denote, 指實 'chi-shat.
Denounce, 控告 huung'-ko'.
Dense, 稠密 ch'au-mat.
Dentist, 牙科醫生 nga-foh-i-,shang.
Deny, 不認 pat-ying', 'm-ying', 話唔係 wa-'m-hai', (one's self) 克己 hak-'ki, 捨己 'she-'ki.
Depart, 別去 pit-hue', 行離 hang-li, 離去 li-hue'.

Department, 該管 koi-'koon, 職守 chik-'shau, 所屬 shoh-shuuk, 部 po'.
Depend on, 倚賴 'i-laai', 倚靠 'i-k'aau'.
Deplorable, 可恨 'hoh-han' 堪悲 hom-pi.
Deplore, 悲哀 pi-oi.
Deport, 搬去 poon-hue'.
Deportment, 行為 hang-wai, (correct) 容儀 yuung-i.
Depose, 革職 kaak'-chik.
Deposit, (a) 當頭 tong'-t'au, (to) 墜落 chui'-lok, (pawn) 按當 ohn'-tong', 押 aat'.
Deposition, (verbal) 口供 'hau-kuung, (from office) 廢 fai', 革職 kaak'-chik.
Depraved, 邪惡 ts'e-ok', 心壞 sum-waai'.
Depreciate, 看低 hohn'-tai, 睇輕 't'ai-heng.
Depress, 壓落 aat'-lok.
Depressed, 困鬱 k'wun'-wut.
Deprive, 奪 tuet, 革去 kaak'-hue'.

Depute, 委託 ʻwai-tʻok᾿.
Deranged, 亂 luen᾿, 癲 tin.
Deride, 戲笑 hiʼ-siu᾿, 嬉笑 hi-siu᾿.
Derive, (obtain) 得倒 tak-ʻto.
Derogate, 損 ʻsuen.
Descend, 下降 ʻha-kong᾿.
Descendants, 後裔 hauʼ-yui᾿.
Describe, 指出 ʻchi-chʻuut, 歷歷表明 lik-lik-ʻpiu-ming, 講清楚 ʻkong-tsʻing-chʻoh, (write) 寫出 ʻse-chʻuut.
Description, (every) 各色 kokʼ-shik.
Desecrate, 褻瀆 sitʼ-tuuk.
Desert, 野 ʻye, 野外 ʻye-ngoi᾿, 郊外 kaau-ngoi᾿.
Desert, (merit), 因果 yan-ʻkwoh, 功勞 kuung-lo.
Desert, (to) 逃脫 tʻo-tʻuet, 走路 ʻtsau-lo᾿, 拋離 pʻaau-li.
Deserve, 應係 ying-hai᾿, 該當 koi-tong, 應分 ying fun᾿.

Design, (to) 計謀 kaiʼ-mau, (a) 意像 iʼ-tseung᾿, 謀畧 mau-leuk, (intention) 主意 ʻchue-i᾿.
Designation, 字號 tszeʼ-ho᾿.
Designate, 稱呼 chʻing-foo.
Desire, 欲 yuuk, 願 uen᾿, 情願 tsʻing-uen᾿, (covet) 貪 tʻaam.
Desist, 止息 ʻchi-sik, 罷了 paʼ-ʻliu, 歇手 hitʼ-ʻshau.
Desk, 寫字臺 ʻse-tszeʼ-ʻtʻoi, (portable) 寫字箱 ʻse-tszeʼ-seung.
Desolate, 孤寒 koo-hohn, 零落 ling-lok.
Despair, 絕望 tsuet-mong᾿, 失望 shat-mong᾿.
Desperate, 無奈何 ʻmo-noi᾿-hoh.
Despise, 藐視 ʻmiu-shi᾿, 侮慢 ʻmoo-maan᾿, 輕忽 hing-fut, 睇不上眼 tʻaiʼ-'m-sheungʼ-ʻngaan.
Despond, 失望 shat-mong᾿.
Despotic, (oppressive) 酷 huuk, (government) 全權政 tsʻuen-kʻuen-chingʼ.

注 释

【得倒】获得，得到。
【走路】逃跑。
【孤寒】荒凉的。
【无奈何】绝望的。
【全权政】独裁，专制。

注释

【擸杂】混乱的。
【讲损】贬低，诋毁。
【行差】偏离，脱离。
【交落】被移交，转移。
【尿淋】糖尿病。

Destination, 去向 *hue-heung*.
Destiny, (fate) 命 *meng*, 數 *sho*.
Destitute, 窮 *k'uung*, 窮困 *k'uung-k'wun*.
Destroy, 毀滅 *‘wai-mit*, 毀爛 *‘wai-laan*, 敗壞 *paai-waai*.
Destruction, 滅亡 *mit-mong*.
Desultory, 擸雜 *laap-tsaap*, 無層次 *‘mo-ts‘ang-ts‘ze*.
Detach, 分開 *fun-hoi*.
Detail, (in) 逐一 *chuuk-yat*, (to) 逐一逐二講 *chuuk-yat-chuuk-*i*-‘kong*.
Detain, 留住 *lau-chue*, 揯阻 *k‘ang-‘choh*.
Detect, 察出 *ch‘aat-ch‘uut*, 訪出 *‘fong-ch‘uut*.
Deter, 攔阻 *laan-‘choh*.
Deteriorate, 舊壞 *kau-waai*, 衰壞 *shui-waai*.
Determination, 決意 *k‘uet-i*.
Determine, 定 *ting*, 決 *k‘uet*.
Detest, 恨惡 *han-oo*, 厭惡 *im-oo*, 憎惡 *tsang-oo*.

Detract, 講損 *‘kong-‘suen*.
Devastation, 荒廢 *fong-fai*.
Develope, 舒開 *shue-hoi*, 伸發 *shan-faat*, 發開 *faat-hoi*.
Deviate, 行差 *hang-ch‘a*.
Device, 計 *kai*, *kai*.
Devil, 魔鬼 *moh-‘kwai*.
Devise, 計謀 *kai-mau*, 籌畫 *ch‘au-waak*.
Devoid of, 無 *‘mo or moo*.
Devolve, 交落 *kaau-lok*.
Devoted, 仰慕 *‘yeung-moo*, 心慕 *sum-moo*, 深服 *shum-fuuk*.
Devotion, 誠敬之禮 *shing-king-chi-‘lai*, 虔敬 *k‘in-king*.
Devour, 硬吞 *ngaang-t‘un*.
Devout, 誠心 *shing-sum*, 虔敬 *k‘in-king*.
Dew, 露水 *lo-‘shui*, 霧 *mo*.
Dexterous, 巧手 *‘haau-‘shau*.
Diabetes, 尿淋 *niu-lum*.
Diabolical, 惡妖 *ok-iu*, 兇惡 *huung-ok*.
Diagnose, 診 *‘ch‘an*.

Diagonal, 斜線 ts'e-*sin⁾, 對角線 tui⁾-kok⁾-*sin⁾.
Diagrams, (the eight) 八卦 paat⁾-kwa⁾.
Dial, 日晷 yat-ᶜkwai, 日窺 yat-ᶜk'wai.
Dialect, 土話 ᶜt'o-*wa⁾, 土談 ᶜto-t'aam.
Dialogue, 問荅 mun⁾-taap⁾, 相論 seung-luun⁾.
Diameter, 徑線 king⁾-*sin⁾.
Diamond, 金剛石 kum-kong-shek, 鑽石 tsuen⁾-shek.
Diarrhœa, 痾 oh, 水瀉 ᶜshui-se⁾.
Diary, 日記 yat-ki⁾.
Dice, 色子 shik-ᶜtsze.
Dice-playing, 擲色 chaak-shik.
Dictate, 囑咐 chuuk-foo⁾, 主張 ᶜchue-cheung, (to a writer) 口授 ᶜhau-shau⁾.
Dictionary, 字典 tsze⁾-ᶜtin, 字彙 tsze⁾-ᶜlui.
Dictum, 硬話 ngaang⁾-*wa⁾.

Die, (to) 死 ᶜsze, (said of men) 過世 kwoh⁾-shai⁾, 身故 shan-koo⁾.
Diet, (to) 戒口 kaai⁾-ᶜhau.
Differ, 爭 chaang, 有分別 ᶜyau-fun-pit.
Difference, 差 ch'a, 分別 fun-pit, 爭 chaang.
Different, 不同 'm-t'uung, (very) 差得遠 ch'a-tak-ᶜuen.
Difficult, 難 naan, 惡做 ok⁾-tso⁾.
Difficulty, 艱難 kaan-naan.
Diffident, 信不過 suun⁾-'m-kwoh⁾.
Diffuse, 佈散 po⁾-saan⁾, 播揚 poh⁾-yeung.
Dig, 掘 kwut.
Digest, 消化 siu-fa⁾.
Dignified, 威嚴 wai-im.
Dignity, 威儀 wai-i, 威風 wai-fuung.
Digress, 支離 chi-li.
Dike, 基堢 ki-pok⁾.
Dilapidated, 頹壞 t'ui-waai⁾.

注 释

【色子】骰子。
【硬话】权威意见。
【戒口】忌口。
【支离】偏离。
【基堢】堤防, 堤坝。

注 释

【抠稀】稀释。
【酒凹】酒窝。
【吧闭】喧闹。
【污糟】肮脏。
【撞板】同"碰壁"。比喻做事或说话受到阻碍或遭拒绝，也指事情行不通。

DIR　69　DIS

Dilate, 撑開 ch'aang-hoi, (expatiate) 講詳細 ḳong-ts'eung-sai.

Dilatory, 遲慢 ch'i-maan, (*maan).

Dilemma, 兩難 'leung-naan.

Diligent, 勤力 k'an-lik, 勤 k'an.

Dilute, 攪水 'kaau-'shui, 摳稀 k'au-hi.

Dim, 矇矓 muung-luung, 矇 muung.

Dimensions, 長闊 ch'eung-foot, 度量 to'-leung'.

Diminish, 減少 'kaam-'shiu.

Diminutive, 細微 sai'-mi, sai'-mi.

Dimple, 酒凹 'tsau-nup.

Din, 嘈响 ts'o-'heung, 吧閉 pa-pai.

Ding-dong, 玎璫 ting-tong.

Dinner, 大餐 taai'-ts'aan.

Dip, 蘸 chaam', 沉下 ch'um-*ha, 浸下 yum-ha, tsim.

Direct, 正直 ching'-chik, (to) 指點 'chi-'tim, 指教 'chi-kaau', 管理 'koon-'li.

Direction, 去向 hue'-heung', 方向 fong-heung'.

Directly, 即刻 tsik-haak, 即時 tsik-shi.

Dirt, 泥土 nai-'t'o, (dung) 屎 'shi.

Dirty, 汚糟 oo-tso, 鐪鮓 la'-cha, (to) 整污糟 'ching-oo-tso.

Disabled, 無能 mo-nang.

Disabuse the mind, 開茅塞 hoi-maau-sak.

Disadvantage, 受虧 shau'-fai, 不直 pat-chik.

Disaffected, 不輸服 'm-shue-fuuk.

Disagree, 不對 'm-tui', 唔啱 'm-ngaam, 相爭 seung-chaang.

Disagreeable, 醜 'ch'au, 揩 k'ang', 淰 sum'.

Disappear, 失去 shat-hue'.

Disappoint, 不遂願 pat-sui'-uen', 撞板 chong'-paan, 不趁願 'm-ch'an'-uen'.

Disapprove, 不中意 'm-chuung-i'.

英粤字典　69

DIS	70	DIS

Disaster, 凶事 huung-sze’.
Disavow, 不認 'm-ying’.
Disband, 散班 saan’-paan.
Disburse, 使費 ‘shai-fai’, 使 ‘shai, 支 chi, 出 ch‘uut.
Discard, 除免 ch‘ue-‘min, 除出 ch‘ue-ch‘uut.
Discern, 睇破 ‘t‘ai-p‘oh’.
Discernment, 聰明 ts‘uung-ming.
Discharge, 出 ch‘uut, 放 fong’, (duty) 盡本分 tsuun’-‘poon-fun’.
Disciple, 門生 moon-‘shang, 學生 hok-‘shaang.
Discipline, 教法 kaau’-faat’, (exercise) 練習 lin’-tsaap.
Disclose, 敗露 paai’-lo’, 露出 lo’-ch‘uut.
Discomfit, 打敗 ‘ta-paai’.
Discomfort, 不爽快 'm-‘shong-faai’.
Discomposed, 淹悶 im-moon’.
Disconcerted, 失愕 shat-ngok.
Disconsolate, 憂憶 yau-yik, 憂鬱 yau-wat.

Discontented, 不滿意 pat-‘moon-i’ 不知足 pat-chi-tsuuk, 喬扭 k‘iu-‘nau.
Discontinue, 止了 ‘chi-‘liu, 斷 ‘t‘uen, 間斷 kaan-‘t‘uen.
Discordant, 不和 pat-woh, 唔啱 'm-‘ngaam.
Discount, 扣頭銀 k‘au’-t‘au-*ngan, 扣銀水 k‘au’-ngan-‘shui, 扣 k‘au’.
Discountenance, 免相與 ‘min-seung-‘ue, 唔同埋 'm-t‘uung-maai.
Discourage, 丟 — 駕 tiu — ka’, 落 — 臺 lok — t‘oi, 勸止 huen’-‘chi.
Discouraged, 喪氣 song’-hi’.
Discourse, 議論 ‘i-luun’, 論 luun’.
Discover, 尋見 ts‘um-kin’, 考明 ‘haau-ming, 查出 ch‘a-ch‘uut.
Discredit, (disbelieve) 不信 'm-suun’, 思疑 sze-i.
Discreet, 仔細 ‘tsze-sai’.

注 释

【散班】解散。
【睇破】看破。
【淹悶】不安。
【扣头银】折扣。
【免相与】不赞成。
【丢驾】丢脸。

注释

【解用】解开，理清。
【出】剥夺（某人的）继承权。
【深啉】阴沉。
【落箱】解散（队伍等），旧时指戏班在某处演出完毕装箱要离去。

Discrepancy, 不對之處 pat-tui⁾-chi-chʻue⁾, 不相對處 ʼm-seung-tuiˊ-chʻue⁾.
Discrepant, 不對 pat-tuiˊ, ʼm-tuiˊ.
Discretion, 謹慎 ʻkan-shanˊ, (at your) 隨你主意 tsʻue-ʻni-ʻchue-i.
Discretionary, 隨便 tsʻue-*pinˊ, 任意 yumˊ-i.
Discriminate, 分明 fun-ming, 分別 fun-pit, 辨別 ʻpinˊ-pit.
Discuss, 辯論 pinˊ-luunˊ.
Disdain, 藐視 ʻmiu-shi.
Disease, 疾病 tsat-pengˊ, 病症 pengˊ-chingˊ.
Disengage, Disentangle, } 解出 ʻkaai-chʻuut, 解用 ʻkaai-lut.
Disengaged, 得閒 tak-haan.
Disgrace, 污辱 oo-yuuk, 羞辱 sau-yuuk.
Disguise, 假扮 ʻka-paanˊ.
Disgust, 憎厭 tsang-imˊ.
Disgusting, 可惡 ʻhoh-ooˊ.
Dishes, 碗碟 ʻoon-tip.

Disheartened, 心恢 sum-fooi.
Dishevel, 散亂 ʻsaan-luenˊ.
Dishonest, 無真誠 ʼmo-chan-shing, 無真實 ʼmo-chan-shat.
Dishonour, (to), 辱 yuuk.
Dishonourable, 無體面 ʼmo-ʻtʻai-min.
Disinclined, 不想 ʼm-ʻseung, 不願 ʼm-uenˊ.
Disinherit, 出 chʻuut.
Disinterested, 無私心 ʼmo-sze-sum.
Disjoint, 挫歪骨節 tsʻoh⁾-ˊme-kwut-tsit, 整開骨節 ʻching-hoi-kwut-tsit.
Disk, 輪 luun.
Dislike, 嫌 im.
Dismal, 深啉 shum-lum.
Dismay, 大驚 taaiˊ-king.
Dismembering, (a punishment) 凌遲 ling-chʻi.
Dismiss, 使—去 ʻshai, — hueˊ, 不用 pat-yuungˊ, 放 fong, (clear out. —I dismiss you) 落箱 lok-ʻseung.

Disobedient, 悖逆 pooi`-yik.	Dispose, (arrange) 安排 ohn-p'aai.
Disobey, 違背 wai-pooi`, 不聽話 'm-t'eng-wa`.	Disposition of mind, 品格 `pun-kaak`, 品性 `pun-sing`, 皮氣 p'i-hi`.
Disobliging, 無照應 mo-chiu`-ying` 噉情 ngaak-ts'ing.	Dispute, 辯駁 pin`-pok`.
Disordered, 亂 luen`.	Disquietude, 無平安 mo-p'ing-ohn.
Disorderly, 佬噪 `lo-`ts'o, 鹵莽 `lo-`mong, 妄 `mong, 立亂 laap-luen`.	Disregard, 不顧 'm-`koo.
	Disreputable, 失體 shat-`t'ai, 不好意思 'm-`ho-i`-sze, 下流 ha`-iau.
Disown, 不認 'm-ying`.	
Disparage, 講低 `kong-tai.	Disrepute, 無名聲 mo-ming-shing, 不興 'm-hing.
Disparity, 差 ch'a.	
Dispatches, 文書 mun-shue.	Disrespectful, 不恭敬 'm-kuung-king`.
Dispensary, 藥館 yeuk-`koon, (a shop) 藥材舖 yeuk-ts'oi-`p'o.	Dissatisfied, 不知足 'm-chi-tsuuk`, 不滿意 'm-`moon-i`.
Dispense, 施 shi, (with) 免 `min.	Dissemble, 詐造 cha`-tso`, 詐成 cha`-shing, 詐假意 cha`-`ka-i`, cha`-`ka-i`.
Disperse, 離散 li-saan`.	
Dispirit, 喪志 song`-chi`.	Disseminate, 佈散 po`-saan`, 傳布 ch'uen-po`, 散開 saan`-hoi.
Displace, 搬亂 poon-luen`.	
Displaced, 離位 li-*wai`.	
Display, 顯見 `hin-in`, 彰明 cheung-ming.	Dissent, 懷異意 waai-i-i`, 唔信從 'm-suun`-ts'uung.
Displeased, 不歡喜 'm-foon-`hi.	
Disposal, 管理 `koon-li.	

注释

【见淡】厌恶。
【利水药】利尿剂。
【寐水】潜水。
【筊杯】又称"筊贝""杯筊",是中国远古民间信仰中的一种寻求神灵指示的工具。原用蚌壳投掷于地,视其俯仰情形,断其吉凶。后改用竹子或木片做成蚌壳状替代。

Dissimilar, 不似 'm-ts'ze.
Dissipate, 散 saan'.
Dissipated, ⸺
Dissolute, 放肆 fong'-sze', 放蕩 fong'-tong, 花消 fa-siu.
Dissolve, 化開 fa'-hoi, 消散 siu-saan'.
Dissuade, 勸戒 huen'-kaai'.
Distant, 遠 'uen, 隔遠 kaak-'uen.
Distaste, 見淡 kin'-t'aam.
Distend, 張開 cheung-hoi, 撐開 chaang-hoi.
Distil, 烝 ching, 甑 tsang'.
Distinct, 分明 fun-ming, 明白 ming-paak.
Distinguish, 分別 fun-pit.
Distinguished, 出衆 ch'uut-chuung', 超羣 ch'iu-k'wun.
Distorted, 歪 waai, 'me.
Distract the mind, 分心 fun-sum, (crazed) 喪心 song-sum.
Distress, 艱難 kaan-naan, 急逼 kup-pik, (want) 坳嶭 aau-ai.

Distribute, 分派 fun-p'aai'.
District, 縣 uen'.
Distrust, 思疑 sze-i.
Disturb, 攪動 'kaau-tuung', 攪亂 'kaau-luen'.
Disturbance, (make) 生事 shang-sze'.
Ditch, 溝渠 kau-k'ue, 坑 haang.
Diuretic, 利水藥 li'-'shui-yeuk.
Dive, 寐水 mi'-'shui.
Diverge, 分支 fun-chi, 叉口 ch'a-'hau.
Divers, 幾個 'ki-koh', 不止一個 'm-'chi-yat-koh', 不一 pat-yat.
Diverse, 幾樣 'ki-*yeung', 不同 'm-t'uung.
Divert, 引開 'yan-hoi, (the mind) 開心 hoi-sum.
Divide, 分開 fun-hoi.
Divination, 占卜 chim-puuk.
Divine, (of God) 上帝(的)嘅 Sheung'-tai'-ke'.
Divining blocks, 筊杯 kaau'-pui.

Division, (a) 一段 yat-tuen`, 一分 yat-fun`, 一股 yat-`koo.
Divorce, 休棄 yau-hi`, 出 ch'uut, 分妻 fun-ts'ai.
Divulge, 話人知 wa`-yan-chi.
Dizzy, 暈 wun`, 頭暈 t'au-wun, t'au-wun, t'au-wun.
Do, 做 tso`, 行 hang, 爲 wai, (don't) 不好 'm-`ho, 咪 `mai.
Dock, (for ships) 船澳 shuen-o`, 做船涌 tso`-shuen-ch'uung.
Doctor, 醫生 i-`shaang.
Doctrine, 教 kaau`, 道理 to`-`li.
Documents, 書契 shue-k'ai`, 文書 mun-shue.
Dodder, 無葉籐 mo-ip-t'ang.
Dodge, 用計 yuung`-*kai`.
Doe, 麀 yau, 麋 mi.
Dog, 狗 `kau, 犬 `huen.
Dog fish, 跌倒沙 tit`-to-sha.
Dog-rose, 棠罌花 t'ong-aang-fa.

Dogged, 古板 `koo-`paan, 硬頸 ngaang`-`keng.
Dogmatic, 執意 chup-i`, 固執 koo`-chup.
Doleful, 晶屭 pai`-ai`.
Dolichos, 葛 koht.
Doll, 公仔 kuung-`tsai.
Dollar, 銀錢 ngan-*ts'in, 大元 taai`-uen.
Dolt, 鷚仔 ngau`-`tsai.
Domestic, 家 ka, (servants) 家人 ka-yan.
Dominate, 揸權柄 cha-k'uen-ping`.
Dominoes, 骨牌 kwut-*p'aai.
Done, 做完 tso`-uen, 完 uen.
Donkey, 驢 *lue.
Dooms-day, 歸結日子 kwai-kit`-yat-`tsze, 審判日 `shum-p'oon`-yat.
Door, 門 moon, (-way) 門口 moon-`hau.
Dose, (a) 劑 tsai.
Dot, 點 `tim.
Dotage, 老懵懂 `lo-`muung-`tuung.

注 释

【船澳】船坞。
【硬颈】固执。
【晶屭】忧郁。
【鷚仔】笨蛋，傻瓜。
【揸权柄】统治，掌握权力。
【老懵懂】老糊涂。

注 释

【三口两脷】两面三刀，一口两舌。指当面一套背后一套，玩弄欺骗手法。
【恰瞓眼】打瞌睡。
【螳蝐】蜻蜓。
【一淡】一口（饮料）。

Dote on, 溺愛 nik-oiʾ.
Dotted, 一點點 yatʾ-ʿtim-ʿtim.
Double, 兩倍 ʿleung-ʿpʻooi, (ADJ.) 雙 sheung, 孖 ma, (meaning) 雙關話 sheung-ʿkwaan-ʿwa, (to) 加一倍 ka-yatʾ-ʿpʻooi, (to fold) 摺 chipʾ.
Double flower, 雙托花 sheung *tʻok-ʿfa.
Double-tongued, 三口兩脷 saam-ʿhau-ʿleung-li ʾ.
Doubt, 思疑 sze-i, 疑惑 i-waak.
Doubtful, 不定 ʾm-tingʾ.
Doubtless, 無錯 ʿmo-tsʻohʾ.
Dough, 發麵 faatʿ-minʾ.
Dove, 鴿 kopʾ, 班鳩 ʿpaan-ʿkau.
Dove-tailed, 交指榫 kaau-ʿchi-ʿsuun, 鬥筍 tauʾ-suunʾ.
Down, (feathers) 氈毛 yuung-mo, (on the skin) 寒毛 hohn-mo, 幼毛 yauʾ-mo.
Down, (-ward) 下 haʾ, 落 lok.

Down stairs, 樓梯下 lau-tʻai-haʾ, (go) 落樓 lok-*lau.
Dowry, 妝奩 chong-lim.
Doze, (to) 恰瞓眼 hapʾ-ʿngaan-funʾ.
Drab, (a colour) 栗色 luut-shik.
Drag, 拉 laai, 搲 mangʾ, ʿmang, 拖 tʻoh.
Dragon, 龍 luung, (a) 條龍 tʻiu-luung.
Dragon-fly, 螳蝐 tʻong-ʿmi.
Drain, (to, land) 開寳 hoi-tauʾ, (a) 暗渠 omʾ-kʻuc, 陰溝 yum-kau.
Drake, 鴨公 aapʾ-ʿkuung.
Draught, (a drink) 一淡 yat-taamʾ.
Draught, a rough, 草稿 ʿtsʻo-ʿko, (wind) 通風處 tʻuung-fuung-shueʾ.
Draw, 拉 laai, 搲 mangʾ, (towards) 攀 maan, (pictures) 寫 ʿse, (water) 汲 kʻap, 打 ʿta, 拂 fut, (a sword) 拔 pat, 取出 ʿtsue-chʻuut, (to influence) 引 ʿyan.

Drawer, 櫃桶 kwai⁾-ʿt'uung.	Drink, 飲 ʿyum.
Drawing-room, 客廳 haak⁾-ʿt'eng.	Drip, 滴滴落來 tik-tik-lok-lai.
Drawl, 拉長聲講 laai-ch'eung-sheng-ʿkong.	Drive, (away) 逐去 chuuk-hue⁾, 趕逐 ʿkohn-chuuk, (push) 推 t'ui, (a horse) 駛 ʿshai.
Dread, 畏懼 wai⁾-kue⁾, 慌怕 fong-p'a⁾.	
Dreadful, 利害 li⁾-hoi⁾.	Drizzle, 落雨微 lok-ʿue-ʿmi.
Dream, 夢 muung⁾, (to) 發夢 faat⁾-muung⁾.	Droll, 好趣 ʿho-ts'ue⁾, (a laughing stock) 笑柄 siu⁾ peng⁾.
Dreary, 蔽翳 pai⁾-ai⁾.	Drollery, 趣話 ts'ue⁾-wa.
Dredge, (to) 撈 laau.	Dromedary, 獨峰駝 tuuk-fuung-t'oh.
Dregs, 渣滓 cha-ʿtsze, 脚 keuk⁾.	Droop, 垂 shui, (decay) 衰 shui.
Drench, 濕透 shup-t'au⁾, 濕嗮 shup-saai⁾.	Drop, (a) 滴 tik, (to stop) 放落 fong⁾-lok, (fall) 跌落 tit⁾-lok.
Dress, 裝扮 chong-paan⁾, (to) 着衣服 cheuk-i-fuuk.	
Dressing-case, 鏡奩 keng⁾-lim, 鏡粧 keng⁾-ʿchong.	Dropsy, 水腫 ʿshui-ʿchuung, 蠱脹 ʿkoo-cheung⁾.
Dried up, 涸乾 k'ok⁾-kohn, 乾嗮 kohn-saai⁾.	Dross, 屎 ʿshi, 渣滓 cha-ʿtsze, (of silver) 密佗僧 mat-t'oh-sang.
Drift, to, 漂流 p'iu-lau.	Drought, 天旱 t'in-ʿhohn.
Drifting, 蒲蒲泛 p'o-p'o-faan⁾ (p'aan⁾).	Drown, 沉死 ch'um-sze⁾ 溺死 nik-ʿsze, 浸死 tsum⁾-ʿsze.
Drill, (to) 鑽 tsuen⁾, (a) 鑽子 tsuen⁾-ʿtsze, (practice) 習鍊 tsaap-lin⁾, 操 ts'o.	

注 释

【柜桶】抽屉。
【拉长声讲】慢吞吞地说。
【蔽翳】沉闷,枯燥,愁闷。
【蒲蒲泛】漂流,漂浮物。
【落雨微】毛毛细雨。

注 释

【眼瞓】困，瞌睡的。
【贱艺】苦工。
【烂酒人】醉鬼。
【蒲荞】浮萍。
【钝胎】傻瓜。

Drowsy, 眼瞓 ˈngaan-ˌfun, 瞓瘟 fun’-wun, hapˈngaan.
Drub, 棒打 ˈp‘aang-ˌta.
Drudgery, 贱艺 tsin’-ngai’.
Drugs, 药材 yeuk-ts‘oi.
Drum, 鼓 ˈkoo, (a) 一面鼓 yat-min’-ˈkoo.
Drum-stick, 鼓槌 ˈkoo-*ch‘ui.
Drunk, 醉酒 tsui’-ˈtsau.
Drunkard, 烂酒人 laan’-ˈtsau-yan.
Dry, 乾 kohn, 旱 ˈhohn, 爽 ˈshong, (to) 整乾 ˈching-kohn, (in the sun) 晒乾 shaai’-kohn, (at the fire) 焙 pooi’, (in the air) 晾乾 long’-kohn.
Duality, (the two modes of nature) 两仪 ˈleung-i, 阴阳 yum-yeung.
Duck, 鸭 aap’, (wild) 水鸭 ˈshui-*aap’, (Muscovy) 番鸭 faan-aap’.
Duck-weed, 蒲荞 p‘o*-k‘iu.
Due, 该当 koi-tong, 当还 tong-waan, (owing) 欠 him’.

Dug, (a) 奶头 ˈnaai-t‘au.
Duke, 公爷 kuung-ye.
Dull, 鸗 ngau’, 钝 tuun’, 鸗豆 ngau’-tau’, (gloomy) 阴阴沉沉 yum-yum-ch‘um-ch‘um, 阴翳 yum-ai’, (tint) 瘀 ˈue.
Duly, 依期 i-k‘i.
Dumb, 痖口 ˈa-ˈhau.
Dumfound, 吓亲 haak’-ts‘an, 吓到呆 haak’-to’-ngoi.
Dummy, 痖口 ˈa-ˈhau, 痖仔 ˈa-ˈtsai.
Dumpling, 水饺子 ˈshui-ˈkaau-tsze, 馄饨 wun’-t‘un.
Dun, (to) 催逼 ts‘ooi-pik, 逼攞 pik-ˈloh.
Dunce, 钝胎 tuun’-t‘oi.
Dung, 粪 fun’, 屎 shi, (to) 落粪 lok-fun’.
Dungeon, 地牢 ti’-lo.
Dung-hill, 粪堆 fun’-tui.
Duped, 上当 sheung-tong’, 中计 chuung’-kai’.
Duplicity, 二心 i’-sum, 三口两脷 saam-ˈhau-ˈleung-li.

| DYN | 78 | EAR |

Durable, 衿使 k'um-ʿshai, 哈得耐 k'um-tak-noiʾ.
During,——之耐——chi-noiʾ,——咁耐——komʾ-noiʾ.
Dusk, 黃昏 wong-fun, 挨晚 aai-*ʿmaan.
Dust, 塵 ch'an, 塵埃 ch'an-oi, (to) 拂塵 fut-ch'an, faakʾ-ch'an, 揚 ʿyeung.
Duster, 拂塵布 faakʾ-ch'an-poʾ, (feather-) 毛掃 mo-ʿso.
Dutiful, 純良 shuun-leung, 順從 shuunʾ-ts'uung.
Duty, 本分 ʿpoon-funʾ, (custom) 餉銀 ʿheung-*ngan.
Dwarf, 矮人 ʿai-yan, (to) 屈古樹 wutʾ-ʿkoo-shueʾ.
Dwell, 居 kue, 居住 kue-chueʾ.
Dwelling house, 住家屋 chueʾ-ka-uuk.
Dwindle, 漸漸縮 tsimʾ-tsimʾ-shuuk.
Dye, 染色 ʿim-shik.
Dynamite, 炸藥 chaʾ-yeuk.

Dynasty, 朝 ch'iu, 國朝 kwokʾ-ch'iu.
Dysentery, 紅痢 huung-liʾ, 紅白痢 huung-paakʾ-liʾ.
Dyspepsia, 停食 t'ing-shik, 不消化 pat-siu-faʾ.
Dysury, 小便不通 ʿsiu-pinʾ-pat-t'uung.

E

Each, 每 ʿmooi, 各 kokʾ, (each other) 相—— seung——.
Eager, 懇切 ʿhan-tsʾit, 嫩 nat.
Eagle, 神鷹 shan-ying.
Ear, 耳躲 ʿi-tö, 耳仔 ʿi-ʿtsai.
Ear of corn, 穗 suiʾ, 一苕穀 yat-k'uung-kuuk.
Ear-ring, 耳環 ʿi-*waan.
Ear-wax, 耳屎 ʿi-ʿshi, 耳油 ʿi-yau.
Ear-wig, 蚰蜒 yau-in.
Earl, 伯 paakʾ.
Early, 早 ʿtso.

注 释

【衿得耐】耐用。
【咁耐】那么久。
【纯良】忠实的,顺从的。
【停食】消化不良。

注 释

【髟口】屋檐，檐口。
【滚起】沸腾。
【不同人】怪人。
【注神】入迷。
【转头风】小旋风。

Earn, 賺 chaan', *chaan'.
Earnest, 懇誠 ʿhan-shing, 熱中 ie-chuung'.
Earth, 地 ti', (matter) 坭土 nai-ʿtʻo.
Earthen-ware, 瓦器 ʿnga-hi', 缸瓦 kong-ʿnga, (fine) 磁器 tsʻze-hi'.
Earthquake, 地震 ti'-chan'.
Earth-worm, 地龍 ti'-luung, 黃犬 wong'-ʿhuen.
Ease, 安 ohn, 安樂 ohn-lok (with) 流利 lau-li' (lai'), (to) 放鬆 fong'-suung, (nature) 出恭 chʻuut-ʿkuung, 大便 taai'-pin'.
East, 東 tuung, 東邊 tuung-pin, 東方 tuung-fong.
Easy, 容易 yuung-i', (comfortable) 自在 tsze'-tsoi'.
Eat, 食 shik, 吃 yaak.
Eaves, 髟口 yum-ʿhau, 髟頭 yum-*tʻau, 簷口 im-ʿhau.
Eaves-dropping, 門外打聽 moon-ngoi'-ʿta-tʻeng'.
Ebb, 水乾 ʿshui-kohn.

Ebony, 烏梅木 oo-mooi-muuk, (Chinese) 酸枝 suen-ʿchi.
Ebullition, 滚起 ʿkwun-ʿhi.
Eccentric, 出規矩外 chʻuut-kʻwai-ʿkue-ngoi', 不同人 pat-tʻuung-yan, 'm-tʻuung-yan-ti'.
Echo, 回响 ooi-ʿheung, 應聲 ying'-sheng, 撞聲 chong'-sheng.
Eclipse, 蝕 shik.
Ecliptic, 黃道 wong-to'.
Economical, 儉 kim', 儉用 kim'-yuung', 慳廉 haan-lim.
Economize, 儉用 kim'-yuung', 惜 sik.
Ecstasy, 注神 chue'-shan, 神游極 shan-yau-kik.
Eddy, 回旋 ooi-suen, (water) 倒槽水 ʿto-tsʻo-ʿshui, (wind) 轉頭風 ʿchuen-tʻau-fuung.
Edge, (of a knife) 口 ʿhau, 鋒 fuung, (side) 邊 pin, (near the) 呢 mun'.

Edict, 札諭 chaat'-ue', 上諭 sheung-ue'.	Egregiously, 太甚 t'aai'-shum'.
Edify, 輔德 foo'-tak, 建德 kin'-tak, 養心 ʻyeung-sum.	Egret, 白鷺 paak-lo'.
	Eight, 八 paat'.
	Eighth, 第八 tai'-paat'.
Edit, 校訂 kaau'-ting'.	Either, 或 waak.
Educate, 教養 kaau'-ʻyeung.	Eject, 趕出 ʻkohn-chʻuut, 出 chʻuut.
Educated, 讀書 tuuk-shue, 學文 hok-mun.	Elaborate, 費心機 fai'-sum-ki.
Eel, 鱔魚 ʻshin-ue, (congor) 海鰻 ʻhoi-maan'.	Elapsed, 過了 kwoh'-ʻliu, kwoh'-hiu.
Effect, 效驗 haau'-im', 所致 ʻshoh-chi', 所成 ʻshoh-shing, 所便然 ʻshoh-ʻshai-in, 果 ʻkwoh.	Elastic, 韌 ngan', 有靭力 ʻyau-ngau'-lik.
	Elated, 志氣昂昂 chi'-hi'-ngong-ngong.
Effeminate, 女人形 ʻnue-*yan-ying.	Elbow, 手睜 ʻshau-chaang.
Effervesce, 發滾 faat'-ʻkwun.	Elbow-chair, 圈手椅 huen-ʻshau-ʻi.
Efficacious, 功效 kuung-haau', 靈 leng.	Elder than, 大於 taai'-ue, 老過 ʻlo-kwoh'.
Effluvia, 穢氣 wai'-hi'.	Elders, 長老 ʻcheung-ʻlo.
Effort, (make an) 奮力 ʻfun-lik, 出力 chʻuut-lik.	Eldest son, 長子 ʻcheung-ʻtsze, 大仔 taai'-ʻtsai.
Egg, 蛋 *taan', 卵 ʻluun, 蟲 chʻuun.	Elect, 揀 ʻkaan, 選 ʻsuen.
Egg-plant, 苦瓜 ʻfoo ʻkwa, 矮瓜 ʻai-ʻkwa.	Electric eel, 火鱔 ʻfoh-ʻshin.
Egg-shell, 蛋殼 *taan'-hok'.	Electric telegraph, 電報 tin'-po'.

注释

【輔德】教诲，陶冶，开导，启发。

【女人形】像女人一样的，柔弱的。

Egg-plant:茄子。译为"苦瓜"属误译。

【手睜】手肘。

注释

【大砂蹄】象皮病，一种因血丝虫感染引起的疾病。
【合用】合适的，符合条件的。
【省文】省略语。
【好口角】口才好。
【落船】上船。

ELK　　81　　EMB

Electricity, 電氣 tin’-hi’.
Electro-plate, 電鍍(金) tin’-to’-(kum).
Elegant, 靚 leng’, 幽幽雅雅 yau-yau-ʻnga-ʻnga, 文雅 mun-ʻnga.
Elements, 元質 uen-chat, (the five) 五行 ʻng-hang, (of learning) 初學 ch‘oh-hok, 學之始基 hok-chi-ch‘i-ki.
Elephant, 象 tseung’.
Elephantiasis, 大砂蹄 taai’-sha-t‘ai, 赤瘋 ch‘ik’-fuung.
Elevate, 舉 ʻkue.
Elevated, 高昂 ko-ngong.
Eleven, 十一 shap-yat.
Eleventh, 第十一 tai’-shap-yat.
Elf, 妖怪 iu-kwaai’, 馬騮精 ʻma-ʻlau-tsing.
Eligible, 合用 hop-yuung’.
Ellipse, 長圓形 ch‘eung-uen-ying, 橢圓 ʻt‘oh-uen.
Elliptical language, 省文 ʻshaang-mun.
Elk, 麋鹿 mi-luuk.

Elm, 榆 ue.
Elope, 私跳 sze-t‘o, 走路 ʻtsau-lo’.
Eloquence, 口才 ʻhau-ts‘oi.
Eloquent, 好口角 ʻho-ʻhau-kok’.
Else, (besides) 另外 ling’-ngoi’, (if not) 若不是 yeuk-pat-shi’, 若唔係 yeuk-ʻm-hai’, (then) 就係 tsau’-hai’.
Elsewhere, 第二處 tai’-i’-shue’, tai’-shue’.
Elude, 逃脫 t‘o-t‘uet’, 逃甪 t‘o-lut.
Elysium, 極樂世界 kik-lok-shai’-kaai’.
Emaciated, 瘦損 shau’-ʻsuen.
Emancipate, 放 fong’, 釋放 shik-fong’.
Embankment, 基 ki, 基堡 ki-pok’.
Embargo, 禁止行船 kum’-ʻchi-hang-shuen.
Embark, 落船 lok-shuen.
Embarrass, 揯阻 k‘ang’-ʻchoh, 拮据 kat-kue’-(ʻk‘ö), 累 lui’.

Embarrassment, 煩難 faan-naan.
Embassador, 欽差 yum-ch'aai.
Embellish, 修飾 sau-shik.
Embers, 火剩 ʻfoh-shing’.
Embezzle, 私取 sze-ts'ue.
Emblem, 喻表 ue’-ʻpiu.
Embossed, 浮凸 fau-tut.
Embowel, 劏肚 t'ong-ʻt'o.
Embrace, 懷抱 waai-ʻp'o.
Embrasure, 埤堄 ʻp'ai-ngai, 城人 sheng-*yan.
Embroider, 繡花 sau’-fa.
Embroil, 鬧亂 naau’-luen’.
Embryo, 胚 ʻp'ooi.
Emendation, 改正處 ʻkoi-ching’-ch'ue’.
Emerald, 呂宋綠 Lui’-suung’-luuk, 鸚鵡綠 ying-ʻmoo-luuk, (an) 綠玉 luuk-yuuk.
Emerge, 出來 ch'uut-lai, 出現 ch'uut-in’.
Emergency, 急切時候 kup-ts'it’-shi-hau’.
Emetic, 發嘔藥 faat’-ʻau-yeuk.

Emeu, 食火鷄 shik-ʻfoh-ʻkai.
Emigrate, 出外方住 ch'uut-ngoi’-fong-chue’.
Eminent, 高 ko, 尊 tsuen.
Emolument, 俸祿 ʻfuung-luuk.
Emotion, 情 ts'ing, 情動 ts'ing-tuung’.
Emperor, 皇帝 wong-tai’.
Emphatic, 懇聲 ʻhan-sheng.
Empire, (the world) 天下 t'in-ha’.
Empiric practice, 斷估工夫 tuen’-ʻkoo-kuung-foo, 估吓試吓 ʻkoo-ʻha-shi-ʻha.
Employ, 任用 yum’-yuung’, 使 ʻshai.
Employer, 事頭 sze’-*t'au.
Employment, 事業 sze’-ip.
Empower, 俾權 ʻpi-k'uen.
Empress, 皇后 wong-hau’.
Empty, 空虛 huung-hue, 空 huung, 吉 kat (a euphemism for huung), (to) 整空 ʻching-huung.
Emulate, 賽勝 ts'oi’-shing’, 賽贏 ts'oi’-yeng, 鬥效 tau’-haau’.

注 釋

【火剩】余火。
【劏肚】剖開。
【斷估工夫】经验主义。
【事头】老板。事头婆，即老板娘。
【俾权】授权。

注释

【机器】引擎，发动机。

Enable, 令——能 ling²——nang.
Enact, 設 ch'it², 作 tsok².
Enamel, 磁器油 ts'ze-hi²-yau, (COL.) 哴油 ʿlong-*yau.
Encamp, 劄營 chaap²-ying.
Enchantment, 迷魂陣 mai-wan-chan².
Encircle, } 圍埋 wai-maai,
Enclose, } 圍住 wai-chue².
Encoffin, 收殮 shau-ʿlim.
Encompass, 圍住 wai-chue².
Encore, 再演 tsoi²-ʿin.
Encounter, 遇 ue².
Encourage, 勉勵 ʿmin-lai², 勸勉 huen²-ʿmin, 鼓舞 ʿkoo-ʿmoo.
Encroach, 侵佔 ts'um-chim².
Encumber, 累贅 lui²-chui².
Encyclopedia, 類書 lui²-shue.
End, 收尾 shau-ʿmi (ʿmi), 終 chuung, (either) 頭 t'au.
Endanger, 累——險 lui²——ʿhim.
Endeavour, 出力 ch'uut-lik, 試 shi².

Endless, 無窮 mo-k'uung, 無盡 mo-tsuun².
Endowments, 品質 ʿpun-chat, 才 ts'oi, (property) 營業 sheung-ip.
Endure, (last) 存 ts'uen, 袊 k'um, (bear) 忍耐 ʿyan-noi², 耐得 noi²-tak.
Enemy, 仇敵 ch'au-tik, 對敵 tui²-tik.
Energy, 力 lik, 勢力 shai²-lik.
Enervated, } 衰弱 shui-yeuk.
Enfeebled, }
Enforce, 勒令 lak-ling², 使 ʿshai, 必使 pit-ʿshai.
Engage, 任用 yum²-yuung², (to marry) 定親 ting²-ts'an.
Engaged, (occupied) 有事 ʿyau-sze², 不得閒 'm-tak-haan.
Engagement, (agreement) 約 yeuk², 約信 yeuk²-suun², (business) 事幹 sze²-kohn².
Engine, 機器 ki-hi².
Engineer, chief, 大計 taai²-*kai², second, 二計 i-*kai².

England, 英吉利國 Ying-kat-li⁾-kwok⁾, 英倫 Ying-lun.	Ensign, 旗 k'i.
English, 英 Ying.	Ensure, 保領 ῾po-῾ling.
Engraft, 劗樹 ts'im-shue⁾, 接枝 tsip⁾-chi.	Entangle, 揹住 k'ang⁾-chue⁾, k'waang⁾-chue⁾, 絞亂 ῾kaau-luen⁾.
Engrave, 雕刻 tiu-hak.	Enter, 入 yup, 進入 tsuun⁾-yup, (on life) 出身 ch'uut-shan.
Engross, 攬埋 ῾laam-maai.	
Enigma, 啞謎 ῾a-*mooi, 背語 pooi⁾-῾uc.	Enterprising, 好逞奇 ῾ho-῾ch'ing-k'i, 肯作肯爲 ῾haang-tsok⁾-῾haang-wai.
Enjoin, 叮篤 teng-tuuk.	
Enjoy, 享 ῾heung.	Entertain, 招接 chiu-tsip⁾, 看待 hohn-toi⁾.
Enlarge, 發大 faat-taai⁾, 整大 ῾ching-taai⁾.	Enthusiasm, 苦志 ῾foo-chi, 烈熱之氣 lit-it-chi-hi⁾.
Enlighten, 照光 chiu⁾-kwong.	
Enlist, 招 chiu.	Entice, 引誘 ῾yan-῾yau, (or urge to) 摟 lau.
Enmity, 仇怨 ch'au-uen⁾.	
Ennui, 懈倦 haai⁾-kuen⁾.	Entire, 十全 shap-ts'uen.
Enormous, (great) 甚大 shum⁾-taai⁾.	Entirely, 齊嘥 ts'ai-saai⁾, 一槩 yat-k'oi⁾, 盡地 tsuun-*ti⁾.
Enough, 够 kau⁾, 足 tsuuk.	Entitled to 應得 ying-tak.
Enquire, 訪問 ῾fong-mun⁾.	Entrails, 臟腑 tsong⁾-῾foo, (ox's) 牛雜 ngau-tsaap.
Enrage, 激怒 kik-no⁾, 激嬲 kik-nau.	Entranced, 入幻境 yup-waan⁾-῾king.
Enraptured, 了不得歡喜 ῾liu-pat-tak-foon-῾hi.	Entrapped, 入圈套 yup-huen-t'o⁾.
Enrich, 令—富 ling—foo⁾.	

注 释

【叮笃】叮嘱。
【了不得欢喜】狂喜。
【揹住】纠缠。
【好逞奇】具有冒险精神的。
【齐嘥】全部。

注释

【时症】流行病。
【发羊吊】癫痫。
【值咁多钱嘅】值那么多钱的。

Entreat, 懇求 ʻhan-kʻau.	Equinox, 日夜平分 yat-yeʼ-pʻing-fun, (vernal) 春分 chʻun-fun, (autumnal) 秋分 tsʻau-fun.
Entry, 入路 yup-loʼ.	
Enunciate, 講出 ʻkong-chʻut.	
Envelop, 包住 paau-chue.	
Envelope, (of a letter) 信函 suunʼ-haam, 信套 suunʼ-*toʼ, 信封 suunʼ-fung.	Equipped, (dressed out) 全身披掛 tsʻuen-shan-pʻi-kuaʼ.
	Equitable, 公平 kung-pʻing.
Envy, 嫉妒 tsat-toʼ, 妒忌 toʼ-kiʼ, 眼紅 ʻngaan-hung.	Equivalent, 值咁多錢嘅 chik-kom²-toh-*tsʻin-ke².
	Equivocate, 講雙關話 ʻkong-sheung-kwaan-*wa².
Epicure, 膏梁子弟 ko-leung-ʻtsze-taiʼ.	Erase, 刮去 kwaatʼ-hueʼ, 搽去 *chʻa-hueʼ.
Epidemic, 時症 shi-chingʼ.	
Epidendrum, 吊蘭 tiuʼ-*laan.	Erect, 立直 laap-chik, 豎起 shueʼ-ʻhi, (to build) 起 ʻhi, (upright) 企 ʻki.
Epilepsy, 發羊吊 faatʼ-yeung-tiuʼ.	
Epistle, 信札 suunʼ-chaatʼ.	Err, 差失 chʻa-shat, 失誤 shatʼ-ʼngʼ, 致誤 chiʼ-ʼngʼ.
Epitaph, 墓誌 mooʼ-chiʼ.	
Epithet, 別號 pit-hoʼ.	Error, 錯 tsʻohʼ.
Epitome, 大畧 taaiʼ-*leuk.	Eruption, (on the skin) 出疹 chʻutʼ-ʻchʻan, 瘢疹 paanʻ-ʻchʻan.
Equal, 等 ʻtang, 相等 seung-ʻtang, 均平 kwun-pʻing.	
	Erysipelas, 癉疽 ʻtaan-tsue.
Equally, 均 kwun, 平 pʻing.	Escape, 走得甩 ʻtsau-tak-lut, 脫離 tʻuetʼ-li, (a way of) 去路 hueʼ-loʼ.
Equanimity, 心定 sum-tingʼ.	
Equator, 赤道 chʻikʼ-toʼ.	Escort, 護送 ooʼ-suungʼ.

Especially, 特要 tak-iu̵’, 更係 ‵kang-hai’, 至緊要 chi’-‵kan-iu̵.	Europe, 歐羅巴 Au-loh-pa.
Essay, (an) 文章 mun-cheung.	Evacuate, 搬空 poon-‵huung, (bowels) 解手 ‵kaai-‵shau. 出恭 ch‛ut-‵kuung.
Essence, 精華 tsing-wa, 精髓 tsing-‵sui.	Evade, 推甩 t‛ui-lut.
Essential, 必須 pit-sue.	Evaporate, 升散 shing-saan’.
Establish, 建立 kin’-laap, 立定 laap-ting’.	Evasive, 旁敲側擊 p‛ong-haau-chak-kik, 閃縮 ‵shim-shuuk.
Estate, 基業 ki-ip.	Even, 平 p‛ing, (number) 雙數 ‵sheung-sho’, (also) 亦 yik, 都 too.
Esteem, (consider) 以爲 ‵i-wai, (respect) 尊重 tsuen-chuung’.	Evening, 晚 ‵maan, (towards) 挨晚 aai-*maan, (dark) 晚黑 ‵maan-hak.
Estimate, 筭度 suen’-tok, 量度 leung-tok.	Evening-star, 長庚星 ch‛eung-kang-‵sing.
Et cetera, 又有添 yau’-‵yau-t‛im.	Event, 事情 sze’-ts‛ing, (important) 大事 taai’-sze’.
Eternal, 永遠 ‵wing-‵uen.	Eventually, 收尾 shau-‵mi.
Etiquette, 小禮 ‵siu-‵lai, 小節 ‵siu-tsit, 儀注 i-chue’.	Ever, 不歇 pat-hit, (eternally) 永遠 ‵wing-‵uen, (any time) 幾時 ‵ki-shi.
Eunuchs of the palace, 太監 t‛aai’-kaam’.	Ever-green, 週年青 chau-nin-ts‛ing.
Euphemism, 吉祥話 kat-ts‛eung-*wa, 雅緻話 ‵nga-chi-*wa.	Everlasting, 永 ‵wing, 永世 ‵wing-shai’.

注 释

【算度】估计。
【又有添】等等（表示列举未尽）。
【雅致话】委婉语。
【长庚星】金星。
【周年青】常绿（植物）。

注释

【样样野】每个东西。
【乜野都系】每个都是。
【啱啱】刚好。
【讲得太过】夸张。
【抄爆】惹怒。

Every, 個個 ‚koh'-koh', (N.B.—*Every* is expressed by repeating the noun), 每 ‚mooi.
Everything, 樣樣野 yeung'-yeung' ye, (-is) 乜野都係 mat'-ye-too-hai.
Everywhere, 到處 to'-ch'ue', 周圍 ‚chau-wai.
Evidence, 證據 ching'-kue', 憑 ‚p'ang, (verbal) 口供 ‚hau-kuung.
Evident, 明白 ‚ming-paak.
Evil, 惡 ok'.
Ewe, 羊母 ‚yeung-‚moo.
Ewer, 水瓶 ‚shui-p'eng.
Exact, 合 hop, 正 ching', (COL.) 啱啱 ‚ngaam-‚ngaam.
Exact, (to) 抽剝 ‚ch'au-mok, (extort) 勒索 lak-sok', 逼勒 pik-lak.
Exaggerate, 講得太過 ‚kong-tak-t'aai'-kwoh', 極言 kik-in.
Exaggeration, 太過 t'aai'-kwoh'.
Exalt, 舉高 ‚kue-ko.

Examination, (literary) 考試 ‚haau-shi'.
Examine, 考究 ‚haau-kau, (judicially) 審問 ‚shum-mun', 盤問 p'oon-mun'.
Example, 樣子 yeung'-‚tsze, (effect of) 風化 ‚fuung-fa'.
Exasperate, 抄爆 ch'aau-paau'.
Exceed, 勝過 shing'-kwoh'.
Exceedingly, 太過 t'aai'-kwoh', 太甚 t'aai'-shum'.
Excel, 贏 ‚yeng, 勝過 shing'-kwoh'.
Excellency, (a title) 大人 taai'-yan, 憲臺 Hin'-t'oi.
Excellent, 極好 kik-‚ho.
Except, (to) 除去 ch'ue-hue', 不計 pat-kai', (unless) 苟不 ‚kau-pat, 倘若不 ‚t'ong-yeuk-'m.
Excess, 過當 kwoh'-tong, 過度 kwoh'-to'.
Excessively, 過頭 *kwoh'-t'au.
Exchange, 兌換 tui'-oon'.

| EXE | 88 | EXP |

Excite, 撩惹 ‛liu-⸌ye, 慫恿 ‛suung-‛yuung, 聳起 ‛suung-‛hi, 驚動 king-tuung⸌.
Exclaim, 呼喊 foo-haam⸌.
Exclude, 除出 ch‛ue-ch‛uut.
Excrement, 屎 ‛shi.
Excrescence, 疣贅 yau-chui⸌, 贅瘤 chui⸌-*lau.
Excruciating, 慘 ‛ts‛aam.
Exculpate, 表白 ‛piu-paak.
Exculpation, 解說 ‛kaai-shuet⸌, 推諉 t‛ui-wai.
Excuse, (to) 見諒 kin⸌-leung⸌, (make an) 托辭 t‛ok⸌-ts‛ze, 倘塞 ‛t‛ong-sak.
Execute, 做成 tso⸌-shing, 辦成 paan⸌-shing.
Execution, 正法 ching⸌-faat⸌, (ground) 法場 faat⸌-ch‛eung.
Executioner, 殺手 shaat⸌-‛shau.
Executive council, 議政局 ‛i-ching⸌-*kuuk.
Executor, 受托之人 shau⸌-t‛ok⸌-chi(ke⸌)-yan 承辦人 shing-paan⸌-yan.

Exempt, 免 ‛min.
Exercise, (motion) 行動 hang-tuung⸌, (practice) 習練 tsaap-lin⸌.
Exert, 奮 ‛fun, 發奮 faat⸌-‛fun, (strength), 奮力 ‛fun-lik.
Exhalation, 所出之氣 ‛shoh-ch‛uut-chi-hi⸌.
Exhaust, 盡 tsuun⸌, 使盡 ‛shai-tsuun⸌.
Exhibit, 發現 faat⸌-in⸌, 顯示 ‛hin-shi⸌.
Exhilarated, 爽神 ‛shong-shan.
Exhort, 勸 huen⸌.
Exigency, 緊急 ‛kan-kup.
Exist, 在 tsoi⸌, 有 ‛yau, 存 ts‛uen.
Exit, (way) 去路 hue⸌-lo⸌, 出處 ch‛uut-ch‛ue⸌.
Exorbitant, 太過 t‛aai⸌-kwoh⸌, 多得嚌 toh-tak-tsai⸌.
Exorcise, 逐鬼 chuuk-‛kwai.
Expand, 張開 cheung-hoi.
Expanse, 浩蕩 ho⸌-tong⸌, 廣闊處 ‛kwong-foot⸌-shue⸌.

注 釋

【撩惹】激起。
【爽神】使……高兴，使……愉快。
【多得嚌】太多了。
【逐鬼】驱邪。

注 释

【使费】花费。
【游观】探索。
【浅露】表情的，表现的；微微露出。
【特登】特地。

Expect, 望 mong², 待 toi², 料 liu², 料必 liu²-pit.
Expedient, (convenient) 便宜 pin²-i, (an) 計 kai².
Expel, 趕出 ʿkohn-chʻuut.
Expend, 使費 ʿshai-fai².
Expense, 使用銀 ʿshai-yuung²-*ngan.
Experienced, 老練 ʿlo-*lin², 慣熟 kwaan²-shuuk, (hand) 老手 ʿlo-ʿshau.
Experiment, 試驗 shiʾ-im², 比併 ʿpi-pʻing².
Expert, (hand) 巧手 ʿhauu-ʿshau, (at) 善精 shin²-tsing.
Expiate, 贖 shuuk.
Expire, 呼 foo, 噴氣 pʻun²-hiʾ, (die) 絕氣 tsuet-hiʾ, 斷氣 ʿtʻuen-hiʾ, 盡 tsuun², (time) 滿 ʿmoon.
Explain, 解 ʿkaai.
Explanation, 解說 ʿkaai-shuet, 解法 ʿkaai-faat.
Expletive, 虛字 hue-tszeʾ.
Explicity, 明明白白 ming-ming-paak-paak.

Explode, 炸 chaʾ, 爆出 paau²-chʻuut.
Explore, 遊觀 yau-koon, 探索 tʻaam²-shaak², 巡查 tsʻuun-chʻa.
Explosion, 嘭 paang, paang.
Export, 裝(貨)出口 chong-(fohʾ) chʻuut-ʿhau.
Expose, 顯露 ʿhin-loʾ, 攻詰 kuung-kʻit.
Expostulate, 諫 kaan², 勸諫 huen²-kaan².
Expound, 講解 ʿkong-ʿkaai.
Express, (to) 講出 ʿkong-chʻuut, (an) 千里馬 tsʻin-ʿli-ʿma.
Expression, 詞語 tsʻze-ʿue, (of face) 氣色 hiʾ-shik.
Expressive, (open as the face) 淺露 ʿtsʻin-loʾ.
Expressly, 特登 tak-ʿtang.
Expunge, 搽去 *chʻa-hueʾ.
Exquisite, 妙 miuʾ, 妙極 miuʾ-kik.
Extant, 所存 ʿshoh-tsʻuen.
Extempore, to speak, 順口講 shuun²-ʿhau-ʿkong.

Extend, 伸開 shan-hoi, (widen) 伸闊 shan-foot, (lengthen) 伸長 shan-ch'eung.	Eye, 眼 ʻngaan, 眼目 ʻngaan-muuk.
Extensive, 廣闊 ʻkwong-foot.	Eye-ball, 眼珠 ʻngaan-ʻchue, 眼核 ʻngaan-wat.
Extenuate, 減輕 ʻkaam-heng.	Eye-brow, 眼眉 ʻngaan-mi.
Exterior, 外面 ngoiʼ-minʼ.	Eye-lash, 眼翕毛 ʻngaan-yup-*mo.
Exterminate, 剿滅 ʻtsiu-mit.	Eyelid, 眼蓋 ʻngaan-koiʼ.
External, 外 ngoiʼ.	Eye-service, 裝米面工夫 chong-*mai-*minʼ-kuung-foo, 光面工夫 kwong-*minʼ-kuung-foo.
Extinguish, 滅 mit, 熄 sik, (by blowing) 吹滅 ch'ui-mit.	
Extort, 勒索 lak-sokʼ.	
Extract, 脫出 t'uetʼ-ch'uut, 拔出 pat-ch'uut.	**F**
Extraordinary, 格外 kaakʼ-ngoiʼ.	Fable, 寓言 ueʼ-in, 小說 ʻsiu-*shuetʼ.
Extravagant, 奢 ch'e, 無節制 mo-tsitʼ-chaiʼ, (expense) 花費 fa-faiʼ, (price) 太貴 t'aaiʼ-kwaiʼ.	Fabric, (texture) 織做之物 chik-tsoʼ-chi-mat, chik-tsoʼ-keʼ-ʻye.
	Fabricate, 杜撰 toʼ-chaanʼ.
Extreme, 極 kik.	Fabulous, 虛誕 hue-taanʼ.
Extremely, 至極 chiʼ-kik, 甚 ʻshum.	Face, 面 minʼ, (to) 對面 tooiʼ-minʼ, 當面對 tong-minʼ-tooiʼ, (to see) 覿面 tik-minʼ, 見面 kinʼ-minʼ.
Extricate, 脫甪 t'uetʼ-lut.	
Exult, 歡喜到跳 ʻfoon-ʻhi-toʼ-t'iuʼ.	

注释

【转色】褪色。
【残晓】已褪色的，凋谢的。
【信德】信念，信仰。
【诈假意】假装。
【狎习】熟悉的。

FAI　91　FAM

Face to face, 面晤 min²-'ng², 兩面相向 ʻleung-min²-seung-heung.
Facile, 容易 yuung-i².
Facility, 順便 shuun²-*pin².
Fac-simile, 摹成似眞 mo-shing-tsʻze-chan.
Fact, 實事 shat-sze².
Faction, 黨 ʻtong, 黨羽 ʻtong-ʻue.
Factory, 行 *hong.
Faculty, 能幹 nang-kohn².
Fade, 殘毀 tsʻaan-ʻwai, (as colour) 轉色 ʻchuen-shik.
Faded, 殘曉 tsʻaan-hiu.
Fagged, 困倦 kʻwun²-kuen², 够倦 kau²-kuen², kooi².
Faggot, (a) 一把柴 yat-pa-chʻaai.
Fail, 廢 fai², (become bankrupt) 倒行 ʻto-*hong, 倒灶 ʻto-tso².
Faint, (to) 昏迷 fun-mai, 失魂 shat-wun, (feeble) 軟弱 ʻnen-yeuk 力盡 lik-tsuun².

Fair, (clear) 清 tsʻing, 晴 tsʻing, (pretty) 清秀 tsʻing-sau², (just) 公道 ʻkuung-to², (-wind) 順風 shuun²-fuung, (tide) 順水 shuun²-ʻshui.
Fairy, 仙 ʻsin, 神仙 shan-ʻsin, 野仙 ʻye-ʻsin, (female) 仙女 ʻsin²-*nue.
Fairy-land, 蓬萊仙境 pʻuung-loi-sin-ʻking.
Faith, 信德 suun²-tak.
Faithful, 忠心 chuung-sum.
Falcon, 獵鷹 lip-ying, 鸇 ʻchuen.
Fall, 跌 tit², 慣倒 kwaan²-ʻto, (COL.) tap.
False, 假 ʻka.
Falsehood, 大話 taai²-wa², 謊言 ʻfong-in.
Falsify, 詐假意 chaʻ-ʻka-i (ʻka-i) 整假 ʻching-ʻka.
Fame, 名聲 ming-shing, 名 ming.
Familiar, 狎習 haap-tsaap, 喵橋 ʻngaam-*kʻin, (too) 褻狎 sit²-haap.

FAR 92 FAT

Family, 家 ka, 家眷 ka-kuen, 家口 ka-ʿhau, (how is your?) 寶眷平安呀 ʿpo-kuen-pʻing-ohn-a? (well, thank you) 家小都托賴 ka-ʿsiu-too-tʻokʾ-laaiʾ.
Famine, 飢荒 ki-fong.
Famishing, 餓到死噉 ngohʾ-toʾ-ʿsze-ʿkom, 餓得急 ngohʾ-tak-kup.
Fan (a) 把扇 ʿpa-shinʾ, (to) 打扇 ʿta-shinʾ, 撥 pʻootʾ.
Fanatic, 信到狂 sunn-toʾ-kʻwong, 信到癲 sunn-toʾ-tin.
Fancy, 幻想 waanʾ-ʿseung, 夢想 muungʾ-ʿseung, (suit the) 如意 ne-iʾ, (rare) 玩 oonʾ.
Fanners, 風櫃 fuung-kwaiʾ.
Far, 遠 ʿuen.
Farce, (a) 弄戲一出 luungʾ-hiʾ-yat-chʻuut.
Fare, (money) 水腳 ʿshui-keukʾ, 腳錢 keukʾ-*tsʻin.
Farewell, 望你平安 mongʾ-ʿni-pʻing-ohn.

Farm, 田庄 tʻin-chong, (to) 耕田 kang-tʻin.
Farmer, 農夫 nuung-foo.
Fascinating, 有引 ʿyau-ʿyan.
Fashion, (the) 時欵 shi-foon, (a) 樣 *yeung.
Fashionable, 依時欵 i-shi-foon, 時興 shi-hing.
Fast, (to) 禁食 kumʾ-shik, 食齋 shik-chaai.
Fast, (quick) 快 faaiʾ, 趕快 ʿkohn-faaiʾ, (firm) 堅實 kin-shat.
Fasten, 綁緊 ʿpong-ʿkan, 整實 ʿching-shat, (a door) 閂 shaan.
Fastidious, 難悅 naan-uet, 俺尖 im-tsim.
Fat, 肥 fi, (SUB.) 油 yau, 膏油 ko-yau.
Fate, 天命 tʻin-mingʾ, 定數 tingʾ-shoʾ.
Father, 爸 fooʾ, 爸親 fooʾ-tsʻan, (COL.) ʿlo-tau, 老子 ʿlo-ʿtsze.
Father-in-law, 外爸 ngoiʾ-*fooʾ, 岳丈 ngok-*cheungʾ, (wife's) 家翁 ka-yuung.

注 释

【餓到死噉】餓得要死。
【弄戲一出】一出鬧劇。
【水腳】船費，運費。
【有引】迷人的，吸引人的。
【俺尖】挑剔。

注 释

【挪撚】奉承。
【规银】费用。

FEE 93 FEN

Fathom, (10 feet) 丈 cheung⌐, (to) 測度 ch'ak-tok.
Fatigue, 困倦 k'wan⌐-kuen⌐.
Fatten, 養肥 ʿyeung-fi.
Fault, 不是處 pat-shi⌐-ch'ue⌐, 毛病 mo-peng⌐, 弊病 pai⌐-peng⌐, 過失 kwoh⌐-shat.
Favour, 恩 yan, 人情 yan-ts'ing, (to) 帮襯 pong-ch'an⌐.
Favourable, 順 shuun⌐.
Favourite, 寵愛 ʿch'uung-oi⌐.
Fawn, (to) 挪撚 noh-ʿnun, 撥馬尾 p'oot⌐-ma-ʿmi.
Fear, 怕 p'a⌐, 恐怕 ʿhuung-p'a⌐.
Feasible, 可以 ʿhoh-ʿi.
Feast, 筵席 in-tsik, 酒席 ʿtsau-tsik.
Feather, 羽毛 ʿue-mo, 雀毛 tseuk⌐-mo.
February, 英二月 Ying-i⌐-net.
Feces, 屎 ʿshi, (refuse) 渣滓 cha-ʿtsze.
Fee, 規銀 k'wai-*ngan, (secret) 規 k'wai.

Feeble, 軟弱 ʿuen-yeuk.
Feed, 養 ʿyeung, 養口 yeung-ʿhau, (give food to) 喂 wai⌐, 饎 hi⌐, (fatten) 養肥 ʿyeung-fi.
Feel, 覺 kok⌐, 見 kin⌐, (with the hand) 摸 ʿmoh.
Feeling, 情 ts'ing.
Feign, 詐 cha⌐, 佯爲 yeung-wai.
Felicity, 福 fuuk.
Fell, 斬 ʿchaam, 倒—落來 ʿto——lok-lai.
Fellow, 同伴 t'uung-poon⌐, (common) 佬 ʿlo.
Fellowship, 相交 seung-kuau.
Fellow-townsman, 鄉親 heung-ts'an.
Felony, 死罪 ʿsze-tsui⌐, 大罪 taai⌐-tsui⌐.
Felt, 毛氈 mo-ʿchin, 鞋氈 haai-ʿchin.
Female, 母 ʿmo, 嫲 ʿna, (woman) 女 ʿnue, (gender) 陰類 yum-lui⌐.
Fence, 籬笆 li-pa, 圍 *wai.
Fence (to) 舞劍 ʿmoo-kim⌐.
Fencing, 劍術 kim⌐-shuut.

| FET | 94 | FIG |

Fender, 圍 *wai, (ship's) 艃 ‚leng.
Ferment, 發酵 faat‛-kaaüʼ, (spoil) 發 faat‛.
Fern, 黃狗毛 wong-‛kau-‚mo, 井底荽 ‛tseng-‛tai-sai, 簹萁 lóng-ki, (edible) 蕨 k‛uet‛.
Ferocious, 勢兇 shai‛-huung.
Ferocity, 殘殺之性 ts‛aan-shaat‛-chi-sing‛.
Ferret, 白獴獵 paak-muung-kwai‛.
Ferry, 渡頭 to‛-t‛au.
Ferry-boat, 橫水渡 waang-‛shui-*to‛.
Fertile, 沃 yuuk, 肥 fi.
Fervent, 熱 it.
Fester, 生瘡 shang-ch‛ong.
Festival, 節期 tsit‛-k‛i.
Fetch, 擰――來 ning――lai.
Fetid, 臭 ch‛au‛.
Fetters, 桎梏 chat-kuuk, (hand-) 手繚 ‛shau-liu, (feet-) 腳繚 keuk‛-liu.
Fetus, 胚 p‛ooi, 胚胎 p‛ooi-t‛oi.

Fever, 發熱 faat‛-it, (intermittent) 打擺子 ‛ta-‛paai-‛tsze.
Feverish, 殷 heng‛.
Few, 少 ‛shiu, 些少 se-‛shiu.
Fib, 詐僞呆 cha‛-‚ngi-‚ngoi.
Fibres, 紋 mun, 絲 sze.
Fickle, 無定性 mo-ting‛-sing‛, (COL.) fa-fik.
Fiction, 小說 ‛siu-*shuet‛.
Fictitious, 假 ‛ka.
Fiddle, (two stringed) 二絃 i‛-*in, (to) 研二絃 ngaan-i‛-*in.
Fidelity, 忠心 chuung-sum.
Fidgety, 瑣碎 ‛soh-sui‛.
Fie! 啋 ts‛oi! ch‛ö!
Field, 田 t‛in.
Fiend, 惡鬼 ok‛-‛kwai.
Fierce, 猛烈 ‛mang-lit.
Fife, 橫笛 waang-*tek.
Fifth, 第五 tai‛-‛ng.
Fig, 無花菓 mo-fa-‛kwoh.
Fight, 打架 ‛ta-ka‛, (in war) 打仗 ‛ta-cheung‛ (cheung‛), 交戰 kaau-chin‛.
Figurative, 比喻 ‛pi-uc‛.

注 释

【黃狗毛】蕨。
【橫水渡】轮渡。
【拧来】拿来。
【诈伪呆】撒小谎。

注释

【揾着】发现，找到。
【小家种】过分注意的。
【炮像】应为"炮仗"，鞭炮。
【水车】消防车。

FIN 95 FIR

Figure, 形像 ying-tseung', (of speech) 譬喻 pʻi'-ue'.
File, (a tool) 把鉎 ⸢pa-tsʻoh', (to) 鉎卟 tsʻohʻ-⸢ha, (papers) 疊埋 tip-maai.
File fish, 剝皮洋 mokʻ-pʻi yeung.
Filial, 孝順 haauʻ-shuunʻ.
Fill, 放滿 fongʻ-⸢moon, 打滿 ⸢ta-⸢moon.
Fillet of beef, 牛柳 ngau-⸢lau.
Film, 膜 mok, 衣膜 i-mok.
Filter, 隔清 kaakʻ-tsʻing, 濾 lueʻ, (a) 砂漏 sha-*lauʻ.
Filth, 穢物 waiʻ-mat.
Filthy, 污穢 oo-waiʻ, 污糟 oo-tso.
Fin, 翅 chʻi'.
Final, 結尾 kitʻ-⸢mi (⸤mi), 收尾 shau-⸤mi.
Finally, 終然 chuung-in, 究竟 kauʻ-⸢king.
Find, 揾着 ⸢wan-cheuk, (by accident) 遇着 ueʻ-cheuk, (-out) 查出 chʻa-chʻuut.

Fine, 幼細 yauʻ-saiʻ, (elegant) 靚 leng', 妙 miu', 講究 kong-kau.
Fine, (to) 罰銀 faatʻ-*ngan.
Finery, 浮華之物 fau-wa-chi-mat.
Finger, 手指 ⸢shau-⸢chi.
Finger-glass, 手盅 ⸢shau-⸤chuung.
Finger-ring, 戒指 kaaiʻ-⸢chi.
Finical, 小家種 ⸢siu-ka-⸤chuung.
Finish, 做完 tsoʻ-uen.
Finite, 有限 ⸢yau-haanʻ.
Fir, 杉 chʻaam', 松 tsʻuung.
Fire, 火 ⸢foh, (to) 燒 shiu, (a gun) 鈉炮 naatʻ-pʻaauʻ.
Fire-arms, 火炮 ⸢foh-pʻaauʻ, (foreign muskets) 洋鎗 yeung-⸤tsʻeung.
Fire-crackers, 炮像 pʻaauʻ-*tseung'.
Fire-engine, 水車 ⸢shui-chʻe.
Fire-fly, 螢火 ying-⸤foh.
Fire-wood, 柴 chʻaai.
Fire-works, 烟花 in-fa, (to burn) 燒烟火 shiu-in-⸢foh.

Firm,	主固 'chue koo', 堅定 kin-ting', 堅硬 kin-ngaang'.	
Firm, (a)	公司 kuung-sze, 行 *hong.	
Firmament,	穹蒼 k'uung-ts'ong.	
First,	第一 tai'-yat.	
First-born,	頭長 t'au-'cheung.	
First-rate,	頂好 'ting-'ho.	
Fish,	魚 ue, *ue, (a) 一條魚 yat-t'iu-*ue, (to) 打魚 'ta-*ue, 羅魚 'loh-*ue, 拗魚 'aau-*ue, (angle) 釣魚 tiu'-*ue.	
Fisherman,	羅魚人 'loh-ue-yan.	
Fishy smell,	魚腥 ue-seng.	
Fissure,	鑵隙 la'-kwik.	
Fist,	拳頭 k'uen-t'au.	
Fistula,	生穿 shang-ch'uen.	
Fit,	着 cheuk, (a) 一塲 yat-ch'eung, (fainting) 昏迷一塲 fun-mai-yat-ch'eung.	
Fitch,	小荳 'siu-*tau'.	
Five,	五 'ng.	
Fix,	定實 ting'-shat.	

Fixed number,	額數 ngaak-sho'.	
Flabby,	鬆呔 suung-p'au'.	
Flag, (a)	旗 k'i, (to) 衰頹 shui-t'ui.	
Flag-staff,	旗杆 k'i-kohn.	
Flag-stone,	石板 shek-'paan.	
Flagitious,	兇悍 huung-hohn'.	
Flagrant,	明妄 ming-'mong, 當面 tong-min'.	
Flail,	打禾棒 'ta-woh-'p'aang.	
Flake,	片 p'in'.	
Flame,	火尾 'foh-'mi, 火焰 'foh-im'.	
Flank,	軟脅 'uen-hip.	
Flannel,	小絨 'siu-*yuung.	
Flap,	撳 'im, 蓋撳 koi'-'im.	
Flapping,	拍拍吓 p'aak-p'aak-*ha.	
Flash, (to)	閃 'shim, 爍 ship'.	
Flask,	鐏 'tsuun.	
Flat,	平正 p'ing-ching', (thin) 扁 'pin, (ground) 低地 tai-ti', (insipid) 淡淡地 t'aam-*t'aam-*ti'.	

注 釋

【头长】应为"头生",指长子或长女。

【生穿】瘻管,细管。

Fitch: 艾鼬,又称"艾虎""地狗",是鼬科鼬属的小型毛皮动物。译为"小豆"属误译。

【松吓】松弛的,没气力的。

【拍拍吓】拍动,拍打。

注释

【映转处】炫耀，招摇。
【飞咁快】飞逝的，短暂的。
【下爬轻轻】"下爬"应为"下巴"。比喻说话轻浮，好夸海口。

FLI　　　97　　　FLO

Flatter, 阿媚奉承 oh-mi²-fuung⁻-shing.
Flattery, 諂媚 ⸢ch'im-mi⸥.
Flatulent, 食滯發氣 shik-chai²-faat²-hi².
Flaunt, 映轉處 ⸢yeung-⸢chuen-shue⸥.
Flavour, 氣味 hi²-mi².
Flaw, 瑕疵 ha-ts'ze.
Flax, 蔴 ma.
Flay, 剝皮 mok-p'i.
Flea, 狗虱 ⸢kau-shat, 跳虱 t'iu²-shat.
Flee, 逃走 t'o-⸢tsau, 走去 ⸢tsau-hue².
Fleet, 跑得快 ⸢p'aau-tak-faai², 速 ts'uuk, (a) 一幫 yat-pong.
Fleeting, 飛咁快 fi-kom²-faai².
Flesh, 肉 yuuk.
Fleur-de-lis, 蝴蝶花 oo-*tip-fa.
Flexible, 柔軟 yau-⸢uen, 屈得 wat-tak.
Flighty, 兩頭跳 ⸢leung-t'au-t'iu², 桃撻 t'iu-t'aat².
Flinch, 畏縮 wai²-shuuk.

Fling, 投 t'au, 揼 wing.
Flint, 火石 ⸢foh-shek.
Flippant, 油嘴 yau-⸢tsui, 下爬輕輕 ha²-p'a-heng-heng.
Float, 浮 fau, 蒲 p'o.
Flock, 羣 k'wun.
Flog, 鞭打 pin-⸢ta, (bamboo) 打板子 ⸢ta-⸢paan-⸢tsze.
Flood, (the) 洪水 huung-⸢shui.
Flood-tide, 水大 ⸢shui-taai².
Flooding, 血崩 huet²-pang, 血山崩 huet²-shan-pang.
Floor, 樓板 *lau-⸢paan, (ground-) 地臺 ti²-t'oi.
Floss-silk, 絲絨 sze-yuung.
Flounder, 左口魚 ⸢tsoh-⸢hau-*ue, 鰽閉魚 tsang²-pai²-ue.
Flour, 麵粉 min²-⸢fun, (1st) 澄麵 tang²-min², (2nd) 標麵 piu-min², (3rd) 灰麵 fooi-min².
Flourishing, 茂盛 mau²-shing².
Flow, 流 lau.

Flower, 花 *fa*, (a) 一朶花 yat-ʽtoh-*fa*.	Fold (for sheep) 羊欄 yeung-laan, (to) 摺 *chip*ʾ, (one) 單 ʽ*taan*, (two or more) 倍 ʽpʽooi.
Fluctuating, 不定得 ʾm-tingʾ-*tak*, 兩頭流 ʽleung-tʽau-lau.	
Fluent, 流利 lau-liʾ (laiʾ).	Foliage, 葉茂 ip-mauʾ.
Fluid, 水嗷樣 ʽshui-ʽkom-yeung.	Follow, 跟從 kan-tsʽuung, 隨後 tsʽui-hauʾ.
Flurry, 慌忙 fong-mong.	Folly, 戇氣 ngongʾ-hiʾ, 呆事 ngoi-szeʾ.
Flush, 發紅 *faat*ʾ-huung.	Foment, 熱淋 it-lum.
Flute, 簫 siu, 橫笛 waang-*tek.	Fond of, 痛愛 tʽuungʾ-oiʾ.
Flutter, (to) 撲翼 pʽokʾ-yik, (in a) 心亂 sum-luenʾ, 着急 cheuk-*kup*, 頻撲 pʽan-pʽokʾ.	Fondle, 懷撫 waai-ʽfoo, 撫抱 ʽfoo-pʽo.
	Food, 食物 shik-mat, 伙食 ʽfoh-shik, 野食 ʽye-shik.
Fly, (to) 飛 *fi*, (a) 烏蠅 ʽoo-ʽying, (blue bottle) 青蠅 tsʽing-ying, 金烏蠅 ʽkam-ʽoo-ʽying.	Fool, 呆人 ngoi-yan, 蠢子 ʽchʽuun-tszeʾ.
	Foolish, 蠢鈍 ʽchʽuun-tuunʾ.
	Foolishly, 莽 ʽmong.
Foam, 浮漚 fau-*au*, (at the mouth) 吐沫 tʽoʾ-moot.	Foolhardy, 冒險 moʾ-ʽhim.
Foe, 敵 tik.	Foot, 腳 keukʾ, 足 tsuuk, (measure) 尺 chʽekʾ.
Fog, 矇霧 muung-moʾ, 迷霧 mai-moʾ.	Footprint, 腳印 keukʾ-yanʾ.
	Footstep, 腳跡 keukʾ-tsik.
Foist in, 亂入 luenʾ-yap, 涵入 wan-yap.	Foot-stool, 腳踏凳 keukʾ-taap-tangʾ.

注 释

【不定得】波动。
【水嗷样】液体，像水一样的。
【呆事】愚蠢。
【热淋】煽动，挑拨。
【怀抚】爱抚，抚摸。

注释

【缩手】克制。
【点盐指】应为"睫盐指"，食指的俗名。
【来路货】舶来品，进口货。
【头人】领班。
【上昼】上午。
【抵填】罚款。

Fop, 裝腔 ₍chong-₎hong.
For, (ADV.) 因 yan, 因為 yan-wai, (PREP.) 代 toi', 替 t'ai, 為 wai'.
Forbear, 縮手 shuuk-'shau, 忍住 'yan-chue'.
Forbearance, 忍耐 'yan-noi'.
Forbid, 禁止 kum'-'chi.
Force, 力 lik, (to) 強 'k'eung, 逼 pik.
Forced, 勉強 'min-k'eung.
Forceps, 鐵鉗 t'it'-*k'im, 鉗仔 *k'im-'tsai.
Ford, (to) 步涉 po'-ship', kaang'.
Fore, 前 ts'in, 先 sin.
Forearm, 手肘 'shau-'chaau.
Forefinger, 二指 i'-'chi, 點鹽指 'tim-im-'chi.
Forego, 丟開 tiu-hoi, 放下 fong'-ha.
Forehead, 額頭 ngaak-t'au.
Foreign goods, 來路貨 loi-*lo'-foh'.
Foreign nation, 外國 ngoi'-kwok'.

Foreigner, 外國人 ngoi'-kwok'-yan, (European) 洋人 yeung-yan, (the Chinese call foreigners) 番人 faan-yan, (with a little more respect) 老番 'lo-faan, (and in contempt) 番鬼 faan-'kwai.
Foreknow, 預先知到 ue'-sin-chi-to'.
Foreman, 頭人 t'au-yan, 亞總 a'-tsuung, 攬頭 'laam-*t'au.
Forenoon, 上晝 sheung'-chau'.
Forerunner, 先驅 sin-k'ue, 先鋒 sin-fuung.
Foresee, 先見 sin-kin', 早知 'tso-chi, 大早知到 taai'-'tso-chi-to'.
Forest, 樹林 shue'-lum.
Forethink, 預先估 ue'-sin-'koo, 預料 ue'-liu'.
Forfeit, 抵填 'tai-t'in.
Forge, (a) 打鐵爐 'ta-t'it'-lo.
Forge, (to) 假冒 'ka-mo'.

Forgery, 託名僞書 t'ok'-ming-ngai'-shue.
Forget, 忘記 mong-ki'.
Forgetful, 不上心 'm-'sheung-sum, 無記性 'mo-ki'-sing'.
Forgive, 赦免 she'-'min.
Fork, (a) 枝叉 chi-ch'a.
Forked, 了叉 'a-ch'a.
Forlorn, 孤獨 koo-tuuk.
Form, (shape) 模式 moo-shik, 式 shik, (body) 形像 ying, tseung'.
Formality, mere 虛禮 hue-'lai.
Formosa, 臺灣 T'oi-waan.
Former, (time) 在先 tsoi'-sin.
Formerly, 從前 ts'uung-ts'in, 起先 'hi-sin, 舊時 kau'-shi.
Fornication, 私情 sze-ts'ing, 苟合 'kau-hop.
Forsake, 遺棄 wai-hi', 棄 hi', 拋離 p'aau-li.
Forsooth, 眞個 chan-koh'.
Fort, 炮臺 p'aau'-*t'oi.
Forth, 出 ch'uut.

Fortify, 築城 chuuk-sheng, 築營壘 chuuk-ying-'lui, 起炮臺 'hi-p'aau'-*t'oi.
Fortitude, 堅忍 kin-'yan, 堅心 kin-sum, 剛強 kong-k'eung.
Fortunate, 吉 kat, 好命 'ho-meng'.
Fortunately, 好彩 'ho-ts'oi.
Fortune, 造化 tso'-fa', 命 meng', 運數 wan'-sho'.
Fortune-teller, 算命人 suen'-meng'-yan.
Forward, (go) 上前 'sheung-ts'in, (bold) 大胆 taai'-'taam.
Foster, 養 'yeung.
Foul, 汚穢 oo-wai', 汚糟 oo-tso, (wind) 逆風 ngaak-fuung.
Found, (metals) 鑄 chue', (establish) 鼎建 'ting-kin'.
Foundation, 基址 ki-'chi, 基 ki, 墻脚 ts'eung-keuk', (stones) 地牛礈 ti'-ngau-chum.
Foundling, 執倒嘅仔 chup-'to-ke'-'tsai.

注 释

【真个】真的, 确实。
【好彩】幸运的。
【执倒嘅仔】拾到的孩子, 弃儿。

注释

【喷水景】喷泉。
【嬲嫋】暴躁的,倔强的。
【放甩】自由的。
【焦积】烦躁的。

FRA　　101　　FRI

Fountain, 泉源 ts'uen-uen, 源頭 uen-t'au, (artificial) 噴水景 p'un-'shui-king.
Four, 四 sze'.
Four-square, 四方 sze'-fong-ke'.
Fourth, 第四 tai'-sze', (a) 四分一 sze'-fun'-yat.
Fowl, 鷄 kai, (generally) 雀鳥 tseuk-'niu.
Fowling-piece, 鳥鎗 'niu-ts'eung.
Fox, 狐狸 oo-*li.
Fractious, 嬲嫋 nau-nat.
Fragment, 碎片 sui'-p'in'.
Fragrant, 馨香 hing-heung.
Frail, 脆弱 ts'ui'-yeuk.
Frame, (a) 架 ka'.
France, 法蘭西 Faat'-laan-sai, 法國 Faat'-kwok'.
Frank, 坦易 't'aan-i', 直白 chik-paak.
Frankincense, 乳香 'ue-heung.
Frantic, 癲狂 tin-k'wong.
Fraternity, 結義兄弟 kit'-i'-hing-tai'.
Fraud, 騙局 p'in'-kuuk.

Freak, 出奇事 ch'uut-k'i-sze', 新樣 san-*yeung'.
Freckled, 斑點 paan-'tim, paan-'tim-ke'.
Free, 自由 tsze'-yau, 自主 tsze'-'chue, 無拘管 mo-k'ue-'koon.
Free, (to) 放甩 fong-lat.
Freely, 隨便 ts'ui-*pin', (gratuitously) 白白 paak-paak, (willingly) 甘心 kom-sum.
Freeze, 結冰 kit'-ping, 冷硬 'laang-ngaang', 凍 tuung'.
Freight, 水脚 'shui-keuk'.
Frequent, (to) 常時來往 sheung-shi-loi-'wong.
Frequently, 屢次 lue'-ts'ze', 多賬 toh-cheung'.
Fresh, 新鮮 san-sin, (water) 淡 t'aam, taam'.
Fretful, 焦積 tsiu-tsik.
Friction, 相磨 seung-moh.
Friday, 禮拜五 'lai-paai-'ng.
Friend, 朋友 p'ang-'yau.
Friendly, 相好 seung-'ho.

Frighten, 嚇怕 haak'-p'a'.
Frightful, 可怕 ‘hoh-p'a'.
Fringe, 絮 *sue, 纓 ying.
Frisk, (to) 跳轉處 t'iu'- ‘chuen-shue'.
Frith, 河口 hoh-‘hau.
Frivolous, 輕浮 hing-fan.
Frog, 蛤姆 kop'-na, 田雞 t'in-kai.
Frolic, 戲耍 hi'-sha, 反斗 ‘faan-‘tau.
From, 由 yau, 從 ts'uung, 自 tsze', (distant) 去 hue', 離 li.
Front, 前頭 ts'in-t'au, 前邊 ts'in-pin (pin'), (to) 面向 min'-heung'.
Frontier, 境界 ‘king-kaai'.
Frost, 霜降 seung-kong'.
Froth, 泡 ‘p'o.
Frown, 縐埋眉頭 tsau'-maai-mi-t'au.
Frugal, 省儉 ‘shaang-kim'.
Fruit, 菓子 ‘kwoh-‘tsze, 菓實 ‘kwoh-shat.
Fruitful, 豐盛 fuung-shing'.
Fruit-tree, 菓木 ‘kwoh-muuk.

Frustrate, 破敗 p'oh'-paai', (good) 孤負 koo-foo'.
Fry, 煎炒 tsin-‘ch'aau, 蘇 ch'aau'.
Frying-pan, 鑊 wok.
Fuel, 柴 ch'aai, 柴火 ch'aai-foh.
Fulfil, 成就 shing-tsau', 踐 tsin, 應驗 ying'-im'.
Fulfilment, 應驗 ying'-im'.
Full, 滿 ‘moon, 盈 ying.
Fully, 嘥 saai', 盡地 tsuun'-*ti'.
Fume, (rage) 鬧 naau', 生氣 shang hi'.
Fumigate, 燻 fan.
Fun, 頑笑 waan-siu', 戲耍 hi'-sha.
Function, (office,) 職 chik, (use) 用處 yuung'-‘ch'ue'.
Fund, 嘗銀 sheung-*ngan, 嘗項 sheung-hong'.
Fundamental, 根本 kan-‘poon.
Funeral, 送葬 suung'-tsong', 喪事 song'-sze'.
Fungus, 香信 heung-suun', 菌 ‘k'wun, ‘k'an, (on trees) 木耳 muuk-‘i.

注 释

【反斗】顽皮，淘气。
【境界】这里指边疆。
【闹】骂。
【香信】菌类。

注释

【卷埋】收拢，卷起来。
【家伙】家具。
【宿宿地】发霉的。
【嘮嘈】喋喋不休地。

Funnel, 漏砵 lau’-poot’, (chimney) 煙通 in-t‘uung.
Fur-dress, 裘 k‘au, 皮衣 p‘i-i, (sable) 貂鼠皮 tiu-ʿshue-p‘i.
Furbish, 擦光 ts‘aat’-kwong.
Furious, 暴 po’, 兇暴 huung-po’.
Furl, 捲埋 ʿkuen-maai.
Furlough, 假 ka’, (to ask) 告假 ko’-ka’, (to give) 放假 fong’-ka’.
Furnace, 爐 lo, 灶 tso’, (portable) 風爐 fuung-*lo.
Furnish, 給 k‘up, 備辦 pi’-paan’, 齊備傢伙 ts‘ai-pi’-ka-ʿfoh.
Furniture, 傢伙 ka-ʿfoh.
Furrow, 犁路 lai-lo’, 田溝 t‘in-kau.
Further, 更遠 kang’-ʿuen, 再進 tsoi’-tsuun’.
Furthermore, 而且 i-ʿch‘e.
Fury, 怒狂 no’-k‘wong.
Fuse, 燒鎔 shiu-yuung.
Fussy, 浮躁 fau-ts‘o’.
Fusty, 宿宿地 suuk-suuk-*ti’, yik.

Futile, 虛徒 hue-t‘o.
Future, 將來 tseung-loi, 來 loi, 後 hau’.

G

Gabble, 嘮嘈 lo-ts‘o.
Gable, 金礨 kum-kai’, 墻礨 ts‘eung-kai’.
Gad about, 開逛 haan-k‘waang’.
Gad-fly, 牛蝱 ngau-mong.
Gag, 鉗口 k‘im-ʿhau, 塞口 sak-ʿhau.
Gage, (a) 準則 ʿchuun-tsak.
Gaiety, 繁華 faan-wa.
Gain, 利 li’, 利息 li’-sik, (to) 賺 chaan’, 贏 yeng, 獲 wok.
Gait, 舉動 ʿkue-tuung’.
Galangal, 艮薑 leung-keung.
Gale, 大風 taai’-fuung.
Gall, 膽 ʿtaam, 膽汁 ʿtaam-chup.
Gall-nut, 五倍子 ʿng-ʿp‘ooi-ʿtsze, 沒石 moot-shek.

GAN 104 GAR

Gallant, (heroic) 英雄 ying-huung.
Gallery, 樓臺 lau-t'oi, 樓 *lau.
Gallipot, 冚盅 hom'-ˌchuung.
Gallon, (a) 一斗 yat-ˈtau.
Gallop, 跑 p'aau.
Gallows, 縊架 ai'-*ka'.
Gambier, 薯莨 shue-leung.
Gamble, 賭錢 ˈto-*ts'in.
Gambler, 賭棍 ˈto-kwun'.
Gambling-house, 番攤館 ˌfaan-t'aan-ˈkoon.
Gamboge, 籘黃 t'ang-wong.
Gambol, 隨處跳 ts'ui-ch'ue'-t'iu'.
Game, (a) 博局 pok'-kuuk, 博戲 pok'-hi', (to play) 戲耍 hi'-ˈsha, (make of) 舞弄 ˈmoo-luung'.
Game, (meat) 野味 ˈye-*mi.
Gammon, 嘴滑 ˈtsui-waat, (to) 噆 t'um'.
Gammon, (ham) 火腿 ˈfoh-ˈt'ui.
Gander, 鵝公 ngoh-ˌkuung.
Gang, 隊 tui'.

Gangrene, 肉死 yuuk-ˈsze.
Gaol, 監房 kaam-fong.—Superindendent of, 司獄官 sze-yuuk-koon.
Gaoler, 司獄 sze-yuuk, 禁子 kum'-ˈtsze, 看監 hohn-ˌkaam.
Gap, 山口 shaan-ˈhau, 一個口 yat-koh'-ˈhau.
Gape, 擘大個口 maak'-taai'-koh'-ˈhau, (and stare) 擘口定眼 maak'-ˈhau-ting'-ngaan.
Garble, 講歪 ˈkong-ˈme, 半吞半吐 poon'-t'un-poon'-t'o'.
Garden, 園 uen, *uen.
Gardener, 園丁 uen-ˌting.
Gardenia florida, 白蟾花 paak-shim-fa, 黃梔 wong-chi.
Gargle, 漱口 sau'-ˈhau, ˈlong-ˈhau.
Garland, 花冠 fa-koon.
Garlic, 青蒜 ts'ing-*suen', 大蒜 taai'-*suen', 蒜頭 suen'-t'au.

注释

【冚盅】带盖的陶瓷罐。
【縊架】绞刑架。
【番摊馆】赌场。
【随处跳】雀跃。
【肉死】坏疽。
【擘大个口】张大嘴巴。
【擘口定眼】嘴巴张着，目不转睛地看。

> 注 释
>
> 【石班】石斑鱼。
> 【看门公】看门人。
> 【积埋】积聚在一起。
> 【睇定眼】直勾勾地盯着。

Garment, 衣服 i-fuuk, 衣裳 i-sheung.
Garoupa, 石班 shek-ₒpaan.
Garret, 貼脊頂樓 tʻipʾ-tsekʾ-ₒting-lau, 樓仔 *lau-ₒtsai, 閣仔 kokʾ-ₒtsai.
Garrison, 兵 ₒping, 屯兵 tʻuen-ₒping.
Garrulous, 沉贅 chʻum-chuiʾ.
Garter, 襪帶 mat-taaiʾ.
Gas, (coal-) 煤氣 mooi-hiʾ.
Gas-light, 煤燈 mooi-ₒtang.
Gash, 傷口 ₒsheung-ₒhau.
Gasp, 喘氣 ʻchʻuen-hiʾ, 抽氣 ₒchʻau-hiʾ.
Gate, 門 ₒmoon, (with bars) 閘門 chaapʾ-ₒmoon, (rolling) 走櫳 ʻtsau-*luung.
Gate-keeper, 看門公 hohnʾ-ₒmoon-ₒkuung.
Gather, 積埋 tsikʾ-maai, 收拾 ₒshau-shupʾ, 聚埋 tsueʾ-maai.
Gaudy, 排場 pʻaai-chʻeung.
Gauze, 紗 ₒsha, 機紗 ki-sha, 亮紗 leungʾ-ₒsha.
Gay, 奢華 ₒchʻe-wa, (person) 好奢華 hoʾ-ₒchʻe-wa.

Gaze, 睇定眼 ʻtʻai-ₒting-ʻngaan, (at) 定眼睇住 tingʾ-ʻngaan-ʻtʻai-chueʾ.
Gazelle, 羚羊 ling-yeung.
Gazette, 通報 tʻuung-poʾ, (Peking-) 京報 King-poʾ, 京抄 King-ₒchʻaau.
Gecko, 蛤蚧 kopʾ-*kaai, 雷公蛇 lui-ₒkuung-*she.
Gelatine, 膠 ₒkaau.
Geld, 閹 ₒim, 割勢 kohtʾ-shaiʾ.
Gem, 玉 *yuuk, 寶石 ʻpo-shek.
Gender, (to) 生 ₒshaang.
Genealogy, 族譜 tsuuk-ʻpʻo, 世系 shaiʾ-haiʾ.
General, 總共 ʻtsuung-kuungʾ, 通 ₒtʻuung.
General, (a) 將軍 tseungʾ-ₒkwun.
Generally, 大凡 taaiʾ-ₒfaan, 大約 taaiʾ-*yeukʾ.
Generate, (as animals) 傳種 chʻuen-ₒchuung, (produce) 生 ₒshaang.
Generation, 世代 shaiʾ-toi

GER 106 GIN

Generous, 慷慨 'k'ong-k'oi', 大量 taai'-leung, 四海 sze'-'hoi.
Genial, 溫和 wan-woh.
Genii, 神仙 shan-,sin.
Genius, 英才 ying-ts'oi.
Genteel, 斯文 sze-mun.
Gentian, 黃連 wong-lin.
Gentle, 溫柔 wan-yau.
Gentleman, (in character) 君子 kwun-'tsze, (a teacher) 先生 sin-shang, 老師 'lo-sze, (an old) 老爺 'lo-ye, (young) 相公 seung'-kuung.
Gentlemen! 列公 lit-,kuung.
Gently, (lightly) 輕輕地 heng-heng-*ti' (slowly) 慢慢地 maan'-maan'-*ti'.
Gentry, 紳襟 shan-k'um, 紳士 shan-sze'.
Genuine, 眞 chan.
Geography, 地理 ti'-'li.
Geomancy, 風水 fuung-'shui.
Geometry, 幾何 'ki-hoh, 丈量 cheung'-leung.
Geranium, 香葉 heung-ip.

Germ, 芽 nga, (seed) 仁 yan, ngan.
German-silver, 白銅 paak-t'uung.
Germany, 德國 Tak-kwok'.
Germinate, 發芽 faat'-nga, 爆哄 paau'-muuk'.
Get, 得到 tak-'to, 攞到 'loh-'to, 攞得 'loh-tak, 得 tak.
Ghost, 鬼 'kwai.
Giant, 偉丈夫 'wai-cheung'-foo, 長人 ch'eung-yan.
Giblets, 蒲胵 p'o-c'hi'.
Giddy, 頭暈 t'au-wan' (,wan), (light) 佻撻 t'iu-t'aat'.
Gift, (a) 送俾 suung'-,pi, suung'-,pi-ke 送禮 suung'-'lai, (from a superior) 賜 ts'ze'.
Giggle, 笑嬉嬉 siu'-hi-hi.
Gild, (to) 鍍金 to'-,kum, 黐金 ch'i-,kum.
Gills, 鰓 soi.
Gimlet, 手鑽 'shau-tsuen'.
Gin, (snare) 圈套 huen-t'o'.

注 释

【列公】先生。
【偉丈夫】偉人。
【蒲胵】雜碎，内臟。
【送俾】送給。

注释

【俾】给。
【津液之核】腺体。
【车料】玻璃研磨。
【烧料】玻璃烧制。
【玄明粉】芒硝。
【利口】油嘴滑舌的。
【手笠】手套。

| GLA | 107 | GLO |

Ginger, 薑 keung, (preserved) 糖薑 t'ong-keung, (stem) 子薑 ,tsze-keung.
Ginseng, 人參 yan-shum.
Gipsies, (Chinese) 三姑六婆 saam-koo-luuk-p'oh.
Gird, (to) 束住 ch'uuk-chue', 箍住 k'oo-chue'.
Girdle, 腰帶 iu-*taai', 褲頭帶 foo'-t'au-*taai'.
Girl, 女仔 ‛nue-‛tsai, (servant) 妹仔 mooi-‛tsai.
Girth, 肚帶 ‛t'o-*taai'.
Give, 俾 ‛pi, (present) 送俾 suung-‛pi.
Gizzard, 腎 ‛shan, (skin of the) 脺肶 p'i-c'hi.
Glad, 歡喜 foon-‛hi.
Glance, (to) 閃 ‛shim, (at) 睇一吓 ‛t'ai-yat-‛ha — 一睇 yat-‛t'ai.
Glands, 津液之核 tsuum-yik-chi-wat.
Glare, 光猛 kwong-‛mang.
Glaring, 明明 ming-ming.
Glass, 玻璃 ‛poh-‛li, (a tumbler) 玻璃杯 ‛poh-‛li-‛pooi.

Glass-grinding, 車料 ch'e-*liu'.
Glass-melting, 燒料 shiu-*liu'.
Glauber-salts, 玄明粉 uen-ming-‛fun.
Glazed, 光滑 kwong-waat, 玻璃光 ‛poh-‛li-kwong, (glass put in) 鑲玻璃 seung-‛poh-‛li.
Glib, 利口 li-‛hau, (slippery) 滑 waat.
Glide, 流 lau, 慢流 maan'-lau.
Glimmer, 微光閃 mi-kwong-‛shim.
Glitter, 發光 faat'-kwong, (show) 光華 kwong-wa.
Globe, 球 k'au, (the) 地球 ti-k'au.
Gloomy, 晦氣 fooi-‛hi, (weather) 天色暗 t'in-shik-om', 烏雲 oo-wan.
Glorify, 歸榮 kwai-wing.
Glory, 榮 wing, 榮光 wing-kwong.
Glossy, 閃靚 ‛shim-leng'.
Gloves, 手笠 ‛shau-lup.

英粵字典

Glow-worm, 放光蟲 fong-kwong-*ch'uung.	GOD, 上帝 SHEUNG'-TAI', (the gods) 諸上帝 chue-sheung'-tai', 鬼神 ʿkwai-shan.
Glue, 牛皮膠 ngau-pʻi-kaau.	
Glutton, 大食王 taai'-shik-wong, (VULG.) 大食鬼 taai'-shik-ʿkwai.	Godown, 貨倉 foh'-ts'ong.
	Goitre, 大頸疱 taai'-keng-pʻaau.
Gluttonous, 貪喫 tʻaam-yaak.	Gold, 金 kum, 黃金 wong-ʿkum.
Gnash, (the teeth) 咬牙 ʿngaau-nga, 切齒 tsʻit'-ʿchʻi.	Gold-leaf, 金薄 kum-pok.
	Gone, 去了 hue'-liu, hue'-hiu, 無咯 ʿmo-lok.
Gnat, 虻虫 mong-chʻuung, 蚊 ʿmun.	Gong, 鑼 *loh, (a) 一面鑼 yat-min'-*loh.
Gnaw, 齧 nget, 啽 luun.	Gonorrhea, 白濁 paak-chuuk.
Go, 去 hue', 往 ʿwong, 行 hang, (be off) 扯 ʿchʻe.	Good, 好 ʿho, 善 shin'.
	Good-bye, (to the remaining) 坐丫 *tsoh'-a, (to the going) 好行 ʿho-haang.
Goal, 準頭 ʿchuun-tʻau.	
Goat, 山羊 shaan-*yeung, 草羊 ʿtsʻo-*yeung, 羊咩 yeung-ʿme.	Goose, 草鵝 ʿtsʻo-*ngoh, (wild) 鴈鵝 ngaan'-*ngoh.
Gobble, 吞 tʻun, 挰聲吞 luet-sheng-tʻun, ʿtsʻuun.	Gore, (to) 觸傷 chʻuuk-sheung, 抄 chʻaau.
	Gorgeous, 榮華 wing-wa.
Go-between, 中人 chuung-*yan, 媒 mooi, (female) 媒婆 mooi-*pʻoh.	Gormandize, 食太過 shik-tʻaai'-kwoh.
	Gospel, 福音 fuuk-yum.
Goblet, 壺 *oo, 鍾 chuung.	

注释

【贪喫】贪吃。

【挰声吞】"咕"地一声吞下去。

【大颈疱】甲状腺肿。

【白浊】淋病。

【坐丫】再见。

注释

【巷婆】爱说长道短的人。
【脚风】痛风。
【了哥】八哥。
【脚色】等级。
Grampus: 逆戟鲸。

Gossamer, 草蛛網 ‚ts'o-chue-‛mong, 遊絲 yau-sze.
Gossip, 閒談 haan-t'aam, 是非 shi'-fi, (to) 聞風捉影 mun-fuung-chuuk-'ying, (a) 巷婆 hong'-*p'oh.
Gouge, (a) 啉鑿 lum-tsok.
Gouge, (to), 鑿 tsok, 挖 waat'.
Gourd, 匏瓜 p'aau-‚kwa, 葫蘆 oo-*loo, (snake-) 絲瓜 ‚sze ‚kwa.
Gout, 脚風 keuk'-fuung.
Govern, 管理 'koon-‛li, 治 chi'.
Government, 國家 kwok'-ka, 皇家 wong-ka, 國政 kwok'-ching', 治 chi', —Offices 督憲署 'tuuk-hin'-‛shue.
Governor General, 督憲 tuuk-hin', 總督 ‛tsuung-tuuk, 制台 chai'-t'oi, (the Supreme) 主宰 ‛Chue-‛tsoi.
Gown, 長衫 ch'eung-‚shaam, 袍 *p'o.

Grace, (mercy) 恩典 yan-‛tin.
Graceful, 斯文 sze-mun, 雅 ‛nga.
Gracious, 恩 yan.
Grackle, 了哥 ‚liu-koh.
Gradation, 次等 ts'ze'-‛tang.
Grade, 脚色 keuk'-shik.
Gradually, 漸漸 tsim'-*tsim', 漸次 tsim'-ts'ze'.
Graduate, (of 1st deg.) 秀才 sau'-*ts'oi, (of 2nd) 舉人 ‛kue-yan, (of 3rd) 進士 tsuun'-sze', (of 4th) 翰林 hohn'-lum, (to) 登科 tang-foh, (1st) 入學 yup-hok, (2nd) 扳桂 p'aan-kwai'.
Graft, (to) 劉 ts'im, (to slip) 駁 pok'.
Grain, 穀 kuuk, (a) 粒 nup, (of wood) 紋 mun.
Grammar, 作文法 tsok'-mun-faat'.
Grampus, 鯨魚 k'ing-ue.
Granary, 穀倉 kuuk-ts'ong.
Grand, 高大 ko-taai', 大 taai', 巍巍 ngai-ngai.

Grand-father, 祖父 ʻtso-fooʼ 公爺 kuung-ye, 亞公 aʼ-kuung, (mother) 祖母 ʻtso-ʼmo, 亞婆 aʼ-pʻoh, (child) 孫 suen, ʻsuen.
Granite, 青石 tsʻing-shek, 花剛青 fa-ʻkong-tsʻeng, 白石 paak-shek.
Grant, 許准 ʻhue-ʻchuun.
Grapes, 葡提子 pʻo-tʻai-ʻtsze.
Graphic, 形容得出 ying-yuung-tak-chʻuut.
Grasp, 揸 cha.
Grass, 草 ʻtsʻo.
Grass-cloth, 蔴布 ma-poʼ, 夏布 haʼ-poʼ.
Grass-hopper, 蚱蜢 chaʼ-ʻmang, 草蜢 ʻtsʻo-ʻ*mang.
Grate, (a) 鐵火爐 tʻit-ʻfoh-lo, (to) 刮 kwaat, 擦 tsʻaatʼ, 刮沙 kwaatʼ-sha.
Grateful, 感恩 ʻkom-yan, 感謝 ʻkom-tseʼ.
Grater, 磨 mohʼ, *mohʼ.
Gratified, 快悅 faaiʼ-uet.
Gratify, 悅 uet.

Grating, (noise) 刮刮聲 kwit-kwit-sheng, (an iron) 鐵柱 tʻitʼ-ʻchʻue.
Gratis, 白白 paak-paak.
Gratitude, 感心 ʻkom-sum.
Gratuity of money, 贈銀 tsangʼ-*ngan.
Grave, (a) 墳墓 fun-mooʼ, 塚墓 ʻchʻuung-mooʼ.
Grave, (sedate) 莊敬 chong-king, 嚴肅 im-suuk, (heavy) 重 ʻchʻuung.
Gravestone, 墓碑 mooʼ-pi.
Graveclothes, 壽衣 shauʼ-i.
Gravel, 砂 sha, 砂石 sha-shek, (a disease) 砂痳 sha-lum.
Graving-tool, 懺刀 tsaamʼ-to.
Gravitation, 相汲力 seung-kʻup-lik.
Gravy, 醬 tseungʼ, 汁 chup.
Gray, 褐色 hohtʼ-shik, 灰色 fooi-shik, (hair) 白髮 paak-faatʼ.
Grease, 膏油 ko-yau.

注釋

【形容得出】生動的，輪廓分明的。
【快悅】稱心的。
【相汲力】引力。

注释

【为食】贪吃。
【希利尼】现译为"希腊人，希腊语"。
【不入世】缺乏处事经验的人，容易受骗的人。
【交关】剧烈的。
【噬起床牙】咧嘴笑。
【髀摺】腹股沟。

Greasy, 肥膩 fi-ni', 油膩 yau-ni'.
Great, 大 taai'.
Great-grand-father, 曾祖 tsang-‘tso, (-son) sak.
Greedy, 貪心 t‘aam-sum, (of food) 爲食 wai'-shik.
Greek, 希利尼 Hi-li-ni.
Green, 綠色 luuk-shik, 青綠 ts‘ing-luuk.
Greenhorn, 不入世 ’m-yup-shai'.
Greens, 青菜 ts‘ing-ts‘oi', 波菜 poh-ts‘oi'.
Greet, 問候 mun'-hau'.
Gridiron, 鐵鈀 t‘it'-*p‘a.
Grief, 憂悶 yau-moon'.
Grievance, 委曲 ‘wai-huuk.
Grievous, (heavy) 重 ch‘uung, (lamentable) 可哀 ‘hoh-oi.
Grievously, 交關 kaau-kwaan.
Griffin, or unicorn, 麒麟 k‘i-*luun.
Grill, 炒 ‘ch‘aau.
Grimace, 歪面 ‘me-min'.
Grin, 噬起牀牙 shai'-‘hi-ch‘ong-nga.
Grind, 磨 moh.
Grinding, (noise) 啥啥聲 ngum'-ngum'-sheng.
Grindstone, 磨刀石 moh-to-shek.
Gripes, 扭痛 ‘nau-t‘uung'.
Gristle, 脆骨 ts‘ui'-kwut.
Grits, 麥頭 mak-t‘au, 麥碎 mak-sui.
Gritty, 帶沙 taai'-sha.
Groan, 嘆氣 t‘aan'-hi', 吽吽聲 ’ng-‘ng-sheng, 硬硬聲 ngang-ngang-sheng.
Grocery, (a) 雜貨舖 tsaap-foh'-p‘o.
Groin, 髀摺 ‘pi-chip'.
Groom, 馬夫 ‘ma-foo.
Groove, (a) 一條坑 yat-t‘iu-haang, (to) 入柳 yup-‘lau.
Grope, 摩探 moh-t‘aam', 摸 ‘moh.
Gross, 粗 ts‘o, (large) 粗大 ts‘o-taai'.
Grotesque, 古怪 ‘koo-kwaai'.
Ground, 地 ti', 土 ‘t‘o.

GUA 112 GUL

Ground-nut, 花生 fa-,shang, 地豆 ti'-*tau'.
Groundless, 無根無本 mo-kan-mo-‘poon.
Grounds, (dregs) 渣滓 cha-‘tsze.
Group, 隊 tui', 堆 tui, (to) 成隊 shing-tui'.
Grovelling, 下作 ha'-tsok', 卑陋 pi-lau'.
Grow, 生長 shaang-‘cheung, 長大 ‘cheung-taai', 生 shaang.
Growl, 胡胡聲 oo-oo-sheng.
Grub, 蠐螬 ts'ai-ts'o, 地底蟲 ti'-‘tai-ch'uung.
Grudge, 吝惜 luun'-sik, (a) 私怨 sze-uen'.
Gruel, 粥 chuuk.
Gruff, 粗魯 ts'o-‘lo.
Grumble, 晗沈 ngum-ch'um.
Grunt, 嚙嚙聲 nguet-nguet-sheng.
Guano, 鳥糞 ‘niu-fun'.
Guarantee, (to) 包 paau.
Guard, 守 ‘shau, 護衛 oo'-wai', (against) 防 fong.

Guard-boat, 巡船 ts'uun-*shuen.
Guardian, 養主 ‘yeung-‘chue.
Guava, 番石榴 faan-shek-*lau.
Gudgeon, 白鴿魚 paak-kop'-*ue.
Guess, 猜 ch'aai, 試猜 shi'-ch'aai, 猜度 ch'aai-tok, haai.
Guest, 人客 yan-haak'.
Guide, 引路 ‘yan-lo'.
Guild, 行 hong, 會館 ooi'-‘koon.
Guile, 詭譎 ‘kwai-kwut, 詭計 ‘kwai-kai'.
Guilt, 罪辜 tsui'-koo.
Guilty, 有罪 ‘yau tsui'.
Guise, 貌 maau', 裝扮 chong-paan'.
Guitar, 琵琶 p'i-*p'a.
Gulf, 大灣 taai'-waan, (an abyss) 深淵 shum-uen.
Gull, (a) 鷗 au (to) 欺騙 hi-p'in', 欺弄 hi-luung'.
Gullet, 咽喉 in-hau, 喉嚨 hau-luung.

注 释

【无根无本】无根据的。
【下作】卑下人。
【晗沈】抱怨，嘟嚷。
【包】保证。
【养主】监护人，保护人。

注 释

【坎坑】水沟。
【黄画】黑线鳕。
【疾口】争论。
【远远叫】招呼，向……
　　　欢呼。

Gully, 坎坑 ʻhaang-ʻhom.
Gulp, 硬吞 ngaang'-tʻun.
Gum, 樹膠 shue'-kaau.
Gum-benjamin, 安息香 ohn-sikˋ-ʻheung.
Gums, 牙齦肉 nga-kan-yuuk.
Gun, (fowling-piece) 鳥鎗 ʻniu-ʻtsʻeung, (cannon) 炮 pʻauu'.
Gun-cap, 銅帽子 tʻuung-mo'-tsze.
Gun-powder, 火藥 ʻfoh-yeuk.
Gun-powder-tea, 小珠茶 ʻsiu-chue-chʻa.
Gush, 噴溢 pʻun'-yat.
Gust, 陣風 chan'-fuung, 口風 ʻhau-fuung, 閃山風 ʻshim-shaan-fuung.
Gut, 腸 chʻeung.
Gutta-percha, 硬樹膠 ngaang'-shue'-kaau.
Gutter, 溝渠 kau-kʻue.
Gymnastics, 打把寳 ʻta-ʻpa-shat, 練工夫 lin'-kuung-fou.
Gypsum, 石膏 shek-ko.
Gyves, 腳鐐 keukˋ-liu.

H

Ha! 喺 ʻhai!
Habit, 慣例 kwaan'-lai', (in the) 慣習 kwaan'-tsaap, 做慣 tso'-kwaan'.
Habitable, 住得 chue'-tak, chue'-tak-ke'.
Hack, (to) 斸 teuk, 削 seuk'.
Haddock, 黃畫 wong-*waak.
Hades, 陰間 yum-kaan, 陰府 yum-ʻfoo.
Haft, 柄 pingˋ, pengˋ.
Haggard, 瘦壞 shau'-waai', 醜樣 ʻchʻau-*yeung'.
Haggle, 疾口 tsat-ʻhau.
Hail, 雹 pok, (a fall of) 落雹 lok-pok.
Hail, (to) 遠遠叫 ʻuen-ʻuen-kiu', 招 chiu.
Hair, 毛 mo, (of the head) 頭髮 tʻau-faatˋ.
Hair-breadth, 一毫 yat-ho, 絲毫 sze-ho, (-escape) 啱啱得甩 ʻngaam-ʻngaam-tak-lut.

| HAM | 114 | HAN |

Hair-cloth, 毛布 mo-po'.
Hair-gum, (used by women) 鉋花 p'aau-fa.
Hair-pin, 髻頭針 kai'-*t'au-chum, (clasp) 簪 ,tsaam.
Halberd, 斧鉞 ,foo-uet.
Hale, (to) 拉 ,laai, 拖 t'oh.
Hale, (healthy) 壯健 chong'-kin.
Half, 半 poon'.
Halibut, 將軍甲 tseung-kwun-kaap'.
Hall, 廳 ,t'eng, 堂 t'ong, 館 ,koon.
Halo, 汞 huung', 暈 wan'.
Halt, (to) 停脚 ,t'ing-keuk', (limp) 趷脚 kat-keuk'.
Halter, 馬籠頭 ,ma-luung-,t'au, (noose) 老鼠結 ,lo-,shue-lit, 生結 ,shaang-lit.
Ham, 火腿 ,foh-,t'ui.
Hamlet, 村 ,ts'uen.
Hammer, 鐵鎚 t'it'-*ch'ui, (to) 鎚 ,ch'ui, 打 ,ta, 揼 ,tum.
Hammock, 吊牀 tiu'-,ch'ong.

Hamper, (a) 籠 ,luung, 篢 ,lau, (to) 逼窄 pik-chaak', 窒手脚 chat-,shau-keuk.
Hand, 手 ,shau.
Hand-bill, 招帖 ,chiu-t'ip, 街招 ,kaai-,chiu.
Hand-cuffs, 手繚 ,shau-liu.
Handful, (a) 一揸 yat-,cha.
Handicraft, 手作 ,shau-tsok', 手藝 ,shau-ngai'.
Hand-kerchief, 手巾 ,shau-,kan, 汗巾 hohn'-,kan.
Hand-writing, 筆跡 pat-tsik.
Handle, (to) 抖 tau', 摩 ,moh, ,moh.
Handle, (a) 條柄 t'iu-peng'.
Handmaid, 婢 ,p'i.
Handsome, 精綏 ,tsing-,chi.
Handy, 抵手 ,tai-,shau, (convenient) 便當 pin'-tong'.
Hang, 吊 tiu', 懸掛 uen-kwa', (up) 掛起 kwa'-,hi, (down the head) 嗒低頭 tap-tai-*t'au, (by the neck) 吊頸 tiu'-,keng.

注释

【黄脚鸡】指被色诱的男人。此译法并不贴切，"hanger-on"译为"跟屁虫"更好。

【整硬】变硬。

【争的】几乎不，刚刚；差点儿。

【崩口】兔唇。

HAR　　115　　HAT

Hanger-on, 黄脚鸡 wong-keuk'-ᶜkai.
Hanker after, 贪 t'aam, 恋 luen'.
Happen, 遇有 ue'-ᶜyau, 遇着 ue'-cheuk.
Happily, 幸 hang', 好彩 ᶜho-ᶜts'oi.
Happiness, 福 fuuk.
Happy, 有福 ᶜyau-fuuk.
Harass, 难为 naan-wai.
Harbour, (a) 港口 ᶜkong-ᶜhau, (to) 窝藏 woh-ts'ong, 隐藏 ᶜyan-ts'ong.
Harbour Master, 船政厅 shuen-ching-ᶜt'eng.
Hard, 坚硬 kin-ngaang', 硬 ngaang', (difficult) 难 naan, (hearted) 忍心 ᶜyan-sum.
Harden, 整硬 ᶜching-ngaang'.
Hardship, 艰难 kaan-naan.
Hardly, 争的 ᶜchaang-ᶜti, 难 naan, 仅 ᶜkan.
Hardy, 强健 k'eung-kin'.
Hare, 野兔 ᶜye-t'o'.
Harelip, 崩口 pang-ᶜhau.

Harlot, 娼妓 ch'eung-ki'.
Harm, 害 hoi', 伤 sheung.
Harmony, 和 woh.
Harness, 器具 hi'-kue', (to a horse) 配置 p'ooi'-chi'.
Harp, 筝 chang.
Harpoon, 镖 piu.
Harrow, 耙 p'a, 犁耙 lai-p'a.
Harsh, 倔 kwut, 嘊 haai, 刻薄 haak'-pok.
Hart, 鹿公 luuk-ᶜkuung.
Harts-horn, 鹿茸 luuk-yuung.
Harvest, 收割时候 shau-koht'-shi-hau, 秋收 ts'au-shau, 收成 shau-shing.
Hash, 斩伤 ᶜchaam-sheung, 切烂 ts'it'-laan'.
Hasp, (hook) 钩 ngau, (for a padlock) 锁牌 ᶜsoh-p'aai.
Haste, 急切 kup-ts'it'.
Hasten, 趁快 ᶜkohn-faai'.
Hasty, 急 kup.
Hat, 帽 *mo, (put on) 戴帽 taai'-*mo.
Hatch, (a) 舱门 ts'ong-moon, (to) 孵 po', (artificially) 焙 pooi'.

Hatch-way, 艙口 ts'ong-ʻhau.	Healthy, 爽神 ʻshong-shan, 强壯 k'eung-chong', 壯 chong'.
Hatchet, 斧頭 ʻfoo-*t'au.	Heap, 堆 tui, (up) 堆埋 tui-maai, 堆起 tui-ʻhi, 重重叠叠 ch'uung-ch'uung-tip-tip.
Hate, 恨怒 han'-no', 怨恨 uen'-han', 憎 tsang.	
Hateful, 可惡 ʻhoh-oo'.	
Haughty, 大腔 taai'-ʻhong, 驕傲 kiu-ngo'.	Hear, 聽 t'eng, 聽聞 t'eng-mun, 聽見 t'eng-kin'.
Haul, 扯 ʻch'e.	Hearken, 俾耳聽 ʻpi-i-t'eng.
Have, 有 ʻyau.	
Havoc, 殘害 ts'aan-hoi'.	Hearsay, 風聞 fuung-mun.
Hawk, 鷹 ying.	Hearse, 喪車 song-kue.
Hawker, 販仔 faan'-ʻtsai, 小販 ʻsiu-*faan'.	Heart, 心 sum.
	Heart-burn, 心酸 sum-suen, 發嘞酸 faat'-laak'-suen, 翻口 faan-k'au'.
Hawthorn, 枳 ʻchi.	
Hazard, 危險 ngai-ʻhim, (to) 敢 ʻkom, 冒 mo', 拚 p'oon', 冒險 mo'-ʻhim.	Hearth, 火爐底 ʻfoh-lo-ʻtai.
	Heartily, (willing) 甘心 kom-sum.
Haze, 雲霧 wan-moo'.	
Hazel-nut, 榛 yui.	Hearty, 爽快 ʻshong-faai', 眞心 chan-sum.
He, 佢 ʻk'ue.	
Head, 頭 t'au, 首 ʻshau.	Heat, 熱 it, 熱氣 it-hi', (to) 燒熱 shiu-it, 整熱 ʻching-it.
Headache, 頭痛 t'au-t'uung', 頭瘠 t'au-ts'ek'.	
Headstrong, 硬頸 ngaang'-ʻkeng.	Heathen, 教外異民 kaau'-ngoi'-i'-mun.
Heal, 醫 i, 醫好 i-ʻho.	

注 释

【大腔】傲慢的。
【枳】山楂。
【榛】榛子。
【佢】(粤语中指)他、她、它等。
【硬頸】顽固的。
【俾耳听】倾听。

注 释

【猬】刺猬。
【脚踭】脚踝。
【藜芦】百合科藜芦属多年生草本植物，可入药。

HEL 117 HER

Heave, (pull) 扯 ‘ch‘e, (throw) 投 t‘au, (swell) 冲起來 ch‘uung-‘hi-lai.
Heaven, 天 t‘in, (the abode) 天堂 t‘in-t‘ong.
Heavy, 重 ‘ch‘uung.
Hebrew, 希伯來 Hi-paak‘-loi.
Hedge, 籬笆 li-pa, 笏籬 lak-li.
Hedge-hog, 猬 wai’, 箭猪 tsin’-‘chue.
Heed, 顧住 koo’-chue’.
Heedless, 不留心 ’m-lau-sum.
Heel, 脚踭 keuk’-chaang.
Heifer, 牛母仔 ngau-‘moo-‘tsai.
Heighten, 起高 ‘hi-ko, 整高 ‘ching-ko.
Heir, 嗣子 tsze’-‘tsze, 冡子 ch‘uung-‘tsze, (to) 承業 shing-ip.
Hell, 地獄 ti’-yuuk.
Hellebore, 黎蘆 lai-lo.
Helm, 舵 ‘t‘oh, 舦 ‘t‘aai, 舦筒 ‘t‘aai-t‘uung.

Helmsman, 梢公 shaau-kuung.
Helmet, 頭盔 t‘au-k‘wai.
Help, 帮助 pong-choh’, 照顧 chiu’-koo’, (no) 無奈何 ‘mo-noi’-hoh.
Helping-hand, 幫手 pong-‘shau.
Hem, 邊骨 pin-kwut, (to) 挑邊骨 t‘iu-pin-kwut.
Hem and ha, e-e-a’-a’.
Hemp, 麻 ma.
Hen, 鷄母 kai-‘moo, 鷄姆 kai-‘na.
Hence, 故此 koo’-‘ts‘ze, (away) 離此 li-‘ts‘ze, 離呢處 li-ni-shue’.
Henceforth, 自今以後 tsze’-kum-‘i-hau’.
Her, 個女人 koh’-‘nue-*yan, 佢 ‘k‘ue, (poss.) 佢嘅 ‘k‘ue-ke’.
Herald, 宣令官 suen-ling’-koon, 宣報 suen-po’.
Herb, 草菜 ‘ts‘o-ts‘oi.
Herbalist, 探藥先生 ‘ts‘oi-yeuk-sin-shang.
Herd, 羣 k‘wun.

	HES	118	HIL	

Herdsman, 牧人 muuk-yan, (of cows) 牧牛人 muuk-ngau-yan.

Here, 呢處 ni-ch'ue, ni-shue.

Hereafter, 此後 'ts'ze-hau', 嗣後 tsze-hau'.

Heresy, 異端 i'-tuen, 邪教 ts'e-kaau'.

Heretofore, 從來 ts'uung-loi, 向來 heung'-loi.

Hermit, 離世獨居之人 li-shai'-tuuk-kue-ke'-yan, 山人 shaan-yan.

Hernia, 小腸氣 'siu-ch'eung-hi'.

Hero, 英雄 ying-huung, 豪傑 ho-kit.

Heron, 白鷺 paak-lo'.

Herring, 鱛魚 ts'o-*ue, 鯠魚 ch'i-*ue, 黃魚 wong-*ue.

Herring-bone (in sewing) 隔骨 kaak'-kwut.

Hesitate, 踟躇 ch'i-ch'ue, 思疑 sze-i, (in speaking) 嗯嗯 luun-chuun, 拐喀 lak-k'ak.

Heterodoxy, 異教 i'-kaau'.

Hew, (to) 斸 teuk', 削 seuk', 劈 p'ek'.

Hibernate, 潛藏 ts'im-ts'ong.

Hibiscus, (rosa) 紅花 huung-fa, (mutab) 芙蓉 foo-yuung, (manihot) 黃蜀葵 wong-shuuk-k'wai, (Syriaca) 佛桑 fut-song.

Hiccough, 打嘶嗌 'ta-sze-yik.

Hide, (to) 匿埋 nik-maai, 藏埋 ts'ong-maai.

Hide, (a) 皮張 p'i-cheung, 隻皮 chek'-p'i.

Hideous, 醜貌 'ch'au-maau', 醜惡 'ch'au-ok'.

High, 高 ko, (on high) 上高 sheung'-ko, 在上 tsoi'-sheung'.

High-water, 水大定 'shui-taai'-ting'.

Hill, 山 shaan, 陵 ling.

Hilly, 崎嶇 k'i-k'ue, 多山 toh-shaan.

注 释

【小肠气】疝气。
【潜藏】指动物冬眠。
【打嘶嗌】打嗝。
【皮张】隐藏。
【水大定】高水位的，满潮的。

注 释

【佢嘅】他的。
【修史人】历史学家。
【到呢处】到这里。

Hilt, 條柄 t'iu-,peng', 柯 oh.
Him, 佢 ,k'ue.
Himself, 佢自己 ,k'ue-tsze-,ki.
Hinder, 阻 ,choh, 欄阻 laan-,choh.
Hindermost, 末後 moot-hau', 收尾 shau-mi.
Hinge, 鉸 kaau'.
Hint, 謎語 mai-,ue, (to) 打暗號 ,ta-om-*ho', (at) 暗指 om'-,chi.
Hip, 大腿 taai'-,t'ui, 大髀 taai'-,pi.
Hippocampus, 海馬 ,hoi-,ma.
Hippopotamus, 河馬 hoh-,ma.
Hire, (house, &c.) 租 ,tso, 賃 yum', (men) 任用 yum'-yuung', (wages) 工人 ,yan-,kuung, 工銀 ,kuung-*ngan.
His, 佢嘅 ,k'ue-ke'.
Hiss, 嘶嘶 ,sze-,sze, 嚌臺 ,ch'aai-t'oi.

Historian, 修史人 ,sau-,sze-yan.
History, 史記 ,sze-ki', (national) 綱鑑 ,kong-kaam'.
Hit, 打着 ,ta-cheuk, 捧親 ,p'uung-ts'an, (with a stone) 掟親 teng'-ts'an.
Hither, 到呢處 to'-,ni-shue'.
Hitherto, 向來 heung'-,loi, 至到今 chi'-to'-,kum, 平素 ,p'ing-so'.
Hive, 蜜蜂籠 mat-,fuung-*luung.
Hoard, (to) 積蓄 tsik-ch'uuk.
Hoarseness, 沙聲 ,sha-,sheng.
Hoax, 戲弄 hi'-luung'.
Hobgoblin, 妖怪 ,iu-kwaai', 馬騮精 ,ma-,lau-,tsing.
Hoe, (to) 鎊 ,pong, (a) 張鎊 ,cheung-,pong, 鋤頭 ,ch'oh-,t'au.
Hog, 猪 ,chue.
Hog's lard, 猪油 ,chue-,yau.
Hoist, 扯 ,ch'e, 扯起 ,ch'e-,hi, 上 ,sheung, 扯上 ,ch'e-,sheung.

HON 120 HOR

Hold, (to) 把守 ‵pa-‵shau, 把持 ‵pa-ch‵i, 執 chup, 揸住 cha-chue‵, (contain) 裝 chong, 藏得 ts‵ong-tak, 入得 yup-tak, (fast) 定實 ting‵-shat.

Hold, (ship's) 艙 ts‵ong.

Hole, 孔 ‵huung, 窿 luung.

Holiday, (to give) 放假 fong‵-ka‵, (a gala day) 高興日子 ko-hing-yat-‵tsze.

Hollow, 空韃 huung-‵luung, 凹 nup.

Hollyhock, 葵花 k‵wai-fa.

Holy, 聖 shing‵.

Home, 家 ka, (at) 在家 tsoi‵-ka, (go) 歸 kwai, 翻歸 faan-kwai, 回家 ooi-ka.

Home-made, 家欄 ka-*laan, ka-*laan-ke‵.

Hone, 潮石 ch‵iu-shek.

Honest, 老實 ‵lo-shat.

Honey, 蜜糖 mat-t‵ong.

Honey-comb, 蜜房 mat-fong, 蜜竇 mat-tau‵.

Honey-suckle, 金銀花 kum-ngan-fa.

Hongkong, 香港 Heung-‵kong.

Honour, 尊貴 tsuen-kwai‵, (to) 敬重 king‵-chuung‵.

Hood, 雪帽 suet‵ *mo‵, 頭蓋 t‵au-k‵oi‵.

Hoof, 蹄 t‵ai.

Hook, 鉤 kau, nyau.

Hoop, (to) 箍 foo, k‵oo, (a) 條篾 t‵iu-mit, (iron-) 鐵箍 t‵it-foo (k‵oo).

Hoot, 喝 hoht, 喝聲 hoht-sheng.

Hop, 單脚跳 taan-keuk‵-t‵iu.

Hope, 望 mong‵, 指望 ‵chi-mong‵.

Hoppo, 關部 kwaan-poo‵, 海關 ‵hoi-‵kwaan.

Horizon, 地平 ti‵-p‵ing, (visible) 天脚 t‵in-keuk‵.

Horn, 角 kok‵, (edible deer's) 鹿茸 luuk-yuung.

Hornet, 鶯蜂 ‵ang-fuung, 木蜂 muuk-fuung.

Horrible, 淒慘 ts‵ai-‵ts‵aam.

Horror, 觳觫 huuk-ts‵uuk.

注 释

Hollyhock: 蜀葵,又名"一丈红",多年生草本植物,根、茎、叶、花、种子等可用作药材。

【潮石】磨刀石。

注释

【牛喉】（消防车的）胶皮管。
【喜客】好客。
【行吓望吓】边走边看。
【拉杂埋】挤成一团。
【宏宏声】嗡嗡声，哼声。

HOU 121 HUM

Horse, 馬 ʻma, (a) 一隻馬 yat-chek⸴-ʻma.
Horse-racing, 跑馬 ʻpʻaau-ʻma, 鬥馬 tau⸴-ʻma.
Horse-radish, 辣根 laat-kan.
Horse-shoe, 馬夾 ʻma-kaap⸴.
Horse-whip, 馬鞭 ʻma-pin.
Hose, 襪 mat, (of a fire engine) 牛喉 ngau-hau.
Hospitable, 喜客 ʻhi-haak⸴, ʻhi-haakʼ-keʼ.
Hospital, 醫館 i-ʻkoon.
Host, 主家 ʻchue-ka, (troop) 軍 kwun.
Hostages, 質 chiʼ, (to exchange) 交質 kaau-chiʼ.
Hot, 熱 it, (feverish) 燬 hingʼ.
Hotel, 客寓 haak-ueʼ, 酒店 ʻtsau-tim⸴.
Hound, 獵狗 lip-ʻkau.
Hour, 點鐘 ʻtim-chuung, (quarter of an) 刻 haakʼ.
House, 屋 uuk, 屋企 uuk-ʻkʻi, (a) 一間屋 yat-kaan-uuk, (mercantile) 行 *hong.
Household, 家室 ka-shat, (domestics) 家人 ka-yan.

Hovel, 寮 *liu.
Hover about, 徘徊 (pʻooi-ooi) 行吓望吓 hang-ʻha-mong-ʻha, (as a bird) 飛飛吓 fi-fi-ʻha.
How, 點 ʻtim, 點樣 ʻtim-*yeungʼ, 何 hoh.
How many? 幾多 ʻki-toh 多少 toh-ʻshiu.
However, 雖然 sui-in.
Howl, 嗥嗥聲 ho-ho-sheng, 叫 kiuʼ.
Hubbub, 喧鬧 huen-naauʼ, 吧閉 pa-paiʼ.
Huddled, 拉雜埋 lai-tsaap-maai.
Huff, (in a) 生氣 shaang-hiʼ.
Hull, (of a ship) 船身 shuen-ʻshan.
Hull rice, 舂米 chuung-ʻmai.
Hum, 宏宏聲 wang-wang-sheng, 轟轟聲 kwaang-kwaang-sheng.
Human, 人類 yan-luiʼ, yan-luiʼ-keʼ, (relations) 人倫 yan-luun.

Humane, 慈心 ts'ze-sum, 腹心 fuuk-sum.	Hurricane, 風颶 fuung-kue', fuung-kau'.
Humanity, (benevolence) 仁 yan.	Hurry, (to) 催逼 ts'ui-pik, (in a) 忙迫 mong-pik, 緊急 'kan-kup.
Humble, 謙遜 him-suun', (to) 令—謙卑 ling'—him-pi, (one's self) 自謙 tsze'-him.	Hurt, 傷 sheung, (by a knock) 坎親 'hom-ts'an.
Humbly, 伏 fuuk, 匍伏 p'o-fuuk.	Husband, 丈夫 cheung'-foo, (COL.) 老公 'lo-kuung.
Humbug, (a) 下馬威 ha'-'ma-wai, (to) 噤 t'um'.	Husbandman, 農夫 nuung-foo, 耕田人 kang-t'in-yan.
Humility, 謙遜 him-suun', 謙遜之心 him-suun'-ke'-sum.	Hush, 禁默 kum'-mak, (hush!) 咪聲 'mai-sheng.
Humorous, 好調笑 'ho-t'iu-siu', 好講笑 'ho-'kong-siu'.	Hush-money, 揞焙手 'om-pooi'-'shau.
Hump-back, 陀背 t'oh-pooi'.	Husks, 糠 hong, 糠粃 hong-p'i.
Hump, bullock's 牛肩 ngau-kin.	Husky voice, 沙聲 sha-sheng.
Hundred, 百 paak'.	Hut, 茅屋 maau-uuk.
Hundredth, 第百 tai'-paak'.	Hyacinth, (stone) 赤瑪瑙 ch'ik-'ma-'no.
Hunger, 饑餓 ki-ngoh'.	Hymn, 神詩 shan-,shi, 聖詩 shing'-,shi.
Hungry, 肚餓 't'o-ngoh'.	Hyper, 太過 t'aai'-kwoh'.
Hunt, 打獵 'ta-lip.	Hypocrite, 僞善 ngai'-shin', 假善 'ka-shin'.
Hurrah! 好 'ho!	Hyson-tea, 熙春茶 hi-ch'uun-ch'a.

注释

【下马威】欺骗，显示威力。
【咪声】安静。
【揞焙手】封口费。
【太过】极度兴奋的。

注 释

【牛膝草】又称神香草、柳薄荷，一种多年生草本药用植物。
【讲法】成语，惯用语。
【窄心】狭隘的，吝啬的。
【显达】卓越的，杰出的。
【学效】仿效。

Hyssop, 牛膝草 ngau-sat-‘ts‘o.

I

I, 我 ‘ngoh.
Ice, 冰 ping’, 冰凍 ping-tuung’, (commonly called in Canton) 雪 suet’ (snow).
Idea, 意 i’, 意思 i’-sze’, 想頭 ‘seung-t‘au, 想像 ‘seung-tseung’.
Identical, 相同 seung-t‘uung, 同一個 t‘uung-yat-koh’.
Idiom, 講法 ‘kong-faat’.
Idiomatic, 講得去 ‘kong-tak-hue’, 依講法 i-‘kong-faat’.
Idiot, 呆人 ngoi-yan.
Idiotic, 痴呆 ch‘i-ngoi.
Idle, 閒 haan, (to) 偷閒 t‘au-haan.
Idol, 菩薩 p‘oo-saat’.
If, 若 yeuk, 倘若 ‘t‘ong-yeuk, 若係 yeuk-hai’.
Ignis fatuus, 鬼火 ‘kwai-‘foh.
Ignite, 着火 cheuk-‘foh.

Ignorant, 無知 mo-chi, 無見識 mo-‘kin’-shik.
Iguana, 蛤蚧 kop’-kaai.
Ill, (sick) 有病 ‘yau-peng’, (bad) 不好 ’m-‘ho.
Illegal, 犯法 faan’-faat’, 不合法 ’m-hop-faat’.
Illegitimate, }私 sze, 不法 pat-faat’
Illicit,
Illiberal, 窄心 chaak’-sum.
Ill-natured, 猛性 ‘mang-sing’, 嬲嬫 nau-nat.
Illness, 病 peng’.
Illuminate, (with lamps) 張燈 cheung-tang, (enlighten) 照光 chiu’-kwong.
Illustrate, 表明 ‘piu-ming.
Illustrious, 顯達 ‘hin-taat.
Ill-will, 恨 han’.
Image, 偶像 ‘ngau-tseung’.
Imagine, 懸想 uen-‘seung, 想 ‘seung.
Imbecile, 懦弱 noh’-yeuk.
Imbue, 沾 chim, 洽 haap.
Imitate, 學效 hok-haau’.
Immaculate, 無瑕疵 ‘mo-ha-ts‘ze.

IMP　　124　　IMP

Immaterial, 無形無像 mo-ying-mo-tseung⸲, (unimportant) 無相干 ⸲mo-seung-kohn.
Immediately, 卽時 tsik-shi, 登時 tang-shi.
Immense, 極大 kik-taai⸲.
Immerse, 沉 chum⸲, 浸 tsum⸲.
Imminent, the matter is, 事在旦夕 sze⸲-tsoi⸲-taan⸲-tsik.
Immoderate, 過頭 ⸲kwoh-t'au, 過當 kwoh⸲-tong⸲.
Immodest, 無禮 ⸲mo-⸲lai, 失禮 shat-⸲lai, 無廉恥 ⸲mo-lim-⸲ch'i.
Immoral, 不端正 'm-tuen-ching⸲.
Immortality, 永生 ⸲wing-shang.
Immutable, 不易 pat-yik.
Imp, 鬼仔 ⸲kwai-⸲tsai.
Impair, 損 ⸲suen.
Impart, 傳 ch'uen, 傳俾 ch'uen-⸲pi.
Impartial, 公平 kuung-p'ing.
Impatient, 着急 cheuk-kup, 無忍耐 ⸲mo-⸲yan-noi⸲.

Impeach, 告 ko⸲, 告狀 ko⸲-*chong, 禮 ⸲lai.
Impede, 耽誤 taam-'ng⸲, 阻住 ⸲choh-chue⸲.
Impediment, 防碍 fong-ngoi⸲.
Impel, 推 t'ui, 催逼 ts'ui-pik, 擁去 ⸲uung-hue⸲.
Impending, 臨近 lum-⸲k'an.
Imperative, 少不得 ⸲shiu-pat-tak.
Imperfect, 不周全 pat-chau-ts'uen, 有缺 ⸲yau-k'uet.
Imperfection, 缺乏 k'uet-faat.
Imperial, 御 ue⸲, 欽 yum, 皇家 wong-ka.
Imperious, 霸氣 pa⸲-hi⸲.
Impertinent, 犯分 faan⸲-fun, 越禮犯分 uet-⸲lai-faan⸲-fun, 僭分 ts'im⸲-fun, (not concerned) 不關涉 'm-kwaan-ship⸲.
Impetuous, (disposition) 性急 sing⸲-kup.
Impervious, 不得透 'm-tak-t'au⸲.

注　釋

【无形无像】无形的，非实体的。
【无相干】无关紧要的，不重要的。
【鬼仔】顽童。
【犯分】无礼的，不得体的。
【不得透】不能参透的。

注 释

【硬不和】难以调解的。
【硬系】绝对。
【不歇求】强求。
【断无】不可能的。
【困入监/收监】关押，监禁。
【不着】不对, 不恰当。
【无思量】轻率的, 不小心的。

IMP　　125　　IMP

Implacable, 硬不和 ngaang⟩-'m-woh.
Implement, 器 hi⟩, 器具 hi⟩-kue⟩.
Implicate, 拖累 t'oh-lui⟩, 株連 chue-lin, 牽連 kohn-lin.
Implicitly, 無二心 mo-i-sum, 硬係 ngaang⟩-hai⟩.
Implied meaning, 意在言外 i⟩-tsoi⟩-in-ngoi⟩, 內意 noi⟩-i⟩.
Implore, 懇求 ʿhan-kʻau.
Imply, 暗指 om⟩-chi.
Import, (goods) 載——入口 tsoi⟩——yup-ʿhau.
Important, 緊要 ʿkan-iu⟩.
Importune, 呃 ngai, 不歇求 pat-hit-kʻau.
Impose, 加 ka, (upon) 欺騙 hi-pʻin⟩.
Impossible, 斷無 tuen⟩-mo, tuen⟩-mo-keʿ, 勢不得 shai⟩-'m-tak.
Impostor, 光棍 kwong-kwun⟩.
Imposts, 稅鈔 shui⟩-chʻaau⟩.

Impotence, 無能 ʿmo-nang.
Impracticable, 不做得 'm-tso⟩-tak.
Impress, 打印 ʿta-yan⟩, (the mind) 打動 ʿta-tuung⟩, 激 kik.
Imprison, 困入監 kʻwun⟩-yup-ʿkaam, 收監 shau-ʿkaam.
Imprisoned, 坐監 ʿtsʻoh-ʿkaam.
Improbable, 難信 naan-suun⟩, 難有 naan-ʿyau, 不似真 'm-tsʻze-chan.
Improper, 不着 'm-cheuk.
Improve, 越好 uet-ʿho, 做更好 tso⟩-kang⟩-ʿho, (the time) 愛惜光陰 oi⟩-sik-kwong-yum.
Imprudent, 無思量 ʿmo-sze-leung.
Impudent, 不識避忌 'm-shik-piʿ-kiʿ, 放肆 fong⟩-sze⟩, 無忌憚 ʿmo-kiʿ-taan⟩.
Impure, 不潔淨 'm-kitʿ-tsing⟩.

| INC | 126 | INC |

In, (to be) 在 tsoi᾽, 喺 ῾hai, 喺處 ῾hai-shue᾽, 向處 ῾heung-shue᾽, (into) 入 yup.
Inaccurate, 有錯 yau-ts῾oh᾽.
Inadequate, 不夠 ’m-kau᾽.
Inadmissible, 不歸得埋 ’m-kwai-tak-maai.
Inadvertence, 錯誤 ts῾oh᾽-’ng, 失覺 shat-kok.
Inadvertently, 不覺 ’m-kok᾽.
Inattentive, 不用心 ’m-yuung᾽-sum.
Inauspicious, 不吉 pat-kat, 不利市 ’m-li᾽-shi᾽.
Inborn ⎱ 生在內 shaang-
In-bred ⎰ ’tsoi᾽-noi᾽, 天然 t῾in-in, 生成 shaang-sheng.
Incalculable, 不可勝數 pat-῾hoh-shing-῾sho, 無窮 mo-k῾uung.
Incapable, 不能 ’m-nang, 不會 ’m-῾ooi.
Incarnation, 降生 kong᾽-shang.
Incense, (to) 激怒 kik-no᾽.
In῾cense, 香 ῾heung, (sticks) 線香 sin᾽-῾heung, 腳香 keuk᾽-῾heung.

Incessant, 不歇 pat-hit.
Incest, 親屬相姦 ts῾an-shuuk-seung-kaan.
Inch, 寸 ts῾uen᾽.
Incident, 事情 sze᾽-ts῾ing, 偶然事 ῾ngau-in-sze᾽.
Incidental, 偶然 ῾ngau-in, 額外 ngaak-*ngoi᾽.
Incision, 刀傷 to-sheung, 刀路 to-lo.
Incite, 勉勵 ῾min-lai᾽.
Incivility, 無禮 mo-῾lai.
Inclined, 偏歪 p῾in-῾me, 側的 chak-ˌti, (the mind) 心向 sum-heung, 肯 ῾hang.
Inclose, (in a letter) 加封 ka-fuung, (by a fence) 圍埋 wai-maai.
Include, 包在內 paau-tsoi᾽-noi᾽, 包括 paau-k῾oot.
Incoherent talk, 譜話 ngaam᾽-wa᾽.
Income, 入息 yup-sik.
Incomparable, 無雙 mo-sheung, 無比併 ῾mo-῾pi-p῾ing᾽.
Incompatible, 不共得埋 ’m-kuung᾽-tak-maai.

注 释

【不归得埋】难以承认的。
【不歇】连续不断的。
【谵话】语无伦次。
【入息】收入。
【不共得埋】不能相容的。

注释

【菢蛋】孵化。
【唔医得】不能医治的。
【不甩得】去不掉的。
【赔翻】赔偿，补偿。

Incompetent, 不勝任 'm-shing-yum'.
Incomplete, 不齊 'm-ts'ai.
Incomprehensible, 不可測識 pat-ʻhoh-chʻak-shik.
Incongruous } 不對 pat-tui', 唔啱 'm-ngaam.
Inconsistent
Inconstant, 無常 mo-sheung, 不定 pat-ting'.
Incontinent, 不自制 'm-tsze'-chai'.
Inconvenient, 不方便 'm-fong-pin'.
Incorrect, 錯 ts'oh'.
Incorrigible, 頑梗不化 waan-ʻkang-pat-fa'.
Incorruptible, 不壞得 'm-waai'-tak, 不買囑得 'm-ʻmaai-chuuk-tak.
Increase, 加多 ka-toh, 加增 ka-tsang, 添 t'im.
Incredible, 不可信 pat-ʻhoh-suun', 不入信 'm-yup-suun'.
Incubate, 菢蛋 po'-*taan.
Incumbent, 本分 ʻpoon-fun', ʻpoon-fun'-ke'.

Incur, 致 chi', 致到 chi'-to', 招 chiu, 招惹 chiu-ʻye.
Incurable, 唔醫得 'm-i-tak, 無法 ʻmo-faat'.
Indebted, 欠 him', 欠債 him'-chaai'.
Indecent, 非禮 fi-ʻlai, 粗 ts'o.
Indecision, 無決意 ʻmo-kʻuet'-i'.
Indeed, 眞正 chan-ching', 實 shat, 委實 ʻwai-shat, 實在 shat-tsoi'.
Indefatigable, 無倦 ʻmo-kuen'.
Indefinite, 不限定 'm-haan-ting'.
Indelible, 不甩得 'm-lut-tak.
Indemnify, 賠翻 pʻooi-faan.
Independent, 自立 tsze'-laap, 不靠 pat-kʻaau', 另自 ling'-tsze'.
Index, 目錄 muuk-luuk.
India, 印度國 Yan'-to'-kwok'.
Indian corn, 粟米 suuk-ʻmai, 包粟 paau-suuk.

| IND | 128 | INE |

Indian ink, 墨 mak.
India-rubber, 象皮 tseung’-p‘i, 印度樹膠 Yan’-to’-shue’-kaau.
Indicate, 指示 ‘chi-shi’.
Indict, 告狀 ko’-*chong’.
Indifferent, 薄情 pok-ts‘ing, 冷淡 ‘laang-taam’, (any way) 隨隨便便 ts‘ui-ts‘ui-pin’-pin’ (*pin’).
Indigestion, 食滯 shik-chai’.
Indignant, 憾恨 hom’-han’.
Indignation, 惱恨 nau-han’.
Indigo, 藍靛 laam-tin’, (the tree) 藍樹 laam shue’.
Indirect, 非直頭 fi-chik-t‘au, ’m-hai’-chik-t‘au.
Indiscreet, 不仔細 pat-‘tsze-sai’.
Indiscriminately, 無分彼此 ‘mo-fun-‘pi-‘ts‘ze.
Indispensable, 必需 pit-sue, pit-sue-ke’, 少不得 ‘shiu-pat-tak.
Indisposed, 欠安 him’-ohn, 不自在 ’m-tsze’-tsoi’, 渧 nup, (disinclined) 不想 ’m-‘seung.

Indissoluble, 不化得開 ’m-fa’-tak-hoi, 不離得開 ’m-li-tak-hoi.
Indistinct, 不明白 ’m-ming-paak, 未清楚 mi-ts‘ing-‘ch‘oh.
Individual, 位 wai’, (an) 一個人 yat-koh’-yan, (thing) 件 kin’, (See A.), (by itself) 另自 ling’-tsze’.
Indivisible, 不分得 ’m-fun-tak.
Indolent, 躲懶 ‘toh-‘laan.
Indomitable, 不認輸 put-ying’-shue.
Induce, 誘 ‘yau, 招引 chiu-‘yan.
Indulge, 姑息 koo-sik, 縱慣 tsuung’-kwaan’, 放縱 fong’-tsuung’.
Indulgent, 寬大 foon-taai’, (self) 自眼 tsze’-ha’, 自縱 tsze’-tsuung’.
Industrious, 勤工 k‘an-kuung.
Inefficacious, 不靈 pat-leng, ’m-leng, 不應 ’m-ying’.

注 釋

【食滯】消化不良。
【非直头】不直接。
【渧】不舒服的，不愿意的。
【勤工】勤奋。

注释

【不会郁】不会动。
【不便宜】不适当，不明智。
【推度】推断。
【地狱嘅】地狱的，恶魔的，像地狱似的。

INF 129 INF

Inert, 懶 ʻlaan, 不會郁 ’m-ʻooi-yuuk.
Inestimable, 無價寶 ʻmo-kaʼ-ʻpo.
Inevitable, 不免得 ’m-ʻmin-tak, 無奈何 ʻmo-noiʼ-hoh.
Inexcusable, 無可推諉 ʻmo-ʻhoh-tʻui-wai, 無可恕 ʻmo-ʻhoh-shueʼ.
Inexhaustible, 無窮盡 ʻmo-kʻuung-tsuunʼ.
Inexpedient, 不便宜 ’m-pinʼ-i.
Inexperienced, 生手 shaang-ʻshau.
Inexplicable, 無可解 ʻmo-ʻhoh-ʻkaai.
Inexpressible, 言不能盡 in-pat-nang-tsuunʼ, 講不了 ʻkong-’m-ʻliu.
Inextricable, 解不出 ʻkaai-pat-chʻuut, ʻkaai-’m-lut.
Infamous, 臭 chʻauʼ, 醜 ʻchʻau.
Infant, 嬰兒 ying-i, 亞蘇仔 aʼ-soʼ-tsai.

Infantry, 步兵 pooʼ-ping.
Infatuated, 瘋癲 fuung-tin, 入迷魂陣 yup-mai-wan-chanʼ.
Infect, 染 ʻim, 感染 ʻkom-ʻim.
Infectious, 會染 ʻooi-ʻim, 感染 ʻkom-ʻim, ʻkom-ʻim-keʼ.
Infer, 推度 tʻui-tok, 類推 ʻlui-tʻui.
Inferior, 下等 haʼ-ʻtang, 呀 yai, (goods) 呀貨 yai-fohʼ.
Infernal, 地獄嘅 tiʼ-yuuk-ʻkom.
Infest, 紛擾 fun-ʻiu.
Infinite, 無窮 mo-kʻuung, 無限 mo-haanʼ.
Infirm, 衰弱 shui-yeuk.
Inflame, 撥猛火氣 pʻootʼ-ʻmang-fohʼ-hiʼ.
Inflammation, 結熱 kitʼ-it.
Inflate, 鼓起 ʻkoo-ʻhi, (magnify) 張大 cheung-taaiʼ.
Inflexible, 堅硬 kin-ngaangʼ.
Inflict, 加 ka.

Influence, 勢子 *shai'-tsze*, (example) 風化 *fuung-fa'*, (to) 感動 ‛*kom-tuung'*, 化 *fa'*.
Infold, 包裹 *paau-‛kwoh*.
Inform, 話—知 *wa'—chi*, 通知 *t'uung-chi*.
Infuriated, 嬲嬲爆 *nau-nau-paau'*.
Infuse, (tea) 冲茶 *ch'uung-ch'a*, (METAPH.) 浸入去 *tsum'-yup-hue'*.
Ingenious, 精乖 *tseng-kwaai*, 精巧 *tsing-‛haau*.
Ingenuous, 無私心 ‛*mo-sze-sum*, 直白 *chik-paak*, 慷慨 ‛*k'ong-k'oi*, 光明正大 *kwong-ming-ching'-taai'*.
Ingot, 錠 *ting'*, 元寶錠 *uen-‛po-ting'*.
Ingratitude, 忘恩 *mong-yan*.
Ingulf, 吞陷 *t'un-haam'*.
Inhabit, 居 *kue*.
Inhabitant, 居民 *kue-mun*.
Inhale, 吸 *k'up*, 嗽入 *shok'-yup*.

Inherent, 生在內 *shang-tsoi'-noi'*, 自內有 *tsze'-noi'-‛yau*.
Inherit, 承 *shing*, 嗣 *tsze'*.
Inheritance, 家業 *ka-ip*.
Inhuman, 無人性 ‛*mo-yan-sing'*, 狼心 *long-sum*.
Inimitable, 不及得 ‛*m-k'aap-tak*.
Iniquitous, 無道 ‛*mo-to*.
Initiate, 開例 *hoi-lai'*, (introduce) 引進 ‛*yan-tsuun'*, 引入 ‛*yan-yup*.
Injure, 害 *hoi'*, 損害 ‛*suen-hoi'*, 傷害 *sheung-hoi'*.
Injurious, 利害 *li'-hoi'*.
Ink, 墨 *mak*, (liquid) 墨水 *mak-‛shui*.
Ink-stand, 墨水池 *mak-‛shui-ch'i*.
Ink-stone, 墨硯 *mak-in'* (*in'*).
Inland, 內地 *noi'-ti'*.
Inlay, 鑲 *seung*.
Inlet, 入處 *yup-ch'ue'*.
Inmost, 至深 *chi'-shum*, (heart) 深心 *shum-sum*.

注 釋

【勢子】影响，势力。
【嬲嬲爆】狂怒的。
【不及得】无法模仿的，比不上的。
【墨水池】应为"墨水台"。

注释

【新入】创新。
【新冲之事】创新。
【暗剌】暗讽,讽刺,影射。
【了不得咁多】无数的。
【好查问】好问的,好奇的。

INS 131 INS

Inn, 歇店 *hit'-tim'*, 客舘 *haak'-ʻkoon*.
Innate, 天然 *tʻin-in*, 生在內 *shang-tsoi'-noi'*.
Inner, 內 *noi'*.
Innocent, 無罪 *ʻmo-tsui'*.
Innocuous, 無毒 *ʻmo-tuuk*.
Innovate, 新入 *san-yup*.
Innovation, 新冲之事 *san-chʻuung-chi-sze'*.
Innuendo, 暗剌 *omʻ-tsʻze'*.
Innumerable, 不可勝數 *pat-ʻhoh-shing-ʻsho*, 了不得咁多 *ʻliu-pat-tak-komʻ-toh*.
Inoculate, 種痘 *chuungʻ-*tanʻ*.
Inordinate, 無節制 *ʻmo-tsitʻ-chai'*, 濫 *laamʻ*.
Inquest, 驗屍 *imʻ-shi*.
Inquire, 訪問 *fong-mun'*.
Inquisitive, 好查問 *hoʻ-chʻa-mun'*.
Insane, 發癲 *faatʻ-tin*.
Insatiable, 無厭 *ʻmo-imʻ*, 不知足 *ʻm-chi-tsuuk*.
Inscription, 碑文 *pi-mun*, 扁額 *ʻpin-ngaak*.

Inscrutable, 不可測 *pat-ʻhoh-chʻak*.
Insect, 蟲 *chʻuung*, 細腰蟲 *saiʻ-iu-chʻuung*.
Insecure, 不穩 *ʻm-ʻwan*.
Insensible, 無知覺 *ʻmo-chi-kok*, 痳痹 *ma-muuk*, 不省人事 *ʻm-ʻsing-yan-sze'*.
Inseparable, 觧不開 *ʻkaai-ʻm-hoi*, 不分得 *ʻm-fun-tak*.
Insert, 插入 *chʻaapʻ-yup*, 入 *yup*, 鑲 *seung*.
Inside, 裏頭 *ʻlue-tʻau*, 裏面 *ʻlue-min'*, 內 *noi'*.
Insidious, 多變 *toh-pinʻ*, 奸猾 *kaan-waat*.
Insignificant, 微毫 *mi-ho*, 微末 *mi-moot*, 虛 *hue*.
Insincere, 不至誠 *ʻm-chiʻ-shing*.
Insinuate, 讒佞 *tsʻaam-ning'*, 偷偷入 *tʻau-tʻau-yup*.
Insipid, 淡 *taamʻ*, *tʻaam*, 無味道 *ʻmo-miʻ-to'*.

INS 132 INS

Insist, 勒令 lak-ling᾿, 必要 pit-iu᾿.
Insnare, 陷害 haam᾿-hoi᾿, 籠絡 luung-lok᾿.
Insolent, 傲慢 ngo᾿-maan᾿, 侮慢人嘅 ῾moo-maan᾿-yan-ke᾿.
Insoluble, 不化得 ᾿m-fa᾿-tak, 不解得 ᾿m-῾kaai-tak.
Insolvent, 債墩 chaai᾿-tun.
Insomuch, 致于 chi᾿-ue, 致到 chi᾿-to᾿, 甚至 shum᾿-chi᾿.
Inspect, 查察 ch῾a-ch῾aat᾿, 監 kaam, 督 tuuk.
Inspector, 監督 kaam-tuuk.
Inspire, 吸氣 k῾up-hi᾿, (divinely) 默牖 mak-῾yau.
Inspirit, 悚起 ῾suung-῾hi, 聳動 ῾suung-tuung᾿.
Instable, 不穩 ᾿m-῾wan.
Instance, (for) 比如 ῾pi-ue.
Instant, 片刻 p῾in᾿-haak᾿.
Instead, (of) 替代 t῾ai᾿-toi᾿.
Instep, 脚背彎 keuk᾿-pooi᾿-waan.
Instigate, 唆悚 soh-῾suung.

Instil, 浸入去 tsum᾿-yup-hue᾿.
Instinct, 性情 sing᾿-ts῾ing, 本性 ῾poon-sing᾿.
Institute, 設 ch῾it᾿.
Instruct, 教 kaau᾿.
Instruction, 教訓 kaau᾿-fun᾿, 教令 kaau᾿-ling᾿.
Instrument, 器具 hi᾿-kue᾿.
Insubordination, 違逆 wai-yik.
Insufferable, 不忍得 ᾿m-῾yan-tak, ᾿m-῾yan-tak-ke᾿.
Insufficient, 不够 ᾿m-kau.
Insult, 欺負 hi-foo᾿, 凌辱 ling-yuuk, 侮慢 ῾moo-maan᾿.
Insuperable, 過不得 kwoh᾿-pat-tak, kwoh᾿-᾿m-tak-ke᾿, 不過得去 ᾿m-kwoh᾿-tak-hue᾿.
Insupportable, 當不起 tong-pat-῾hi, tong-᾿m-῾hi-ke᾿.
Insurance, 保險 ῾po-῾him.
Insure, 買保險 ῾maai-῾po-῾him.
Insurrection, 作亂 tsok᾿-luen᾿.

注 释

【不化得】不能溶解的。
【債墩】破产者。
【唆悚】唆使,教唆。
【浸入去】渗透。
【过不得】不可逾越的。

注 释

【代求】调解，求情。
【引动个心】引起兴趣的，令人关注的。
【万国公法】即国际法。美国人惠顿（Henry Wheaton）著的 *Elements of International Law*，由在北京同文馆执教的美国人丁韪良（W.A.P.Martin）译后出版，定名为《万国公法》，是中国刊印的第一部中文的西方国际法著作。

INT 133 INT

Integrity, 純厚 shuun-hau', 剛正 kong-ching'.
Intelligence, 見識 kin'-shik, (news) 聲氣 sheng-hi'.
Intelligent, 聰明 ts'uung-ming.
Intelligible, 明白 ming-paak.
Intemperance, 放恣 fong'-ts'ze', 縱恣 tsuung'-ts'ze', 無度 mo-to'.
Intend, 意欲 i'-yuuk, 欲想 yuuk'-seung.
Intense, 極甚 kik-shum'.
Intention, 意思 i'-sze', 意 i'.
Intentioned, 有意 yau-i', 故意 koo'-i'.
Intentness, 專心 chuen-sum.
Inter, 葬埋 tsong'-maai.
Intercalary, 閏 yuun'.
Intercede, 代求 toi'-k'au.
Intercept, 攔截 laan-tsit.
Interchange, 相換 seung-oon', 交易 kaau-yik.
Intercourse, 交接 haau-tsip', 往來 wong-loi.
Interdict, 禁戒 kum'-kaan'.
Interest, 利息 li'-sik, 利錢 li'-ts'in.

Interest, (to move) 打動 ta-tuung', (concern) 關 kwaan.
Interesting, 引動个心 yan-tuung'-koh'-sum.
Interfere, 涉 ship', 理 'li, 打理 'ta-'li, (meddle) 插手 ch'aap'-'shau, 插嘴 ch'aap'-'tsui.
Interim, 時間 shi-kaan.
Interior, 內地 noi'-ti', 裏頭 'lue-t'au.
Interlace, 交加 kaau-ka.
Interleave, 隔紙 kaak'-'chi.
Intermediate, 中間 chuung-kaan.
Intermission, 停息之間 t'ing-sik-chi-kaan.
Intermit, 間歇 kaan'-hit'.
Internal, 內 noi'.
International law, 萬國公法 maan'-kwok'-kuung-faat'.
Interpolate, 混入字句 wan'-yup-tsze'-kue'.
Interpose, 入中間 yup-chuung-kaan, 入其中 yup-k'i-chuung.

INT 134 INT

Interpret, 傳話 ch'uen-*wa', 解 ‘kaai.
Interpreter, 通事 t'uung-*sze', 傳供 ch'uen-kuung, (official) 繙譯官 faan-yik-koon.
Interrogate, 盤問 p'oon-mun'.
Interrupt, 阻斷 ‘choh-t'uen, 阻定 ‘choh-ting', 攪轉處 ‘kaau-‘chuen-shue'.
Intersect, 相交 seung-kaau.
Interstice, 疏罅 shoh-la'.
Interval, 間 kaan.
Intervene, 入中間 yup-‘chuung-kaan.
Interview, 面見 min'-kin'.
Intestines, 腸 ch'eung, *ch'eung.
Intimate, 相熟 seung-shuuk, 親 ts'an, 親近 ts'an-kan', (to) 告知 ko'-chi.
Intimidate, 恐嚇 ‘huung-haak', 嚇壓 ha-aat', (in order to extort) 嚇霸 ha-pa'.
Into, 入 yup, 入內 yup-noi'.

Intolerable, 難容 naan-yuung, 不容得 'm-yuung-tak, 不抵得 'm-‘tai-tak.
Intoxicated, 醉酒 tsui'-‘tsau.
Intoxicating, 會醉人 ‘ooi-tsui'-yan, ‘ooi-tsui'-ke'.
Intractable, 不受教 'm-shau'-kaau'.
Intrenchment, 營壘 ying-‘lui.
Intrepid, 膽生毛 ‘taam-shaang-mo.
Intricate, 錯雜 ts'ok'-tsaap.
Intrigue, 詭詐 ‘kwai-cha'. (to) 挑唆 t'iu-soh, 奸計 kaan-kai'.
Introduce, 引入 ‘yan-yup, 引進 ‘yan-tsuun', 引見 ‘yan-kin', (a subject) 提起 t'ai-‘hi, 挈 k'it'.
Introduction, (to a book) 小引 ‘siu-‘yan, (recommendation) 荐書 tsin'-shue.
Intrude, 搪揬 t'ong-tat, 插入 ch'aap'-yup, 撞入去 chong'-yup-hue'.
Intrusive, 躁暴 ts'o'-po'.

注 釋

【通事】解释者，口译者。
【疏罅】空隙，裂缝。

注 释

【潦水】洪水。
【补力】滋补。
【不伤犯得】不能侵犯的。
【不做得主】义务的，强制的。

Intrust, 托 *t'ok*, 交托 *kaau-t'ok*.	Inveterate, 舊無改 *kau-'mo-'koi*, 根深柢固 *kan-shum-'tai-koo*, 久病難醫 *'kau-peng-'naan-i*.
Intuitively, (to know) 生而知之 *shang-i-chi-chi*.	
Inundate, 水漲 *'shui-cheung*, 水浸 *'shui-tsum*, 水浸嗮 *'shui-tsum-saai*.	Invidious, 招妒忌 *chiu-to'-ki'*.
	Invigorate, 補力 *'po-lik*.
Inundation, 潦水 *'lo-'shui*.	Invincible, 無敵 *'mo-tik*.
Invade, 侵入去 *ts'um-yup-hue'*.	Inviolable, 不傷犯得 *'m-sheung-faan'-tak*.
Invalid, 病壞 *peng'-waai'*.	Invisible, 無形可見 *'mo-ying-'hoh-kin'*.
Invaluable, 無價寶 *mo-ka'-'po*.	Invitation-card, 請帖 *'ts'eng-'t'ip*.
Invariable, 不易 *pat-yik*.	Invite, 請 *'ts'eng*.
Inveigh, 鬧 *naau'*.	Invoice, 貨單 *foh'-taan*.
Inveigle, 鈎引 *kau-'yan*.	Invoke, 呼籲 *foo-yeuk*.
Invent, 製造 *chai'-tso'*.	Involve, 拖累 *t'oh-lui*, 連累 *lin-lui*.
Inventory, 物業單 *mat-ip-taan*.	
Invert, 倒轉 *'to-'chuen*.	Involuntary, 不做得主 *'m-tso'-tak-'chue*.
Inverted, 顛倒 *tin-'to*.	Inward, 內 *noi'*.
Invest, with, 加 *ka*, (money for profit) 出息 *ch'uut-sik*, (in property) 置寶業 *chi'-shat-ip*.	Ipomœa, 錦屏風 *'kum-p'ing-fuung*, (reptans) 甕菜 *ung'-ts'oi'*.
	Iris, 眼睛 *ngaan-tsing*, 烏睛 *oo-tsing*, (flower) 亡憂花 *mong-yau-fa*.
Investigate, 查察 *ch'a-ch'aat*, 追究 *chui-kau*.	

英粵字典

Iron, 鐵 t'it, (for clothes) 熨斗 t'ong-'tau, (to) 熨 t'ong.	Irritable, 嬲嬲 nau-nat, 火頸 'foh-'keng.
Ironically, to speak, 鑿人 tsok-yan, 反倒轉講 'faan-'to-'chuen-'kong.	Irritate, 激嬲 kik-nau, 撩起 'liu-'hi.
Irony, 杯奬話 pooi-'tseung-*wa'.	Irritated, 谷氣 kuuk-hi'.
	Is, 係 hai', 是 shi', (there is) 有 'yau.
Irrational, 無情理 'mo-ts'ing-'li.	Isinglass, 魚膠 ue-kaau.
Irrecoverable, 不得翻 'm-tak-faan.	Island, 海島 'hoi-'to, 海洲 'hoi-chau.
Irregular, 亂 luen', 無法度 'mo-faat'-to, 不齊 'm-ts'ai.	Isolated, 另自 ling'-tsze'.
	Issue, (to) 發 faat', 出 ch'uut.
Irrelevent, 丫丫開 a-a-hoi', nga-nga-hoi.	Isthmus, 山腰 shaan-iu.
	It, 佢 'k'ue.
Irremediable, 無奈何 'mo-noi'-hoh, 無法可救 'mo-faat'-'hoh-kau'.	Itch, 癩 laai'.
	Itching, 痕 han, 痕癢 han-yeung.
	Itinerary, 路程 lo'-ch'ing.
Irresistible, 無人敵得住 'mo-yan-tik-tak-chue'.	Ivory, 象牙 tseung'-nga.
	Ivy, 藤 t'ang, 長春藤 ch'eung-ch'uun-t'ang.
Irresolute, 無主意 'mo-'chue-i', 無定性 'mo-ting'-sing'.	**J**
	Jabber, 孜孜咱咱 tsze-tsze-tsa-tsa.
Irrigate, 灌漑 koon'-k'oi', 淋瀨 lum-laai'.	Jacana, 白勝鷄 paak-shing'-kai.

注 釋

【鑿人】諷刺別人。
【杯奬話】反語，諷刺。
【丫丫開】不相干的。
【谷气】生气，憋气。
Isthmus: 地峡，指穿过水体连接两块陆地的狭长陆地。译为"山腰"属误译。
【孜孜咱咱】急切而含糊地说。

注释

【狗牙样】锯齿状。
【谵话】行语，土话。
【牙关骨】颚骨。
【力逼】猛拉，猛推。

JAR 137 JES

Jacinth, 赤玉 ch'ik-yuuk.
Jack-fruit, 波羅蜜 poh-loh-mat.
Jackal, 野狗 ʻye-ʻkau, 狗貛 ʻkau-foon.
Jack-daw, 烏雀 oo-tseuk'.
Jacket, 短衫 ʻtuen-shaam.
Jadestone, 璧 pik, 玉石 yuuk-shek.
Jagged, 狗牙樣 ʻkau-nga-*yeungʻ.
Jail, 監房 kaam-fong.
Jailer, 司獄 sze-yuuk, 看監 ʻhohn-ʻkaam, 禁子 kumʻ-ʻtsze.
Jam, 糖菓 t'ong-ʻkwoh, (to) 逼 pik, 逼實 pik-shat, 逼緊 pik-ʻkan.
Jangle, 吵鬧 ʻch'aau-naauʻ.
January, 英正月 Ying-ching-uet.
Japan, 日本國 Yat-ʻpoon-kwokʻ.
Jar, (a) 埕 ch'ing, 塔 t'aapʻ, 罌 ʻaang, 瓶 *p'eng, 甕缸 uungʻ-kong, (to) 相撞 seung-p'uungʻ, 爭拗 chaang-aauʻ.

Jargon, 譫話 ngaamʻ-waʻ.
Jasper, 碧玉 pik-yuuk.
Jatropha, 桐樹 t'uung-shueʻ.
Jaundice, 黃疸 wongʻ-t'aan.
Jaunt, 出遊 ch'uut-yau.
Java-sparrow, 和鵠 ʻwoh-kuuk.
Javelin, 手箭 ʻshau-tsinʻ, 標 piu.
Jaw, 牙牀 nga-ch'ong.
Jaw-bone, 牙關骨 nga-kwaan-kwut.
Jay, 鵲 ts'euk.
Jealous, 妒忌 toʻ-kiʻ.
Jealousy, 嫉妒 tsat-toʻ.
Jeer, 戲弄 hiʻ-luungʻ, 欺笑 hi-siuʻ, 譏誚 ki-ts'iuʻ.
JEHOVAH, 耶和華 YE-WOH-WA.
Jelly, 菓汁 ʻkwoh-chup, (animal) 糕 ko, (generally) 凍 ʻtuung.
Jeopardy, 危險 ngai-ʻhim.
Jerk, 力逼 lik-pik, 扭 ʻnau.
Jessamine, 茉莉花 moot-liʻ-fa.
Jest, 講笑 ʻkong-siuʻ.
Jesting, 笑話 siuʻ-*waʻ.

| JOI | 138 | JUD |

JESUS, 耶穌 YE-*SOO*.
Jet, (fossil) 黑玉 *hak-yuuk*, (of water) 射水 *she*ʾ-ʿ*shui*, 浙水線 *chit*ʾ-ʿ*shui-sin*ʾ.
Jetty, 馬頭 ʿ*ma*-**t*ʿ*au*.
Jew, 猶太人 *Yau-t*ʿ*aai*ʾ-*yan*.
Jewel, 珍寶 *chan-*ʿ*po*, 寶玉 ʿ*po-yuuk*.
Jigger, 沙虱 *sha-shat*.
Jingall, 銃 *ch*ʿ*uung*ʾ.
Jingle, 响動聲 ʿ*heung-tuung*ʾ-*sheng*, (COL.) *kwing-kwang*, *kwang-lang*.
Job, (a) 一件工夫 *yat-kin*ʾ-*kuung-foo*.
Job-work, 散工 ʿ*saan-kuung*.
Jog, 搂 *p*ʿ*uung*ʾ, (along) 躊躊吓 ʿ*ch*ʿ*au-ch*ʿ*au-ha*.
Joggle, 挈 *ngo*.
Join, 連 *lin*, 合埋 *hop-maai*, 附貼 *foo*ʾ-*t*ʿ*ip*ʾ.
Joint, 節 *tsit*ʾ, (ginglymus) 骨計 *kwat-*kai*ʾ.
Joint-stock, 合本 *hop*-ʿ*poon*.
Joist, 樓陣 **lau-chan*ʾ, 桁 *haang.

Joke, (to) 講笑 ʿ*kong-siu*ʾ, 調笑 *t*ʿ*iu-siu*ʾ, 打諢 ʿ*ta-wun*ʾ.
Jolly, 福相 *fuuk-seung*ʾ, 寬容 *foon-yuung*, 爽快 ʿ*shong-faai*ʾ.
Jolt, 嘌蕩 *p*ʿ*iu-tong*ʾ, 移移郁 *i-i-yuuk*.
Jonquil, 水仙花 ʿ*shui-ʿsin-fa*.
Jostle, 挵郁 *p*ʿ*uung*ʾ-*yuuk*.
Jot, 點 ʿ*tim*.
Journal, 日記 *yat-ki*ʾ.
Journey, 路程 *lo*ʾ-*ch*ʿ*ing*, 程 *ch*ʿ*ing*.
Jovial, 快活 *faai*ʾ-*oot*.
Joy, 喜樂 ʿ*hi-lok*.
Jubilee, 禧年 *hi*-*nin*.
Judea, 猶太國 *Yau-t*ʿ*aai*ʾ-*kwok*.
Judge, 按察司 *ohn*ʾ-*ch*ʿ*aat*ʾ-*sze*, 審事官 ʿ*shum-sze-koon*, (to) 審判 ʿ*shum-p*ʿ*oon*ʾ.
Judgment-day, 審判日子 ʿ*shum-p*ʿ*oon*ʾ-*yat-*ʿ*tsze*.
Judicious, 好打筭 ʿ*ho-*ʿ*ta-suen*ʾ.

注 释

【挈】轻摇。
【移移郁】使颠簸、摇晃。
【拼郁】推撞，争夺。
【禧年】周年庆祝（尤指50或25周年纪念）。
【审事官】法官。
【审判日子】基督教中所说的世界末日。

注释

【耳瓶】水壶。
【斥法】戏法，杂耍。
【大眼鸡】船。
【䑀】翻倒，倾覆。
【快利】锐利的，敏锐的。

JUR　　139　　KEE

Jug, 耳瓶 ʻi-*pʻeng.
Jugglery, 斥法 chʻik-faat'.
Juice, 汁 chup, 汁漿 chup-tseung.
Jujube, 棗 ʻtso.
July, 英七月 Ying-tsʻat-uet.
Jumble, 打混 ʻta-wun', 混亂 wun'-luen'.
Jump, 跳 tʻiu', up and down, 喐喐吓 ngup-ngup-*ha'.
Junction, 相交處 seung-kaau-chʻue'.
June, 英六月 Ying-luuk-uet.
Jungle, 叢林 tsʻuung-lum.
Junior, 少年 shiu'-nin, 少 shiu', 後生 hau'-shaang.
Juniper, 扁柏 ʻpin-pʻaak'.
Junk, 船 shuen, 大眼雞 taai'-ʻngaan-ˌkai.
Jupiter, (planet) 木星 muuk-ˌsing.
Jury, 秉公之人 ʻping-ˌkuung-chi-yan, 陪審官 pʻooi-ʻshum-ˌkoon.

Just, 公平 ˌkuung-pʻing, 公道 ˌkuung-to', (ADV.) 僅 ʻkan, 啱啱 ˌngaam-ˌngaam, 剛啱 ˌkong-ˌngaam.
Justice, 公道 ˌkuung-to', 公義 ˌkuung-i', (to do) 秉公 ʻping-ˌkuung, Chief 按察司 ohn'-chʻaat-sze,—of peace 紳士 ˌshan-sze'.
Justify, 以為義 ʻi-wai-i'.
Jut-out, 凸出來 tut-chʻuut-lai.
Juvenile, 嫩 nuen'.

K

Kaleidoscope, 萬花筒 maan'-ˌfa-tʻuung.
Kalpa, 劫 kip'.
Keel, 䑀 ngo.
Keen, 快利 faai'-li', 爽利 ʻshong-li', 關係 ˌkwaan-hai'.
Keep, 守 ʻshau, 留 lau, 收埋 ˌshau-maai, 常有 ˌsheung-ʻyau, 存 tsʻuen.

Keeper, 看守人 hohn-ˈshau-yan.	Kiln, 窰 iu, 燒窰 shiu-iu.
Keepsake, 表記 ˈpiu-ki⸴.	Kind, (sort) 類 lui⸴, 樣 yeung⸴, *yeung⸴, 種 ˈchuung.
Kerchief, 巾 kan.	Kind, (good) 好心田 ˈho-sum-tʻin, 腹心 fuuk-sum.
Kernel, 核 wat, 仁 yan, ngan, 粒 nup.	Kindle, 起火 ˈhi-ˈfoh, 着火 cheuk-ˈfoh, 透火 tʻau⸴-ˈfoh.
Kerosine, 煤油 mooi-yau, 火水 ˈfoh-ˈshui.	
Ketchup, 豉油 shi⸴-yau.	Kindness, 惠愛 wai⸴-oi⸴.
Kettle, 提壺 tʻai-*oo, 煲 po.	Kindred, 親戚 tsʻan-tsʻik.
Key, 鎖匙 ˈsoh-shi.	King, 王 wong.
Key-hole, 鎖匙眼 ˈsoh-shi-ˈngaan.	King-crab, 鱟 hau⸴.
	Kingdom, 國 kwok.
Khan, 可汗 ˈhoh-hohn⸴.	Kingfisher, 釣魚郎 tiu⸴-ue-long, (feathers of) 翠毛 tsʻui⸴-mo.
Kick, 踢 tʻek⸴.	
Kid, 山羊仔 shaan-*yeung-ˈtsai.	Kiss, 啜面朘 chuet-min⸴-ˈchue, 親嘴 tsʻan-ˈtsui.
Kidnap, 拐帶 ˈkwaai-taai⸴.	Kitchen, 廚房 chʻue-*fong, (opsonium) 送 suung⸴.
Kidnapper, 拐帶佬 ˈkwaai-taai⸴-ˈlo, 拐子佬 ˈkwaai-ˈtsze-ˈlo.	Kite, (bird) 鳶 uen, (paper) 紙鷂 ˈchi-*iu, (to fly) 放紙鷂 fong⸴-ˈchi-*iu.
Kidney, 內腎 noi⸴-shan⸴, (of beasts) 腰子 iu-ˈtsze.	Knapsack, 背袋 pooi⸴-*toi⸴.
	Knave, 光棍 kwong-kwun⸴.
Kill, 殺 shaat, 殺死 shaat⸴-sze, 打死 ˈta-ˈsze, 整死 ˈching-ˈsze, (animals) 劏 tʻong.	Knead, 搓 chʻaai (COL.) nuuk.
	Knee, 膝 sat, 膝頭哥 sat-tʻau-koh.

注释

【表记】纪念品。
【拐带佬】人贩子。
【啜面脧】亲脸蛋。
【纸鹞】风筝。

注 释

【粒凸】鼓起。
【号标】商标。

KOH 141 LAC

Knee-pan, 膝頭骨 sat-t'au-kwut.
Kneel, 屈膝 wat-sat, 跪下 kwai'-ha'.
Knife, 刀 to, (a) 一張刀 yat-‿cheung-‿to, 一把刀 yat-‿pa-‿to.
Knight, 巴圖魯 pa-t'o-‿lo.
Knit, 桃織 t'iu-chik, (the brows) 皺眉頭 tsau'-mi-t'au.
Knob, 粒珠 nup-‿chue, 粒凸 nup-tuet, 粒頂 nup-‿teng, 鈕 ‿nau.
Knock, 打 ‿ta, 拍 p'aak', 揿 ‿hom.
Knocking, (COL.) pop-pop.
Knot, (to) 打結 ‿ta-kit', ‿ta-lit', (a) 結頭 kit'-t'au, lit'-t'au, (in wood) 罌 ‿ang, (any thing small) 粒 nup.
Know, 知 chi, 知到 chi-to', 識 shik, 識得 shih-tak.
Knowledge, 見識 kin'-shik.
Knuckle, 拳頭骨 k'uen-t'au-kwut.
Kohl rabi, 芥蘭頭 kaai'-*laan-t'au.

L

Label, 號標 ho'-piu, 號頭紙 ho'-t'au-‿chi.
Laborious, 辛苦 san-‿foo, 勤苦 k'an-‿foo.
Labour, 工夫 kuung-foo, (to) 做工夫 tso'-kuung-foo, 勞力 lo-lik, (in-) 臨產 lum-‿ch'aan.
Labourer, 工人 kuung-yan.
Labyrinth, 曲折 huuk-chit'.
Labrus, 黃花魚 wong-fa-*ue.
Lac, 紫梗 ‿tsze-‿kang.
Lace, 織線衣邊 chik-sin'-i-‿pin, 花邊 fa-‿pin, 線帶 sin'-*taai'.
Lacerate, 抓爛 ‿chaau-laan'.
Lack, 少 ‿shiu, 欠 him', 無 ‿mo.
Lacker, 漆 ts'at, (ware) 漆器 ts'at-hi'.
Lad, 細蚊仔 sai'-‿mun-‿tsai, 童 t'uung, 後生 hau'-‿shaang.

Ladder, 梯 ,t'ai, (a hand-) 手梯 ‚shau-t'ai.
Lade, (to load) 落貨 lok-foh², (to lift) 扂 foo², 舀 ‚iu, 拂 fut.
Ladle, 杓 sheuk², 勺 cheuk², 殼 hok².
Lady, 娘 ‚neung, 師奶 sze-‚naai, 奶奶 ‚naai-‚naai, 夫人 ‚foo-yan.
Lady's maid, 梳頭媽 ‚shoh-‚t'au-*‚ma.
Lag, 落後便 lok-hau²-pin².
Lake, 湖 ‚oo.
Lamb, 緜羊仔 min-*‚yeung-‚tsai, 羔 ‚ko.
Lame, 跛腳 pai-keuk².
Lament, 嘆惜 t'aan²-sik, 哭訴 huuk-so².
Lamentable, 可哀 ‚hoh-oi.
Lamp, 燈 ‚tang, 盞燈 ‚chaan-‚tang, 枝燈 chi-‚tang, 眼燈 *‚ngaan-‚tang.
Lamp-chimney, 燈筒 ‚tang-*t'uung.
Lamp-shade, 燈罩 ‚tang-chaau².

Lamp-wick, 燈心 ‚tang-sum.
Lamp-black, 烏烟 ‚oo-in.
Lampoon, 白抄 paak-‚ch'aau.
Lance, 鎗矛 ‚ts'eung-maau.
Lancet, 開瘡刀 ‚hoi-‚ch'ong-‚to.
Land, 地 ti², (cultivated) 田 ‚t'in, (by) 旱路 ‚hohn-lo², (to) 上岸 ‚sheung-ngohn².
Landing-place, 步頭 po²-‚t'au, 馬頭 ‚ma-t'au.
Landlord, 屋主 uuk-‚chue, 地主 ti²-‚chue, (of an inn) 店主 tim²-‚chue.
Landscape, 光景 ‚kwong-‚king, 山水景 ‚shaan-‚shui-‚king.
Lane, 巷 *hong², 冷巷 ‚laang-*hong².
Language, 話 *wa², (speech) 口音 ‚hau-yum.
Languid, 神倦 ‚shan-kuen², 懺倦 p'aai²-kuen².
Lank, 凹 nup, 凹 nep².
Lantern, 燈籠 ‚tang-luung.
Lap, 膝頭處 sat-t'au-shue², 衫被 ‚shaam-p'i, (to) 舔 ‚lim, (COL.) ‚laai.

注 释

【师奶】妇人。
【梳头妈】女佣。
【白抄】讽刺文章。
【步头】登陆处，渡口。
【神倦】倦怠的。

注释

【衿】翻领。
【船左】左舷。
【赞得过】值得赞赏的。

LAT　　143　　LAW

Lapel, 衿 ͵yum.
Lapse, 過 kwoh⌐.
Larboard, 船左 shuen-‵tsoh.
Lard, 豬油 chue-yau.
Large, 大 taai⌐.
Lark, 百鴒 paak⌐-ling, 山麻雀 shaan-ma-tseuk⌐.
Larkspur, 彩雀花 ‵ts‵oi-tseuk-fa.
Larva, 蠘蠘 ts‵ai-ts‵o, 蟲 ch‵uung.
Lascivious, 淫亂 yum-luen⌐.
Lash, 鞭 pin.
Last, 末 moot, 尾 ‵mi, 收尾 shau-‵mi, (year, &c.) 昨 tsok, 舊 kau⌐, (to) 久存 ‵kau-ts‵uen, 留 lau, 衿 k‵um.
Last, (a) 鞋楦 haai-huen⌐.
Latch, (a door-) 門軌 moon-‵kwai.
Late, 遲 ch‵i, 慢 maan⌐, (in the day) 晏 aan⌐, 挨晚 ͵aai-‵maan, aai-*‵maan, (at night) 夜 ye⌐.
Lately, 近來 kan⌐-loi, 就先 tsau⌐-sin.

Latest, 至後 chi⌐-hau⌐, 至新 chi⌐-san.
Lath, 木片 muuk-p‵in⌐, 桷 kok⌐.
Lath and plaster wall, 假墻 ‵ka-ts‵eung.
Lathe, 車牀 ch‵e-ch‵ong.
Latitude, 地緯度 ti⌐-‵wai-to⌐.
Lattice, 欖核格 ‵laam-wat-kaak⌐, 象眼籬 tseung⌐-‵ngaan-li.
Laudable, 讚得過 tsaan⌐-tak-kwoh⌐.
Laudanum, 鴉片酒 a-p‵in⌐-‵tsau.
Laugh, 笑 siu⌐.
Laughable, 好笑 ‵ho-siu⌐.
Laughing stock, 笑柄 siu⌐-peng⌐, 酸梅 suen-*‵mooi.
Laurel, 桂 kwai⌐, 丹桂 taan-kwai⌐.
Lavish, 破費 p‵oh⌐-fai⌐.
Law, 法律 faat⌐-luut, 律例 luut-lai⌐, (to go to) 打官司 ‵ta-koon-sze.
Lawyer, 狀師 chong⌐-‵sze.

LEA　144　LEA

Law-suit, 官訟 koon-tsuung'. 案件 ohn'-*kin'.
Lawsonia, 指甲花 'chi-kaap'-fa.
Lax, 鬆 suung, (morally) 心鬆 sum-suung.
Laxative, 微利藥 mi-li'-yeuk.
Lay, (to) 放下 fong'-ʿha, (up) 藏 ts'ong, 藏埋 ts'ong-maai, 擠埋 chai-maai.
Layer, 層 ts'ang.
Lazy, 懶惰 ʿlaan-toh'.
Lead, 鉛 uen, 黑鉛 hak-uen, (the) 泵鉈 tum'-*t'oh.
Lead, (to) 引 ʿyan, 引導 ʿyan-to', 帶 taai', (by the hand) 拖 t'oh, 拖住 t'oh-chue'.
Leader, 頭目 t'au-muuk.
Leaf, 葉 ip, (of a book) 篇 p'in.
Leaf-fan, 葵扇 k'wai-shin'.
League, (combine) 聯合 luen-hop.
League, (10 'li) 塘汛 t'ong-suun', 甫路 ʿp'o-lo'.
Leak, 漏水 lau'-ʿshui, 滲漏 shum'-lau'.
Lean, 瘦 shau', (to) 極側 chaap-chak, (upon) 倚着 ʿi-cheuk, 挨埋 aai-maai.
Leap, 跳 t'iu', (over) 躐 naam'.
Leap-frog, 跳猪肉臺 t'iu-chue-yuuk-*t'oi.
Learn, 學 hok, (and practice) 學習 hok-tsaap, (begin to) 上學 ʿsheung-hok.
Learned, 博學 pok'-hok.
Lease, 批 p'ai, (to) 租賃 tso-yum'.
Least, 至小 chi'-ʿsiu, (the least quantity) 的咁多 tik-kom'-toh, (not the) 無的 ʿmo-tik.
Leather, 熟皮 shuuk-p'i.
Leave, (to) 離別 li-pit, 離 li, (things) 漏 lau', 嚫 laai', (alone) 由得 yau-tak, (to take) 告別 ko'-pit, (to ask for) 請假 ʿts'eng-ka', (permission) 許准 ʿhue-ʿchuun.

注　釋

【微利药】泻药。
【挨埋】挨在一起。
【跳猪肉台】跳山羊，跳背游戏。
【的咁多】一点点。

注 释

【下风便】背风处。
【牛蜞】水蛭，蚂蟥。
【丢眼角】抛媚眼。
【使左咋】左撇子。
【依例】合法的。
【幽頞】狐猴。

LEG　145　LEO

Leaven, 酵 *kaau*ʾ, 酒餅 ʿtsau-ʿpeng, (to) 發酵 faatʾ-ʿkaau.
Lecherous, 好嫖 hoʾ-pʿiu.
Lecture, 講書 ʿkong-shue.
Ledge, (on a wall) 級 ngap, (of rocks) 石檯 shek-tʿoi.
Ledger, 登記簿 tang-ki-*poʾ.
Lee, 下風便 haʾ-fuung-*pinʾ.
Leech, 牛蜞 ngau-kʿi, 蜞姆 kʿi-ʿna.
Leek, 韭菜 ʿkau-tsʿoi.
Leer, 丟眼角 tiu-ngaan-*kok.
Lees, 渣 cha, 肌 ngan.
Left, the 左 ʿtsoh, (what is) 餘剩 ue-shingʾ.
Left handed 使左咋 ʿshai-ʿtsoh-ʿyaau.
Leg, 脚 keuk, 小腿 ʿsiu-ʿtʿui, (calf) 脚瓜 keukʾ-kwa, 脚囊 keukʾ-ʿnong.
Leg of mutton, 羊髀 yeung-ʿpi.
Legacy, 遺囑財物 wai-chuuk-tsʿoi-mat.
Legal, 依例 i-laiʾ.

Legation, 欽差衙門 yum-chʿaai-nga-*moon.
Legend, 古語 ʿkoo-ʿue.
Leggings, 套褲 tʿoʾ-fooʾ.
Legislate, 設例 chʿit-laiʾ.
Legislative council, 定例局 tingʾ-laiʾ-kuuk.
Legitimate, (proper) 正 chingʾ, 着 cheuk.
Leisure, 閒 haan, 閒暇 haan-haʾ, (at) 得閒 tak-haan.
Leisurely, 慢慢 maanʾ-*maanʾ.
Lemon, 檸檬 ning-ʿmuung.
Lemonade, 檸檬水 ning-ʿmuung-ʿshui.
Lemur, 幽頞 yau-aat.
Lend, 借去 tseʾ-hue, 借過 tseʾ-kwohʾ.
Lengthwise, 從長 tsʿuung-chʿeung, 長便 chʿeung-pinʾ, 掂 tim.
Lenient, 寬恕 foon-shueʾ.
Lens, 玻璃鑒 poh-li-suiʾ.
Lentil, 扁豆 ʿpin-*tau.
Leopard, 金錢豹 kum-tsʿin-pʿaauʾ.

LEV　146　LI

Leprosy, 痲瘋 ma-fuung.
Leprous, 發瘋 faat-fuung.
Less, 小 ʽsiu, 更小 kangˌ-ʽsiu, 少 ˌshiu.
Lessen, 減少 ʽkaam-ˌshiu.
Lesson, 課 fohˌ, (daily-) 日課 yat-fohˌ.
Lest, 恐怕 ʽhuung-pʻaˌ, 免致 ʽmin-chiˌ.
Let, 由得 yau-tak, 任 yumˌ, 俾 ʽpi, (go) 放 fongˌ, (loose) 鬆 suung, (alone) 咪鬥 ʽmai-tauˌ, (rent) 出賃 chʻuut-yumˌ.
Lethargy, 沉瘤 chʻum-kooi.
Letter, (character) 字 tszeˌ, (epistle) 封信 fuung-suunˌ, 書信 shue-suunˌ, (rigid following of the) 解死 ʽkaai-ʽsze.
Lettuce, 生菜 shang-tsʻoi.
Levee, 坐朝 tsohˌ-chʻiu, ʽtsʻoh-chʻiu.
Level, 平 pʻing, 平正 pʻing-chingˌ, (to find the) 打平水 ʽta-pʻing-ʽshui.
Lever, 千斤柝 tsʻin-kan-tak, 撟柝 kiuˌ-tak.

Lever-watch, 騎馬鏢 kʻe-ˌma-ˌpiu.
Levity, 輕薄 hing-pok.
Lewdness, 嫖 pʻiu.
Liable, (for) 是問 shiˌ-munˌ, (to) 有——險 ʽyau ——ʽhim.
Liar, 講大話嘅 ʽkong-taaiˌ-waˌ-keˌ.
Libel, 壞名 waaiˌ-ming.
Liberal, 仁厚 yan-hauˌ, 四海嘅 szeˌ-ʽhoi-keˌ, (in politics) 達權 taat-kʻuen.
Liberate, 釋放 shik-fongˌ.
Liberty, 自由 tszeˌ-yau.
Library, (the room) 書房 shue-*fong, (the books) 書籍 shue-tsik.
License, (a) 執照 chup-chiuˌ, (to) 任從 yumˌ-tsʻuung.
Licentious, 放縱 fongˌ-tsuungˌ, 淫泆 yum-yat.
Lichen, 苔 tʻoi, 石耳 shek-ʽi.
Li-chi, 荔枝 laiˌ-chi, (best sorts) 糯米柿 nohˌ-ʽmai-tsʻze, 黑葉 hak-*ip.

注 释

【沉瘤】沉睡。
【坐朝】早朝,指皇帝早晨接见大臣。

注释

【怕系啩】恐怕是，大概是。

【趷脚】跛脚。

Lick, (to) 舐 ⸌lim, 舐 shaai, (the fingers) 吮手指 ⸌shuen-⸌shau-⸌chi.

Lid, 蓋 koi⸍, (put on a) 冚住 hom⸍-chue⸍.

Lie, (down) 眠下 min-ha⸍, 瞓倒處 fun⸍-⸌to-shue⸍, (to tell) 講大話 ⸌kong-taai⸍-wa⸍, (a) 謊言 ⸌fong-in, 大話 taai⸍-wa⸍.

Lieutenant, 副 foo⸍.

Life, 生 ⸌shaang, 生命 ⸌shaang-meng⸍, 性命 sing⸍-ming⸍.

Lift, 抽起 ch'au-⸌hi, 舉起 ⸌kue-⸌hi, (off or up) 掀 ⸌k'in, 揭 k'it⸍.

Light, (not heavy) 輕 ⸌heng, (in colour) 淺 ⸌ts'in, (the light) 光 kwong, (bring a) 點火來 ⸌tim-⸌foh-lai, (to light) 點 ⸌t'im, 透 t'au⸍, (alight) 落 lok.

Lighthouse, 燈塔 ⸌tang-t'aap⸍.

Lightning, 電光 tin⸍-kwong, 閃電 ⸌shim-tin, 靚火 leng⸍-⸌foh.

Like, (resembling) 好似 ⸌ho-ts'ze, (to) 中意 chuung-i⸍.

Likely, 大概 taai⸍-k'oi⸍, 怕係啩 p'a⸍-hai⸍-kwa⸍.

Likeness, 眞 ⸌chan, 相 *seung⸍, 像 *tseung⸍.

Likewise, 亦 yik, 又 yau⸍.

Lilac, 青蓮色 ts'ing-*lin-shik.

Lily, 百合花 paak⸍-hop-fa, (water-) 蓮花 lin-fa.

Limb, 肢體 chi-⸌t'ai.

Lime, 灰 ⸌fooi, 殼灰 hok⸍-fooi, 石灰 shek-fooi, (fruit) 檸檬 ning-⸌muung.

Lime-stone, 灰石 fooi-shek.

Limit, 界限 kaai⸍-haan⸍, 限 haan⸍.

Limited, 有限 yau-haan⸍.

Limp, (a) 趷脚 kat-keuk⸍.

Limpet, 扁螺 ⸌pin-*loh.

Line, 線 sin⸍, (stroke) 畫 waak.

Linen, 蔴布 ma-po⸍.

Linger, 逗遛 tau⸍-lau.

Linguist, 通事 t'uung-*sze⸍.

Lining, 裡布 ⸌li-po⸍, 裏 ⸌li.

LIT 148 LOA

Link, (a) 連環 lin-waan, (to) 扣連 k'au-lin.
Linseed, 胡麻子 oo-ma-tsze, (oil) 胡子油 oo-tsze-yau.
Lint, (cloth) 搣絨布 wa-*yuung-po.
Lintel, 條楣 t'iu-mi.
Lion, 獅子 sze-tsze.
Lip, 口唇 hau-shuun.
Liquid, 水類 shui-lui.
Liquidate, (accounts) 清數 ts'ing-sho.
Liquor, (spirits) 酒 tsau.
Liquorice, 甘草 kom-t'so.
List, 條目 t'iu-muuk.
Listen, 細聽 sai-t'eng, 靜聽 tsing-t'ing, 聽下 t'eng-ha, 打聽 ta-t'eng.
Listless, 無心聽 mo-sum-t'eng.
Literally, 正講 ching-kong, 字面 tsze-*min, 正面 ching-*min.
Literary, 學文 hok-mun, 斯文 sze-mun.
Literati, 讀書人 tuuk-shue-yan, 紳士 shan-*sze.

Literature, 文墨 mun-mak.
Litharge, 陀僧 t'oh-sang.
Litigation, 爭訟 chaang-tsuung.
Little, 細 sai, 小 siu, (a) 的 tik, (a very) 的咁多 tik-kom-toh.
Live, 生 shaang, 活 oot, (dwell) 住 chue.
Live stock, 畜牲 chuuk-shang, 生口 shaang-hau.
Livelihood, 過日 kwoh-yat, (seeking a) 搵頭路 wan-t'au-lo, 搵計 wan-kai.
Lively, 活潑 oot-p'oot.
Liver, 肝 kohn, (COL.) yuun.
Livid, 青黑 ts'eng-hak.
Lizard, 蚺蛇 im-*she.
Lo! 睇嗱 t'ai-na!
Loach, 烏魚 oo-ue.
Load, (a) 擔 taam, 擔子 taam-tsze, 載 tsoi, (to) 裝貨 chong-foh.
Load-stone, 攝石 ship-shek.
Loaf, 麵頭 min-t'au, 麵包 min-paau.
Loafer, 摘腳 lo-*keuk.

注 釋

【水类】液体。
【清数】清算。
【搵头路】讨生活,谋生。
【睇嗱】看啊。
【乌鱼】泥鳅。
【摄石】磁铁,磁石。

注 释

【门口厅】大厅，会客室。
【辩论之理】现译为"逻辑"。
【关顾吓】仔细地看。

Loan, 借債 *tseʾ-chaaiʾ*, (put out to) 出借 *chʻuut tseʾ*.
Loathe, 憎懨 *tsang-imʾ*.
Loathsome, 可惡 ʻ*hoh-oo*ʾ.
Lobby, 門口廳 *moon-*ʻ*hau-*ʻ*tʻeng*.
Lobe, (ear-) 耳朵 ʻ*i-*ʻ*toh*, 耳尖 ʻ*i-tsim*, ʻ*i-*ʻ*teung*.
Lobster, 龍蝦 *luung-*ʻ*ha*.
Local, 一方 *yat-fong*, *yat-fong-keʾ*, (of this place) 土 ʻ*tʻo*, 本地 ʻ*poon-**tiʾ.
Lock, (a) 把鎖 ʻ*pa-*ʻ*soh*, (with a latch or bolt) 軌銷 ʻ*kwai-*ʻ*soh*, (of a canal) 水閘 ʻ*shui-chaap*, (to) 銷埋 ʻ*soh-maai*.
Locust, 蝗蟲 *wong-chʻuung*.
Lodge, (to) 歇宿 *hitʾ-suuk*, 住 *chueʾ*, (house) 歇店 *hitʾ-timʾ*, 寓 *ueʾ*.
Lodger, 歇客 *hitʾ-haakʾ*.
Lofty, 高 *ko*.
Log, 木頭 *muuk-tʻau*.
Logic, 辯論之理 *pinʾ-luunʾ-chi-*ʻ*li*, 辯論法 *pinʾ-luunʾ-faatʾ*.

LOGOS, 道 *TOʾ*.
Loins, 腰 *iu*, 小腌 ʻ*siu-*ʻ*im*.
Loiter, 逗遛 *tauʾ-lau*, 囉囉鑽 *loh-loh-tsuenʾ*.
Lonely, 冷落 ʻ*laang-lok*, 孤獨 *koo-tuuk*.
Long, (in space) 長 *chʻeung*, (in time) 長久 *chʻeung-*ʻ*kau*, 久 ʻ*kau* 耐 *noi, *noi*, (to) 戀慕 *luenʾ-mooʾ*, 渴想 *hohtʾ-*ʻ*seung*.
Long-ells, 嗶機 *pitʾ-*ʻ*ki*.
Longevity, 長壽 *chʻeung-shauʾ*.
Longitude, 地經度 *tiʾ-king-toʾ*.
Longsuffering, 忍耐 ʻ*yan-noi*ʾ.
Look, 看 *hohnʾ*, 睇 ʻ*tʻai*, (carefully) 關顧吓 *kwaan-kooʾ-*ʻ*ha*, (down upon) 睥睨 *pʻai-*ʻ*ngai*.
Looking-glass, 面鏡 *minʾ-kengʾ*.
Look-out, (place) 望樓 *mongʾ-lau*.
Loom, (a) 一架機 *yat-ka-*ʻ*ki*.

Loop, 紐圈 ʿnau-huen, 紐眼 ʿnau-ʿngaan.		Lounge, (to) 散逸 ʿsaan-yat, 閒散 haan-ʿsaan.
Loop-hole, 狗竇 ʿkau-tau, 墻口 ts'eung-ʿhau, 漏罅 lauʾ-laʾ.		Louse, 虱 shat, 虱乸 shat-ʿna.
Loose, 鬆 sung, 散 ʿsaan, (to) 鬆開 sung-hoi, 解角 ʿkaai-lut.		Lout, 懶佬 ʿlaan-ʿlo.
		Love, 愛 oiʾ, (tenderly) 愛惜 oiʾ-sik, (reverently) 敬愛 kingʾ-oiʾ.
Lop off, 割去 koht'-hueʾ.		Love-apple, 金錢桔 kum-ts'in-kat.
Loquacious, 多口 toh-ʿhau.		
Loquat, 櫨橘 lo-kwut, 枇杷菓 p'i-p'a-ʿkwoh.		Low, 低 tai, 矮 ʿai, 卑 pi, (water) 水乾慢 ʿshui-kohn-maan.
Lord, 主 ʿchue.		Low, (to) 牛吽 ngau-kiuʾ.
Lose, 失 shat, 遺失 wai-shat, (in trade) 貼本 shitʾ-ʿpoon, (in a game) 輸 shue.		Loyal, 忠信 chuung-sunʾ.
		Lubber, 劣弱人 luetʾ-yeuk-yan, 大冬瓜 taaiʾ-tuung-kwa.
Loss, 傷壞 sheung-waaiʾ, 虧缺 fai-k'uetʾ.		
		Lubberly, 生沙虱 shang-sha-shat, 大不用 taaiʾ-patʾ-yuungʾ.
Lost, 不見 ʾm-kinʾ, 失了 shat-ʿliu, shat-hiu, 亡 mong.		
		Lubricate, 潤滑 yuunʾ-waat, 整滑 ʿching-waat.
Lots, (cast) 抽籤 ch'au-ts'im, 拈籌 nim-*ch'au.		
		Lucid, 明亮 ming-leungʾ, 明朗 ming-ʿlong.
Lotion, 洗藥 ʿsai-yeuk.		
Lottery, 白鴿票 paak-kopʾ-piu, 賭票 ʿto-piu, (to open a) 開票 hoi-piu.		Lucifer-match, 自來火 tszeʾ-loi-ʿfoh.
Lotus, 蓮花 lin-fa.		
Loud, 大聲 taaiʾ-sheng.		

注 释

【多口】多话的，多嘴。
【狗竇】狗窝。
【白鸽票】源于清代赌鸽的一种彩票。赛鸽时每只鸽子按《千字文》中的天、地、玄、黄、宇、宙、洪、荒、日、月等字顺序编号，赌鸽时所猜字号若与比赛结果相同，则为赢家。
【大冬瓜】比喻傻大个。
【生沙虱】粗笨的，笨拙的。

> 注 释

【好彩数】幸运的。
Lucubration: 应译为"冥思苦想"（通常指在夜里）。
【好叹】享受的。

Luck, 造化 tso²-fa², 命運 ming²-wan², (good) 好彩數 ʿho-ʿtsʿoi-sho².
Luckily, 好彩 ʿho-ʿtsʿoi.
Lucky, 吉 kat, 幸 hang², 有彩 ʿyau-ʿtsʿoi.
Lucrative, 發財 faat²-tsʿoi-ke².
Lucubration, 靜夜作文 tsing²-ye²-tsok²-mun.
Ludicrous, 好笑 ʿho-siu².
Luff, 扳舵 pʿaan-tʿoh, maan-tʿaai.
Luggage, 行李 hang-ʿli.
Lugubrious, 愁苦 shau-ʿfoo, 晦氣 fooi²-hi².
Lukewarm, 半冷半熱 poon²-laang-poon²-it, 冷煖間 ʿlaang-ʿnuen-kaan.
Lull, 畧息 leuk-sik.
Lumbago, 腰骨痛 iu-kwut-tʿuung².
Luminaries, (the 3) 三光 saam-kwong.
Luminous, 光明 kwong-ming.
Lump, 塊 faai², 俗 kau², (to) 攝埋 laap²-maai.

Lunatic, 發癲 faat²-tin.
Lungs, 肺家 fai²-ka, 肺腑 fai²-foo.
Lurch, 打側 ʿta-chak.
Lurk, 埋伏 maai-fuuk.
Luscious, 甘味 kom-mi², 甜淰淰 tʿim-num-num.
Lust, 慾火 yuuk-ʿfoh, (after) 貪饕 tʿaam-tʿo.
Lustre, 光 kwong, 光滑 kwong-waat.
Lustring, 絹 kuen².
Luxuriant, 蔢蔢蔢蔢 poh²-poh²-soh-soh.
Luxurious, 好歎 ʿho-tʿaan², 嬌樂 kiu-lok, 奢侈 chʿe-chʿi.
Lychnis, 虞美人 ue-ʿmi-*yan.
Lycopodium, 卷柏 ʿkuen-pʿaak².
Lye, 鹼水 ʿkaan-ʿshui, (sediment) 鹼沙 ʿkaan-sha.
Lyre, 三絃 saam-*in, (to play) 彈三絃 tʿaan-saam-*in.
Lyrics, 詞曲 tʿsze-kʿuuk.

M

Macao, 澳門 $O^{\rangle}$-*moon.
Macaroni, 通心粉 t'uung-sum-fun, 粉條 ⸢fan-*t'iu.
Mace, (one) 一錢 yat-ts'in. (of nutmegs) 荳蔲花 tau⸥-k'au⸥-fa.
Macerate, 漚 au⸥.
Machination, 機謀 ki-mau.
Machine, 機器 ki-hi⸥.
Mackerel, 鯎魚 ch'i-*ue.
Macroura, 蝦 ⸢ha.
Maculate, 染汚 ⸢im-oo, 玷 tim⸥.
Mad, 狂 k'wong, 發狂 faat⸥-k'wong.
Madam, (respectfully) 奶奶 naai-*naai.
Madder, 茜草 sin⸥-⸢ts'o.
Made, 做了 tso⸥-⸢liu, tso⸥-hiu, tso⸥-ke⸥.
Maggots, (to breed) 生蛆 shang-ts'ue, 生蟲 shang-ch'uung.
Magic, 巫術 moo-shuut.

Magistrates, 官府 koon-⸢foo, —Police, 巡理府 ts'uun-⸢li-⸢foo.
Magnanimous, 豪俠 ho-haap.
Magnates, 大人家 taai⸥-yan-ka.
Magnet, 攝石 ship⸥-shek, 南針 naam-⸤chum.
Magnificent, 浩大 ho⸥-taai⸥, 華麗 wa-lai⸥.
Magnify, 影大 ⸢ying-taai⸥, 整大 ⸢ching-taai⸥.
Magnitude, 若干大 yeuk-kohn-taai⸥.
Magnolia, (fuscata) 含笑花 hom-siu⸥-fa, (conspicua) 玉蘭 yuuk-laan, (pumila) 夜合 ye⸥-*hop.
Magpie, 喜鵲 ⸢hi-ts'euk⸥.
Mahogany, (Chinese) 森木 ⸤shum-muuk, (flower—pride of India) 苦楝花 ⸢foo-lin-fa.
Mahommedanism, 囘囘教 Ooi-*ooi-kaau⸥.
Maid, (servant) 使妹 ⸢shai-⸢mooi, (old) 老女 ⸢lo-*nuc.

注释

【漚】浸泡。
【影大】放大。
Mahommedanism:拼写错误,应为Mohammedanism, 指伊斯兰教。
【使妹】女佣。

注 释

【法条】应为"发条",指机械中的主发条。
【揸大旗】扛大旗,比喻掌权。
【生螆】癞疥。

MAL 153 MAN

Maiden, 童女 t'uung-ʻnue.
Mail, (armour) 甲冑 kaap'-chau'.
Mail, (letter carrying) 驛 yik, 帶信 taai'-suun'.
Maim, 殘缺 ts'aan-k'uet'.
Main, (principal) 大 taai', 正 ching', (the bulk) 大體 taai'-t'ai, (most important) 最要 tsui'-iu'.
Main-spring, 法條 fuat'-*t'iu.
Maintain, 固守 koo'-ʻshau, 保存 ʻpo-ts'uen, 保住 ʻpo-chue'.
Maize, 包粟 paau-suuk.
Majestic, 威嚴 wai-im.
Majority, (of age) 成丁 shing-ting.
Make, 做 tso', 整 ʻching, 作 tsok', (a story) 安是安非 ohn-shi'-ohn-fi, (trouble) 生事 shaang-sze', (away with) 收拾 shau-shup.
Maker, 造者 tso'-ʻche.
Malaria, 山嵐瘴氣 shaan-laam-cheung'-hi'.

Male, 男 naam, 男人 naam-*yan, (of beasts) 公 kuung, (generally) 陽類 yeung-lui'.
Malevolent, 黑心 hak-sum.
Malicious, 兇惡 huung-ok'.
Malignant, 惡毒 ok'-tuuk.
Malleable iron, 熟鐵 shuuk-t'it'.
Mallet, 木槌 muuk-*ch'ui.
Mallows, 葵 k'wai.
Mamma, 媽媽 ma-ʻma.
Man, 人 yan, *yan.
Man-of-war, 兵船 ping-shuen.
Manacles, 手鐐 ʻshau-liu.
Manage, 辦理 paan'-li.
Manager, 總理 ʻtsuung-li, 揸品 cha-ʻpun, 揸大旗 cha-taai'-k'i.
Manchu, 滿洲 Moon-ʻchau.
Mandarin, 官府 koon-ʻfoo, (dialect) 官話 koon-*wa'.
Mane, (horse's) 馬鬃 ʻma-tsuung.
Mange, 生螆 shaang-tsze.
Mangle, (a) 碾布具 shin'-po'-kue', (to spoil) 殘 ts'aan.

MAN 154 MAR

Mango, 檬菓 mong-ʽkwoh.
Mangosteen, 山竹菓 shaan-chuuk-ʽkwoh.
Manhood, 成人 shing-yan.
Maniac, 狂 kʽwong.
Manifest, 明白 ming-paak, (to) 顯明 ʽhin-ming, (a) 貨單 fohʼ-ˎtaan.
Manila, 小呂宋 ʽSiu-ʽlue-suung.
Manis, 穿山甲 chʽuen-shaan-kaapʼ.
Mankind, 人類 yan-luiʼ.
Manly, 君子 kwan-ʽtsze, kwun-ʽtsze-keʽ.
Manner, 樣 yeungʼ, *yeungʼ.
Manners, 禮 ʽlai.
Mansion, 宅 chaak, 府 ʽfoo.
Mantis, 馬郞蚣 ʽma-long-*kʽong.
Mantle, 大蓼 taaiʼ-ˎlau.
Mantlepiece, 火爐額 ʽfoh-lo-ngaak.
Manual labour, 手作 ʽshau-tsok.
Manufacture, 製做 chaiʼ-tsoʼ.

Manure, 糞 funʼ, (to) 落糞 lokʼ-funʼ.
Manuscript, 手抄 ʽshau-chʽaau, 寫嘅 ʽse-keʽ.
Many, 多 toh.
Map, 圖 tʽo, 地圖 tiʼ-tʽo.
Maple, 楓樹 fuung-shueʼ.
Mar, 損壞 ʽsuen-waaiʼ, ˎte.
Marble, 花粉石 fa-ʽfun-*shek, 雲石 wun-*shek, (white) 白粉石 paak-ʽfun-*shek.
March, 英三月 Ying-saam-uet, (to) 步師 poʼ-sze, 齊步行 tsʽai-poʼ-hang.
Mare, 馬母 ʽma-ʽmo.
Margarite, 珍珠 chan-chue.
Margin, 邊 pin.
Marines, 水師 ʽshui-sze.
Mariners, 水手 ʽshui-ʽshau.
Mark, 記號 kiʼ-hoʼ, 畫 waak, (to) 打印 ʽta-yanʼ, 打號 ʽta-hoʼ, (observe) 睇眞 ʽtʽai-chan.
Market, 市 ʽshi.
Market-place, 市頭 ʽshi-*tʽau, 欄 ˎlaan (town) 墟 hue.

> 注 释
>
> 【下沙】沼泽。
> 【埠头】渡头，引申为集市。
> 【守死善道】牺牲，殉道。
> 【笑面殼】面具。

Marking-line, 墨斗 mak-ʻtau.
Marquis, 侯 hau.
Marriage, 婚姻 fun-yan.
Marrow, 髓 sui.
Marry, (a wife) 娶 tsʻueʼ, 取心抱 ʻtsʻue-sum-pʻo, (a husband) 嫁 kaʼ, (a couple) 成親 shing-tsʻan.
Mars, (planet) 火星 ʻFoh-sing, (the god of war) 武帝 ʻmoo-taiʼ, (Chinese) 關帝 Kwaan-taiʼ.
Marsh, 下沙 haʼ-sha, 沙灘 sha-ʻtʻaan, 澤 chaak.
Mart, 埠頭 fanʼ-tʻan.
Marten, 貂鼠 tiu-ʻshue.
Martial, 武 ʻmoo.
Martyrdom, 守死善道 ʻshau-ʻsze-shinʼ-to.
Marvel, 奇事 kʻi-szeʼ, (to) 詫異 chʻaʼ-i.
Marvel of Peru, 胭脂花 in-chi-fa.
Masculine gender, 陽類 yeung-luiʼ.
Mash, 搓爛 chʻaai-laanʼ.

Mask, 笑面殼 siuʼ-minʼ-hokʼ.
Mason, 泥水人 nai-ʻshui-yan, (stone-) 石匠 shek-*tseungʼ.
Mass, 團 tʻuen, 俗 kauʼ, (people) 下民 haʼ-mun, 庶民 shueʼ-mun.
Massacre, 屠戮 tʻo-luuk, 殺戮 shaatʼ-luuk.
Massive, 厚大 hauʼ-taaiʼ.
Mast, 枝桅 chi-wai.
Master, 事頭 szeʼ-*tʻau, 主人公 ʻchue-yan-kuung, 主 ʻchue, (teacher) 先生 sin-shang, 師傅 sze-*foo.
Masticate, 嚼 tseukʼ, tsiuʼ.
Mat, 席 tsek, (of bamboo) 箞 taatʼ, (cushion) 墊 tinʼ.
Mat-shed, 棚廠 pʻaang-ʻchʻong.
Match, 火紙 ʻfoh-ʻchi, (Lucifer) 火柴 ʻfoh-chʻaai.
Match, (a mate) 偶 ʻngau.
Match-maker, 媒婆 mooi-*pʻoh.

| MEA | 156 | MED |

Mate, (chief) 伙長 ˊfoh-ˊcheung, (2nd) 二伙 iˋ-ˊfoh, (generally) 伙計 ˊfoh-kiˊ.

Materials, 材料 tsʻoi-liuˋ, 物料 mat-liuˋ.

Matrix, (for type) 銅板模 tʻuung-ˊpaan-moo.

Matter, 質 chat, (affair) 事幹 szeˋ-kohnˋ, (no) 無乜緊要 ˊmo-mat-ˊkan-iuˋ, (from a boil) 膿 nuung.

Matter of fact, 事實 szeˋ-shat.

Mattress, 牀褥 chʻong-*yuuk.

Mature, 成熟 shing-shuuk.

Maxim, 箴規 chum-kʻwai.

May, (can) 得 tak, 可以 ˊhoh-ˊi, (I, or we, wish) 願 uenˋ.

Maze, 紛紛 fun-fun.

Meadow, 草塲 ˊtsʻo-chʻeung.

Meal, (a) 餐 tsʻaan, (flour) 粉 ˊfun.

Mealy-mouthed, 口聰 ˊhau-chʻi.

Mean, (base) 鄙陋 ˊpʻi-lauˋ, 賤 tsinˋ, (to hit the) 得中 tak-chuung, (to) 意係 iˋ-haiˋ, (the doctrine of the) 中庸 chuung-yuung.

Meaning, 意思 iˋ-szeˋ.

Means, 資本 tsze-ˊpoon, (method) 法 faatˋ.

Means, (by no) 斷唔係 tuenˋ-'m-haiˋ.

Meanwhile, 同時 tʻuung-shi.

Measles, 痲症 *ma-chingˋ, 出痲 chʻut-*ma.

Measure, (to) 度 tok, 量度 leungˋ-tok, (a) 量 leungˋ, 度量 toˋ-leungˋ, (foot-) 尺 chʻekˋ.

Meat, 肉 yuuk.

Mechanic, 工匠 kuung-tseungˋ.

Mechanism, 機器 ki-hiˋ.

Meddle, 尋事 tsʻum-szeˋ, 打理 ˊta-ˊli.

Mediator, 中保 chuung-ˊpo.

Medicine, 藥材 yeuk-tsʻoi, (science of) 醫學 i-hok.

注释

【行状】一种记述死者世系、生平、生卒年月、籍贯、事迹的文章。
【下役】仆人。
【羽斜】美利奴羊毛。

Meditate, 默想 mak-‘seung.
Medusa, 水母 ‘shui-‘mo.
Meek, 謙和 him-woh.
Meet, (to) 遇着 ue’-cheuk, 接着 tsip’-cheuk, (by appointment) 聚會 tsue’-ooi’.
Meeting, 會 ooi’, 聚集 tsue’-tsaap.
Melancholy, 悶悶 moon’-moon’.
Mellow, 熟腍 shuuk-num.
Melody, 佳音 kaai-yum.
Melon, 瓜 kwa.
Melt, 鎔化 yuung-fa’.
Member, 股 ‘koo, (church-) 兄弟 hing-tai’.
Members, 百體 paak’-t‘ai.
Membrane, 衣膜 i-mok.
Memoir, 行狀 hang-chong’.
Memorial, 奏本 tsau’-‘poon.
Memory, 記性 ki’-sing’.
Mencius, 孟子 Mang’-‘tsze.
Mend, 補 ‘po, 修整 sau-‘ching.
Menial, 下役 ha’-yik.
Menses, 月經 uet-king.
Mental, 心內 sum-noi’.

Mention, 講及 ‘kong-k‘aap.
Mercantile, 生意 shang-i’, 買賣 ‘maai-maai’.
Mercenary, 求利 k‘au-li’.
Merchant, 商人 sheung-yan.
Merciful, 哀憐 oi-lin, 慈 ts‘ze, 慈心 ts‘ze-sum.
Merciless, 狠心 long-sum.
Mercury, 水銀 ‘shui-ngan, (planet) 水星 ‘Shui-sing.
Mercy, 慈悲 ts‘ze-pi, 憐憫 lin-‘mun.
Merely, 不過 pat-kwoh’, 獨係 tuuk-hai’, ——呗 chek.
Merge, 褪埋 t‘an’-maai.
Meridian, 子午線 ‘tsze-‘ng-sin’, (-lines) 經線 king-sin’.
Merino, 羽斜 ‘ue-ts‘e.
Merit, 功勞 kuung-lo, 功 kuung, (to) 應得 ying-tak, 功勞應得 kuung-lo-ying-tak.
Merry, 喜笑 ‘hi-siu’, 好趣 ‘ho-ts‘ue’.
Merry-andrew, 雜脚 tsaap-keuk’, 丑 ‘ch‘au.

| MIC | 158 | MIL |

Mesh, 網眼 ʻmong-ʻngaan.
Mess, (medley) 擸雜 laap-tsaap.
Mess together, 同孿 tʻung-tsʻuen'.
Message, 報信 po'-suum'.
Messenger, 差人 cʻaai-yan, (official) 委員 ʻwai-uen.
Metal, 金類 kum-lui'.
Metaphor, 借語 tse'-ne, 借意 tse'-i'.
Metempsychosis, 輪囘 luan-ooi.
Meteor, 流星 lau-ʻsing, 墜星 chui'-ʻsing.
Method, 方法 fong-faat', 法子 faat'-tsze.
Metonomy, 借講 tse'-ʻkong.
Metropolis, 京城 king-sheng, 京都 king-too.
Mettle, 精氣 tsing-hi'.
Mew, } 坳聲 ngaau-sheng.
Mewl,
Miasma, 瘴氣 cheung'-hi', (damp) 濕氣 shap-hi', 濕瘴 shap-cheung'.
Mica, 千層紙 tsʻin-tsʻang-ʻchi.

Microcosm, 小天地 ʻsiu-tʻin-ti'.
Microscope, 顯微鏡 ʻhin-mi-keng'.
Mid, 中 chung.
Mid-day, 晏晝 aan'-chau'.
Middle, 中間 chung-ʻkaun.
Middle-man, 媒人 mooi-*yan.
Middle-woman, 媒婆 mooi-*pʻoh.
Middling, 嘛嘛哋 ma-*ma-ti'.
Midnight, 半夜 poon'-ye'.
Mid-summer, 夏至 ha'-chi', 端陽 tuen-yeung.
Mid-way, 半路 poon'-lo'.
Midwife, 接生婆 tsip-shang-*pʻoh, 穩婆 ʻwan-*pʻoh, 執媽 chup-ʻma.
Might, 能 nang.
Mighty, 大能 taai'-nang.
Migratory, 依時來往 i-shi-loi-ʻwong.
Mild, 溫良 wan-leung.
Mildew, 霉 mooi, 漚霉 au'-mooi.

注 释

【擸杂】混乱。
【晏昼】中午，正午。
【嘛嘛地】一般般。
【大能】有力的，伟大的。

注释

【嫋娜】裊娜。
【香花菜】薄荷。
【异迹】奇迹。
【唖碎】琐碎。
【悭财人】守财奴。

Mile, (36/100 of an English) 里 ʻli.
Military, 武 ʻmoo.
Milk, 乳 ʻue, 嬭 ʻnaai, (COL.) ʻnin.
Mill, 磨 mohʼ, *mohʼ.
Millet, 小米 ʻsiu-ʻmai, 粟 suuk.
Million, 百萬 paakʼ-maanʼ.
Mimic, 學 hok.
Mince, 切細 tsʻitʼ-saiʼ.
Mincing, 嫋娜 ʻniu-ʻnoh.
Mind, 心 sum, (to) 顧住 kooʼ-chueʼ.
Mindful, 有細心 ʻyau-saiʼ-sum, (you are) 有心 ʻyau-sum.
Mine, (to) 掘 (金) 竉 kwut- (kum-) ʻluung, (a) 礦 kʻwongʼ.
Minister, (to) 執事 chup-szeʼ, 司事 sze-szeʼ, (a) 臣 shan, (prime) 宰相 ʻtsoi-seungʼ.
Mint, 香花菜 heung-fa-tsʻoi, (a) 錢局 tsʻin-kuuk.
Minus, 減 ʻkaam.

Minute, 細微 saiʼ-mi, (of time) 分時 fun-shi.
Miracle, 異跡 iʼ-tsik.
Mire, 泥濘 nai-paanʼ.
Mirror, 面鏡 minʼ-kengʼ.
Mirth, 快樂 fuaiʼ-lok.
Miscarriage, 小產 ʻsiu-ʻchʻaan.
Miscellaneous, 零星 ling-sing, 雜 tsaap, 拾碎 shup-suiʼ, 唖碎 sup-sui.
Mischief, 故傷 kooʼ-sheung, 損害 ʻsuen-hoiʼ.
Miser, 慳財人 haan-tsʻoi-yan, 慳壞 haan-waaiʼ.
Miserable, (as a miser) 自賤 tszeʼ-tsinʼ, (poor) 拗憊 aau-ai.
Misery, 苦楚 ʻfoo-ʻchʻoh, 悽涼 tsʻai-leung.
Misfortune, 不幸 patʼ-hangʼ, 苦命 ʻfoo-mengʼ, 凶事 huung-szeʼ.
Misinterpret, 解錯 ʻkaai-tsʻohʼ.
Mislead, 引錯 ʻyan-tsʻohʼ.
Misprint, 印錯 yanʼ-tsʻohʼ.

Misrepresent, 講歪 ʻkong-ʻme.
Miss, (young lady) 姑娘 koo-neung, (to) 失 shat, 唔中 ʻm-chuung.
Missionary, 傳教人 chʻuen-kaauʾ-yan, (society) 傳教會 chʻuen-kaauʾ-ooi.
Misspend, 浪費 longʾ-fai.
Mist, 烟霧 iu-moo, 霞霧 ha-moo, 雲霧 wan-moo.
Mistake, 估錯 ʻkoo-tsʻoh, (a) 錯 tsʻoh, *tsʻoh, 錯過 tsʻoh-kwoh.
Mister, (Mr) 先生 sin-shang, ——公 ——kuung.
Mistress, (Mrs) 奶奶 naai-*naai, (of a household) 事頭娘 szeʾ-tʻau-neung, 主人娘 ʻchue-yan-neung, 主母 ʻchue-ʻmoo, (of a school) 女師 ʻnue-sze, (a kept) 老契 ʻlo-kʻai.
Misunderstand, 不會意 ʻm-ooiʾ-i, 聽錯 tʻeng-tsʻoh.
Mix, 攪勻 ʻkaau-wan, 調和 tʻiu-woh, 摳勻 kʻau-wan.

Moan, 嗟嘆 tse-tʻuanʾ, 嘆氣 tʻuanʾ-hi.
Mob, 百姓鬧亂 paakʾ-sing-naauʾ-luen.
Mock, 戲弄 hiʾ-luungʾ, 訕笑 shaanʾ-siu.
Model, 模樣 moo-yeungʾ, moo-*yeung.
Moderate, 不多不少 pat-toh-pat-ʻshiu, 適中 shuk-chuung, 中和 chuung-woh, (to) 調勻 tʻiu-wan.
Modern, 今 kum, 新 san, (times) 近世 kanʾ-shaiʾ.
Modest, 有廉恥 ʻyau-lim-ʻchʻi, 知羞 chi-sau, 謙退 him-tʻui.
Modify, 改削 ʻkoi-seukʾ.
Moist, 濕 shup, 腍 num.
Moisten, 潤 yunʾ.
Mole, 田鼠 tʻin-ʻshue, (on the skin) 黑疵 hak-tsʻze-黑痣 hak-chiʾ.
Mole-cricket, 土狗 ʻtʻo-ʻkau.
Molest, 難為 naan-wai.
Moment, 片刻 pʻinʾ-hak, 頃刻 ʻkʻing-hak.

注 释

【马骝】猴子。
【荳家】垄断者。
【荳货】垄断。
【猜梅】应为"猜枚"，一种行酒令的方式。
【典主】承受抵押者。

MOP　　161　　MOR

Monastery, (Tau.) 觀 *koon*ʼ, (Bud.) 寺 *tsze*ʼ, (Rom.) 修道院 *sau-to*ʼ-*uen*ʼ.
Monday, 禮拜一 ʻ*lai-paai*-*yat*.
Money, 錢 *tsʻin*, *tsʻin*, 銀錢 *ngan-*tsʻin*, *ngan*.
Mongol, 蒙古 *Muung-*ko*o.
Mongrel, 雜種 *tsaap-*chuung*.
Monkey, 馬騮 ʻ*ma-*lau*.
Monomania, 心病狂 *sum-peng*ʼ-*kʻwong*, 因事病狂 *yan-sze*ʼ-*peng*ʼ-*kʻwong*.
Monopolist, 荳家 ʻ*tuun-*ka*.
Monopolize, 荳貨 ʻ*tuun-foh*ʼ.
Monstrous, 怪祟 *kwaai*ʼ-*sui*ʼ.
Month, 月 *uet*.
Monument, 牌坊 *pʻaai-fong*, 碑記 *pi-kiʼ*.
Mood, 心情 *sum-tsʻing*, 情景 *tsʻing-*king*.
Moody, 鼓氣 ʻ*koo-hi*ʼ.
Moon, 月 *uet*, (light) 月光 *uet-*kwong*.
Moor, (to) 灣泊 *waan-pok*, 灣劄 *waan-chaap*ʼ.
Mop, 布拂 *po*ʼ-*fut*.

Mope, 發悶 *faat*ʼ-*moon*ʼ.
Morally, 依情理 *i-tsʻing-*li*.
Morals, 行爲 *hang-wai*, 德行 *tak-hang*, (good) 善德 *shin*ʼ-*tak*.
More, 添 *tʻim*, 多 *toh*, (COMP. DEG.) 更 *kang*ʼ, 重 *chuung*ʼ.
Moreover, 更兼 *kang*ʼ-*kim*, 況且 *fong*ʼ-*chʻe*, 而且 *i-*chʻe*.
Morning, 早 ʻ*tso*, 朝 *chiu*, (good) 早晨 ʻ*tso-shan*, (-star) 啟明星 ʻ*kʻai-ming-*sing*.
Morose, 陰沉 *yum-chʻum*.
Morra, 猜梅 *chʻaai-mooi*.
Mortal, 會死 ʻ*ooi-*sze*.
Mortally, 致死 *chi*ʼ-*sze*ʼ.
Mortar, 泥 *nai*, (a) 舂坎 *chuung-*hom*.
Mortgage, (a house) 典屋 ʻ*tin-uuk*, 當屋 *tong*ʼ-*uuk*.
Mortgagee, 典主 ʻ*tin-*chue*.
Mortification, 枯廢 *foo*ʼ-*fai*ʼ, 腐 *foo*ʼ, (gangrene) 肉死 *yuuk-*sze*, (of spirit) 憔悴 *tsʻiu-sui*ʼ.

Mortise, 榫眼 ʽsuun-ʽngaan.	Mould, (a) 模式 moo-shik.
Mosquito, 蚊 ʽmun.	Mouldy, 發毛 faatʾ-mo.
Mosquito-curtain, (a) 一堂蚊帳 yat-tʽong-ʽmun-cheungʾ.	Mound, 土堆 tʽo-ʽtui, 封土 fuung-tʽo.
Moss, 苔蘚 tʽoi-ʽsin, 莓苔 mooi-tʽoi, 青苔 tsʽeng-tʽoi.	Mount, (to) 上 ʽsheung, 升上去 shing-sheung-hueʾ.
Most, (of quality) 至 chiʾ, 十分 shap-fun, (of quantity) 至多 chiʾ-toh.	Mountain, 山 shaan.
	Mourn, 弔喪 tiuʾ-song, 哀哭 oi-huuk.
Mostly, 大概 taaiʾ-*kʽoi, 大約 taaiʾ-*yeukʾ, 大體 taaiʾ-ʽtʽai.	Mourning, 喪服 song-fuuk, (put on) 着服 cheukʾ-fuuk.
	Mouse, 鼠仔 ʽshue-ʽtsai, 石鼠 shek-ʽshue.
Moth, 蛾 ngoh, 燈蛾 tang-*ngoh.	Mouth, 口 ʽhau.
Mother, 老母 ʽlo-*ʽmoo, (respectfully) 母親 ʽmoo-tsʽan.	Mouthful, (a) 一口 yat-ʽhau, 一啖 yat-taamʾ.
	Move, 郁動 yuuk-tuungʾ, (remove) 搬 poon.
Mother-in-law, 外母 ngoiʾ-*ʽmoo.	Mow, 鏟 ʽchʽaan.
Mother-of-pearl, 雲母殼 wan-ʽmoo-hokʾ.	Moxa, 艾茸 ngaaiʾ-yuung.
	Much, 多 toh.
Mother-wort, 益母草 yik-ʽmoo-ʽtsʽo.	Mud, 坭 nai.
	Muddy, 濁 chuuk, 泥湴 nai-paanʾ, 漚耨 auʾ-nauʾ, (style) 拖泥帶水 tʽoh-nai-taaiʾ-ʽshui.
Motion, 動 tuungʾ.	
Motive, 起見 ʽhi-kinʾ, 念頭 nimʾ-tʽau.	
Motto, 題句 tʽai-kueʾ.	Muff, 拱手套 ʽkuung-ʽshau-tʽoʾ.

注　释

【起见】动机。
【模式】模具。
【发毛】发霉。
【郁动】移动。

注释

【啥沉】咕哝,发牢骚。
【生痄腮】流行性腮腺炎。
【四海嘅】丰厚的,慷慨的。
【吹打佬】演奏乐器的人,乐师。
【摩啰人】伊斯兰教徒。
【洽坏】陈腐的,放太久导致闷坏和发霉的。
【唔声】不出声。

Mug, 水筒 ʿshui-*tʿuung.
Mulberry, (tree) 桑樹 song-shueʾ.
Mule, 騾馬 lohʾ-ʿma.
Mullet, 黃尾鯔 wong-ʿmi-tsʿai, 白尾鯔 paak-ʿmi-tsʿai.
Multiply, 乘 shing, (increase) 生多 shaang-toh.
Multitude, 衆 chuungʾ, (the) 庶民 shueʾ-mun, 大衆百姓 taaiʾ-chuungʾ-paakʾ-singʾ.
Mumble, 啥沉 ngum-chʿum.
Mummery, 詭馬事 ʿkwai-ʿma-szeʾ.
Mumps, 生痄腮 shangʾ-chaʾ-soi.
Munificent, 厚重 hauʾ-chuungʾ, 四海嘅 szeʾ-ʿhoi-keʾ.
Murder, 兇殺 huung-shaatʾ.
Murderer, 兇手 huung-ʿshau.
Murex, 刺螺 tsʿzeʾ-*loh.
Murmur, 論蠢 luunʾ-chuunʾ, (at) 怨嘆 uenʾ-tʿaanʾ.
Muscle, (of the body) 肌膚 ki-foo, 瘦肉 shauʾ-*yuuk.

Mushroom, 菌 ʿkʿwun, ʿkʿan.
Music, 樂音 ngok-yum.
Musicians, 吹打佬 chʿui-ʿta-ʿlo, (respectfully) 樂師 ngok-sze.
Musk, 麝香 sheʾ-heung.
Musk-melon, 香瓜 ʿheung-ʿkwa.
Musket, 鳥鎗 ʿniu-tsʿeung.
Muslin, 棉紗 min-sha.
Mussel, (shell fish) 黃沙蜆 wong-ʿsha-ʿhin, 蜆 ʿhin.
Mussulman, (Moor) 摩囉人 ʿMoh-ʿloh-yan, (Mohammedan) 囘子 Ooiʾ-ʿtsze.
Must, 必 pit, 必定 pit-tingʾ, 必要 pit-iuʾ, 是必 shiʾ-pit.
Mustaches, 髭 tsze, 八字鬚 paatʾ-tszeʾ-so.
Mustard, 芥末 kaaiʾ-moot, 芥辣 kaaiʾ-laat, (seed) 芥子 kaaiʾ-ʿtsze.
Muster, 板 ʿpaan.
Musty, 糠隨 ʿhong-tsʿue 洽壞 up-waaiʾ.
Mute, 唔聲 ʾm-sheng, 啞口 ʿa-ʿhau.
Mutilate, 殘害 tsʿaan-hoiʾ.

| NAK | 164 | NAT |

Mutiny, 叛逆 poon'-yik.
Mutter, (COL.) ‚kong-nge-nge-sheng, t'up-t'up-sheng.
Mutton, 羊肉 yeung-yuuk.
Mutual, 相 seung, 交相 kaau-seung-ke', 彼此 ‚pi-ts‚ze.
Muzzle, 口 ‚hau, 嘴 ‚tsui, (to) 笠住口 lup-chue'-‚hau.
My, mine, 我嘅 ‚ngoh-ke'.
Myriad, 萬 maan'.
Myrrh, 沒藥 moot-yeuk.
Myself, 我自己 ‚ngoh-tsze'-‚ki, 本身 ‚poon-shan, (I feed myself) 我食自己 ‚ngoh-shik-tsze'-‚ki.
Mysterious, 奧妙 o'-miu', 難明 naan-ming.
Myth, 古語 ‚koo-‚ue.

N

Nail, 釘 ‚teng, (a) 一口釘 yat-‚hau-‚teng, (finger-, &c.) 甲 kaap', 爪 ‚chaau.
Naked, 赤 ch‚ik, 光 ‚kwong, (stark) 脫赤肋 t'uet-ch‚ik'-lak.

Nakedness, (destitution) 赤貧 ch‚ek-p‚un.
Name, 名 ming, *meng, (to) 改名 ‚koi-*meng.
Namely, 卽 tsik.
Nankeen, cloth, 紫花布 ‚tsze-fa-po', 赤布 ch‚ik-po'.
Nanking, 南京 Naam-king.
Nap, 毛 mo, 絨頭 yuung-t'au, (sleep) 哈吓 hap-‚ha.
Napkin, 布仔 po'-‚tsai, (table-) 茶巾 ch'a-‚kan.
Narcissus, 水仙花 ‚shui-sin-fa.
Narcotic, 迷藥 mai-yeuk.
Narrate, 述出來 shuut-ch'uut-lai.
Narrow, 窄 chaak', (tight) 挟 kip.
Nasturtium, 荷葉蓮 hoh-ip-lin.
Nasty, 臭 ch'au'.
Nation, 邦 pong, 國 kwok'.
Native, 本地 ‚poon-*ti', 土 t'o.

注 释

【笠住口】把嘴巴封住的。
【古语】神话。
【哈吓】打盹，小睡。

注释

Nautilus:现译为"鹦鹉螺"。

【无唔得】必要的。

【死骨】骨疽。

【补联婆】修补衣服的女人。

【对面话头】否定的,相反的。

Natural, 天生 t'in-shang, t'in-shang-ke', 本性 ‘poon-sing'.
Naturally, 自然 tsze'-in, 天然 t'in-in.
Nature, 性 sing'.
Naughty, 頑皮 waan-p'i, 不好 'm-‘ho, k'waai'.
Nausea, 會嘔 ‘ooi-‘au, 想嘔 ‘seung-‘au.
Nautilus, 浮水螺 fau-‘shui-*loh.
Naval, (troops) 水師 ‘shui-sze, (officer) 水師官 ‘shui-sze-koon.
Nave, 輪心 luun-sum.
Navel, 肚臍 ‘t'o-ts'ze, (string) 臍帶 ts'ze-‘taai.
Navigate, 駛船 ‘shai-shuen.
Nay, 唔係 'm-hai', 不是 pat-shi'.
Near, 近 kan', ‘k'an, 附近 foo'-kan'.
Near-sighted, 近視眼 kan'-*shi'-‘ngaan.
Nearly, 差不多 ch'a-pat-toh, 將近 ‘tseung-kan'.

Neat, 齊整 ts'ai-‘ching, (clean) 乾淨 kohn-tseng'.
Necessary, 必要 pit-iu' 定必 ting'-pit, 無唔得 mo-'m-tak.
Neck, 頸 ‘keng.
Neck-lace, 頸鍊 ‘keng-*lin'.
Necktie, 頸領 ‘keng-‘leng.
Necrosis, 死骨 ‘sze-kwut.
Need, 須 sue, 須要 sue-iu'.
Needle, 眼針 ‘ngaan-chum, (magnetic) 南針 naam-chum.
Needle-woman, 補聯婆 ‘po-luen-*p'oh.
Needless, 不使 'm-‘shai, 不要 'm-iu'.
Needy, 窮乏 k'uung-fat.
Nefarious, 醜惡 ‘ch'au-ok'.
Negative, 對面話頭 tui'-min'-wa-t'au, (positive &—) 有無 ‘yau-mo.
Neglect, 忘却 mong-k'euk', 失記 shat-ki', 失覺 shat-kok', 不顧 'm-koo'.
Negligent, 忽畧 fut-leuk.
Negotiate, 辦理 paan'-‘li.

| NET | 166 | NIC |

Neigh, (嘶風 sze-fuung), 馬叫 ʽma-kiu'

Neighbour, 隣人 luun-yan, 街坊 ʽkaai-fong.

Neighbours, 隣里 luun-ʽli, 四隣 sze'-ʽnun.

Neighbouring, 隣近 luun-kan', 隔離 kaak'-li.

Neighbourly, 好相與 ʽho-seung-ʽue.

Neither——nor, 不是——又不是 pat-shi'——yau'-pat-shi', 唔係——又唔係 'm-hai'——yau'-'m-hai', ——都唔係 too-'m-hai'.

Nephew, 姪子 chat-ʽtsze.

Neptune, 龍王 Luung-wong.

Nerve, 腦氣筋 ʽno-hi-kan.

Nervous, (timid) 無志氣 ʽmo-chi-hi, (irritable) 內傷頸 noi'-sheung-ʽkeng.

Nest, 巢窩 chʽaau-woh, 竇 tau'.

Net, 網 ʽmong, 張網 cheung-ʽmong, (lifting) 罾 tsang.

Nettle rash, 風騥 fuung-naan'.

Neutral, 兩不相涉 ʽleung-pat-seung-ship'.

Neutralize, (medicine) 解藥 ʽkaai-yeuk, (poison) 解毒 ʽkaai-tuuk.

Never, (past) 未有 mi'-ʽyau, 原來無 uen-loi-mo, 總無 ʽtsuung-mo, (to come) 終不 chuung-pat, 永遠無 ʽwing-ʽuen-ʽmo.

Nevertheless, 雖然 sui-in.

New, 新 san.

News, 新聞 san-*mun, 聲氣 sheng-hi'.

Newspaper, 新聞紙 san-mun-ʽchi.

Next, 第二 tai'-i', 次 tsʽze', 對下 tui'-ha', (day, &c.) 明日 ming-yat, &c., (near to) 近住 kan'-chue'.

Nice, 好 ʽho, 好樣 ʽho-*yeung', 雅潔 ʽnga-kit', (particular) 仔細 ʽtsze-sai', (too) 俺尖 im-tsim.

Nickname, 花名 fa-*meng, 混名 wan'-*meng.

注 釋

【隔离】旁边。
【好相与】好相处的。
【脑气筋】神经。
【风騥】风疹。
【好样】好看的。

注 释

【悭】节省。
【鬼责】鬼压身。
【瞓衫】睡衣。
【虱乸孻】虱子幼虫。
【晏昼】中午。

NOB 167 NOT

Niece, 姪女 chat-ʽnue.
Niggardly, 悭 haun, 鄙吝 ʽpʽi-luun.
Night, 夜晚 yeʼ-ʽmaan.
Night-mare, 夢壓 muungʼ-aatʼ, 鬼責 ʽkwai-chaakʼ.
Night-dress, 瞓衫 funʼ-ʽshaam.
Nimble, 輕快 hing-faaiʼ, 快捷 faaiʼ-tsit.
Nine, 九 ʽkau.
Nineteen, 十九 shap-ʽkau.
Ninety, 九十 ʽkau-shap.
Ninth, 第九 taiʼ-ʽkau.
Nip, 揰 nip, 鉗 kʽim, 搣 mit.
Nippers, 鉗 *kʽim.
Nipple, 奶頭 ʽnaai-tʽau.
Nirvana, 湼盤 nip-pʽoon.
Nit, 虱乸孻 shat-ʽna-chʽuun.
Nitre, 鹹硝 haam-siu, 硝 siu.
No, 不是 pat-shiʼ, 唔係 ʼm-haiʼ, 無 ʽmo.
Nobility, 爵 tseukʼ.
Noble, 尊貴 tsuen-kwaiʼ, (minded) 慷慨 ʽkʽong-kʽoi, 光明正大 kwong-ming-chingʼ-taaiʼ.

Nod, 點頭 ʽtim-tʽau, 低頭 tai-tʽau, 瞌頭 ngup-*tʽau.
Noise, 聲響 sheng-ʽheung.
Noisome, 毒 tuuk.
Noisy, 嘈鬧 tsʽo-naauʼ.
Nominal, (merely) 有名無實 ʽyau-meng-mo-shat, 掛名 kwaʼ-*meng.
Nominate, 題名 tʽai-meng.
None, 無 ʽmo.
Nonsense, 譫話 ngaamʼ-waʼ, 糊說 oo-shuetʼ.
Noon, 晏晝 aanʼ-chauʼ, 正午 chingʼ-ʽng.
Noose, 生結 shany-litʼ, 老鼠耳 ʽlo-ʽshue-ʽi, 老鼠掘 ʽlo-ʽshue-kʽekʼ, (to) 掘住 kʽekʼ-chueʼ.
Nor, (see Neither).
North, 北 pak, (N. E., &c.) 東北 tuung-pak, &c.
Nose, 鼻 piʼ, 鼻哥 piʼ-koh.
Nosegay, 鮮花球 sin-fa-*kʽau.
Nostril, 鼻孔 piʼ-ʽhuung, 鼻籠 piʼ-ʽluung.
Not, 不 pat, 非 fi, 唔 ʼm.

Notable, 出衆 ch'uut-chuung, 非常 fi-sheung.
Notch, 割口 koht-'hau, (a) 缺 k'uet, 崩口 pang-'hau.
Note, (to) 記 ki, 記住 ki-chue, (sound) 音 yum, (a paper) 一張字 yat-cheung-tsze, (money) 銀紙 ngan-'chi.
Notepaper, 箋 'tsin.
Nothing, 無乜野 'mo-mat-'ye, 無物 'mo-mat, 無野 'mo-'ye.
Notice, (to) 覺 kok, 顧 koo, 知見 chi-kin, 見得 kin-tak, 睇見 't'ai-kin.
Notification, 報單 po-taan.
Notify, 報知 po-chi.
Notion, 想頭 'seung-t'au.
Notoriety, 起名 'hi-*meng.
Notwithstanding, 雖然 sui-in.
Noun, 實字 shat-tsze.
Nourish, 養 'yeung, 養育 'yeung-yuuk.

Novel, (a) 小説 'siu-*shuet.
Novelty, 新樣 san-*yeung, 新事 san-sze, (a) 新出物 san-ch'uut-mat.
November, 英十一月 Ying-shap-yat-uet.
Novice, 亞初 a-ch'oh.
Now, 如今 ue-kum, 家下 ka-'ha, 而家 i-ka.
Noxious, 惡 ok, 毒 tuuk.
Nozzle, 嘴 'tsui.
Nudity, 脱赤肋 t'uet-ch'ik-lak.
Nugatory, 虛徒 hue-t'o.
Nugget, 金頭 kum-t'au.
Nuisance, 污糟 oo-tso, 臭物 ch'au-mat.
Null and void, 廢字紙 fai-tsze-'chi.
Numbed, 痲痺 ma-muuk, 痲痺 ma-pi.
Number, 數 sho, (No.) 第 tai.
Numeral, 數目字 'sho-muuk-tsze.
Numerically, 照數 chiu-sho.

注 釋

【銀紙】紙币。
【无乜野】没什么。
【想头】想法。
【亚初】新手。
【脱赤肋】裸体。
【金头】天然金块。
【污糟】脏的。
【照数】数字上的。

注释

【亚妈】护士。
【恕树园】苗圃。
【拜诡】敬礼,尊敬。
【顺情】体贴的。

OAK   169   OBL

Nun, (3 kinds) 三姑 saam-koo, (viz.) 尼姑 ni-koo, 道姑 to'-koo, 齋姑 chaai-koo, (Rom. Cath.) 修道女 sau-to'-'nue.
Nunnery, 庵堂 om-t'ong.
Nurse, 亞媽 a'-*ma, (wet) 奶媽 'naai-ma, 濕媽 shup-ma, (dry) 乾媽 kohn-ma, (to) 餵奶 wai'-'naai, (carry) 抱 p'o.
Nursery-garden, 恕樹園 'nun-shue'-*uen.
Nut, 核子 hat'-'tsze.
Nut-crackers, 核子鉗 hat'-'tsze-k'im.
Nutmeg, 荳蔻 tau'-k'au'.
Nutshell, 菓子殼 'kwoh-'tsze-hok'.
Nux-vomica, 馬前 'ma-ts'in.

O

Oak, 橡 tseung', 櫟 lik.
Oakum, 碎纜料 sui'-laam'-*liu', 麻根 ma-kan, (used by Chinese) 竹絲 chuuk-sze.

Oar, 枝槳 chi-'tseung.
Oath, 誓願 shai'-uen', 盟誓 mang-shai'.
Oatmeal, 粗麥粉 t'so-mak'-'fun.
Obedient, 聽話 t'eng'-wa', t'eng'-wa'-ke'.
Obeisance, 拜詭 paai'-kwai'.
Obey, 遵 tsuun, 聽話 t'eng'-wa'.
Object, 物件 mat-kin', (of a verb) 所 —— 'shoh ——, (aim) 意向 i'-heung', 志向 chi'-heung'.
Object, (to) 頂駁 'ting-pok', (as an inferior) 駁嘴 pok'-'tsui.
Obligation, 本分 'poon-fun', (a debt) 賬 cheung'.
Oblige, (force) 監 kaam, 強 'k'eung.
Obliged, (much) 多得 toh-tak, 足領 tsuuk-'ling.
Obliging, 順情 shuun'-ts'ing.
Oblique, 斜 ts'e, ts'e'.
Obliterate, 滅去 mit-hue'.

Oblivion, 忘沒 mong-moot.
Oblong, 長方 ch'eung-fong, 日字樣 yat-tsze-*yeung'.
Obloquy, 凌辱 ling-yuuk.
Obscene, 粗口 ts'o-ʻhau.
Obscure, 幽杳 yau-ʻmiu.
Obsequies, 喪禮 song-ʻlai.
Obsequious, 伏順 fuuk-shuun', 謙讓 him-yeung, 陰柔 yum-yau, (to the rich) 白鴿眼 paak-kop'-ʻngaan.
Observe, 睇 ʻt'ai, 觀 koon, (keep) 守 ʻshau.
Obstinate, 皮氣硬 p'i-hi-ngaang, 固執 koo'-chup, 拗頸 aau'-ʻkeng.
Obstruct, 阻住 ʻchoh-chue', 壅滯 ʻyuung-chai', 塞住 sak-chue'.
Obstruction, 防礙 fong-ngoi', 阻塞 ʻchoh-sak.
Obtain, 得到 tak-ʻto.
Obtrusively, 自擅 tsze'-shin', 擅權 shin'-k'uen.
Obtuse, 鈍 tuun'.

Obviate, 免 ʻmin, 免得 ʻmin-tak.
Obviously, 當面 tong-min'.
Occasion, 機會 ki-ooi', (time) 排 *p'aai, (no) 不使 'm-ʻshai, (to) 使 ʻshai.
Occasional, 或時 waak-shi.
Occult, 秘密 pi'-mat.
Occupation, 事業 sze'-ip, 工夫 kuung-foo.
Occupy, (take possession of) 據 kue', 住 chue'.
Occur, 遇有 ue'-ʻyau—
Occurrence, 事 sze'.
Ocean, 洋海 yeung-ʻhoi.
Ochre, 石黃 shek-wong, 赭石 ʻche-shek, 雌黃 ts'ze-wong.
October, 英十月 Ying-shap-uet.
Ocular, 眼見 ʻngaan-kin'.
Oculist, 眼醫 ʻngaan-i, 眼科醫生 ʻngaan-ʻfoh-i-ʻshang.
Odd, (single) 奇 ki, 單 taan, 零 leng, (strange) 古怪 ʻkoo-kwaai', 奇 k'i.

注释

【得人恨】讨厌，憎恶。
【干犯】冒犯。
Officer: 官员。译为"官府"属误译。
【丢眼角】抛媚眼。

| OFF | 171 | OMI |

Ode, 詩 shi.
Odious, 可惡 ʻhoh-oo⸴.
Odium, (incur) 得人恨 tak-yan-han⸴.
Odour, 香氣 heung-hi⸴, (bad) 臭氣 chʻau⸴-hi⸴.
Of, ── 之 ──chi, ── 嘅 ── ke⸴, (course) 自然 tsze⸴-in, (made of) 俾 ── 做 ʻpi ──tso⸴.
Off, 去 hue⸴, 離 li, (distant) 遠 ʻuen, (off the stage) 過造 kwoh⸴-tso⸴, (be off) 踎喇 liu-la.
Offence, 罪 tsui⸴, (to take) 見怪 kin⸴-kwaai⸴.
Offend, 干犯 kohn-faan⸴.
Offer, 許 ʻhue, 許口 ʻhue-ʻhau, (a price) 出 chʻuut, 還 waan, (present) 送 suung⸴, 獻 hin⸴, (promise) 應承 ying-shing.
Office, (building) 寫字樓 ʻse-tsze⸴-*lau, 館 ʻkoon, 房 *fong, (situation) 職 chik.
Officer, 官府 koon-ʻfoo.
Official, 官 koon.

Officious, 多事 toh-sze⸴, toh-sze⸴-ke⸴.
Often, 多次 toh-tsʻze⸴, 屢次 lue⸴-tsʻze⸴.
Ogle, 丟眼角 tiu-ʻngaan-*kok⸴.
Oh! 眯呀 ai-ya!
Oil, 油 yau.
Oiled cloth, 油布 yau-po⸴.
Oiled paper, 油紙 yau-ʻchi.
Ointment, 膏藥 ko-yeuk.
Old, 老年 ʻlo-nin, 老 ʻlo, (things) 舊 kau⸴.
Olea fragrans, 桂花 kwai⸴-fa.
Oleander, 夾竹桃 kaap-chuuk-tʻo.
Olibanum, 乳香 ʻue-heung, 桃乳 tʻo-ʻue.
Olive, 橄欖 ʻkom-ʻlaam, (foreign) 水翁子 ʻshui-yuung-ʻtsze.
Omelet, 雞蛋餅 kai-taan⸴-ʻpeng.
Omen, 兆頭 chiu⸴-tʻau.
Omit, 漏 lau⸴, 瀨 laai⸴, 遺失 wai-shat.

| OPA | 172 | OPP |

Omnipotent, 無所不能 mo-῾shoh-pat-nang, 全能 ts῾uen-nang.

Omnipresent, 無所不在 mo-῾shoh-pat-tsoi᾿.

Omniscient, 無所不知 mo-῾shoh-pat-chi.

On, 上 sheung᾿, (to be) 在 — 上 tsoi᾿ —— sheung᾿, 喺 ῾hai.

Once, 一回 yat-ooi, 一晌 yat-῾sheung, 一排 yat-*p῾aai, (at) 卽時 tsik-shi.

One, 一 yat, 一個 yat-koh᾿, (single-) 單 taan.

One sided, 偏 p῾in, 一偏 yat-p῾in.

Onion, 葱頭 ῾ts῾uung-t῾au.

Only, 單 taan, 獨 tuuk, 但 taan᾿, 獨係 tuuk-hai᾿, 祇 ῾chi.

Onset } 力攻 lik-kuung.
Onslaught }

Onward, 向前 heuug᾿-ts῾in.

Ooze, 滲漏 shum᾿-lau᾿.

Opaque, 不透光 ᾿m-t῾au᾿-kwong.

Open, 開 hoi, (fix open) 撐開 ch῾aang᾿, (out) 敷開 foo-hoi, (-faced) 率眞 suut-chan, (-handed) 手指疏 ῾shau-῾chi-shoh, (wide apart) 疏 shoh.

Operation, 作爲 tsok᾿-wai, 工夫 kuung-foo, (surgical) 割症 koht᾿-ching᾿.

Ophthalmia, 眼症 ῾ngaan-ching᾿.

Opiate, 致睡藥 chi᾿-shui᾿-yeuk.

Opinion, 意見 i᾿-kin᾿.

Opium, 鴉片 a-p῾in᾿.

Opium-shop, 烟館 ᾵in-῾koon, 鴉片館 a-p῾in᾿-῾koon.

Opopanax, 獨活糕 tuuk-oot-ko.

Opponent, 對頭 tui᾿-*t῾au, 敵手 tik-῾shau.

Opportunely, 恰好 hap-῾ho, 啱 ᾵ngaam.

Opportunity, 機會 ki-ooi᾿.

Oppose, 對 tui᾿, 拒 ῾k῾ue, 抗拒 k῾ong᾿-῾k῾ue, 擋住 ῾tong-chue᾿, 對住 tui᾿-chue᾿.

注 释

【手指疏】大方的，慷慨的。
【割症】外科手术。
Opopanax: 金合欢，愈伤草，一种可以医治伤口的植物。原译"独糕"应为"独活膏"，是治疗皮肤病的药物，属误译。

注 释

【定系】还是。
【高谈士】演说家。
【停当】有秩序的；整齐的。
【好睇】好看。
【孤哀子】孤儿。

Opposite, 對面 *tui*ʼ-minʼ, (contrary) 相反 seungʼ-ʻfaan.
Oppress, 強壓 kʻeung-aatʼ, 困逐 kʻwunʼ-chuuk.
Opprobrious, 鄙薄 ʻpʻi-pok.
Optional, 隨便 tsʻui-*pinʼ, (for) 隨在 tsʻui-tsoiʼ, 隨得 tsʻui-tak.
Opulent, 豐富 fuung-fooʼ.
Or, 或 waak, 抑或 yik-waak, (-else) 定係 tingʼ-hai.
Orach, 萊草 loi-ʻtsʻo (?).
Oral, 口講 ʻhau-ʻkong, ʻhau-ʻkong-keʼ.
Orange, 橙 *chʻaang, (loose skinned) 柑 ʻkom, (small smooth) 桔 kat, (red) 硃砂桔 chue-sha-kat.
Orang-outang, 猩猩 ʻsing-ʻsing.
Orator, 高談士 ʻko-tʻaam-szeʼ.
Orb, 輪 luun, 球 kʻau.
Orbit, 週道 chau-toʼ.
Orchard, 菓園 ʻkwoh-uen.
Orchis, 蘭花 laan-fa, 石仙桃 shek-sin-tʻo.

Order, (arrangement) 次第 tsʻzeʼ-taiʼ, 次序 tsʻzeʼ-tsueʼ, 層次 tsʻang-tsʻzeʼ, (to) 吩咐 fun-fooʼ.
Orderly, 停當 tʻing-tongʼ.
Ordinary, 平常 pʻing-sheung.
Ordure, 糞 funʼ.
Ore, 礦 kʻwaangʼ.
Organ, (musical) 大風琴 taaiʼ-fuung-kʻum, (any) 器 hiʼ.
Orifice, 口 ʻhau, 竅 kʻiuʼ, 籠 ʻluung, 眼 ʻngaan.
Origin, 原頭 uen-tʻau, 原本 uen-ʻpoon.
Originally, 原本 uen-ʻpoon, 原來 uen-loi.
Originate, 創做 chongʼ-tso, 初起 chʻoh-ʻhi.
Oriole, 黃鳥 wong-ʻniu, 黃鶯 wong-ʻang.
Ornament, 文飾 mun-shik, (to) 粧飾 chong-shik.
Ornamental, 好睇 ʻho-ʻtʻai, 花 fa.
Orphan, 孤哀子 koo-oi-ʻtsze, 哀仔 oi-ʻtsai.
Orpiment, 雄黃 huung-wong.

OUT 174 OVE

Orthodox, 正教 ching'-kaau'.
Oscillate, 搖擺 iu-ʿpaai.
Osprey, 鶚 ngok.
Os-pubis, 交骨 kaau-kwut.
Ostensible, 名為 ming-wai.
Ostentatious, 賣弄 maai'-luung', 弄巧 luung'-ʿhaau, 揮霍 fai-fok'.
Ostracion, 牛魚 ngau-ue.
Ostrich, 鴕鳥 t'oh-ʿniu.
Other, 第二 tai'-i', 別個 pit-koh', 別 pit, 他 t'a, (provinces) 外江 ngoi-ᴄkong.
Otherwise, 別樣 pit-yeung', 若唔係 yeuk-'m-hai'.
Otter, 山獺 shaan-ch'aat', (sea-) 海獺 ʿhoi-ch'aat'.
Ought, 應當 ying-tong, 應該 ying-koi, (not) 不可 pat-ʿhoh, 不好 'm-ʿho.
Ounce, (Chinese) 兩 ʿleung, (Eng.) 七錢五 ts'at-ts'in-ʿng.
Our, 我地嘅 ʿngoh-ti'-ke'.
Out, 出 ch'uut, 外 ngoi'.
Outcry, 喊苦 haam'-ʿfoo.

Out-house, 外廠 ngoi'-ᴄch'ong, 外屋 ngoi'-uuk, (built on) 㧿仔屋 me-ᴄtsai-uuk.
Out-let, 去路 hue'-lo'.
Outrage, 橫暴 waang-po'.
Outrageous, 無度 ʿmo-to'.
Outside, 外 ngoi', 外頭 ngoi'-t'au, 外面 ngoi'-min', 外便 ngoi'-pin'.
Outward, 向外 heung'-ngoi', (appearance) 外貌 ngoi'-maau'.
Oval, 鵝蛋樣 ngoh-ᴄch'uun-*yeung'.
Oven, 焗爐 kuuk-lo.
Over, 過 kwoh', (above) 上 sheung', (something over) 有剩 ʿyau-shing'.
Overbearing, 霸氣 pa'-hi'.
Overcast, 起雲 ʿhi-wan.
Overcome, (to) 克制 haak-chai', 制服 chai'-fuuk, 尅 haak.
Overflow, 水滿過 ʿshui-ʿmoon-kwoh'.
Overgrown, 生滿 shang-ʿmoon.

注 釋

【若唔系】否则。
【鹅蟃样】鹅卵型的。
【焗炉】烤箱。
【起云】阴天。

注释

【唔睇】不看。
【越/躙过】跨过。
【枝橈】划桨。
【火船车】明轮船舶的一种推进工具。

OWL 175 PAD

Overhear, 旁聽 p'ong-t'eng.
Overlay, 鋪 p'o, 鍍 to'.
Overlook, 旁視 p'ong-shi', (not see) 唔睇 'm-t'ai, (see Oversee).
Overmuch, 太多 t'aai'-toh, 多過頭 toh-ʻkwoh-t'au.
Overpass, 越 uet, 躙過 naam'-kwoh'.
Overrun, (as types) 褪 t'un'.
Oversee, 督理 tuuk-ʻli, 照管 chiu'-ʻkoon.
Overseer, 監督 kaam-tuuk.
Overspread, 遮蔽 che-pai', 遮蓋 che-k'oi'.
Overthrow, } 打倒 ʻta-ʻto.
Overturn,
Overweening, 過傲 kwoh'-ngo'.
Overwhelm, 沉沒 ch'um-moot.
Overwhelming, 極甚 kik-shum'.
Oviparous, 蛋生 taan'-shang, 卵生 ʻluun-shang.
Owe, 欠 him'.
Owl, 貓兒頭鷹 ʻmaau-i-t'au-ying.

Own, 自已嘅 tsze'-ʻki-ke', 親 ts'an, (confess) 認 ying'.
Owner, 本主 ʻpoon-ʻchue, 原主 uen-ʻchue.
Ox, 牛 ngau, (common) 黃牛 wong-ngau, (steer) 騸牛 shin'-ngau.
Oyster, 蠔 ho.
Oyster-shell windows, 明瓦 ming-ʻnga.

P

Pace, 步 po'.
Pacific Ocean, 太平洋 T'aai'-p'ing-yeung, 南洋 Naam-yeung.
Pacify, 開解 hoi-ʻkaai, 勸息 huen'-sik, 息 sik.
Pack, 收拾 shau-shup, 包好 paau-ʻho, 裝好 chong-ʻho, (off) 落箱 lok-seung.
Paddle, 扒 p'a, (a) 枝橈 chi-*iu.
Paddle-wheel, 火船車 ʻfoh-shuen-ch'e.

Paddy, 禾 woh, (grain) 穀 kuuk.
Padlock, 荷包鎖 hoh-ʻpaau-ʻsoh.
Page, (leaf) 篇 pʻin, (one side of a leaf) 版 ʻpaan.
Pageant, 擺儀仗 ʻpaai-i-cheungʼ.
Pagoda, 塔 tʻaapʼ, (a) 枝塔 chi-tʻaapʼ.
Pail, (water-) 水桶 ʻshui-ʻtʻuung.
Pain, 痛 tʻuungʼ.
Pains-taking, 用心 yuungʼ-sum, 心機 sum-ki.
Paint, 油色 yau-shik, (water colours) 顏色 ngaan-shik.
Painter, 油漆師傅 yau-tsʻat-sze-*fooʼ, 油漆佬 yau-tsʻat-ʻlo, (picture-) 畫工 *waʼ-kuung.
Pair, 對 tuiʼ, 雙 sheung, (to) 配合 pʻooiʼ-hop.
Palace, 宮殿 kuung-tinʼ.
Palate, 腭 ngok, 上腭 sheungʼ-ngok.
Palaver, 虛話 hue-*waʼ.
Pale, 土色 ʻto-shik, 白 paak.

Paling, 欄杆 laan-ʻkohn.
Palisade, 欄檻 laan-laamʼ.
Pall, (for a coffin) 棺罩 koon-chaauʼ.
Pall, (to) 失味 shat-miʼ.
Palliate, 減輕 ʻkaam-heng, 文飾 munʼ-shik.
Palm, 棕樹 tsuung-shueʼ, 桄榔 kwong-long, (cocoanut) 椰樹 ye-shueʼ, (date) 波斯棗 Poh-sze-ʻtso, (fan-) 葵 kʻwai.
Palm of the hand, 手版膛 ʻshau-ʻpaan-tʻong, 掌 ʻcheung.
Palpable, 明明白白 ming-ming-paak-paak.
Palpitate, 跳 tʻiuʼ, (col.) pop-pop-tʻiuʼ.
Palsy, 瘋癱 fuung-ʻtʻaan, 癱瘓 ʻtʻaan-oonʼ.
Paltry, 微賤 mi-tsinʼ.
Pamper, 縱慣口腹 tsuungʼ-kwaanʼ-ʻhau-fuuk.
Pamphlet, 小書 ʻsiu-shue.
Pan, 鐵鑊 tʻit-wok.
Pan-pipe, 笙 shang.

【荷包锁】挂锁。
【摆仪仗】游行，盛会。
【微贱】不足取的，卑鄙的。
【纵惯口腹】骄纵，溺爱。
【铁镬】铁锅。

> 注 释

【瓜样】（房间）有护墙板的，镶框式的。
【戏舞】哑剧。
【较场】阅兵场。
【小绸遮】（女用）遮阳伞。
【包野】包裹，小包。

PAP 177 PAR

Pan-cake, 油煎餅 yau-tsin-ˊpeng.
Pancreas, 甜肉 tʻim-yuuk.
Pander, 窩娼 woh-chʻeung.
Pane, 塊 faaiˋ 片 *pʻinˋ.
Panelled, 瓜樣 ˊkwa-*yeungˋ, 凸朒 tatˋ-ˊkoo, (door) 瓜門 ˊkwa-*moon.
Pang, 暴痛 poˋ-tʻuungˋ 陣痛 chanˋ-tʻuungˋ.
Pangolin, 穿山甲 chʻuen-shaan-kaapˋ.
Panic, 嚇殺 haakˋ-shaatˋ, 嚇死人 haakˋ-ˊsze-yan.
Pansy, 堇菜 ˊkan-tsʻoi.
Pant, 喘 ˊchʻuen.
Panther, 豹 pʻaauˋ.
Pantomime, 戲舞 hiˋ-ˊmoo.
Pantry, 管事房 ˊkoon-szeˋ-*fong.
Papa, 爸爸 pa-pa.
Papaya, 乳瓜 ˊue-ˊkwa, 木瓜 muuk-ˊkwa, 萬壽菓 maanˋ-shauˋ-ˊkwoh.
Paper, 紙 ˊchi.
Paper-money, 銀紙 ngan-ˊchi, (for worship) 元寶 uen-ˊpo, 紙錢 ˊchi-tsʻin.
Paper-mulberry, 楮 ˊchʻue.
Papist, 天主敎徒 Tʻin-ˊchue-kaauˋ-tʻo.
Parable, 譬喻 pʻiˋ-ueˋ.
Parade-ground, 較場 kaauˋ-*chʻeung.
Paradise, 樂園 lok-uen, (bird of) 雀皇 tseukˋ-wong.
Paradoxical, 似相反 ˊtsʻze-seung-ˊfaan.
Paraffine, 煤油 mooi-yau.
Paragraph, 段 tuenˋ, 條 tʻiu.
Parallel, 平排 pʻing-pʻaai, 平行 pʻing-hang.
Paralysis, 癱 ˊtʻaan.
Parapet, 欄圍 laan-wai, 圍墻 wai-tsʻeung.
Paraphernalia, 嫁粧 kaˋ-chong.
Parasite, 寄生 kiˋ-shang.
Parasol, 小綢遮 ˊsiu-chʻau-ˊche.
Parboil, 煮半熟 ˊchue-poonˋ-shuuk.
Parcel, 包野 paauˋ-ˊye.
Parched, 乾燥 kohn-tsʻoˋ.
Parchment, 羊皮紙 yeung-pʻi-ˊchi.

| PAR | 178 | PAR |

Pardon, 赦 $she^{>}$, 赦免 $she^{>}$-$_{<}$min, (beg-) 不該 'm-koi.
Pare, 剝削 p'ai-seuk$^{>}$, (scoop) 挖 waat$^{>}$.
Paregoric, 止痛 $_{<}$chi-t'uung$^{>}$.
Parents, 父母 foo$^{>}$-$_{<}$moo, 兩親 $_{<}$leung-ts'an.
Park, 苑 $_{<}$uen, (an enclosure) 圍 *wai.
Parliament, 上下議院 sheung$^{>}$-ha$^{>}$-i-*uen$^{>}$.
Parlour, 客廳 haak$^{>}$-$_{<}$t'eng.
Parody, 改作笑話 $_{<}$koi-tsok$^{>}$-siu$^{>}$-*wa.
Paroquet, 鸚哥 $_{<}$ang-$_{<}$koh.
Paroxysm, 抽搐 ch'au-ch'uuk$^{>}$, 忽然痛 fut-in-t'uung$^{>}$.
Parrot, 鸚鵡 ying-$^{<}$moo, 鶯哥 $_{<}$ang-$_{<}$koh.
Parrot fish, 鷄公魚 $_{<}$kai-$_{<}$kuung-*ue.
Parry, 擋格 $^{<}$tong-kaak$^{>}$.
Parsee, 白頭人 Paak-t'au-yan, 波斯人 Poh-sze-yan.
Parsimonious, 慳吝 haan-luun$^{>}$.

Parsley, 芫荽 uen-$_{<}$sai.
Parsnip, 葫蘿蔔 oo-loh-paak.
Part, 分 fun$^{>}$, (to) 分開 fun-hoi, (with) 捨 $_{<}$she.
Partake, 有分 $_{<}$yau-*fun$^{>}$.
Partial, 一偏 yat-p'in, yat-p'in-ke$^{>}$.
Participate, 有分 $_{<}$yau-*fun$^{>}$.
Particle, (word) 虛字眼 hue-tsze$^{>}$-$_{<}$ngaan, (small) 微末 mi-moot.
Particular, (special) 特 tak, (important) 要緊 iu$^{>}$-$^{<}$kan, (each) 一一 yat-yat, (careful) 仔細 $^{<}$tsze-sai$^{>}$.
Particularize, 逐一逐二 chuuk-yat-chuuk-i$^{>}$.
Particularly, 特要 tak-iu$^{>}$, 專爲 chuen-wai.
Partition, 隔壁 kaak$^{>}$ pik$^{>}$, 間牆 kaan$^{>}$-ts'eung, (to) 間隔 kaan$^{>}$-kaak$^{>}$.
Partly, 有的係 $_{<}$yau-$_{<}$ti-hai$^{>}$.
Partner, 夥計 $^{<}$foh-ki$^{>}$, 夥伴 $^{<}$foh-poon$^{>}$.

注 释

【风车花】西番莲，多年生常绿攀缘木质藤本植物，有"果汁之王"的美誉。
【火性】易怒的。
【不郁】不动。
【路票】护照。

Partridge, 鷓鴣 *che²-ͺkoo*, 竹絲鷄 *chuuk-ͺsze-ͺkai*.
Party, 羣黨 *k'wan-ͺtong*, 班 *paan*, 幫 *pong*.
Pass, (to) 過去 *kwoh²-hue²*, 行過 *hang-kwoh²*, (a) 關 *kwaan*, (a street-) 街紙 *kaai-ͺchi*, (night-) 夜紙 *ye²-ͺchi*, (mountain) 峽 *haap²*.
Pass a law, 設例 *ch'it²-lai²*, (a time, or place) 過 *kwoh²*.
Passage, 路 *lo²*, 門 *moon*, 冷巷 *ͺlaang-*hong*²*.
Passage-boat, 渡船 *to²-shuen*, **to²*.
Passenger, 搭客 *taap²-haak²*.
Passion, (anger) 怒 *no²*, (desire) 情欲 *ts'ing-yuuk*, (generally) 烈氣 *lit-hi²*, (the seven passions) 七情 *ts'at-ts'ing*.
Passion-flower, 風車花 *ͺfuung-ͺch'e-ͺfa*.
Passionate, 火性 *ͺfoh-sing²-ke²*.

Passive, (not moving) 不郁 *'m-yuuk*, (N.B. signs of the passive, as, 受 *shau²*, 被 *pi²*, 見 *kin²*, &c., should be used sparingly and in each case according to example of *natives*).
Passover, (the) 踰越節 *ue-uet-tsit²*.
Passport, 路票 *lo²-p'iu²*.
Pass-word, 暗號 *om²-*ho²*.
Past, 過了 *kwoh²-ͺliu, kwoh²-hiu*.
Paste, 漿糊 *tseung-oo*, (to) 裱 *ͺp'iu*, 粘 *nim*.
Pasteboard, 裱紙皮 *ͺp'iu-ͺchi-p'i*.
Paster, 裱匠 *ͺp'iu-tseung²*.
Pastor, 牧 *muuk*, (minister) 牧師 *muuk-sze*.
Pastry, 點心 *ͺtim-ͺsum*, 麵食 *min²-shik*, (covered dishes) 麵龜 *min²-ͺkwai*.
Pasture, 牧草 *muuk-ͺts'o*.
Pat, (to) 拍 *p'aak²*.
Patch, 補拿 *ͺpo-ͺim*, (to) 釘補拿 *teng-ͺpo-ͺim*, 補 *ͺpo*.
Patch-work, 摒 *p'ing²*.

Patent, (to grant a) 批准 p'ai-‿chuun-chuen-tso’, (a) 執照 chup-chiu’.
Path, 小路 ‿siu-lo’.
Pathetic, 傷心話 sheung-sum-*wa’, 動情 tuung’-ts'ing.
Patience, 忍耐 ‿yan-noi’.
Patrimony, 基業 ki-ip.
Patron, 帮顧主 pong-koo-‿chue, 主顧 ‿chue-*koo’, 恩主 yan-‿chue.
Patronize, 照顧 chiu’-koo’, 幫襯 pong-ch'an’.
Patter, 滴滴達達 tik-tik-taat-taat.
Pattern, 樣子 yeung’-‿tsze.
Patty, 角仔 kok’-‿tsai, 餃子 kaau-‿tsze.
Pauper, 無倚賴 ‿mo-‿i-laai’.
Pause, 歇吓 hit’-‿ha.
Pave, 砌平石 ts'ai’-p'ing-shek.
Pavement, 石路 shek-lo’, 鋪石路 p'o-shek-lo’, (of bricks) 街磚地 kaai-‿chuen-ti’.

Pavilion, 涼亭 leung-*t'ing, 亭 *t'ing.
Paw, (蹯 faan), 掌 ‿cheung, 爪 ‿chaau.
Pawn, (to) 當 tong’, 當押 tong’-aat’, (a pledge) 當頭 tong’-t'au, (in chess) 卒 tsuut.
Pawn-broker, 當主 tong’-‿chue.
Pawn-shop, 當鋪 tong’-p'o.
Pawn-ticket, 當票 tong’-p'iu.
Pay, 交 (銀) kaau (ngan), 還 waan.
Pay-day, 支銀日期 chi-*ngan-yat-k'i.
Payments, 支 (銀) chi, (ngan).
Peas, (green) 青荳 ts'eng-*tau, 荷蘭荳 Hoh-‿laan-*tau.
Peace, 平安 p'ing-ohn, (international) 和 woh, (general) 太平 t'aai’-p'ing, (keep the) 守分 ‿shau-fun’, 守和 ‿shau-woh, (break the) 失和 shat-woh.

注 释

【角仔】一种广东小吃，又称油角。
【无倚赖】穷人，乞丐。
【歇吓】停顿，歇气。

注释

【担】重量单位，一担为50千克。

【丢书包】学究，书呆子。

【贩仔】小贩。

【塘鹅】鹈鹕。

【新埠】（马来西亚）槟榔屿。1786年英国东印度公司侵占其地后，开辟商埠，故当时称为新埠。

Peach, 桃 *tʻo, (best kind) 鸚嘴桃 ying-ʻtsui-*tʻo.
Peacock, 孔雀 ʻhuung-tseukʼ.
Peacock's feather, 翎 ling, (superior double eyed) 雙眼花翎 sheung-ʻngaan-fa-ling, (next order) 花翎 fa-ling, (inferior) 藍翎 laam-ling.
Peak, 山頂 shaan-ʻteng, 嶺頭 ʻling-tʻau, 山峰 shaan-fuuny.
Pear, 沙梨 sha-*li, (from the north) 雪梨 suetʼ-*li.
Pearl, 珍珠 chan-chue.
Pearl barley, 苡米 ʻi-ʻmai.
Pearl-oyster, 珠蚌 chue-ʻpʻong.
Peasant, 村佬 ʻtsʻuen-ʻlo, 村夫 ʻtsʻuen-foo.
Peat, 地面炭 tiʼ-minʼ-tʻaanʼ.
Pebble, 石礛 shek-chʻuun.
Peck, (to) 啄 teukʼ, teung ; (a) 斗 ʻtau.
Pecul, 擔 taamʼ.
Peculiar, 自己 tszeʼ-ʻki, tszeʼ-ʻki-keʼ, 另自 lingʼ-tszeʼ, 奇特 kʻi-tak.

Pedant, 丟書包 ʻtiu-ʻshue-paau.
Pedler, 販仔 faanʼ-ʻtsai, 担頭仔 taamʼ-*tʻau-ʻtsai.
Peel, (to) 剝皮 mok-pʻi.
Peep, 窺探 kʻwai-tʻaamʼ, 覩 chong, 偷睇 tʻau-tʻai.
Peevish, 嬲嫩 nau-nat.
Peg, 釘杙 teng-tak.
Peking, 北京 Pak-king.
Pekoe-tea, 白毫茶 paak-ho-chʻa.
Pelican, 塘鵝 tʻong-*ngoh.
Pelt, (to) 掟 tengʼ.
Pelvis, 尻骨盤 haau-kwut-pʻoon.
Pen, pencil, 支筆 chi-put, (lead-) 鉛筆 uen-put, (coop) 欄 laan.
Penalty, 刑罰 ying-fat.
Penang, 新埠 San-fauʼ.
Pending, 未定 miʼ-tingʼ.
Pendulum, 擺 ʻpaai.
Penetrate, 透入 tʻauʼ-yup, 深入 shum-yup.
Penguin, 企鵝 kʻi-*ngoh.
Penis, 陽物 yeung-mat, (VULG.) tsʻat.

Penitence, 悔心 fooi-sum.	Percolate, 滲漏 shum-lau.
Pennant, 旒 p'ooi, 旗帶 k'i-taai.	Percussion cap, 銅帽子 t'uung-mo-tsze.
Pension, 養老銀 yeung-lo-*ngan, 太平糧 t'ai-p'ing-leung.	Peremptory, 緊緊 kan-kan.
	Perennial, 週年 chau-nin, chau-nin-ke.
Pensive, 心思思 sum-sze-sze.	Perfect, 成全 shing-ts'uen, 齊 ts'ai.
Penurious, 慳吝 haan-luun.	
Peony, 牡丹花 maau-taan-fa.	Perfectly, 十分 shap-fun.
People, 民 mun, 百姓 paak-sing.	Perfidious, 奸詐 kaan-cha.
	Perforate, 鑽通 tsuen-t'uung, 穿 ch'uen.
Pepper, 胡椒 oo-tsiu, 椒末 tsiu-moot, (red) 花椒 fa-tsiu.	Perform, 行 hang, 做 tso.
	Perfume, 香 heung, 香料 heung-*liu.
Peppermint, 薄荷 pok-hoh.	Pergularia, 夜蘭香 ye-laan-heung.
Perambulate, 巡行 ts'uun-hang.	
Perceive, 覺得 kok-tak, 見 kin.	Perhaps, 或者 waak-che, (it is) 係都唔定 hai-too-'m-ting.
Per cent, 每一百 mooi-yat-paak, (discount three) 九七扣 kau-ts'at-k'au.	Peril, 危險 ngai-him, 危險處 ngai-him-shue.
	Period, (time) 時候 shi-hau, (in writing) 斷句圈 t'uen-kue-huen.
Perceptible, 睇得 t'ai-tak, t'ai-tak-ke.	
Perch, 栖 ts'ai, (to) 踎 mau, (a fish) 鱸魚 lo-*ue, 鹹頭 waak-t'au.	Periodic, 循還 ts'uun-waan, 輪時 lnuu-shi.

注 释

【心思思】心痒痒。Pensive意为"沉思的",与"心思思"并不完全同义。

【睇得】可察觉到的。

【銅帽子】雷管。

【系都唔定】不一定,或许。

【轮时】定期的,周期的。

注释

【誓枉愿】伪誓，伪证。
【人情纸】许可证。
【企直】站直。

Perish, 滅亡 mit-mong, 沈淪 ch'um-luun.
Perishable, 易壞 i'-waai'.
Perjure, 枉誓 ‿wong-shai', 發枉誓 faat'-‿wong-shai'.
Perjury, 誓枉願 shai'-‿wong-uen'.
Permanent, 恆久 hang-‿kau.
Permeate, 通透 t'uung-t'au'.
Permit, 准 ‿chuun, 俾 ‿pi, 許准 ‿hue-‿chuun, 由得 yau-tak.
Permit, (a) 人情紙 yan-ts'ing-‿chi.
Pernicious, 利害 li'-hoi'.
Perpendicular, 豎直 shue'-chik, 企直 ‿k'i-chik, 棟企 tuung'-‿k'e.
Perpetual, 永 ‿wing.
Perpetuate, 常存 sheung-ts'uen.
Perplex, 煩擾 faan-‿iu.
Perplexity, 紛紛 fun-fun, 曲折 k'uuk-chit'.
Persecute, 困逐 k'wun'-chuuk.

Perseverance, 始終如一 ‿c'hi-chuung-ue-yat, 恆心 hang-sum.
Persimmon, 柿 *ts'ze, (soft) 臉柿 num-*ts'ze.
Persist, 硬要 *ngaang'-iu', 不歇要 pat-hit'-iu', 固執 koo'-chup.
Person, 位 wai', 人 yan, (body) 身 shan, (in) 親身 ts'an-shan.
Perspicacious, 聰明 ts'uung-ming.
Perspicuous, 明白 ming-paak.
Perspiration, 汗 hohn'.
Perspire, 出汗 ch'uut-hohn'.
Persuade, 勸服 huen'-fuuk.
Pert, 傷突 t'ong-tat.
Pertinacious, 固執 koo'-chup, 執硬 chup-ngaang'.
Perturb, 擾亂 ‿iu-luen'.
Perturbed, 着忙 cheuk-mong.
Peruvian-bark, 金雞勒 kum-kai-lak.
Pervade, 通暢 t'uung-ch'eung', 暢達 ch'eung'-taat.

Perverse, 乖僻 kwaai-p'ik, 剛戾 kong-lui`, 扭頸 `nau-`keng.
Pervert, 弄壞 luung`-waai`.
Pervious, 透得 t'au`-tak, t'au`-tak-ke`.
Pestilence, 瘟疫 wan-yik.
Pestle, 舂杵 chuung-ch'ue, (for rice) 碓 tui`.
Pet, (child) 寵愛仔 `chuung-oi`-`tsai.
Petal, 花瓣 fa-faan`.
Petition, 禀 `pun.
Petroleum, 石油 shek-yau.
Petted, 縱慣 tsuung`-kwaan`.
Petticoat, 中裙 chuung-k'wun, 內裙 noi`-k'wun.
Pettish } 小嫌 `siu-im, 俺尖 im-tsim.
Petulant
Petuntsze, 白不子 paak-`tuun-`tsze.
Pewter, 鑞錫 laap-sek`.
Phantom, 幻景 waan`-`king.

Pheasant, 山鷄 shaan-kai, (golden) 錦鷄 `kum-kai, (argus) 鸞鷄 luen-kai, (peacock-) 金錢鷄 kum-ts'in-kai.
Phenix, 鳳凰 fuung`-wong.
Phenomenon, 象 tseung`.
Philosopher, 博士 pok`-sze`.
Phlegm, 痰涎 t'aam-in, t'aam-shin.
Phlegmatic, 性慢 sing`-maan`, 閒八 haan-paat`, 慢閒 maan`-haan.
Phonography, (representing sounds merely) 寫白字 `se-paak-tsze`.
Photograph, 影相 `ying-*seung`.
Phrase, 句話 kue`-wa`.
Phthisis, 癆病 lo-peng`.
Physical, 有形 `yau-ying.
Physician, 醫生 i-`shang.
Physiognomy, 相 seung`, (science) 相學 seung`-hok.
Piano, 洋琴 yeung-k'um.

注 释

【透得】能接受的，可渗透的。
【性慢】迟钝的。

注 释

【插手佬】扒手。
【游燕】野餐。
【面龟】馅饼。
【鼠摩】小偷小摸。

Pick, up, 拈起 nim-‘hi, 拾起 shap-‘hi, 執 chup, (the teeth) 莿牙 ts‘ze-nga, (flowers, &c.) 摘 chaak, (choose) 揀 ‘kaan, (tease) 搣 mit, (nibble) 啯 luun, (pierce) 啄 teung.
Pick-axe, 鷄嘴斧 kai-‘tsui-‘foo, 番釘 faan-‚teng.
Picket, (a stake) 樁 chong.
Pickled, 鹹 haam.
Pickles, 酸菓 suen-‘kwoh.
Pick-pocket, 剪綹 ‘tsin-‘lau, ‘tsin-‘nau-‘lo, 插手佬 ch‘aap-‘shau-‘lo.
Picnic, 遊燕 yau-in’.
Picture, 畫 wa’, *wa’, (-frame) 畫架 wa’-ka’.
Picul, 擔 taam’.
Pie, (bird) 喜鵲 ‘hi-ts‘euk’, (pastry) 麵龜 min’-kwai.
Pie-bald, 斑駁 paan-pok’.
Piece, 塊 faai’, 件 kin’, (of cloth) 疋 p‘ut.
Piece-work, 斷件工夫 tuen’-*kin’-kuung-foo.
Pier, 馬頭 ‘ma-t‘au.

Pierce, 劖 ts‘im, 刮 kat, 刮穿 kat-ch‘uen.
Piety, (filial) 孝 haau’, (religion) 虔敬 k‘in-king’.
Pig, 猪 ‚chue, (a) 隻猪 chek’-‚chue.
Pigeon, 白鴿 paak-kop’.
Pigment, 顏料 ngaan-liu’.
Pigmy, 矮佬仔 ‘ai-‘lo-‘tsai.
Pigtail, 條辮 t‘iu-‚pin.
Pike, (a) 一枝鎗 yat-chi-ts‘eung.
Pike, fish, 班魚 paan-ue.
Pile up, 壘起 tip-‘hi, 挪起 lum’-‘hi, 壘 ‘lui, (drive piles) 打椿 ‘ta-chong.
Piles, (disease) 痔瘡 chi’-‚ch‘ong, (wooden) 椿 chong.
Pilfer, 鼠摩 ‘shue-‚moh, 鼠竊 ‘shue-sit’.
Pilferer, 三隻手 saam-chek’-‘shau.
Pilgrim, 遊客 yau-haak’.
Pill, 藥丸 yeuk-*uen.
Pillage, 搶掠 ‘ts‘eung-leuk, 刼掠 kip’-leuk.

Pillar, 條柱 tʻiu-ᶜchʻue, 柱墩 ᶜchʻue-ᶜtun, (monument) 碑 pi.	Pioneer, 開路先鋒 hoi-lo⸌-ᶜsin-ƒuung.
Pillow, 枕頭 ᶜchum-tʻau.	Pious, 虔心 kʻin-sum.
Pilot, 引水人 ᶜyan-ᶜshui-yan, 帶水佬 taai⸌-ᶜshui-ᶜlo, naai⸌-ᶜshui-ᶜlo.	Pip, (of fowls) 雞髆 kai-ᶜkʻang, (seed) 核 wat.
	Pipe, 筒 *tʻuung, (opium-) 鎗 ᶜtsʻeung.
Piloting, 帶船 taai⸌-shuen, naai⸌-shuen.	Pirate, 海賊 ᶜhoi-tsʻaak.
Pimp, 做龜 tso⸌-ᶜkwai.	Pistil, 花蕊 fa-ᶜyui.
Pimple, 粉刺 ᶜfun-tsʻze⸌.	Pistol, 手鎗 ᶜshau-ᶜtsʻeung.
Pin, 頭針 tʻau-chum, 釘 teng.	Piston, (牡 ᶜmau), 榫 suut.
	Pit, 阱 ᶜtseng, 潭 tʻaam, ᶜtʻum.
Pinafore, 圍裙 wai-*kʻwun.	Pitch, 吧碼油 ᶜpa-ᶜma-yau.
Pincers, 鉗 *kʻim.	
Pinch, (to) 攝 nip, 搣 mit.	Pitcher, 水埕 ᶜshui-chʻing.
Pine, (wood) 杉 chʻaam⸌.	Pitcher-plant, 豬籠草 chue-luung-ᶜtsʻo.
Pine, (to) 失志 shat-chiᵎ, 喪氣 song⸌-hi⸌, 消瘦 siu-shau⸌.	Pitch-fork, 禾杈 woh-ᶜchʻa.
	Pith, 樹心 shue⸌-ᶜsum.
Pine-apple, 波羅菓 poh-loh-ᶜkwoh.	Pith-paper, 蓪紙 tʻuung-ᶜchi, 紙蓪 ᶜchi-tʻuung.
Pink, 剪邊羅 ᶜtsin-pin-loh.	Pithy, 有力 ᶜyau-lik, ᶜyau-lik-ke⸌.
Pin-money, 針𥻗銀 chum-ᶜchi-*ngan.	
	Pitted, (pock-) 痘皮 tau⸌-pʻi.
Pinnacle, 頂 ᶜteng.	Pity, 可憐 ᶜhoh-lin, 憐恤 lin-suut, 哀憐 oi-lin.
Pint, (a) 半斤 poon⸌-kan.	

注 释

【引水人/带水人】领航员。
【做龟】拉皮条。
【针黹银】零花钱。

注 释

【会和翻】能和解的。
【㨆埋】折起来。
【攻灰】石膏，灰泥。
【拼辫】扎麻花辫。
【好似真】貌似可信的。

Pivot, 轉樞 ‛chuen-suut.
Placable, 會和翻 ‛ooi-woh-faan.
Placard, 帖 t‛ip’, 揭帖 k‛it’-t‛ip’, (anonymous) 白帖 paak-*t‛ip’, (with a name) 長紅 ch‛eung-huung.
Place, 處 ch‛ue’, 地方 ti’-fong, 定 *teng’, (to) 安置 ohn-chi’, 擠 chai, (one) 一笪 yat-taat’.
Placenta, 胎衣 t‛oi-i, 後人 hau’-*yan.
Placid, 和氣 woh-hi’.
Plagiarism, 抄襲 ch‛aau-tsaap.
Plague, 瘟疫 wan-yik, 黃瘟病 wong-wan-peng’, (to) 難爲 naan-wai.
Plaice, 甑閉魚 tsang-pai’-ue.
Plain, 明白 ming-paak, (even) 平 p‛ing, (unadorned) 樸素 p‛ok’-so’, (a) 平原 p‛ing-uen.
Plaintiff, 原告 uen-ko’.
Plait, 㨆埋 pun’-maai, (fold) 蹙埋 ts‛uuk-maai.

Plan, 方法 fong-faat’, (to) 謀 mau, 謀度 mau-tok.
Plane, (tool) 刨 *p‛aau, (to) 刨 p‛aau.
Planet, 行星 hang-‛sing.
Plank, 橋板 k‛iu-‛paan, 厚木板 hau’-muuk-‛paan.
Plant, (a) 草 ‛ts‛o, (to) 種 chuung’, (rice) 蒔禾 shi’-woh.
Plantago, 車前草 ch‛e-ts‛in-‛ts‛o.
Plantain, 蕉 ‛tsiu, (fragrant) 香牙蕉 heung-nga-‛tsiu, (long) 龍牙蕉 luung-nga-‛tsiu.
Plaster, (to) 攻灰 ‛mun-fooi, 溫 tong’, (medical) 膏藥 ko-yeuk.
Plat, (to) 拼 pun’, (the cue) 拼辮 pun’-‛pin.
Plate, (a) 碟 *tip, 隻碟 chek’-*tip, (to) 鍍 to’.
Platform, 棚 p‛aang, 臺 t‛oi, *t‛oi.
Platina, 白金 paak-‛kum.
Plausible, 好似真 ‛ho-‛ts‛ze-chan.

Play, 反斗 ˊfaan-ˊtau, 頑耍 waan-ˊsha, (TRANS. VERB) 打 ˊta, 弄 luung’, (as a guitar) 彈 t'aan, (as a violin) 研 ngaan, (as a fife) 吹 ch'ui.

Play-acting, 做戲 tso’-hi’.

Play-day, 放假日 fong’-ka’-yat.

Player, 戲子 hi’-ˊtsze.

Plea, 解訴 ˊkaai-so’, 供狀 kuung-chong’.

Pleasant, 爽快 ˊshong-faai’, 得意 tak-i’.

Please, 悅 uet, 樂 lok, (if you) 請 ˊts'eng, (as you) 隨便 ts'ui-*pin’.

Pleased, 歡喜 foon-ˊhi.

Pleasure, 快樂 faai’-lok, (— excursion) 遊嬉 yau-hi.

Plebeian, 俗 tsuuk.

Pledge, 當頭 tong-t'au, (to) 按當 ohn’-tong’, 拚 p'oon’, (in drinking) 酬酢 ch'au-tsok, 敬酒 king’-ˊtsau, 勸酒 huen’-ˊtsau.

Plenipotentiary, 全權 ts'uen-k'uen.

Plentiful, 豐阜 fuung-fau’, 豐足 fuung-tsuuk.

Plethora, 血實 huet’-shat, 壯實 chong’-shat.

Pleurisy, 肺胞膜炎 fai-paau-mok-im.

Pliable, 柔軟 yau-ˊuen, 艮 t'suun-leung, 易轉 i’-chuen.

Plight, (state) 地位 ti’-wai’.

Plod, 勞勞 lo-lo.

Plot, 計策 kai’-ch'aak’, (lot) 塊 faai’.

Plough, (to) 犁 lai, 使 ˊshai, 耕 kang, (a) 把犁 ˊpa-lai.

Ploughshare, 犁頭嘴 lai-t'au-ˊtsui.

Pluck, 摘 chaak, (out) 拔 pat, 猛出來 mang’-ch'uut-lai, (up courage) 揚起心肝 tik-ˊhi-sum-kohn.

Plug, (塞子 sak-ˊtsze), 椊 suut.

Plum, 梅 *mooi, 李 ˊli.

Plumb-line, 吊鉈 tiu’-t'oh, 準繩 ˊchuun-shing.

注 释

【当头】抵押物。
【血实】多血症。
【劳劳】辛勤工作。
【扬起心肝】打定主意，决心。

注 释

【好肉耳】丰满的。
【沈下】陷入，跳进。
【戥正】平衡。

Plume, 翎 ˊling.
Plump, 好肉耳 ˊho-yuuk-ˊi, 肥粒粒 fi-nup-nup.
Plunder, 打劫 ˊta-kipˋ, 搶劫 ˊts'eung-kipˋ.
Plunge, 沈下 chumˋ-ˊha, 投水 t'auˋ-ˊshui, (noise) 泵聲 tumˋ-sheng.
Pluto, 閻羅王 Im-loh-wong.
Ply, 趕緊 ˊkohn-ˊkan, 勤 k'an, 趕起 ˊkohn-ˊhi.
Pocket, 衫袋 shaam-*toiˋ, 袋 *toiˋ.
Pock-marked, 痘皮 tauˋ-p'i.
Pod, 荳莢 tauˋ-kaapˋ.
Poem, 首詩 ˊshau-ˊshi.
Poet, 詩人 shi-yan.
Poignant, 辣 laat.
Point, 尖 tsim, 尖處 tsim-shueˋ, 尖嘴 tsim-ˊtsui, (dot) 點 ˊtim, (point out) 指出 chi-ch'uut, 指點 ˊchi-ˊtim, (to plaster) 批灰 ˊp'ai-fooi.
Poise, 戥正 tangˋ-cheng.
Poison, 毒 tuuk, 毒物 tuuk-mat, (to) 毒死 tuuk-ˊsze.

Poisoned, 服毒 fuuk-tuuk.
Poke, (to) 刺 ts'zeˋ, (stir) 撩起 ˊliu-ˊhi.
Poker, 火棒 ˊfoh-ˊp'aang.
Poke-weed, 菖 fuuk.
Pole, 竿 kohn, 杠 kongˋ, (north) 北極 pak-kik, (south) 南極 naam-kik.
Pole a boat, 撐船 ch'aang-shuen.
Pole-cat, 臭貓 ch'auˋ-ˊmaan.
Polianthes, 玉簪花 yuuk-ˊtsaam-fa.
Police, 差役 ch'aai-yik, (in Hongkong) 綠衣 luuk-ˊi.
Police Court, 巡理府 ts'uun-ˊli-ˊfoo.
Police-office, 巡捕廳 ts'uun-poˋ-ˊt'eng.
Polish, 磨擦 moh-ts'aatˋ, 擦光 ts'aatˋ-kwong, 磨光 moh-kwong.
Polite, 有禮貌 ˊyau-ˊlai-maauˋ, (you are) 好話 ˊho-waˋ.
Politics, 國事 kwok-szeˋ.
Pollen, 花粉 fa-ˊfun.

Pollute, 污糜 oo-mit, 整污 ‵ching-oo.
Polypus, (in the nose) 鼻菌 pi‵-‵k'wun), 鼻蛇 pi'-she.
Pomatum, 頭髮油 t'au-faat'-yau, 香油 heung-yau.
Pomegranate, 石榴 shek-*lau.
Pommel, (to) 搥泵 ch'ui-‵tum.
Pomp, 繁華 faan-wa.
Pomphret, 鯧魚 ts'ong-*ue.
Pompous, 駕子大 ka'-‵tsze-taai'.
Pond, 池塘 ch'i-t'ong.
Ponder, 默想 mak-‵seung, 深想 shum-‵seung, 細想 sai'-‵seung.
Ponderous, 重 ‵ch'uung.
Pond-weed, 藻 ‵tso.
Pongee, 綢 *ch'au.
Pool, 池 ch'i, 水氹 ‵shui-‵t'um.
Poop, 船尾樓 shuen-‵mi-lau.
Poor, 貧窮 p'un-k'uung, 貧寒 p'un-hohn.

Poor health, 不受用 ‵m-shau'-yuung'.
Pop, (a sound) (COL.) pop-sheng.
Pope, 教王 kaau-wong'.
Poppy, 罌粟 ang-suuk, 阿芙蓉 oh-foo-yuung.
Popular, 民愛 mun-oi'.
Population, 戶口 oo'-‵hau.
Porcelain, 瓷 ts'ze, (ware) 瓷器 ts'ze-hi'.
Porch, 頭門拱 t'au-moon-‵kuung.
Porcupine, 箭猪 tsin'-chue.
Pores, 毛孔 mo-‵huung, 竅 k'iu'.
Pork, 猪肉 chue-yuuk.
Porpoise, 猪魚 chue-ue.
Porridge, 麥粉羹 mak-‵fun-kang, 煮熟麥粉 ‵chue-shuuk-mak-‵fun.
Port, (a) 港口 ‵kong-‵hau, 埠頭 *fau'-t'au, (-side) 船左 shuen-‵tsoh.
Port-clearance, 紅牌 huung-p'aai.
Portent, 凶兆 huung-chiu'.

注 释

【担担】行李搬运工。
【西洋国】（清朝时指）葡萄牙。
【鬼迷】着魔的。
【街招】海报，标语。
【展缓】延缓，延迟。
【再笔】附录。

Porter, (at a gate) 看門公 ˏhohn-moon-ˏkuung, (carrier) 挑夫 tʻiu-foo, (to be a) 擔擔 taam-taamʾ.
Portfolio, 書夾 shue-kaapˏ.
Portion, 分子 funʾ-ˏtsze, 分 funʾ, 分額 funʾ-ngaak.
Portland cement, 英坭 ying-*nai.
Portly, 肥壯 fi-chongʾ.
Portmanteau, 背包 pooiʾ-paau.
Portrait, 眞 ˏchan, 像 *tseung, 相 seungʾ.
Portray, 寫眞 ˊse-ˏchan.
Portugal, 西洋國 Sai-yeung-kwokˏ.
Pose, (to) 難 naan.
Position, 地位 tiʾ-waiʾ.
Positively, 一定 yat-ting ʾ, 偏偏 pʻin-pʻin.
Possess, 有 ˊyau, 常有 sheung-ˊyau.
Possessed, (by a demon) 鬼迷 ˊkwai-mai.
Possessions, 所有 ˊshoh-ˊyau.
Possible, 做得 tsoʾ-tak, tsoʾ-tak-ˊke, 能 nang, 得 tak.

Post, (a pillar) 支柱 chi-ˊchʻue, (letter-) 通書信 tʻuung-shue-suunʾ, 驛 yik.
Postage, 酒資 ˊtsau-ˏtsze, 信貲 suunʾ-ˏtsze.
Poster, 街招 ˏkaai-ˏchiu.
Postman, 千里馬 tsʻin-ˊli-ma, (-horse) 快馬 faaiʾ-ˏma.
Postmaster General, 驛務司 Yik-mooʾ-ˏsze.
Post-office, 書信館 shue-suunʾ-ˊkoon.
Postpone, 展緩 ˊchin-oon, 推遲 tʻui-chʻi.
Postscript, 再筆 tsoiʾ-put.
Posture, 形勢 ying-shaiʾ.
Pot, 壺 oo, *oo, (chamber-) 便壺 pinʾ-*oo, (to boil in) 煲 ˏpo, (COL.) tup, (flower-) 花盤 fa-pʻoon.
Potash, 鹻 ˊkaan.
Potatoe, 荷蘭薯 Hoh-ˏlaan-*shue, 薯仔 shue-ˊtsai, (sweet) 番薯 faan-*shue.
Pot-belly, 肥肚腩 fi-tʻo-ˊnaam.

Potency, 勢力 shai²-lik, 功力 kuung-lik.
Pottage, (to make) 煮熟麥粉 ⸢chue-shuuk-mak-⸜fun.
Pottery, 瓦器 ⸢nga-hi², 缸瓦 kong-⸢nga, (-kiln) 瓦窰 ⸢nga-iu.
Pouch, 囊 nong, 袋 *toi².
Poultice, 洽瘡材料 up-⸜ch'ong-ts'oi-liu², (put on, of rice) 俾爛飯洽 ⸢pi-laan²-faan²-up.
Poultry, 雞鴨 kai-aap².
Pounce upon, 搶 ⸢ts'eung.
Pound, (to) 椿 chuung, (rub and grind) 擂 lui, (weight) 磅 p'ong, 十二兩 shap-i²-⸜leung.
Pour out, 斟 chum, 倒出 ⸢to-ch'uut, (in) 潞 lo², 灌入去 koon²-yup-hue².
Pout, 攖脣 ying-shuun.
Powder, 粉 ⸢fun, 末 *moot, (gun-) 火藥 ⸢foh-yeuk, (medicine) 藥散 yeuk-⸢saan.

Power, 才能 ts'oi-nang, 勢力 shai²-lik, 權柄 k'uen-ping².
Pox, (syphilis) 生疔病 shang-teng-peng², 疳瘡 kom-⸜ch'ong.
Practicable, 可用 ⸢hoh-yuung², 使得 ⸢shai-tak, 可以做得 ⸢hoh-⸢i-tso²-tak.
Practical joke, 整頓人 ⸢ching-tun²-yan-ke².
Practice, 習練 tsaap-lin².
Praise, 讚美 tsaan²-⸢mi, 讚羨 tsaan²-sin², 褒獎 po-⸜tseung.
Prance, 跳 t'iu², 跑來跑去 ⸢p'aau-loi-⸢p'aau-hue².
Prate, 支支咋咋 chi-chi-cha²-cha².
Prattle, (COL.) i-i-a-a, ti-ti-te-te, (嘔啞 ⸢au-a).
Prawns, 明蝦 ming-⸜ha.
Pray, 祈禱 k'i-⸜t'o, 祈求 k'i-k'au, (I pray you) 請 ⸢ts'eng.

注 释

【俾爛飯洽】用烂糊的药膏敷上。
【攖脣】撅嘴。
【生疔病】痘,疹。
【整頓人】恶作剧。
【支支咋咋】唠叨,空谈。

> 注 释

【忙速】快速,猛地落下。
【啱啱】正好。
【不俾】不给,排除。
【老辣】早熟的,发育过早的。
【预影】预示,预想。
【落起头】前置。

Preach, 宣傳 suen-ch'uen, 講書 ʿkong-shue, 講道 ʿkong-to'.
Precarious, 險險地 ʿhim-ʿhim-*ti'.
Precaution, 預防 ue'-fong.
Precede, 在先 tsoi'-sin, (go first) 先行 sin-hang.
Precedent, 先起例 sin-ʿhi-lai'.
Precept, 敎訓 kaau'-fun', 規條 k'wai-t'iu, 箴規 chum-k'wai.
Precession of the equinoxes, 歲差 sui'-ch'a.
Precincts, 境界 ʿking-kaai'.
Precious, 寶貝 ʿpo-pooi', 珍寶 chan-ʿpo.
Precipice, 危巖 ngai-ngaam, 山崖 shaan-ngaai.
Precipitate, 忙速 mong-ts'uuk, (to) 傾跌 k'ing-tit'.
Precipitous, 危聳 ngai-ʿsuung.
Precise, 端方 tuen-fong, 端正 tuen-ching', 正經 ching'-king.

Precisely, 正 ching', 啱啱 ʿngaam-ʿngaam.
Preclude, 阻隔 ʿchoh-kaak', 免致 ʿmin-chi', 不俾 'm-ʿpi.
Precocious, 老辣 ʿlo-laat.
Preconceive, 預估 ue'-ʿkoo.
Predecessor, 先任 sin-yum'.
Predetermine, 預定 ue'-ting'.
Predict, 預言 ue'-in, 預先話 ue'-sin-wa'.
Predisposed, 先向 sin-heung'.
Predominate, 贏過 yeng-kwoh'.
Pre-eminent, 出類 ch'uut-lui', 出衆 ch'uut-chuung'.
Pre-engaged, 先應 sin-ying'.
Preface, 書序 shue-tsue'.
Prefect, 知府 chi-ʿfoo.
Prefecture, 府 ʿfoo.
Prefer, 寧愛 ning-oi', 寧願 ning-uen', 更愛 kang'-oi'.
Prefigure, 預影 ue'-ʿying.
Prefix, 落起頭 lok-ʿhi-t'au, 落頭頂處 lok-t'au-ʿting-shue'.

Pregnant, 懷孕 waai-yan', 有身紀 ʻyau-shan-ʻki, 馱胎 tʻoh-tʻoi.
Prejudice, 偏見 pʻin-kin'.
Preliminary, 引起 ʻyan-ʻhi, ʻyan-ʻhi-keʻ.
Premature, 太早 tʻaai-ʻtso, 未熟 mi'-shuuk.
Premeditated, 豫先想出 ueʻ-sin-ʻseung-chʻuut.
Premises, 行 *hong.
Premium, 賞 ʻsheung, (money) 賞銀 ʻsheung-*ngan.
Preoccupy, 先得倒 sin-tak-ʻto, 先取 sin-ʻtsʻue, 住先 chueʻ-sin.
Prepare, 准備 ʻchuun-piʻ, 整備 ʻching-piʻ, 預備 ueʻ-piʻ, 整定 ʻching-tingʻ.
Prepay, 先交銀 sin-kaau-*ngan.
Preponderate, 越重 uetʻ-ʻchʻuung.
Preposterous, 慌唐 fong-tʻong, 不入理 ʼm-yupʻ-ʻli, 怪誕 kwaaiʻ-taanʻ.
Prerogative, 獨權 tuuk-kʻuen.

Presage, (a) 兆頭 chiuʻ-tʻau.
Prescription, 藥方 yeuk-fong.
Presence, 面前 minʻ-tsʻin, (of mind) 淡定 taamʻ-tingʻ, 定見 tingʻ-ʻkinʻ.
Present, (time) 今 kum, (to be) 在 tsoiʻ, (a) 禮物 ʻlai-mat, (to) 送 suungʻ, 獻上 hinʻ-ʻsheung.
Presently, 就家 tsauʻ-ka, 就來 tsauʻ-loi.
Preserve, 守住 ʻshau-chueʻ, 保全 ʻpo-tsʻuen, 存吓 tsʻuen-ʻha.
Preserves, 糖菓 tʻong-ʻkwoh.
President, 會頭 *ooiʻ-tʻau, of a Republic, 總統 ʻtsung-ʻtʻung.
Press, (a) 櫃 kwaiʻ, (oil, &c.) 榨 chaʻ, (printing-) 印書盤 yanʻ-shue-pʻoon.
Press, (to) 壓住 aatʻ-chueʻ, 逼 pik, 搾 chaʻ, 揠 ʻang.
Pressing, 急切 kup-tsʻit.
Prestige, 聲勢 shing-shaiʻ.

注 释

【行】房屋，一般指商铺。
【先得倒】抢先占有，抢先取得。"倒"应为"到"。
【越重】（在重量、数量、力量、影响等）超过，偏重。
【就家】目前。

注释

【胆敢】擅自，冒昧。
【不讲心】不真挚。
【吸三吸四】闪烁其词。

PIR 195 PRI

Presume, 膽敢 'taam-'kom, 逞 'ch'ing, 敢當 'kom-tong, 擅 shin⁾, (on) 恃 'ch'i, 倚恃 'i-shi.
Pretend, 詐 cha⁾, 貌爲 maau⁾-wai, 自稱 tsze⁾-ch'ing, 自己話 tsze⁾-'ki-wa.
Pretty, 好睇 'ho-'t'ai, 靚 leng, 美 'mi, (-well) 幾好 'ki-'ho.
Prevail, 贏 yeng, (abound) 豐盛 fuung-shing⁾.
Prevaricate, 不講心 'm-'kong-'sum, 閃縮 'shim-shuuk, 吸三吸四 ngup-saam-ngup-sze⁾.
Prevent, 阻 'choh, 免致 'min-chi⁾, 不俾 'm-'pi.
Previously, 預先 ue⁾-sin.
Price, 價錢 ka⁾-ts'in, 價 ka⁾.
Prick, 攙刺 'ch'aam-ts'ze⁾, (a) 條刺 t'iu-ts'ze⁾, 管刺 'koon-ts'ze⁾.
Pricking, 瘹 ts'ek.
Prickles, 竻 lak, 刺 ts'ze⁾.
Prickly-heat, 熱痱 it-*fai⁾.

Pride, 傲氣 ngo⁾-hi⁾.
Pride of India, 森木 'shum-muuk, 苦楝 'foo-lin⁾.
Priest, 祭司 tsai⁾-sze, (Bud.) 和尚 woh-*sheung⁾, (Tau.) 道士 to⁾-*sze⁾, (Rom.) 神父 shan-foo⁾.
Prim, 迂腐 hue-foo⁾.
Prime, 第一 tai⁾-yat, 首 'shau, 上等 sheung⁾-'tang.
Prime cost, 本錢 'poon-ts'in.
Prime Minister, 拜相 paai⁾-seung⁾, 宰相 'tsoi-seung⁾.
Primitive, 原本 uen-'poon.
Primrose, 蓮馨花 lin-hing-fa.
Prince, 君 kwun, 親王 ts'an-wong.
Principal, 頭一個 t'au-yat-koh⁾, (-thing) 根本 kan-'poon.
Principally, 大概 taai⁾-*k'oi⁾, 大約 taai⁾-*yeuk⁾.
Principles, 道理 to⁾-'li, 理 'li.
Print, 印 yan⁾.
Printing office, 印書館 yan⁾-shue-'koon.

Prior, 先 sin.		Proceed, 前進 ts'in-tsuun', 上前去 sheung-ts'in-hue', (from) 出 ch'uut, 出乎 ch'uut-oo.

Prior, 先 sin.
Prison, 監房 kaam-fong.
Prisoner, 監犯 kaam-*faan'.
Private, 私家 sze-ka, (secret) 密 mat, 秘密 pi'-mat, 隱 'yan.
Privet, (ligustrum lucidum) 山瑞香 shaan-sui'-heung.
Privilege, 湊巧 ts'au'-'haau.
Privy-council, 內閣 noi'-kok'.
Privy, (a) 廁坑 ts'ze'-haang.
Prize, (a) 賞 'sheung, 賞賜 'sheung-ts'ze', 賞犒 'sheung-ho', (to win a) 贏 yeng.
Prize up, 撬起 kiu'-'hi.
Probably, 或者 waak-'che, (most) 大概 taai'-*k'oi', 怕係啩 p'a'-hai'-kwa'.
Probation, 試驗 shi'-im'.
Probe, (a) 鍼 chum, 探針 t'aam'-chum, (to) 俾針探吓 'pi-chum-t'aam'-'ha.
Proboscis, 象拔 tseung'-pat, 象鼻 tseung'-pi'.

Proceed, 前進 ts'in-tsuun', 上前去 sheung-ts'in-hue', (from) 出 ch'uut, 出乎 ch'uut-oo.
Procession, (idolatrous) 菩薩出遊 p'o-saat'-ch'uut-yau.
Proclaim, 宣傳 suen-ch'uen.
Proclamation, (a) 告示 ko'-shi'.
Proclivity, 偏歸一便 p'in-kwai-yat-*pin'.
Procrastinate, 推遲 t'ui-ch'i, (COL.) 哆吊 'te-tiu', (put off from day to day) 日推一日 yat-t'ui-yat-yat.
Procurator, 承辦人 shing-paan'-yan.
Procure, 搵得 'wun-tak, 得到 tak-'to, 攞到 'loh-'to.
Prodigal, (a) 浪子 long'-'tsze.
Prodigy, 精怪 tsing-kwaai'.
Produce, 出 ch'uut, 生出 shang-ch'uut, 產 'ch'aan.
Profane, 穢褻 wai'-sit'.
Profess, 明認 ming-ying', 自稱 tsze'-ch'ing.

注 釋

【撬起】撬开。
【怕係啩】恐怕是。
【偏归一便】倾向一边。
【搵得】找到。
【攞到】拿到。

注释

【散荡花消】放荡的。
【凸出来】计划, 提议。
【特出】突出。
【揭单】承付票。
【海表】海角。

Profession, (calling) 業 ip, 事業 sze⌐-ip, 脚色 keuk⌐-shik.
Profile, 半邊面 poon⌐-pin-*min⌐, 半面相 poon⌐-min⌐-*seung⌐.
Profit, 利益 li⌐-yik, (to) 賺 chaan⌐, 利 li⌐.
Profitable, 有益 yau⌐-yik, 有賺 ʿyau-chaan⌐.
Profligate, 散蕩花消 ʿsaan-tong⌐-fa-siu, (a) 敗家仔 paai⌐-ka-ʿtsai.
Profound, 深 shum, 深沉 shum-chʻum.
Profusion, 太多 tʻaai⌐-toh.
Prognosticate, 占卜 chim-puuk, 占卦 chim-kwa⌐.
Programme, 預定單目 ue⌐-ting⌐-taan-muuk.
Progress, 前進 tsʻin-tsuun⌐, 上進 ʿsheung-tsuun⌐.
Prohibit, 禁戒 kum⌐-kaai⌐, 禁止 kum⌐-chi.
Project, 凸出來 tut-chʻuut-lai, 發 faat⌐.
Prolapse, 墜落 chui⌐-lok.

Prolong, 拖長 tʻoh-chʻeung, 整長 ʿching-chʻeung, 阻耐 ʿchoh-noi⌐.
Prominence, 凸 tut.
Prominent, 特出 tak-chʻuut.
Promissory note, 揭單 kʻit-ʿtaan.
Promiscuous mixing, 混雜 wan⌐-tsaap.
Promise, 應承 ying-shing, (break a) 食言 shik-in, 失信 shat-suun⌐.
Promontory, 海表 ʿhoi-ʿpiu.
Promote, 助 choh⌐, (a man) 提拔 tʻai-pat.
Prompt, 快捷 faai⌐-tsit, (to) 提醒 tʻai-ʿsing.
Promulgate, 播揚 poh⌐-yeung, 傳講 chʻuen-ʿkong.
Prone to, 偏向 pʻin-heung⌐, 會 ʿooi.
Pronounce, 講出來 ʿkong-chʻuut-lai, 話出 wa⌐-chʻuut.
Pronunciation, 口音 ʿhau-ʿyum, 口鉗 ʿhau-kʻim.
Proof, 憑據 pʻang-kue⌐, (print a) 打稿 ʿta-ʿko.

Prop, (to) 頂起 ‛ting-‛hi, (a) 條撐 t‛iu-ch‛aang.
Propel, 推前 t‛ui-ts‛in, 使——行 ‛shai——hang.
Propensity, 偏向 p‛in-heung, 癖性 p‛ik-sing.
Proper, 着 cheuk.
Property, 產業 ch‛aan-ip, 家業 ka-ip, 財 ts‛oi, (nature) 性 sing, 性格 sing-kaak.
Prophesy, 講未來事 ‛kong-mi-loi-sze.
Prophet, 先知 sin-chi.
Propitiate, 和翻 woh-faan, 挽回 ‛waan-ooi.
Propitious, 慈祥 ts‛ze-ts‛eung, (time, &c.) 吉 kat, 好 ‛ho.
Proportion, (rule of) 比例 ‛pi-lai, 配法 p‛ooi-faat.
Propose, 陳說 ch‛an-shuet, 出主意 ch‛uut-chue-i.
Proprietor, 原主 uen-‛chue, 原人 uen-yan.
Propriety, 禮數 ‛lai-sho.
Prosecute, 告 ko, (pursue) 趕起 ‛kohn-‛hi.

Proselyte, 進教 tsuun-kaau.
Prospect, 光景 kwong-‛king.
Prospect for gold, 探金 t‛aam-‛kum.
Prosper, 興旺 hing-wong, 發達 faat-taat.
Prosperous, 暢盛 ch‛eung-shing.
Prostitute, 娼婦 ch‛eung-‛foo, 文牛 mun-*ngau, (to) 浪用 long-yuung.
Prostrate, 傾倒 k‛ing-‛to, (one's self) 蹼倒處 puuk-‛to-shue, 俯伏 ‛foo-fuuk.
Protect, 保佑 ‛po-yau, 擋梢 maan-shaau.
Protegé, 所照顧 ‛shoh-chiu-koo.
Protest, 告訴 ko-so, 話心不服 wa-sum-‛m-fuuk.
Protestant, (Christianity) 耶穌教 Ye-soo-kaau.
Protract, 拖長 t‛oh-ch‛eung.
Protuberant, 凸 tut, 凸出 tut-ch‛uut.
Proud, 驕傲 kiu-ngo.
Prove, 証實 ching-shat, (verify) 徵驗 ching-im.

注 释

【讲未来事】预言, 预告。

【和翻】劝解, 和解, 抚慰。

【话心不服】不信服, 抗议。

注 释

【化生保养】天意。
【出夜】夜里潜行。
【省枝叶】修剪枝叶。
【发身】发育。
【咪埋口】把嘴缩拢。
【一朕】应为"一阵"。

Proverb, 俗語 tsuuk-*ʻue, 成語 shing-*ʻue, 箴言 chum-in.
Provide, 給 kʻup, 預備 ueʼ-pi, (against) 提防 tʻai-fong.
Providence, 化生保養 faʼ-shang-ʻpo-ʻyeung.
Providential, 天注定 tʻin-chueʼ-tingʼ.
Province, 省 ʻshaang.
Provisions, 糧草 leung-ʻtsʻo, 口糧 ʻhau-leung.
Provoke, 惹 ʻye, 激 kik.
Prowl, 出夜 chʻuut-*yeʼ.
Proxy, 代理 toiʼ-ʻli.
Prudence, 智慧 chiʼ-waiʼ.
Prudent, 會思量 ʻooi-sze-leung, 好打算 ʻho-ʻta-suenʼ.
Prune, (to) 省枝葉 ʻshaang-chi-ip.
Prunes, 梅子 mooi-ʻtsze, (dried) 乾梅 kohn-*mooi.
Prussia, 布國 Poʼ-kwokʼ.
Prussian-blue, 洋靛 yeung-tinʼ.
Pry, 窺探 kʻwai-tʻaamʼ.

Psalms, 聖詩 shingʼ-ʻshi.
Psoriasis, 乾漏 kohn-lauʼ.
Puberty, (female) 天癸 tʻin-kwaiʼ, (male) 成童 shing-tʻuung, (VULG.) 發身 faatʼ-ʻshan.
Public, 公 kuung, (the) 百姓 paakʼ-singʼ.
Public spirit, 公心 kuung-sum, 義氣 iʼ-hiʼ.
Publish, (books, &c.) 出賣 chʻuut-maaiʼ.
Pucker, 縐埋 tsauʼ-maai, (the mouth) 咪埋口 mai-maai-ʻhau.
Pudding, 麵食 minʼ-shik.
Puddle, iron, 炒鐵 ʻchʻaau-tʻitʼ, (make muddy) 攪濁 ʻkaau-chuuk, (water tight) 整坭湴底 ʻching-nai-paanʼ-ʻtai.
Puff, (a) 一朕 yat-chumʼ.
Puffed up, 自滿 tszeʼ-ʻmoon.
Puisne Judge, 副臬司 fooʼ-nip-ʻsze.
Pule, 哇哇 wa-wa.
Pull, (to) 搢 mangʼ, 拉 laai, 扯 ʻchʻe, (down) 拆 chʻaakʼ.

Pulley, 絆羅 luut-‚loh.
Pulp, 鸌 nong.
Pulpit, 講書檯 ‚kong-shue-t'oi.
Pulse, (lentils) 荳 *tau⌐, (the) 脈 mak.
Pulverize, 粉碎 ‚fun-sui⌐.
Pumice, 浮石 fau-shek.
Pummelo, 波碌 poh-luuk, 柚子 yau-‚tsze, 囉柚 loh-*yau.
Pump, 欶筒 shok⌐-t'uung, 拖水泵 t'oh-‚shui-‚tum, (to) 欶 shok⌐.
Pumpkin, 冬瓜 tuung-kwa.
Pun, 雙關取笑 sheung-‚kwaan-‚ts'ue-siu⌐.
Punch, (a) 鐵撞 t'it⌐-chong⌐, 鷄眼鑿 kai-‚ngaan-*tsok.
Punctilious, 執細 chup-sai⌐.
Punctual, 依期 i-k'i.
Punctuate, 點斷 ‚tim⌐-t'uen.
Puncture, 針 chum.
Pungent, 辣 laat.
Punish, 罰 fat, 責罰 chaak⌐-fat.
Punishment, 刑罰 ying-fat.
Punkah, 風扇 fuung-shin⌐.

Puny, 矮細 ‚ai-sai⌐.
Pup, 狗仔 ‚kau-‚tsai.
Pupil, (of the eye) 瞳人 t'uung-*yan, (scholar) 門生 moon-‚shaang, 學生 hok-‚shaang.
Puppet show, 鬼仔戲 ‚kwai-‚tsai-hi⌐.
Purblind, 眼矇 ‚ngaan-muung.
Purchase, 買 ‚maai.
Pure, 清潔 ts'ing-kit⌐.
Purgative, 瀉藥 se⌐-yeuk.
Purgatory, 煉獄 lin⌐-yunk.
Purify, 洗滌 ‚sai-tik, 潔淨 kit⌐-tsing⌐, 整乾淨 ‚ching-kohn-tseng⌐.
Purple, 葡萄靑 p'oo-t'o-‚ts'eng.
Purpose, 主意 ‚chue-i⌐.
Purposely, 特登 tak-‚tang, 故意 koo⌐-i⌐.
Purse, 荷包 hoh-‚paau, 匙插 shi-*ch'aap.
Purser, 寫字人 ‚se-tsze⌐-yan.
Purslane, 猪仔荣 chue-‚tsai-ts'oi.

注释

【耍图】拼图。
【矮佬仔】侏儒。
【撞包先生】冒牌医生。
【量天尺】四分仪。
【失志】胆怯，畏缩，退败。

Pursue, 追趕 chui-῾kohn.
Purvey, 辦伙食 paan-῾foh-shik.
Pus, 膿 nuung.
Push, 推 t῾ui, 擁 ῾uung, (along, as a row of types &c.) 褪 t῾an᾿.
Pusillanimous, 心怯 sum-hip᾿.
Pustule, 小瘡 ῾siu-ch῾ong.
Put, 放 fong, 置 chi᾿, (down) 擠落 chai-lok, (on) 着 cheuk᾿, 按 ohn᾿, 安 ohn, (in) 插 ch῾aap᾿, 入 yup, (out) 出 ch῾uut, (past) 收埋 shau-maai, (away) 除 ch῾ue, (off) 推 t῾ui, 脫 t῾uet᾿.
Putchuk, 木香 muuk-heung.
Putrid, 腐爛 foo᾿-laan᾿.
Putty, 桐油灰 t῾uung-yau-fooi.
Puzzle, (a) 難估之物 naan-῾koo-chi-mat, naan-῾koo-ke-ye, (a toy) 耍圖 ῾sha-t῾o.
Pygmy, 矮佬仔 ῾ai-῾lo-tsai.
Pylorus, 幽門 yau-moon.

Pyramid, 尖方形 tsim-fong-ying, 金字塔 kum-tsze᾿-t῾aap᾿.

Q

Quack, (a) 撞包先生 chong᾿-paau-sin-shang, ch῾ong᾿-paau-seng.
Quadrangular, 四方 sze᾿-fong᾿, sze᾿-fong-ke᾿.
Quadrant, (or sextant) 量天尺 leung-t῾in-ch῾ek᾿.
Quadruped, 走獸 ῾tsau-shau᾿.
Quaff, 飲 ῾yum.
Quail, (a) 鵪鶉 om-shuun.
Quail, (to) 失志 shat-chi᾿.
Quaint, 古怪 ῾koo-kwaai᾿.
Quake, 振動 chan᾿-tuung᾿.
Qualified, (able) 能 nang.
Quality, 等 ῾tang, 品 ῾pun, 腳色 keuk᾿-shik, (of things) 色 shik, 性格 sing᾿-kaak᾿.
Qualm of conscience, 良心自責 leung-sum-tsze᾿-chaak᾿.

Quantity, 數量 sho²-leung², (what?) 多少 toh-⸌shiu.
Quarrel, 爭 chaang, 鬧交 naau²-⸌kaau, 隘交 aai²-⸌kaau.
Quarry, 取石山 ⸌ts'ue-shek-shaan.
Quart, (a) 一斤 yat-kan.
Quarter, (a) 四分之一 sze²-fun²-chi-yat, 一角 yat-kok², (of an hour) 一刻 yat-hak, (of the year) 季 kwai², (of the body) 肢 chi.
Quarter, (to lodge) 歇宿 hit²-suuk.
Quartz, 白火石 paak-⸌foh-shek, 石瑛 shek-ying.
Quash, 拉倒 laai-⸌to, 撲滅 p'ok²-mit.
Quassia, 白木 paak-muuk.
Queen, 皇后 wong-hau².
Queer, 奇怪 k'i-kwaai², 竻特 lak-tak.
Quell, 滅 mit.
Quench, 滅 mit, 救熄 kau²-sik, (thirst) 解 ⸌kaai.
Quest, 尋 ts'um.

Question, 問 mun², (a) 問話 mun²-wa², (doubt) 思疑 sze-i.
Quibble, 盤根問柢 p'oon-kan-mun²-⸌tai, 詰難 k'it-naan, 爭言語 chaang-in-⸌ue.
Quick, 快 faai², 快快 faai²-faai², (sharp) 麻俐 ma-li², (clever) 伶俐 ling-li², (lively) 活潑 oot-p'oot².
Quicken, (in the womb) 胎動 t'oi-tuung².
Quicksand, 浮沙 fau-sha.
Quicksilver, 水銀 ⸌shui-ngan.
Quiet, 安靖 ohn-tsing², (be) 靜靜 tsing²-*tsing².
Quietness, 平安 p'ing-ohn.
Quill, 鵝毛筆 ngoh-mo-pat.
Quilt, 綿被 min-p'i², 綿胎 min-⸌t'oi.
Quilted-coat, 綿衲 min-naap.
Quince, 木瓜 muuk-⸌kwa.
Quinine, 金雞納霜 ⸌kum-kai-naap-seung.
Quinsy, 生鵝喉 shaang-ngoh-hau.

注 释

【鬧交/隘交】吵架。
【取石山】采石场。
【歇宿】住宿，驻扎。
【争言语】争辩。
【生鵝喉】扁桃体炎。

注释

【扭计】闹别扭。
【入柳】槽口接缝处。
【犖色】废物，垃圾。
【囉囉仔】流浪儿。
【揼烂布】收破烂。

Quip, 譏刺 ki-ts'ze'.
Quire, 刀 to, (a) 一刀紙 yat-to-'chi.
Quirk, 扭計 'nau-*kai'.
Quisqualis, 使君子 sze-kwun-'tsze.
Quit, 離去 li-hue', (-hold) 放手 fong'-'shau, 甪手 lut-'shau.
Quite, 十分 shap-fun——嗮——saai', ——完——uen, (not quite) 爭的 chaang-,ti.
Quiz, 試探 shi'-t'aam', 嘲笑 chaau-siu'.
Quote, 引 'yan, 引述 'yan-shuut.

R

Rabbet, (to) 入柳 yup-'lau.
Rabbit, 白兔 paak-t'o'.
Rabble, 下流 ha'-lau.
Rabid, 狂 k'wong, 刁 tiu.
Race, (family) 類 lui', 種 'chuung, (to) 跑 'p'aau.
Rack, (engine) 刑具 ying-kue', (frame) 架 ka'.
Racking, 苦楚 'foo-'ch'oh.
Radiate, 射 she', 光射 kwong-she', 熱射 it-she'.
Radicals, (characters) 部 po' (roots) 根 kan.
Radish, 紅蘿蔔 huung-loh-paak.
Radius, 輻線 fuuk-sin'.
Raffle, 犖色 ngo-shik.
Raft, 桴 *p'aai.
Rafter, 桷 kok', (purlin &) 桁桷 hang-kok'.
Rag, 爛布 laan'-po'.
Ragamuffin, 囉囉仔 ,loh-,loh-'tsai.
Rage, 忿怒 'fun-no'.
Ragged, 藍褸 laam-lue'.
Rag-man, 揼爛布 oon'-laan'-po'.
Rail, (to) 詈罵 li'-ma', (a bird) 竹雞 chuuk-kai.
Railing, 欄杆 laan-,kohn.
Railway, 鐵路 t'it'-lo', 火烟車路 'foh-in-ch'e-lo'.
Rain, 雨 'ue, (to) 落雨 lok-'ue, (-water) 雨水 'ue-shui.

Rainbow, 天蜂 t'in-kong, 虹棋 huung-‗kuung.	Range in rows, 一行行列開 yat-*hong-hong-lit-hoi.
Raise, 起 ‗hi.	Rank, (order) 等級 ‗tang-k'up, 品 ‗pun, (merit) 功名 kuung-ming, (with) 同列 t'uung-lit.
Raisins, 菩提子 p'oo-t'ai-‗tsze.	
Rally, (troops) 合翻埋 hop-faan-maai, (ridicule) 嘲笑 chaau-siu'.	Rank, (growth) 茂 mau', (taste) 臊 so.
Rake, (a man) 花花公子 fa-fa-kuung-‗tsze, 吖嚟㗎吞 oh-‗li-kat-tm', (a tool) 笆 p'a, 耙 p'a-‗ngaau.	Rankle in the breast, 心滾 sum-‗kwan, 到心滾 to'-sum-‗kwan.
	Ransom, 贖 shuuk.
Ram, (a) 羊牯 yeung-‗koo, 羊公 yeung-kuung, (to) 舂 chuung.	Rant, 狂辯 k'wong-pin'.
	Rap, 拍 p'aak', (COL.) pop-pop.
Ramble, 遊行 yau-hang, 去逛 hue'-k'waang', 蹓 ‗liu.	Rape, 強姦 k'eung-kaan.
	Rapid, 急速 kup-ts'uuk, (rapids) 灘 t'aan.
Rampant, 嘈雜 ts'o-tsaap, 高興 ko-hing'.	Rapture, 極喜 kik-‗hi.
	Rare, 希罕 hi-‗hohn, 希奇 hi-k'i.
Rampart, 城墙 sheng-ts'eung.	
Ram-rod, 鳥鎗插 ‗niu-ts'eung-ch'aap', 通條 t'uung-t'iu.	Rarities, 奇物 k'i-mat.
	Rascal, 爛仔 *laan'-‗tsai.
	Rase, 拆平 ch'aak'-p'ing, 洗平 ‗sai-p'ing.
Rancid, 腥 seng, (oil) 饐 yik.	
	Rash, 冒險 mo'-him, 躁暴 ts'o'-po'.
Rancour, 怨毒 uen'-tuuk.	

注 释

【天蜂】彩虹。

【菩提子】菩提树及无患子的果实,常作念佛的数珠。Raisins应译为"葡萄干",译为"菩提子"属误译。

【合翻埋】(军队)召集,集合。

【心滚】心痛。

注 释

【蛇抱笏】覆盆子，悬钩子属植物。
【揅】喧哗，嘎嘎声。
【扯气】死前的喉鸣。
【为食】嘴馋。
【琵琶沙】一种海鱼，学名中国团扇鳐，状似琵琶。

Raspberry, 蛇抱笏 she-‛p‛o-lak.
Rat, 老鼠 ‛lo-‛shue.
Rat-trap, 老鼠籠 ‛lo-‛shue-*luung.
Rate, (price) 價 ka⸴, (of motion) 行法 hang-faat⸴, (first-) 頂好 ‛ting-‛ho.
Rather, 畧畧 leuk-*leuk, 頗 ‛p‛oh, (in preference) 宁可 ning-‛hoh, 更好 kang⸴-‛ho.
Ratify, 批准 p‛ai-‛chuun, 証實 ching⸴-shat.
Rational, 合情理 hop-ts‛ing-‛li.
Rations, 粮食 leung-shik, (daily) 日粮 yat-leung.
Rattan, 沙籘 sha-t‛ang, (shavings) 籘絲 t‛ang-‛sze.
Rattle, 揅 ngo, (a drum) 鈴冧鼓 ‛ling-‛lum-‛koo, (death-) 扯氣 ‛ch‛e-hi⸴.
Rattle-snake, 响尾蛇 ‛heung-‛mi-she.
Ravage, 刧毁 kip⸴-‛wai.

Rave, 喪心 song⸴-sum, 發譫話 faat⸴-ngaam-wa⸴, (in anger) 暴怒 po⸴-no⸴.
Ravelled, 亂 luen⸴.
Raven, 烏鴉 oo-a.
Ravenous, (hungry) 餓得急 ngoh-tak-kup, (greedy) 爲食 wai⸴-shik.
Ravine, 山壑 shaan-k‛ok⸴.
Ravish, 強奪 k‛eung-tuet, (force) 強 ‛k‛eung.
Raw, 生 shaang, shaang-ke⸴.
Ray, (of light) 射光 she⸴-kwong, (a fish) 鯆魚 po-*ue, 琵琶沙 p‛i-p‛a-sha.
Razor, 剃刀 t‛ai⸴-‛to.
Reach, 到 to⸴, 到得 to⸴-tak, (with the hand) 摸到 o-‛to, (out) 伸 shan.
Read, 讀 tuuk, (in silence) 看 hohn⸴, 睇 ‛t‛ai.
Readily, 卽時 tsik-shi, 易易 i⸴-i⸴.
Ready, 備 pi⸴, 齊備 ts‛ai-pi⸴, 便 pin⸴, (money) 現銀 in⸴-*ngan, (made) 現成 in⸴-*shing.

Real, 眞 *chan*.	Recall, 叫 — 翻 *kiu'* — *faan*, (to mind) 想得翻 '*seung-tʌk-faan*.
Really, 果然 '*kwoh*-in, 確實 *k'ok'*-shat.	
Reap, 收割 *shau-koht'*.	Recant, 反口 '*faan*-'*hau*.
Rear, (like a horse) 咢高前蹄 *ngok-ko-ts'in-t'ai*, 椿 ,*chong*, (raise) 養 '*yeung*, *ts'o*.	Recede, 退 *t'ui'*, 褪後 *t'an'-hau'*.
	Receipt, 收單 *shau-,taan*.
	Receive, 接收 *tsip'-shau*, 接到 *tsip'-to'*, 受 *shau'*, (from a superior) 領 '*ling*.
Rear, (the) 尾 '*mi*, 後便 *hau'-pin'*.	
Reason, 道理 *to'-'li*, 情理 *ts'ing-'li*, (a) 緣故 *uen-koo'*.	Recent, 近時 *kan'-shi*, *kan'-shi-ke'*.
	Recently, 近來 *kan'-loi*.
Reasoning, 理論 '*li-luun'*, 辯論 *pin'-luun'*.	Receptacle, 藏 *tsong'*, 房 *fong*, 藏處 *ts'ong-ch'ue'*.
Reasonable, 有道理 '*yau-to'-'li*, 有理 '*yau-'li*, 合理 *hop-'li*.	Recipe, 方法 *fong-faat'*, 方子 *fong-,tsze*.
Reassure, 壯 — 膽 *chong'* — '*taam*.	Reciprocate, 互相交接 *oo'-seung-kaau-tsip'*.
	Recite, 玩誦 *oon'-tsuung'*, 念出 *nim'-ch'uut*.
Rebate, (a groove) 入柳 *yup-'lau*.	Reckless, 刁蠻 *tiu-maan*, 唔打理乜野 '*m-,ta-'li-,mat-'ye*.
Rebel, (to) 作反 *tsok'-'faan*.	
Rebels, 逆賊 *yik-ts'aak*.	Reckon, 點數 '*tim-'sho*, 算 *suen'*.
Rebound, 濺開 *tsaan'-hoi*.	
Rebuke, 責成 *chaak'-shing*.	Reclaim, 攞翻 '*loh-faan*, 救翻 *kau'-faan*.
Rebut, 答倒 *taap'-'to*.	

注 释

【想得翻】回想起来。
【反口】食言。
【唔打理乜野】不顾后果。
【攞翻】拿回来。

注 释

【瞓低】躺下。
【得翻】恢复好了。
【游耍吓】娱乐, 消遣。
【养翻吓】补充营养, 滋养。

Recline, 瞓低 fun'-'tai, 'fun, 挨到 aai-'to, 挨下 aai-'ha.
Recluse, 離世獨居 li-shai'-tuuk-kue.
Recognise, 認 ying'.
Recoil, 褪 t'an', tan', 濺起 tsaan'-'hi.
Recollect, 記起 ki'-'hi, 憶起 yik'-'hi.
Recommend, (a person) 舉薦 'kue-tsin', (advise) 勸 huen'.
Recompense, 報答 po'-taap'.
Reconcilable, 和得翻 woh-tak-faan.
Reconcile, 令——再好 ling'——tsoi'-'ho.
Reconciled, 復和 fuuk-woh.
Reconnoitre, 打探 'ta-t'aam'.
Record, 錄 luuk, (to) 記 ki'.
Recount, 述出來 shuut-ch'uut-lai.
Recover, 得翻 tak-faan, (get well) 病好 peng'-'ho.
Recreate, 遊耍吓 yau-'sha-'ha.

Recrimination, 互相攻訐 oo'-seung-kuung-k'it'.
Recruit, 添補 t'im-'po, (health) 養翻吓 'yeung-faan-ha.
Rectify, 整正 'ching-cheng', 改正 'koi-cheng, 整好 'ching-'ho.
Rectitude, 義氣 i'-hi', 正直 ching'-chik.
Rectum, 直腸 chik-ch'eung.
Recur, 又來 yau'-loi, 來復 loi-fuuk, (in speaking) 再講 tsoi'-'kong.
Red, 紅 huung, 朱 chue.
Redeem, 贖 shuuk, 贖翻 shuuk-faan, (from sin) 贖罪 shuuk-tsui'.
Redound to, 歸翻 kwai-faan.
Redress, a grievance, 申冤 shan-uen, (no) 無法 'mo-faat'.
Reduce, (bring) 令 ling', 致使 chi'-'shai, (diminish) 減 'kaam, (change) 化 fa', 變 pin', (subdue) 打服 'ta-fuuk.

Redundant, 太多無用 t'aai-toh-'mo-yuung, 蛇足 she-tsuuk.

Reed, 蘆葦 lo-'wai, 蘆荻 lo-tek.

Reel and stagger, 行動搖擺 hang-tuung-'iu-paai, (COL.) hang-tak-p'e-p'e-'ha.

Reel of thread, 線轆 sin'-luuk, 車轆 ch'e-luuk.

Refer to, 指 'chi, (speak of) 講及 'kong-k'aap, (apply to) 轉詳 'chuen-ts'eung, 轉問 'chuen-mun'.

Refine, 傾煉 k'ing-lin', 煉 lin'.

Refit, 修整 sau-'ching.

Reflect, 反照 'faan-chiu', 射轉 she'-'chuen, (think) 思想 sze-'seung.

Reform, 變正 pin'-ching', 改惡遷善 'koi-ok'-ts'in-shin'.

Refract, 轉斜 'chuen-ts'e, 撮曲 ts'uet'-k'uuk.

Refrain, 戒 kaai', 忍手 'yan-'shau, 忍口 'yan-'hau.

Refresh, 益補 yik-'po, 滋補 tsze-'po.

Refreshment, 滋補野 tsze-'po-'ye, 點心 'tim-sum.

Refuge, 躲避處 'toh-pi-ch'ue', 避身所 pi'-shan-'shoh.

Refund, 償還 ch'eung-waan.

Refuse, 推辭 t'ui-ts'ze, 不允 'm-'wan, (not receive) 不接 'm-tsip'.

Refute, 駁贏 pok'-yeng.

Regain, 得翻 tak-faan, 贏翻 yeng-fuan.

Regard, 顧住 koo'-chue', (pity) 恤 suut.

Regardless, 不打理 'm-'ta-'li.

Regards, (to express) 問候 mun'-hau'.

Regatta, 鬥船 tau'-shuen.

Regenerate, 更生 kang'-shang, 重生 ch'uung-shang, 翻生 faan-shaang.

Regent, 攝政 ship'-ching'.

Regimen, 戒口 kaai'-'hau.

Regiment, 營 ying, 旗 k'i.

Region, 地方 ti'-fong.

注 释

【叫翻】使恢复。
【复病】病情复发。
【浮凸】免除，减轻。

Register, 紀錄 'ki-luuk, (to) 上冊 'sheung-ch'aak'.
Registrar, 掌案司 'cheung-ohn'-,sze.
Registrar General, (in Hongkong) 華民政務司 wa-man-ching'-moo-,sze.
Regret, 惜 sik, 念惜 nim'-sik, (repent) 悔 fooi', 反悔 'faan-fooi'.
Regular, 有次序 'yau-ts'ze'-tsue', 依法 i-faat', 正 ching'.
Regulate, 定制 ting'-chai', 整好 'ching-'ho.
Regulation, 章程 cheung-ch'ing.
Reign, 爲王 wai-wong, 做王 tso'-wong, (one) 一王之世 yat-wong-chi-shai'.
Rein, (bridle) 轡頭 pi'-t'au.
Rein-deer, 北大鹿 pak-taai'-luuk.
Reinforce, 添補 t'im-'po.
Reinstate, 叫翻 kiu'-faan, 請翻 'ts'eng-faan.
Reject, 丟棄 tiu-hi', 丟抛 tiu-p'aau.

Rejoice, 喜悅 'hi-uet, 歡喜 foon-'hi.
Rejoin, (answer again) 復答 fuuk'-taap'.
Relapse, 復陷 fuuk-haam', (of sickness) 復病 fuuk-peng'.
Relate, 說知 shuet'-chi, 講述 'kong-shuut, (belong to) 屬 shuuk.
Relations, (five) 五倫 'ng-luun, 人倫 yan-luun.
Relation }
Relative } 親戚 ts'an-ts'ik, 相屬 seung-shuuk.
Relax, 放鬆 fong'-suung.
Relaxation, 舒伸 shue-shan.
Release, 釋放 shik-fong'.
Relent, 悔 fooi', 可憐 'hoh-lin.
Relevant, 關涉 kwaan-ship'.
Relief, relievo, 浮凸 fau-tut.
Relieve, (the poor) 救濟 kau'-tsai', (lighten) 減輕 'kaam-heng.
Religion, (doctrine) 教 kaau'.
Religious, 敬虔 king'-k'in.
Relinquish, 捨 'she.

| REM | 210 | REP |

Relish, (to) 知味 chi²-mi², (a) 味道 mi²-to², 滋味 tsze-mi, *mi².

Reluctantly, 勉強 ʻmin-ʻkʻeung.

Rely on, 倚賴 ʻi-laai², 恃 ʻshi.

Remain, 留住 lau-chue², (over) 剩 shing².

Remainder, 餘剩 ue-shing².

Remand, 命—反 ming²—faan, 着—囘去 cheuk²—ooi-hue².

Remark, (see) 睇見 ʻtʻai-kin², (say) 話 wa².

Remarkable, 非常 fi-sheung.

Remedy, 治法 chi²-faat², 醫治 i-faat².

Remember, 記得 ki²-tak, 記住 ki²-chue².

Remind, 提醒 tʻai-ʻseng.

Remiss, 放縱 fong²-tsuung².

Remit, (forgive) 赦免 she²-ʻmin, (send) 寄 ki², (relax) 鬆 suung.

Remnants, 餘碎 ue-sui².

Remonstrate, 責論 chaak²-luun².

Remorse, 痛悔 tʻuung²-fooi².

Remorseless, 殘忍 tsʻaan-ʻyan.

Remote, 遠 ʻuen, 疏 shoh.

Remove, (flit) 搬遷 poon-tsʻin, (put away) 除去 chʻue²-hue², (from office) 革 kaak².

Remunerate, 賠答 pʻooi-taap².

Rend, 裂 lit, 扯裂 ʻchʻe-lit.

Render, (return) 還 waan, (make) 令 ling², 使 ʻshai.

Rendezvous, 聚處 tsue²-chʻue².

Renew } 更新 kang²-san, 改新 ʻkoi-san, 整翻新 ʻching-faan-san.
Renovate

Renounce, 棄絕 hi²-tsuet².

Rent, 租銀 tso-*ngan, 租價 tso-ka², (to) 租 tso; (torn) 爛了 laan²-hiu.

Repair, 修整 sau-ʻching, 補 ʻpo, (go to) 去到 hue²-to².

Repay, 還翻 waan-faan, 賠還 pʻooi-waan.

Repeal, 廢除 fai²-chʻue.

注　释

【睇见】注意到，觉察到。

Remiss:粗心，马虎。译为"放纵"不确。

【还翻】还回去。

注释

【抢翻】抢回来。
【蹓虫】爬虫。
【塊髎】厌恶。
【犹之乎】如同，类似。

Repeat, 再復 tsoi'-fuuk, 重復 ch'uung-fuuk, (a lesson) 背 pooi', 念 nim', 念出 nim'-ch'uut.
Repeatedly, 再三 tsoi'-saam.
Repel, 拒住 'k'ue-chue'.
Repent, 悔恨 fooi'-han', (and mend) 悔改 fooi'-'koi.
Repetition, 贅累 chui'-lui'.
Repine, 怨 uen', 憂怨 yau-uen'.
Replace, 補翻 'po-faan.
Replenish, 滿翻 'moon-faan.
Reply, 對答 tui'-taap', 回音 ooi-yum.
Report, 風聲 fuung-sheng, (give a) 回復 ooi-fuuk, (sound) (COL.) pom.
Repose, 安靜 ohn-tsing'.
Represent, (stand for) 作係 tsok'-hai', 當做 tong-tso', (symbolize) 見意 kin'-i'.
Repress, 禁制 kum'-chai', 遏制 aat'-chai'.
Reprisals, (to make) 搶翻 'ts'eung-faan.
Reproach, 辱罵 yuuk-ma'.

Reprimand } 責成 chaak'-shing, 執責 chup-chaak', (to the face) 斥白 ch'ik-paak, 面斥 min'-ch'ik.
Reptile, 蹓蟲 laan-ch'uung.
Republic, 民主之國 mun-'chue-chi-kwok'.
Repudiate, 棄 hi'.
Repugnant, 相反 seung-'faan, 相攻 seung-kuung, 逆 yik, ngaak.
Repulse, 打退 'ta-t'ui'.
Repulsive, 塊髎 tau-mau.
Reputation, 名聲 ming-shing, 體面 't'ai-min'.
Request, 求請 k'au-'ts'eng.
Require, 須要 sue-iu'.
Requite, 報 po'.
Rescue, 救 kau', 打救 'ta-kau', 救出 kau'-ch'uut.
Research, 考究 'haau-kau'.
Resemblance, 象樣 tseung'-*yeung', 貌 maau'.
Resemble, 似得 'ts'ze-tak, 象似 tseung'-'ts'ze.
Resembling, 猶之乎 yau-chi-oo.

Resentment, 怨恨 uen'-han'.
Reserve, 留有餘 lau-'yau-ue, (to) 存下 ts'uen-'ha.
Reserved, 深沉 shum-ch'um.
Reservoir, 蓄陂 ch'uuk-pi, 陂池 pi-ch'i, 水井 'shui-'tseng.
Reside, 居住 kue-chue'.
Residence, 住家 chue'-ka, 宅 chaak.
Resign, 告退 ko'-t'ui', 辭職 ts'ze-chik, (one's self) 服 fuuk.
Resigned, (submissive) 舒服 shue-fuuk.
Resin, 松明 ts'uung-ming (meng), 松香 ts'uung-heung.
Resist, 抗拒 k'ong'-'k'ue, 頂住 'ting-chue', 敵住 tik-chue', 擋住 'tong-chue'.
Resolute, 堅心 kin-sum.
Resolve, 定意 ting'-i', 立心 laap-sum, 決意 k'uet-i, 主意 'chue-i', (solve) 解開 'kaai-hoi.

Resort, (to a place) 去到 hue'-to', (to a person) 轉向 'chuen-heung', (to a thing, &c.) 轉使 'chuen-'shai, (a place of) 聚處 tsue'-ch'ue', (an escape) 去路 hue'-lo'.
Resound, 響聲 'heung-sheng (echo) 回响 ooi-'heung, 撞聲 chong'-sheng.
Resource, 所倚賴 'shoh-'i-laai', (escape) 去路 hue'-lo'.
Respect, (to) 敬 king', 敬重 king'-chuung', (regard) 顧 koo'.
Respectable, 有體面 'yau-'t'ai-min'.
Respectful, 恭敬 kuung-king'.
Respecting, 論及 luun'-k'ap, 至於 chi'-ue.
Respects, to pay, 拜候 paai'-hau'.
Respiration, 呼吸 foo-k'up.
Respite, 歇時 hit'-shi.
Resplendent, 光朗 kwong-'long.
Respond, 應答 ying'-taap'.

注释

【抖下】休息一下。
【拗颈】倔强的。
【无宁耐】不安宁的。
【开翻手】重新开始。
【卖碎货】零售。
【留翻】保持,保留。
【静中】退休。
【回步】折回,追溯。

RES　　213　　RET

Responsibility, (負荷 foo²-hoh²) 担帶 taam-taai².
Responsible, 是問 shi²-mun².
Rest, 息 sik, 安息 ohn-sik, (to) 歇下 hit²-ʿha, 抖下 ʿt'au-ʿha, (the) 餘剩 ue-shing², ue-shing²-ke², 其餘 k'i-ue, 重有的 chuung-ʿyau-ti.
Restive, 拗頸 aau²-ʿkeng.
Restless, 無宁耐 mo-ning-noi², 俺尖 im-tsim.
Restore, 挽囘 ʿwaan-ooi, 復 fuuk, (save) 救翻 kau-faan.
Restrain, 禁制 kum²-chai², 拘束 k'ue-ch'uuk.
Restriction, 限度 haan²-to².
Result, (in) 終歸 chuung-kwai, (from) 出乎 ch'uut-oo, (the) 關系 kwaan-hai², 效驗 haau²-im².
Resume, 開翻手 hoi-faan-ʿshau, (return to) 做翻 tso²-faan.
Resurrection, 復生 fuuk-shang, fau-shang.

Retail, 賣碎貨 maai²-sui²-foh², 零賣 ling-maai, (trade) 小販 ʿsiu-faan.
Retain, 留翻 lau-faan, 收留 shau-lau.
Retake, (a place) 克復 hak-fuuk, (a prisoner) 捉翻 chuuk-faan.
Retaliate, 還手 waan-ʿshau, 報翻 po²-faan.
Retard, 滯 chai², 阻慢 ʿchoh-maan², 整慢 ʿching-maan².
Retch, 作嘔 tsok²-ʿou.
Retentive memory, 好記性 ʿho-ki²-sing².
Retinue, 跟班 kan-paan.
Retire, 退避 t'ui²-pi², 去 hue², 歸隱 kwai-ʿyan.
Retired, 幽靜 yau-tsing², 背 pooi².
Retirement, 靜中 tsing²-chuung, 隱處 ʿyan-ch'ue².
Retort, to, 還口 waan-ʿhau.
Retrace, 囘步 ooi-po².
Retract, 反口 ʿfaan-ʿhau, 食言 shik-in.

Retreat, 退 t'ui, 走 ʻtsau, (a) 隱處 ʻyan-ch'ue.
Retrench, 減省 ʻkaam-ʻshaang.
Retribution, 報應 poʾ-yingʾ.
Retrieve, 得翻 tak-faan, 贏翻 yeng-faan, 救 kauʾ.
Retrograde, 倒行 ʻto-hang.
Retrospect, 囘顧 ooi-kooʾ.
Return, 返 ʻfaan, 囘 ooi, 翻去 faan-hueʾ, 翻來 faan-*lai, 歸 kwai, (restore) 還 waan.
Reunite, 合翻埋 hop-faan-maai.
Reveal, 啟示 ʻk'ai-shiʾ.
Revel, 鬧酒 naauʾ-ʻtsau.
Revenge, 報仇 poʾ-ch'au, 雪恨 suetʾ-hanʾ.
Revenue, 庫銀 fooʾ-ngan.
Reverberation, 囘勢 ooi-shaiʾ, (sound) 應响 yingʾ-ʻheung.
Reverence, 恭敬 kuung-kingʾ.
Reverend, (honourable) 尊 tsuen, (elderly) 老 ʻlo.
Reverie, 想入神 ʻseung-yup-shan.

Reverse, (the) 相反 seung-ʻfaan, 對面 tuiʾ-minʾ, (to) 倒轉 ʻto-ʻchuen.
Revert, 歸反 kwai-ʻfaan.
Review, 閱 uet, 簡閱 ʻkaan-uet, 評 p'ing.
Revile, 譭罵 ʻwai-maʾ, 講壞 ʻkong-waaiʾ.
Revise, 修改 sau-ʻkoi.
Revive, 復興 fuuk-hing, 復生 fuuk-shang, 再旺 tsoiʾ-wongʾ, (the spirits) 打醒精神 ʻtaʾ-ʻseng-tsing-shan.
Revoke, 反變 ʻfaan-pinʾ, 追囘 chui-ooi, 廢 faiʾ.
Revolt, 背叛 pooiʾ-poonʾ.
Revolting, 凄慘 ts'ai-ʻts'aam.
Revolution, 周 chau, 囘 ooi, (in a state) 變 pinʾ.
Revolve, 簹簹轉 tumʾ-tumʾ-ʻchuen, t'um-t'um-ʻchuen, (旋轉 suen-ʻchuen), (in an orbit) 週轉 chau-chuenʾ.
Revolver, 連還鎗 lin-waan-ts'eung, 對面笑 tuiʾ-minʾ-suiʾ.

注 释

【得翻】恢复,重新得到。
【闹酒】狂欢。
【对面笑】象棋对弈时,双方将、帅不能在棋盘的同一条直线上直接对面,否则先占者得胜。出现这类情况,称为"对面笑"。把"revolver"译为"对面笑",不知何故。

> 注 释
>
> 【叶韵】押韵，协韵，韵脚。
> 【一髼髼】一缕缕。

Reward, 賞 ʽsheung, 賞給 ʽsheung-kʻup, 賞賜 ʽsheung-tsʻzeʼ, 花紅 fa-huung.
Rheumatism, 風濕 fuung-shup.
Rhinoceros, 犀牛 sai-ngau.
Rhubarb, 大黃 taaiʼ-wong.
Rhyme, 叶韻 hipʼ-wunʼ.
Rib, 肋 lak, 肋索骨 lak-shaakʼ-kwut, (ribs) 排骨 pʻaai-kwut.
Ribaldry, 惡聞臭氣 okʼ-mun-chʻauʼ-hiʼ.
Ribbon, 絲帶 sze-taaiʼ.
Rice, 米 ʽmai, (boiled) 飯 faanʼ, (growing) 禾 woh, (paddy) 穀 kuuk, (old man's) 糯米 nohʼ-ʽmai.
Rice-bird, 禾花雀 woh-fa-tseukʼ.
Rice-paper, 通紙 tʻuung-ʽchi.
Rich, 富厚 fooʼ-hauʼ, 富貴 fooʼ-kwaiʼ, (man) 財主 tsʻoi-ʽchue.
Riches, 財帛 tsʻoi-paak.
Rickety, 移移郁 i-i-yuuk.
Rid, 絕了 tsuet-hiu, 甪曉 lut-hiu.

Riddle, (sieve) 篩 ʽshai, (puzzle) 謎 ʽmai, (ask-a) 打物一 ʽta-mat-yat, 打古仔 ʽta-ʽkoo-ʽtsai.
Ride, 騎 kʻe.
Ridge, 條脊 tʻiu-tsekʼ, (in a field) 瀝 lek.
Ridicule, 嘲笑 chaau-siuʼ, 戲笑 hiʼ-siuʼ, (an object of) 笑柄 siuʼ-pengʼ.
Ridiculous, 可笑 ʽhoh-siuʼ.
Rifled, (grooved) 入柳 yup-ʽlau.
Right, 着 cheuk, 正 chingʼ, 本等 ʽpoon-ʽtang, (side) 右 yauʼ.
Righteous, 義 iʼ.
Rigid, 硬 ngaangʼ, 梗 ʽkang.
Rigorous, 嚴緊 im-ʽkan, (森嚴 shum-im).
Rim, 圓邊 uen-pin.
Ring, 環 waan, (finger) 戒指 kaaiʼ-ʽchi, (to) 响 ʽheung, (a bell) 打鐘 ʽta-chuung.
Ring-worm, 癬 ʽsin.
Ringlets, 一髼髼 yat-ʽtsze-ʽtsze.

Rinse, 嗰 ʻlong.
Riot, 亂鬧 luenʼ-naauʼ, 鬧事 naauʼ-szeʼ.
Rip open, 劏開 tʻong-hoi.
Ripe, 熟 shuuk.
Ripple, 波紋 poh-*mun.
Risc, 上 ʻsheung, 起 ʻhi, 興起 hing-ʻhi, (get up) 起身 ʻhi-shan.
Risk, 險 ʻhim, (to) 拚 pʻoonʼ.
Rite, 禮儀 ʻlai-i, 禮文 ʻlai-mun.
Rival, 對頭 tuiʼ-*tʻau.
Rive, 破裂 pʻohʼ-lit, (a) 條裂 tʻiu-lit, 條裂口 tʻiu-lit-ʻhau.
River, 河 hoh, (a) 條河 tʻiu-hoh, 條江 tʻiu-kong, (Canton river is called sea) 海 ʻhoi, 條海 tʻiu-ʻhoi.
Rivet, (to) 轉釘尾 chuenʼ-teng-ʻmi, (mend) 碼翻 ʻma-faan, (a) 兩頭釘 ʻleung-tʻau-ʻteng.
Rivulet, 溪 kʻai, 小河 ʻsiu-hoh, 山坑 shaan-haang.
Roach, 鱒魚 tsʻuun-ue.

Road, 路 loʼ, (high-) 官路 koon-loʼ.
Roam, 遊 yau.
Roar, (哮 haau), 喊 haamʼ, (of thunder) 轟轟聲 kwang-kwang-sheng, (of water) (溯湃 pʻaang-paai), (COL.) pʻop-pʻop-sheng.
Roast, 燒 shiu, (in ashes) 煨 ooi.
Rob, 搶奪 ʻtsʻeung-tuet.
Robber, 賊 *tsʻaak.
Robe, 袍 pʻo.
Robust, 壯肥 fi-chongʼ, 壯健 chongʼ-kinʼ.
Roc, 鵬 pʻaang.
Rock, 磐石 pʻoon-shek, 大石頭 taaiʼ-shek-tʻau, (to) 兩邊擺 ʻleung-pin-ʻpaai.
Rock-fish, 石狗公 shek-ʻkau-ʻkuung.
Rocket, (a) 一枝起火 yat-chi-ʻhi-ʻfoh, (falling) 九龍到地 ʻkau-luung-toʼ-tiʼ, (a, to be caught) 炮頭 pʻaauʼ-tʻau, 花炮 fa-pʻaauʼ.

注释

【嗰】用水冲洗。
【劏開】剖开。
【一枝起火】起火：一种烟花。

注释

【摵椅】摇椅。
【辘】卷，滚动，辗。
【肋喀】不顺畅，崎岖不平。

Rocking-chair, 摵椅 luuk-ʻi.
Rock-work, 假石山 ʻka-shek-shaan.
Rod, 竿 kohn.
Roe, (female deer) 麀 yau, (fish-) 魚鬻 ue-chʻuun.
Rogue, 賊仔 tsʻaak-ʻtsai, 爛仔 *laanʾ-ʻtsai.
Roll, (to) 轆 luuk, (up) 捲埋 ʻkuen-maai, (as water) 滾 ʻkwun, (a) 卷 ʻkuen.
Roller, 碾 ʻchin, 轆 luuk, (for fields) 石滾 shek-ʻkwun.
Rollicking, 反斗 ʻfaan-ʻtau.
Rolling-pin, 研麵棍 ngaan-minʾ-ʻkwun.
Roman Catholic, 天主教 Tʻin-ʻchue-kaauʾ.
Romantic, 虛幻 hue-waanʾ.
Rome, 羅馬 Loh-ʻma.
Roof, 瓦背 ʻnga-*pooiʾ, 屋背 uuk-pooiʾ, (of the mouth) 上嘊 sheungʾ-ngok.
Room, 房 *fong, 廳 ʻtʻeng, (space) 地方 tiʾ-fong, 定 *tengʾ.

Roost, 雞栖 kai-tsʻai, (to) 瞀 mau.
Root, 根 kan, (and branch) 本末 ʻpoon-moot, (and rise) 來歷 loi-lik.
Rootlet, 薑 ʻkʻeung.
Rope, 繩 *shing, 纜 laamʾ, (a) 條繩 tʻiu-*shing.
Rose, 玫瑰花 mooi-kwai-fa, (monthly) 月桂 uet-kwai, (quarterly) 四季春 szeʾ-kwaiʾ-chʻuun.
Rose-apple, 葡萄菓 pʻoo-tʻo-ʻkwoh.
Rose-wood, 花梨木 fa-*li-muuk.
Rosin, 松香 tsʻuung-ʻheung.
Rot, (dry) 枯槁 foo-ʻko, (damp) 霉 mooi.
Rotten, 霉爛 mooi-laanʾ, (putrid) 腐爛 fooʾ-laanʾ, (worm-eaten) 蛀爛 chueʾ-laanʾ.
Rotate, 輪轉 luun-chuenʾ.
Rouge, 脂粉 chi-ʻfun, 胭 in-chi.
Rough, 粗 tsʻo, 嘊 haai, 肋喀 lak-kʻak.

Round, 圓 uen, 當當圈 t'um-t'um-ʻhuen, (turn) 轉 chuen', t'um-t'um-chuen'.	Ruby, 紅寶石 huung-ʻpo-shek.
Rouse, 楊起 tik-ʻhi, 打醒 ʻta-seng, (urge) 鼓舞 ʻkoo-ʻmoo.	Rudd, 鱒魚 ʻts'uun-ue.
	Rudder, 舵 t'oh, 舵 ʻt'aai.
	Rude, 粗 ts'o, 無禮 ʻmo-ʻlai, 鄙劣 ʻp'i-luet, 魯莽 ʻlo-mong.
Rout, 眾人亂聚 chuung'-yan-luen'-tsue', 亂走 luen'-ʻtsau.	Rudiment, 胚 p'ooi, 初做 ch'oh-tso'-ke', (of learning) 小學 ʻsiu-hok.
Route, 道路 to'-lo'.	
Routine, 慣經 kwaan'-king.	Rue, (to) 悔 fooi', (a plant) 臭草 ch'au-ts'o.
Rover, 遊手 yau-ʻshau.	Rueful, 矗厲 pai'-ai.
Row, (rank) 行 hong, 刺 laat.	Ruffian, 兇徒 huung-t'o.
Row, (disturbance) 鬧事 naau'-sze'.	Ruffle, 縐埋 tsau'-maai.
	Rug, (hearth-) 爐口氈 lo-ʻhau-ʻchin.
Row, (to) 櫂 chaau'.	
Rowdy, 匪徒 ʻfi-t'o.	Rugged, 崎嶇 k'i-ʻk'ue, 肋喀 lak-k'ak, 巖磻 ngaam-ts'aam.
Row-lock, 槳脚 ʻtseung-keuk'.	
Rub, 搓 ch'a, 擦 ts'aat', 磨擦 moh-ts'aat', (the hands) 挪挲 noh-soh.	Ruin, 破敗 p'oh'-paai', 崩敗 pang-paai' 敗壞 paai'-waai'.
Rubbish, 廢物 fai'-mat, 爛坭 laan'-nai, 擸撞 laap-saap'.	Rule, 規矩 k'wai-ʻkue, 法度 faat'-to', (to) 管理 ʻkoon-ʻli, (paper) 間線 kaan'-sin'.
Rubble, 蠻石 maan-shek.	

注释

【惯经】日常的，例行的。
【櫂】划（船）。
【绉埋】弄皱。
【矗厲】可怜的，被动的。

注 释

【间尺】尺子。
【翻草】反刍。
【居乡】去乡下，定居乡村。

Ruler, 主宰 ʿchue-ʿtsoi, (an instrument) 間尺 kaanʾ-chʿekʾ.

Rumble, 轟 kwang, (COL.) tʿum-tʿum-sheng.

Ruminate, 翻草 faan-tsʿo, 反齧 ʿfaan-ngit, (reflect) 心思思 sum-sze-sze.

Rummage, 找搵 ʿchaau-ʿwan, 掏亂 lo-luenʾ, chʿaau.

Rumour, 消息 siu-sik, 風聲 fuung-shing, 流風 lau-fuung.

Rump, 尾根 ʿmi-kan, 尾龍骨 ʿmi-luung-kwut.

Rumple, 縐 chʿaau, chʿaau-mang-mang.

Run, 走 ʿtsau, 跑走 ʿpʿaau-ʿtsau, 踢 tek, (as water) 流 lau, (off) 走路 ʿtsau-loʾ.

Runner, (official) 廳差 tʿing-chʿaai.

Running-hand, 草書 ʿtsʿo-shue.

Running-knot, 老鼠耳 ʿlo-ʿshue-ʿi.

Rupture, (See Hernia), (to) 裂 lit.

Rural, 鄉里 heung-ʿli, 鄉下 heung-ʿha.

Rush, (to) 冲突 chʿuung-tat.

Rushes, 燈心草 tang-sum-ʿtʿso, (mat-) 鹹水草 haam-ʿshui-ʿtsʿo.

Russia, 鵝羅斯國 Ngoh-loh-sze-kwokʾ.

Rust, 銹 sauʾ, (to) 生銹 shang-sauʾ.

Rustic, 鄉下 heung-ʿha.

Rusticate, 居鄉 kue-heung.

Rustling, 沙沙聲 sha-sha-sheng, sa-sa-sheng, sö-sö-sheng.

Rut, (軌道 ʿkwai-toʾ), 車轍 chʿe-chʿit.

Rye, 麥 mak, 小麥 ʿsiu-mak.

S

Sabbath, 安息日 Ohn-sik-yat.

Sable, (fur) 黑貂皮 hak-tiu-pʿi.

Sack, 囊 nong, 袋 *toiʾ, (to) 劫空 kipʾ-huung.

| SAG | 220 | SAL |

Sack-cloth, 粗麻布 ts'o-ma-po'.
Sacred, 聖 shing'.
Sacrifice, 祭祀 tsai'-tsze', (to part with) 捨 ʿshe, 拚 p'oon', 拚窮 p'oon'-k'uung.
Sad, 憂悶 yau-moon', 聶屭 pai'-ai', (how!) 可憐 ʿhoh-lin, 可惜 ʿhoh-sik.
Saddle, 鞍 ʿohn, 馬鞍 ʿma-ʿohn.
Safe, 穩當 ʿwan-tong', 妥當 ʿt'oh-tong', 穩陳 ʿwan-chan'.
Safe, (for meat) 風燈 fuung-tang, (an iron) 鐵箱 t'it-seung.
Safflower, (colour) 花紅 fa-huung.
Saffron, 紅藍花 huung-laam-fa.
Sagacious, 伶俐 ling-li'.
Sage, (a) 聖人 shing'-yan, (herb) 來路茶 loi-*lo'-ch'a, 英國茶 Ying-kwok-ch'a.
Sago, 沙穀米 sha-kuuk-ʿmai.

Said, (the) 該 koi.
Sail, 悝 ʿli, 帆 faan, (to) 行船 hang-shuen, 駛 ʿshai, 駛風 ʿshai-fuung, (set-) 開身 hoi-shan, 扯悝 ʿch'e-ʿli.
Sailor, 水手 ʿshui-ʿshau.
Sake of, 爲 wai'.
Salacious, 姣 au.
Salad, 生菜 shang-ts'oi'.
Salary, 俸祿 fuung'-luuk, (a teacher's) 修金 ʿsau-ʿkum.
Sale, 消流 siu-lau, 消路 siu-lo', (for) 出賣 ch'uut-maai', (auction) 出投 ch'uut-t'au, (deed of) 契 k'ai', 張契 cheung-k'ai'.
Salisbury seeds, 白菓 paak-ʿkwoh.
Saliva, 口水 ʿhau-ʿshui.
Sallow, 黃黃白白 wong-wong-paak-paak.
Sally, 走出 ʿtsau-ch'uut.
Salmon, 馬友 ʿma-ʿyau.
Saloon, 客堂 haak'-t'ong.
Salt, 鹽 im, (salted) 鹹 haam, (Epsom) 朴硝 p'ok'-siu. (to) 醃 ip'.

注 释

【稳阵】稳当。
【风灯】此处为误译。Safe 应为"纱橱"，用于存放食品。
【姣】放荡的。
【黄黄白白】气色不好的，灰黄色的。
【马友】马友鱼，是广东湛江徐闻的一种多脂肪的名贵特产鱼类，属马鲅科，学名四指马鲅（Eleutheronema tetradactylum），俗称午笋、祭鱼和鲤后Salmon指鲑鱼。

> 注 释

【好水土】有益健康的。
【作圣】使神圣化。
【心雄】满怀希望的。

| SAN | 221 | SAU |

Saltpetre, 鹹硝 haam-siu, 硝 siu.
Salubrious, 温和 wan-woh.
Salubrity, 好水土 ʻho-ʻshui ʻtʻo.
Salute, (to) 請安 tsʻing-ʻohn, (a) 禮炮 ʻlai-pʻaauʼ.
Salvation, 救 kauʼ, 得救 tak-kauʼ, 救法 kauʼ-faat.
Salve, 膏藥料 ko-yeuk-liuʼ.
Same, 同 tʻuung.
Sample, 樣子 yeungʼ-ʻtsze, 辦 *paanʼ.
Sanctify, 作聖 tsokʼ-shingʼ, 成聖 shing-shingʼ.
Sanction, 准 ʻchuun.
Sand, 沙 sha.
Sandals, (grass-) 草鞋 ʻtsʻo-haai.
Sandal-wood, 檀香 tʻaan-heung.
Sand-stone, 礪石 laiʼ-shek.
Sandwich Islands, 檀香山 Tʻaan-heung-shaan.
Sanguine, 心雄 sum-huung, sum-huung-keʼ.
Sanity, 自在 tszeʼ-tsoiʼ.

Sap, 汁 chup, 蕊 ʻyui, ʻshui, (to undermine) 割地腳 kohtʼ-tiʼ-keuk.
Sapan-wood, 蘇木 soo-muuk.
Sapindus, 無槵樹 mo-*waanʼ-shue, muuk-*waanʼ.
Sapphire, 青玉 tsʻing-yuuk.
Sarcastic, 譏諷 ki-fuungʼ.
Sarcenet, 綢綾 chʻau-ling, (for fans) 紙絹 ʻchi-kuenʼ, (for lanterns) 紗 sha.
Sarsaparilla, 茯苓 fuuk-ling.
Sash, 帶 taaiʼ, 褲頭帶 fooʼ-tʻau-taaiʼ, 腰帶 iu-taaiʼ.
Satin, 緞 *tuenʼ, (native) 八絲緞 paatʼ-sze-*tuenʼ.
Satire, 譏刺 ki-tsʻzeʼ.
Satisfied, 厭足 imʼ-tsuuk, 心足 sum-tsuuk, 見夠 kinʼ-kauʼ.
Saturate, 浸透 tsumʼ-tʻauʼ.
Saturday, 禮拜六 ʻlai-paaiʼ-luuk.
Saturn, (planet) 土星 ʻTʻo-ʻsing.
Sauce, 醬 tseungʼ.
Sauce-pan, 煲 po.

| SCA | 222 | SCA |

Saucer, 茶碟 ch'a-*tip, 茶船 ch'a-*shuen.
Saucy, 輕慢 hing-maan', 傲慢 ngo'-maan', 沙塵 sha-ch'an.
Saunter, 閒遊 haan-yau.
Sausage, 猪腸 chue-*ch'eung, (dried) 臘腸 laap-*ch'eung.
Savage, 蠻 maan, (a) 野人 'ye-yan, 生番 ‵shaang-faan.
Save, 救 kau', 拯救 'ch'ing-kau', 存 ts'uen, (gain) 賺 chaan'.
Saviour, 救世主 Kau'-shai'-chue.
Savour, 味道 mi'-to'.
Saw, (a) 把鋸 'pa-kue', (to) 拉鋸 laai-kue', 鋸 kue'.
Saw-dust, 木糠 muuk-hong.
Saw-mill, 解木廠 ‵kaai-muuk-ch'ong.
Saxifrage, 老虎耳 ‵lo-‵foo-‵i.
Say, 話 wa', (a saying) 語 ‵ue.
Scab, 塊弇 faai'-‵im.

Scabbard, 刀殼 to-hok'.
Scaffold, 搭架 taap'-*ka', 棚 p'aang.
Scald, 爤 luuk.
Scale, (series) 等級 'tung-k'up, (comparative) 配法 p'ooi'-faat'.
Scales, (for weighing) 天平 t'in-p'ing; (of fishes) 魚鱗 ue-luun.
Scaly, (in flakes) 一片片 yat-p'in'-p'in'.
Scandal, (a) 醜事 'ch'au-sze', (to talk) 講是非 ‵kong-shi'-fi.
Scandalized, 見醜 kin'-‵ch'au.
Scandalous, 醜 ‵ch'au, 害情 hoi'-ts'ing, (abusive) 壞名 waai'-meng.
Scanty, 窄窄地 chaak'-*chaak-*ti'.
Scar, 痕 han, 痕迹 han-tsik.
Scarce, 罕有 ‵hohn-‵yau, 希罕 hi-hohn, 少 ‵shiu.
Scarcely, 僅 ‵kan.
Scare, 嚇勢 haak'-shai'.

注释

【生番】未开化的,荒凉的。
【木糠】锯末。
【爤】烫。
【一片片】有鳞的、多鳞的。

注释

【长膊巾】围巾。
【分门】分裂。
【啉哔】责骂。
【觇吓】偷窥。
【淘干净/啃】清除。

Scarf, 長膊巾 ch'eung-pok'-kan, (join on) 駁 pok'.
Scarlet, 大紅 taai'-huung.
Scatter, 散開 saan'-hoi.
Scattered, 星散 sing-saan'.
Scavenger, (street) 掃街 so'-kaai, 倒攬搔 'to-laap-saap', (house-) 倒屎 'to-'shi.
Scenery, 景象 'king-tseung'.
Scent, 香氣 hueng-hi, 香 heung, (to) 鼻聞 pi'-mun.
Scented capers, 珠蘭茶 chue-laan-ch'a.
Sceptical, 多疑 toh-i.
Sceptre, 圭 kwai, (a ladle-shaped) 如意 ue-i'.
Schedule, 冊 ch'aak'.
Scheme, 計謀 kai'-mau.
Schism, 分門 fun-moon.
Scholar, 學生 hok-'shaang, 讀書人 tuuk-shue-yan.
School, 書館 shue-'koon, 學館 hok-'koon, 學堂 hok-t'ong.
School-fellow, 書友 shue-a'yau.

School-master, 先生 sin-shang, (mistress) 女師 'nue-sze.
Science, 學 hok.
Scissors, 鉸剪 kaau'-'tsin.
Scoff, 譏笑 ki-siu'.
Scold, 鬧 naau'.
Scolding, 啉哔 lum-lut, (a) 鬧一場 naau'-yat-ch'eung.
Scoop, (to) 挖 waat'.
Scope, 大意 taai'-i'.
Scorch, 焦 tsiu, 燶 nuung, 燒親 shiu-ts'an.
Scorn, 輕慢 hing-maan', 厭棄 im'-hi', 藐視 'miu-shi'.
Scorpion, 蜂蠍 fuung-hit'.
Scoundrel, 光棍 kwong-kwun'.
Scour, 淘乾淨 t'o-kohn-tseng', 啃 'shaang.
Scourge, 鞭 pin.
Scout, (disdain) 厭棄 im'-hi', (to spy) 覘吓 chong-ha.
Scowl, 嬲色 nau-shik, 縐眉 tsau'-mi.

| SCR | 224 | SEA |

Scraggy, 瘦出骨 ʻshau-chʻuut-kwut.
Scramble, 擒爬 kʻum-pʻa, 手爬爬 ʻshau-pʻa-pʻa.
Scrap, 碎 suiʼ.
Scrape, (to) 刮 kwaatʼ, 刮削 kwaatʼ-seukʼ.
Scratch, 摵 ʻwa, ʻwe, 楢 nyaau, 抓摵 ʻchaau-ʻwa, 搔 so.
Scrawl, 畫花 waak-fa.
Scream } 叫聲 kiuʼ-sheng, 高聲叫 ko-sheng-kiuʼ.
Screech }
Screen, 屏風 pʻing-fuung, 簾 *lim, (to) 遮蓋 che-kʻoiʼ.
Screw, 螺絲 loh-ʻsze, (cork-) 酒鑽 ʻtsau-tsuenʼ, (miser) 蝦鬱鑽 ha-chʻuun-tsuenʼ.
Screw-driver, 螺絲揰 loh-ʻsze-ningʼ.
Screw-steamer, 暗輪船 omʼ-luun-shuen.
Scribble, 亂搽 luenʼ-chʻa.
Scribe, 讀書人 tuuk-shue-yan.

Scrimp, 短少 ʻtuen-ʻshiu.
Scrofula, 瘰癧 ʻloh-lek.
Scroll, 卷 ʻkuen, 手卷 ʻshau-ʻkuen, (a pair of scrolls) 對 tuiʼ.
Scrotum, 腎囊 shanʼ-uong.
Scrub, 刷 shaatʼ, 擦 tsʻaatʼ.
Scruple, (doubt) 思疑 sze-i.
Scrutinize, 查察 cʻha-chʻaatʼ.
Scuffle, 爭鬥 chaang-tauʼ.
Sculk, 竄匿 ʻchʻuen-nik.
Scull, 頭殼 tʻau-hokʼ, (bare) 枯顱頭 foo-lo-tʻau; (of a boat) 櫓 ʻlo, (to) 搖櫓 iu-ʻlo.
Scum, 浮沫 fau-moot, 糜 mi.
Scurf, 老坭 ʻlo-nai, (on the head) 頭坭 tʻau-nai.
Scurrilous, 汚穢 oo-waiʼ.
Scythe, 長鐮 chʻeuug-lim.
Sea, 海 ʻhoi, 洋海 yeung-ʻhoi.
Sea-sickness, 嘔浪 ʻau-long, 暈浪 wanʼ-longʼ.
Sea-weed, 海菜 ʻhoi-tsʻoi.

注 釋

【手爬爬】爬行，攀登。
【亂搽】亂寫，潦草地书写。
【老坭】身上的死皮。
【嘔浪/暈浪】暈船。

注 释

【揸针嘅】女裁缝。
【揾】搜寻，调查。
【唪】隐蔽的，僻静的。
【西席】秘书。
【津液】分泌物。

SEA   225   SED

Seal, (animal) 海獺 ʽhoi-chʽaat’, (to) 印 yan’, 給印 kʽup-yan’, (up) 封 fuung, (-character) 圖書 tʽo-ʽshue, 篆字 suen’-*tsze, (the imperial) 御璽 ue’-ʽsaai.

Sealing-wax, 火漆 ʽfoh-tsʽat.

Seam, (a) 聯骨 luen-kwut, 聯口 luen-ʽhau, (in boarding) 罅 la’, (to) 聯 luen, 縫 fuung, 合埋 hop-maai.

Seamstress, 揸針嘅 cha-chum-ke’.

Search, 搜檢 ʽsau-ʽkim, 揾 ʽwun.

Seared conscience, 喪良心 song’-leung-sum, 無本心 ʽmo-ʽpoon-sum.

Season, 時 shi, (4 seasons) 四季 sze’-kwai’, 四時 sze’-shi.

Seasonable, 着時候 cheuk-shi-hau’.

Seasoning, 落味道 lok-mi’-to’.

Seat, 座 tsoh’, 座位 tsoh’-wai’.

Secluded, 唪 pooi’.

Second, 第二 tai’-i’.

Second-hand, 二檯 i’-*tʽoi.

Secret, 機密 ki-mat, 暗 om’, (a) 隱事 ʽyan-sze’.

Secretary, 西席 Sai-tsik, (private) 幕友 mok-ʽyau, (Colonial-) 輔政司 foo-chingʼ-sze.

Secretion, 津液 tsuun-yik.

Secretly, 私吓 sze-ʽha.

Sect, 教門 kaau’-moon.

Section, 段 tuen’, (a cutting) 截 tsit.

Secure, 穩陳 ʽwan-chan’, 主固 ʽchue-koo’.

Security, 擔保 taam-ʽpo, 擔干紀 taam-kohn-ʽki.

Sedan-chair, 頂轎 ʽting-*kiu’.

Sedan-poles, 轎升 *kiuʼ-ʽshing.

Sedge, 蒲草 pʽo-ʽtsʽo.

Sediment, 渣滓 cha-tsze, 脚 keukʽ.

SEL 226 SEN	
Seditious, 擾亂 ʻiu-luenʼ.	Self-contradictory, 自相矛盾 tszeʼ-ʻseung-mau-tʻuun.
Seduce, 挑引 tʻiuʼ-yan, 誘惑 ʻyau-waak, 引誘 ʻyan-ʻyau.	Self-examination, 自省 tszeʼ-ʻsing.
Sedulous, 勤力 kʻan-lik.	Self-sufficient, 自足 tszeʼ-tsuuk.
See, 見 kinʼ, 睇見 ʻtʻai-kinʼ, (look) 睇吓 ʻtʻai-ha, (after) 看守 hohn-ʻshau.	Self-will, 執拗 chup-aauʼ.
	Selfishness, 私心 sze-sam.
Seed, 種 ʻchuung, 仁 yan, 米 ʻmai.	Sell, 賣 maaiʼ, 賣去 maaiʼ-hueʼ, (offer to) 發賣 faatʼ-maaiʼ.
Seek, 揾 ʻwan, 尋 tsʻum, (ask) 求 kʻau.	Semen, 種 ʻchuung, 精 tsing.
Seem, 似 ʻtsʻze, 顯出 ʻhin-chʻuut, (seems to me) 似覺 ʻtsʻze-kokʼ.	Semi-, 半 poonʼ.
	Send, 寄 kiʼ, (a person) 遣 ʻhin, 打發 ʻta-faatʼ.
Seen, 見過 kinʼ-kwohʼ.	Senior, 長 ʻcheung.
Segar, (Manila) 呂宋烟 ʻLue-suungʼ-ʻin, (a) 一口烟 yatʼ-ʻhau-ʻin.	Senna, 槐葉 waai-ip.
	Sense, 智識 chiʼ-shik, 見識 kinʼ-shik, (common) 情理 tsʻing-ʻli.
Seize, 捉住 chuuk-chueʼ, 霸住 paʼ-chueʼ, 搶 ʻtsʻeung.	
	Senses, (five) 五官 ʻng-koon.
Seldom, 少可 ʻshiu-ʻhoh, 無幾何 ʻmo-ʻki-*hoh.	Sensitive, 情急 tsʻing-kup, 性急 singʼ-kup.
Select, 擇 chaak, 揀 ʻkaan, 選 ʻsuen.	Sensual, 嗜慾 shiʼ-yuuk, 私慾 sze-yuuk.
Self, 自己 tszeʼ-ʻki.	

注 释

【睇吓】看看。
【少可】很少。
【无几何】极为偶尔。
【嗜欲】感觉的, 肉欲的。

注释

【哨人】岗哨，哨兵。
【清平】平静的，安详的。
【下作】卑屈的。
【严紧】严峻的，严厉的。
【阴阳之分】性，性别。
【三黎鱼】西鲱。

Sentence, 句話 *kue*'-wa', (judicial) 批判 *p'ai-p'oon*', 擬定刑 *i-ting*'-ying, 定罰 *ting*'-faat, 辦 paan'.
Sentinel, 哨人 *shaau*'-yan.
Separate, 別開 *pit-hoi*, 分別 *fun-pit*, (ADJ.) 另外 *ling*'-ngoi'.
September, 英九月 *Ying-'kau-uet*.
Sepulchre, 墳墓 *fun-moo*'.
Sequester, 抄 *ch'aau*, 封 *fuung*.
Serene, 清平 *ts'ing-p'ing*.
Serge, 嗶嘰 *put-ki*.
Series, 次第 *ts'ze*'-tai', 列陳 *lit-chan*', 一件件 *yat-kin*'-kin'.
Serious, (person) 莊敬 *chong-king*', (affair) 關系 *kwaan-hai*', 重 *chuung*'.
Serpent, (a) 條蛇 *t'iu-she*.
Servant, 奴僕 *no-puuk*, 使喚人 '*shai-foon*'-yan, (boy) 事仔 *sze*'-*tsai*.
Serve, 服事 *fuuk-sze*'.
Servile, 柔順 *yau-shuun*', 下作 *ha*'-*tsok*'.

Sesamum, 芝蔴 *chi-ma*, 油麻 *yau-ma*.
Set, (to) 立 *laap*, 置 *chi*', 擠 *chai*, (as the sun) 落 *lok*, 入 *yup*, (a) 副 *foo*', (of people) 班 *paan*.
Settle, 定 *ting*', (accounts) 清數 *ts'ing-sho*', (as dregs) 凝 *k'ing*.
Seven, 七 *ts'at*.
Seventh, 第七 *tai*'-*ts'at*.
Sever, 割短 *koht*'-*tuen*.
Several, 幾個 '*ki-koh*', 數 *sho*'.
Severe, 嚴緊 *im-'kan*, 利害 *li*'-*hoi*', (grievous) 重 '*ch'uung*.
Sew, 聯 *luen*, 縫 *fuung*.
Sewer, 坑渠 *haang-k'ue*, 暗渠 *om*-*k'ue*.
Sex, 陰陽之分 *yum-yeung-chi-fun*.
Shabby, 卑賤 *pi-tsin*'.
Shackles, 桎梏 *chat-kuuk*, 繚 *liu*.
Shad, 三黎魚 *saam-laai-*ue*.

SHA 228 SHE

Shaddock, 碌柚 *luuk-*yau*, 柚子 *yau-ʻtsze*.
Shade, 遮陰 *che-yum*, (lamp-) 燈罩 *ʻtang-chaau*ʼ, (a slight) 帶有的 *taai*ʼ-*ʻyau-ʻti*.
Shades, 陰間 *yum-kaan*.
Shadow, 影 *ʻying*.
Shaft, 竿 *kohn*, (handle) 柄 *pengʼ*.
Shaggy, 鬆毛 *suung-mo*, *suung-mo-keʼ*.
Shake, 搖吓 *iu-ha*, 搖動 *iu-tuungʼ*, 挾 *ʻyeung*, (as dice) 揅 *ngo*, (the head) 擰頭 *ningʼ-*tʻau*, (hands) 揸手 *cha-ʻshau*.
Shall, 將來 *tseung-loi*, 必 *pit*.
Shallow, 淺 *ʻtsʻin*.
Shallows, 瀝 *lek*, (rapids) 灘 *tʻaan*.
Sham, 詐僞 *chaʼ-ngaiʼ*, (to) 詐 *chaʼ*.
Shame, 羞 *sau*, 羞恥 *sau-ʻchʻi*, (to feel) 見羞 *kinʼ-sau*, (for another) 見醜 *kinʼ-chʻau*, (disgrace) 醜 *ʻchʻau*.

Shampoo, 泵身 *ʻtum-shan*.
Shape, 式 *shik*, 像 *tseungʼ*, 模樣 *moo-*yeungʼ*, 形 *ying*.
Share, (to) 分數 *fun-shoʼ*, (a) 分子 *funʼ-tsze*, 股分 *ʻkoo-*funʼ*.
Shark, 沙魚 *sha-*ue*.
Sharp, 利 *liʼ*, 快利 *fuaiʼ-liʼ*.
Sharpen, 磨利 *moh-liʼ*.
Shatter, 打碎 *ʻta-suiʼ*.
Shave, 剃 *tʻaiʼ*, (to plane) 刨 *pʻaan*.
Shaving, 刨柴 *pʻaau-*chʻaai*, (gum-shavings) 刨花 *pʻaau-fa*.
Shawl, 答膊蔞 *taapʼ-pokʼ-lau*.
She, he, or it, 佢 *ʻkʻue*.
Sheaf, 禾束 *woh-chʻuuk*, (a) 一把 *yat-ʻpa*.
Shear, 剪 *ʻtsin*.
Shears, 鉸剪 *kaauʼ-ʻtsin*.
Sheath, 鞘 *tsʻiuʼ*, 刀殼 *to-hokʼ*.
Shed, a, 廠 *ʻchʻong*, 篷廠 *pʻuung-chʻong*.

注 释

【松毛】蓬松的。
【拧头】摇头。
【泵身】洗发香波,洗发剂,洗涤剂。
【答膊蔞】披巾。
【禾束】捆,束,扎。

注释

【錯錯諤諤】羞怯的，懦弱的。
【净系】单单是。
【郁】动。
【打冷振】打冷颤，哆嗦。

SHI   229   SHO

Sheep, 羊 *yeung, 綿羊 min-*yeung.
Sheep-fold, 羊欄 yeung-laan.
Sheepish, 錯錯諤諤 ts'ok², ts'ok²-ngok-ngok.
Sheer, 淨係 tseng²-hai².
Sheet, (of a bed) 被單 p'i-taan, (of paper) 張 cheung, (-ropes) 繚繩 liu-shing.
Shelf, 格板 kaak²-paan, 架 ka².
Shell, 螺殼 loh-hok², lö-hok², (of eggs, &c.) 殼 hok².
Shelter, 遮蔽 che-pai, 庇護 pi²-oo², 庇蔭 pi²-yum².
Shepherd, 牧羊人 muuk-yeung-yan, 牧童 muuk-t'uung.
Shepherd's purse, 薺 ts'ai.
Sheriff, 傳票官 ch'uen-p'iu²-koon.
Shield, 牌盾 p'aai-t'uun, (rattan-) 籐牌 t'ang-p'aai.
Shift, (to) 換 oon², 搬 poon, 移 i, (move) 郁 yuuk, (expedient) 計 kai².

Shin, 前臁 ts'in-lim.
Shine, 發光 faat²-kwong, 照 chiu², (upon) 照光 chiu²-kwong.
Ship, 船 shuen, (full rigged) 三枝桅船 saam-chi-wai-shuen.
Ship-building, 裝船 chong-shuen.
Ship-wreck, 破船 p'oh²-shuen.
Shirk, 躲避 toh-pi².
Shirt, 內衫 noi²-shaam, (under) 近身衣 kan²-shan-i, 汗衫 hohn²-shaam.
Shiver, (with cold) 打冷振 ta-laang-chan², (shatter) 打碎 ta-sui².
Shoals, 沙灘 sha-t'aan.
Shock, (shake) 震動 chan²-tuung², (violence) 勢兇 shai²-huung.
Shocking 慘 ts'aam, 傷心 sheung-sum.
Shoe, 鞋 haai, (pair of shoes) 對鞋 tui²-haai.

Shoe-horn, 鞋拔 haai-pat, 鞋抽 haai-ch'au.	Shove, 推擁 t'ui-⸌uung, 擁開 ⸌uung-hoi, (along) 挓 t'an⸍, (pole) 撐 ch'aang.
Shoot, (to) 射 she⸍, 打 ⸌ta, (sprout) 出笋 ch'uut-⸌suun.	Shovel, 鏟 ⸌ch'aan.
Shoots, bamboo-, 竹笋 chuuk-⸌suun.	Show, 俾——睇 ⸌pi——t'ai, (point out) 指示 ⸌chi-shi.
Shop, 舖頭 p'oo⸍-*t'au.	Shower, 陣雨 chan⸍-⸌ue.
Shop-man, 賣貨手 maai⸍-foh⸍-⸌shau, (head) 掌櫃 ⸌cheung-*kwai⸍.	Showy, 排場 p'aai-ch'eung.
	Shred, 爛條 laan⸍-t'iu.
Shore, 岸 ngohn⸍.	Shrew, 惡婆 ok-*p'oh.
Shore up, 撐住 ch'aang-chue⸍.	Shrewd, 麻俐 ma-li⸍.
Short, 短 ⸌tuen, (time) 暫時 tsaam⸍-shi.	Shriek, 叫聲 kiu⸍-sheng.
	Shrike, 伯鷯 paak-liu.
Short-hand, 減筆字 ⸌kaam-put-tsze⸍.	Shrill, 狠響 ⸌han-⸌heung.
	Shrimp, 蝦 ⸌ha.
Short-sight, 近視眼 kan⸍-shi⸍-⸌ngaan.	Shrine, 神龕 shan-⸌hom.
	Shrink, 縮埋 shuuk-maai.
Shot, 彈子 taan⸍-tsze⸍.	Shrivel, 縐 ch'aau.
Should, (ought) 應當 ying-tong.	Shroud, 壽衣 shau⸍-i.
	Shrouding, 收殮 shau-⸌lim.
Shoulder, 肩膊 kin-pok⸍, 膊頭 pok⸍-t'au.	Shrouds, 上桅繩梯 ⸌sheung-wai-*shing-t'ai.
Shoulder of mutton, 羊手 yeung-⸌shau.	Shrub, 矮樹 ⸌ai-shue.
	Shrug the shoulders, 縮膊 shuuk-pok⸍.
Shout, 喝聲 hoht⸍-sheng.	Shudder, 打振 ⸌ta-chan⸍, 戰慄 chin⸍-luut.

注 释

【铺头】商店,店铺。
【卖货手】售货员。
【减笔字】速记。
【排场】炫耀的,卖弄的。
【烂条】碎片。
【打振】发抖,战栗。

注 释

【闪闪缩缩】躲躲闪闪的，狡猾的。
【踢燕】踢毽子。
【瞓晏觉】午睡。
【引气】叹息，叹气。
【好睇】好看的。

SIE　　231　　SIL

Shuffle cards, 洗牌 ‹sai-*p‘aai.
Shuffling, 閃閃縮縮 ‹shim-‹shim-shuuk-shuuk.
Shun, 避 pi›.
Shut, 關 kwaan, 閂埋 ‹shaan-maai, 掩埋 ‹im-maai, 合埋 hop-maai, (lock) 鎖住 ‹soh-chue, (stuff), 塞 sak, (seal) 封 fuung.
Shutters, 窗板 ‹ch‘eung-‹paan.
Shuttle-cock, 踢燕 t‘ek-*in›.
Shy, 畏縮 wai›-shuuk.
Siam, 暹羅國 Ts‘im›-loh-kwok›.
Sick, 有病 ‹yau-peng›, (stomach-) 會嘔 ooi›-‹au, 想嘔 ‹seung-‹au.
Sickle, 鐮 lim.
Side, 邊 pin, 旁邊 p‘ong-‹pin, 側邊 chak-‹pin, (of the body) 小腌 ‹siu-‹im.
Siege, (to lay) 圍住 wai-chue›.
Siesta, 瞓晏覺 fun›-aan›-kaau›.

Sieve, 篩斗 shai-‹tau.
Sift, 篩 shai.
Sigh, 引氣 ‹yan-hi›, 嘆息 t‘aan›-sik.
Sight, 眼見 ‹ngaan-kin›, (power of) 眼力 ‹ngaan-lik.
Sightly, 好睇 ‹ho-‹t‘ai.
Sign, (one's name) 簽名 ts‘im-*meng, (a trace) 影跡 ‹ying-tsik, (an omen) 兆頭 chiu›-t‘au, (a mark) 號 ho›.
Signboard, 招牌 chiu-p‘aai.
Signify, (mean) 有—意思 ‹yau——i›-sze, 意係 i›-hai›, (refer to) 指 ‹chi, (make signs) 示意 shi›-i›, 會意 ooi›-i›, 諧意 haai-i›.
Silence, 寂靜 tsik-tsing›, 無聲 mo-sheng.
Silent, 靜靜 *tsing›-tsing›.
Silently, 靜靜 tsing›-*tsing›.
Silk, (material) 絲 sze, (cloth) 綢 ch‘au, (thread) 絲線 sze-sin.

Silk-worm, 蠶蟲 ts'aam-*ch'uung.
Sill, 棖 ‚ch'aan, ‚ch'aam.
Silly, 呆呆 ngoi-ngoi, 疨食 nup-shik.
Silver, 銀 ngan, *ngan.
Similar, 似 ‚ts'ze, 相似 seung-ts'ze, 好似 ‚ho-ts'ze.
Simper, 冷笑 ‚laang-siu'.
Simple, 朴素 p'ok'-so', (minded) 蠢直 ‚ch'uun-chik, (easy) 容易 yuung-i'.
Simpleton, 呆佬 ngoi-‚lo.
Sin, 罪 tsui', 罪惡 tsui'-ok', (to) 犯罪 faan'-tsui'.
Since, 從——以來 ts'uung——i-loi, (seeing that) 既然間 ki'-in-kaan, (how long?) 起有幾耐 ‚hi-‚yau-‚ki-*noi?
Sincere, 誠實 shing-shat, 真心 chan-sum.
Sinew, 筋 kan.
Sing, 唱 ch'eung', 唱歌 ch'eung'-‚koh.
Singe, 燒燶 shiu-nuung.

Single, 單 ‚taan, 隻 chek'.
Singly, (one by one) 一一 yat-yat, 逐一逐二 chuuk-yat-chuuk-i'.
Single-hearted, 丹心 taan-sum, 赤心 ch'ik-sum.
Singular, 奇異 k'i-i'.
Sinister, 左 ‚tsoh, (bad) 使左挑 shai-‚tsoh-‚t'iu.
Sink, 沈落 ch'um-lok, (as a wall) 坐 tsoh'.
Sinner, 罪人 tsui'-yan.
Sinus, 穴 uet, (bay) 彎 waan.
Sip, 咪 mi, 啜 tsuet'.
Siphon, 角筒 kok'-t'uung.
Sir, 駕上 ka'-sheung', 尊駕 tsuen-ka', (Sirs) 列公 lit-kuung.
Sister, (elder) 亞姐 a'-‚tse, (younger) 亞妹 a'-*mooi.
Sister-in-law, 嬸姆 ‚shum-‚moo, (elder brother's wife) 亞嫂 a'-‚so, (younger brother's wife) 亞嬸 a'-‚shum, (wife's sisters) 亞姨 a'-i, a'-i, (husband's sisters) 亞姑 a'-‚koo.
Sit, 坐 tsoh', ts'oh.

注 釋

【棖】窗台，門檻。
【疨食】笨的；傻瓜。
【起有几耐】自……有多長時間。
【燒燶】燒焦。
【使左挑】不吉利的，不祥的。

> 注 释

【体度】大小，尺寸。
【意笔】素描。
【虾㿪钑】小气鬼。
【市井话】俚语。

Situation, 地位 tiʾ-wai, 所在 ʿshoh-tsoi, (office) 職任 chik-yumʾ.	Skip, 跳 tʿiuʾ, 跳躍 tʿiuʾ-yeuk.
Six, 六 luuk.	Skirt, 衫尾 shaam-ʿmi, (woman's) 裙 kʿwun.
Sixth, 第六 taiʾ-luuk.	Skulk, &c. *See* Sculk, &c.
Size, 體度 ʿtʿai-toʾ, (capacity) 度量 toʾ-leungʾ, (what?) 幾大 ʿki-*taai.	Sky, 蒼天 tsʿong-tʿin, 穹蒼 kʿuung-tsʿong, 天 tʿin, 太空 tʿaai-huung, (in the) 空中 huung-chuung.
Size, (glue) 膠 kaau.	Sky-light, 天窓 tʿin-chʿeung.
Skate, (fish) 鯆魚 poo-ue.	Slab, 塊石 faaiʾ-shek, 石版 shek-ʿpaan, 石碑 shek-pi.
Skate, (to) 碾 shinʾ.	
Skein, 札 chaatʾ, 子 ʿtsze.	
Skeleton, 骨體 kwut-ʿtʿai.	Slabber, 伐伐聲 faat-faat-sheng.
Sketch, 意筆 iʾ-put, (a rough) 草稿 ʿtsʿo-ko, (to) 繪 fooi.	Slack, 鬆 suung, (remiss) 嬾漏 laai-lau, (water) 水漫 ʿshui-maan.
Skewer, 燒肉串 shiu-yuuk-ʿchʿaan (ʿchum).	Slake, 解 ʿkaai, (lime) 發 faat.
Skill, 伎巧 kiʾ-ʿhaau, 才藝 tsʿoi-ngaiʾ.	Slam, 冲撞 chʿuung-chong, 揰 pʿuungʾ.
Skilled, 善精 shinʾ-tsing.	Slander, 譭謗 ʿwai-pʿong, (a) 讒言 tsʿaam-in.
Skim, 撇 pʿitʾ.	
Skin, 皮 pʿi, (to) 剝皮 mok-pʿi.	Slang, 市井話 ʿshi-ʿtseng-waʾ.
Skin (cast off,) 蛻 tʿuiʾ.	
Skin-flint, 蝦㿪鈒 ʿha-chʿuun-chaap.	Slanting, 斜 tsʿe, tsʿeʾ.

| SLE | 234 | SLI |

Slap, 打巴 ʻta-pa, (with the hand) 打巴掌 ʻta-pa-ʻcheung, 摑 kwaakʾ, 拍 pʻaakʾ.

Slash, 斬 ʻchaam, 亂斬 luenʾ-ʻchaam.

Slate, 石版 shek-ʻpaan.

Slattern, 拉狖 laai-taai, 濕霉 shap-mooi.

Slaughter, 殺戮 shaat-luuk, 屠戮 tʻo-luuk, (butcher) 劏 tʻong.

Slave, (female) 奴婢 no-ʻpʻi, (male) 僕 puuk, 奴僕 no-puuk.

Slay, 打死 ʻta-ʻsze.

Sledge, 拖轎 tʻoh-*kiuʾ.

Sleek, 滑澤 waat-chaak.

Sleep, 瞓 funʾ, 睡 shuiʾ, 打睡 ʻta-shui, 瞓覺 funʾ-kauʾ.

Sleepy, 眼瞓 ʻngaan-funʾ, 想瞓 ʻseung-funʾ, hap-ʻngaan.

Sleet, 霰雪 sinʾ-suetʾ.

Sleeve, 袖 tsauʾ.

Sleight of hand, 手法 ʻshau-faatʾ.

Slender, 幼細 yauʾ-saiʾ, 弱 yeuk, 纖 tsʻim, 朴 niu.

Slice, 片 pʻinʾ, 塊 faaiʾ, (to) 切 tsʻitʾ, 脷 lek.

Slide, 蹁 shinʾ.

Slight, (to) 輕忽 hing-fut, (small) 小小 ʻsiu-ʻsiu.

Slim, 纖 tsʻim.

Slime, 泥濘 niʾ-ningʾ, 潺 shaan.

Sling, (for stones) 飛砣 fi-tʻoh, (for carrying) 絡 lok, (of rattan) 籐絡 tʻang-lok.

Slip, (to) 蹁 shinʾ, 失 shat, (fall) 跌 titʾ, (off) 滑甩 waat-lut, (grow from a) 插生 chaapʾ-shang, 駁 pokʾ.

Slippers, 拖鞋 tʻoh-haai.

Slippery, 滑 waat, (character) 白鼻哥 paak-piʾ-ʻkoh, 猾賊 waat-tsʻaak.

Slipstitch, 桶線 ʻtʻuung-sinʾ.

注 释

【湿霉】邋遢地。
【眼瞓】困乏的，欲睡的。
【轻忽】轻微的。
【白鼻哥】又称"白鼻子"。京剧、粤剧等中的丑角儿。

注释

【水朤】水溢出。
【哴水碗】用来冲洗餐具的装水的碗。
【低头屈屈】低着头无精打采的样子。
【嚡褛】褴褛。
【窦板】挡板。
【答口声】咂嘴。
【识几程】一知半解。

Slit, 裂開 lit-hói, (a) 裂 lit, 條裂 t'iu-lit, 條罅 t'iu-la'.

Slop, 水朤 ʿshui-ngan'.

Slop-basin, 哴水碗 ʿlong-ʿshui-ʿoon.

Slope, 斜 ts'e', ts'e.

Sloth, (the) 木狗 muuk-ʿkau, 樹懶 shue'-ʿlaan.

Slothful, 懶惰 ʿlaan-toh.

Slouching, 氹堆 tum'-tui, 低頭屈屈 tai-t'au-wat-wat.

Slovenly, 嚡褛 laai-lue; (in dress) 拉獃 laai-taai.

Slow, 遲慢 ch'i-maan'.

Slowly, 慢慢 maan'-*maan', 摩摩 moh-moh.

Slug, 鼻涕蟲 pi'-t'ai'-ch'uung.

Sluggard, 一身懶骨 yat-shan-ʿlaan-kwut.

Sluice, 寶板 tau'-ʿpaan.

Slur, 玷辱 tim'-yuuk, 瑕疵 ha-ts'ze.

Slush, 泥湴 nai-paan'.

Sluttish, 苟且 ʿkau-ʿch'e.

Sly, 摘滑 lo-waat.

Smack the lips, 答口聲 taap'-ʿhau-sheng, chaap'-ʿhau.

Small, 細小 sai'-ʿsiu,——仔——ʿtsai, (very) 微 mi.

Small-pox, 出痘 ch'uut-*tau', 天行 t'in-hang.

Smalts, 洋青 yeung-ʿts'ing.

Smart, 伶俐 ling-li', 快利 faai'-li', 精巧 tsing-haau, 精 tseng, (to) 痛 t'uung', 見痛 kin'-t'uung'.

Smash, 打碎 ʿta-sui'.

Smattering, to have a, 識幾程 shik-ʿki-ch'ing.

Smear, 塗 t'o, 搽 ch'a, 盪 tong'.

Smell, (generally bad) 臭 ch'au', 隨息 ts'ui-sik, (to) 聞 mun.

Smelt, (to) (銷冶 siu-ʿye), 煉 lin',

Smile, 含笑 hom-siu', 微笑 mi-siu'.

Smite, 打 ʿta.

Smith, 打 (金) 匠 ʿta-(kum-)*tseung'.

Smoke, 烟 in, 火烟 ʻfoh-in, (to, tobacco, &c.) 食烟 shik-in, (emit) 出烟 chʻuut-in, (hams) 燻火 fun-ʻfoh, (blacken) 燢黑 tsʻau-hak.
Smooth, 滑 waat, 縟 nauʾ, (level) 平 pʻing.
Smother, 局死 kuuk-ʻsze.
Smoulder, 尚有的燒 sheungʾ-ʻyau-ti-shiu.
Smuggle, 走私 ʻtsau-sze.
Smuggled goods, 私貨 sze-fohʾ.
Smut, 烏煤 oo-mooi.
Snail, 蝸牛 woh-ngau, 田螺 tʻin-lòh.
Snake, (a) 條蛇 tʻiu-she.
Snap, (break) 斷 ʻtʻuen, (the fingers) 整手卟 ʻching-ʻshau-puuk.
Snapper, fish, 立魚 laap-ue.
Snare, 圈套 huen-tʻoʾ.
Snarl, 嘶牙 shaiʾ-nga.
Snatch, 搶 tsʻeung, 奪 tuet.
Sneaking, 屈氣 wat-hiʾ.
Sneer, 冷笑 ʻlaang-siuʾ.

Sneeze, 打噴嚏 ʻta-pʻanʾ-tʻaiʾ, (COL.) ta-hat-chʻi.
Snipe, 沙隹 sha-chui.
Snobbish, 草恭 ʻtsʻo-ʻmong.
Snore, 扯鼻劓 ʻchʻe-pi-hohn.
Snort, 噴鼻 pʻanʾ-piʾ.
Snout, 嘴 ʻtsui, (pigs) 猪鼻 chue-piʾ.
Snow, 雪 suet.
Snub, (short) 短設設 ʻtuen-chʻit-chʻit (to) 充淡水 chʻuung-tʻaam-ʻshui.
Snuff, 鼻烟 piʾ-in, (a candle) 剪燈花 tsin-tang-fa.
Snug, 安穩 ohn-ʻwan.
So, (in degree) 咁 komʾ, (in kind) 噉 ʻkom, (so and so) 某某 ʻmau-ʻmau, (so forth) 噉之類 ʻkom-chi-luiʾ.
Soak, 浸 tsumʾ, 濕透 shap-tʻauʾ.
Soap, 番䁱 faan-ʻkaan.
Soap-stone, 滑石 waat-shek.
Soar, 高飛 ko-fi.
Sob, 縮氣 shuuk-hiʾ.
Sober, 醒定 ʻsing-tingʾ.

注　释

【局死】窒息。
【尚有的燒】焖烧。
【嘶牙】露齿。
【屈气】不争气的。
【扯鼻劓】打呼噜。
【番䁱】肥皂。
【缩气】啜泣。

注释

【好相与】易交往的，友善的。
【荷兰水】苏打水。
【契弟】鸡奸者。
【钎】焊接。
【独系】单独地。
【打觔斗】翻筋斗。

Sociable, 好相與 ʻho-seung-ʻue.

Society, (a) 會 ooiʼ, (in general) 相與聚集 seung-ʻue-tsueʼ-tsaap.

Sock, See Hose.

Socket, 竇 tauʼ.

Soda-water, 荷蘭水 Hoh-laan-ʻshui.

Sodomy, 鷄姦 kai-kaan, 男色 naam-shik.

Sodomite, 契弟 kʻaiʼ-taiʼ.

Sofa, 匟 kʻong, 睡椅 shuiʼ-ʻi.

Soft, 柔軟 yau-ʻuen, 腍軟 num-ʻuen.

Soil, 坭土 nai-ʻtʻo, (to) 整污 ʻching-oo.

Solanum, 茄 *kʻe.

Solder, 釬 hohnʼ.

Soldering-iron, 鈉鎞 naat-pai (kai).

Soldier, 兵 ping, 兵丁 ping-ting, 兵卒 ping-tsuut.

Sole, (of foot) 脚板 keukʼ-ʻpaan, (of shoe) 鞋底 haai-ʻtai.

Sole, (a fish) 撻沙魚 tʻaatʼ-sha-*ue.

Sole, (only) 單 taan, 獨 tuuk.

Solely, 獨係 tuuk-haiʼ, 不過 pat-kwohʼ.

Solemn, 威嚴 wai-im, 嚴肅 im-suuk.

Solicit, 求 kʻau.

Solicitor, 小狀師 ʻsiu-chongʼ-ʻsze.

Solicitor, (Crown-) 國家狀師 Kwokʼ-ka-chongʼ-ʻsze.

Solicitude, 掛慮 kwaʼ-lueʼ.

Solid, 實 shat, 硬 ngaangʼ.

Solitary, 孤寂 koo-tsik, 獨居 tuuk-kue.

Solstice, (summer) 夏至 haʼ-chiʼ, (winter) 冬至 tuung-chiʼ.

Solve, 解 ʻkaai.

Sombre, 憂色 yau-shik, 陰陰沉沉 yum-yum-chʻum-chʻum.

Some, (有) 的 (ʻyau) ʻti.

Somersault, 打觔斗 ʻta-kan-ʻtau.

| SOR | 238 | SOU |

Something, 野 ‘ye, 閒野 haan-‘ye, 有野 ‘yau-‘ye, 的野 ’ti-‘ye.
Sometimes, 有時 ‘yau-shi.
Somnambulism, 睡中行 shui’-chuung-hang.
Son, 仔 ‘tsai, 子 ‘tsze, 兒 i, (your) 令郎 ling’*long, (my) 小兒 ‘siu-i.
Son-in-law, 女婿 ‘nue-sai’.
Song, 支曲 chi-k‘uuk, 隻歌仔 chek’-koh-‘tsai.
Sonorous, 會响 ‘ooi-‘heung, 响嘅 ‘heung-ke’.
Soon, 就來 tsau’-loi, 無幾耐 ‘mo-‘ki-*noi’, 挨邊 ‘aai-pin.
Soot, 烟煤 in-mooi, 火燂煤 foh-t‘aam-mooi.
Soothe, 安慰 ohn-wai’, 開鬱寧神 hoi-wat-ning-shan, (a child) 啼願 t‘um’-uen’.
Sophistry, 巧辯 ‘haau-pin’.
Soporific, 致睡 chi’-shui’, 致睡嘅 chi’-shui’-ke’.
Sorcery, 巫術 moo-shuut.

Sordid, 簕咁嚡 lak-kom’-haai.
Sore, 損痛 ‘suen-t‘uung’.
Sorrel, 酸迷草 suen-‘mi-‘ts‘o, (in Shi-king) 莫 mo’.
Sorrow, 憂悶 yau-moon’.
Sorrowful, 鼻翳 pai’-ai’.
Sort, 樣 yeung’, 般 poon.
Sot, 爛酒佬 laan’-‘tsau-‘lo.
Sottish, 死爛飲 ‘sze-laan’-‘yum.
Soul, 靈魂 ling-wan.
Sound, (a) 聲音 sheng-yum, (to) 响 ‘heung, (sleep) 瞓稔 fun’-num’, (entire) 全 ts‘uen, 堅固 kin-koo’, (to try) 探 t‘aam’.
Soundly, 重 ‘ch‘uung.
Soup, 湯 t‘ong.
Sour, 酸 suen, (sullen) 鼓氣 ‘koo-hi’.
Source, 源頭 uen-t‘au.
Souse, 撞 chong’, (in water) 洰下 ‘yum-‘ha.
South, 南 naam, (S.E. &c.) 東南 tuung-naam, &c.

注 释

【野】东西。
【睡中行】梦游病。
【无几耐】不久，没有多长时间。
【簕咁嚡】卑劣的。
【烂酒佬】酗酒者。
【瞓稔】睡熟。

注 释

【阔落】宽敞的。
【吕宋】此处应为"西班牙"。"吕宋"指菲律宾群岛中最大的岛屿。
【专登】专门。
【景】景象，奇观。

Southernwood, 青蒿 ts'ing-ho, 同蒿 t'uung-ho, (in Shi-king) 蔞 lau.
Sovereign, 主 ʿchue.
Sow, (to) 撒 saatʾ.
Sow, (a) 猪乸 chue-ʿna.
Soy, 豉油 shiʾ-yau.
Space, 間 kaan, (room) 地方 tiʾ-fong, 笪地方 taatʾ-tiʾ-fong, (all) 週圍 chau-wai.
Spacious, 闊落 footʾ-lok.
Spade, 鏟 ʿch'aan, (a small) 鍫 ts'iu.
Spain, 呂宋 ʿLue-suungʾ.
Span, 楠 naamʾ.
Spanish-flies, 斑蝥 paan-maau.
Spare, (save) 愛惜 oiʾ-sik, 省 ʿshaang, (give away) 捨 ʿshe.
Spark, 火星 ʿfoh-ʿsing (ʿseng), (sparks) 火屎 ʿfoh-ʿshi.
Sparkle, 閃亮 ʿshim-leungʾ, 火飛 ʿfoh-fi.
Sparrow, 麻雀 ma-tseukʾ.

Spasm, 抽筋 ch'au-kan, 拶下 tsaatʾ-ʿha.
Spatter, (with the hand) 澆 kiu.
Spattered, (by walking) 濺污糟 tsaanʾ-oo-tso.
Spawn, 魚翱 ue-ʿch'uun.
Speak, 講 ʿkong, 講說話 ʿkong-shuetʾ-waʾ.
Spear, 竹篙鎗 chuuk-ko-ʿts'eung, (a) 一枝鎗 yat-ʿchi-ʿts'eung.
Special, 特登 tak-ʿtang, 專登 chuen-ʿtang, (extra) 額外 ngaak-ngoiʾ.
Species, 種 ʿchuung.
Specify, 話實 waʾ-shat, 逐一講 chuuk-yat-ʿkong.
Specimen, 樣子 yeungʾ-ʿtsze, 表率 ʿpiu-suut, 辦 *paanʾ.
Specious talk, 巧言 ʿhaau-in.
Speckled, 一點點 yat-ʿtim-ʿtim.
Spectacle, (a) 景 ʿking.
Spectacles, 眼鏡 ʿngaan-keng.

Spectator, 睇見之人 ʻtʻai-kinʼ-chi-yan, ʻtʻai-kinʼ-keʼ.	Spin, 紡績 ʻfong-tsik, 紡線 ʻfong-sinʼ, (round) 擰轉 ningʼ-chuenʼ, 窗窗轉 tʻum-tʻum-chuenʼ.
Speculate, 追想 chui-ʻseung, 圖 tʻo.	Spinage, 波菜 poh-tsʻoi, 波菱菜 poh-ling-tsʻoi, 茛菜 inʼ-tsʻoi.
Speech, 話 waʼ, 說話 shuetʼ-waʼ.	Spindle, (鐵) 紃 (tʻit) tsʻuun.
Speedy, 速 tsʻuuk, 快 faaiʼ.	Spine, 背脊 pooiʼ-tsekʼ.
Spell, (to) 切音 tsʻitʼ-yum.	Spinning-machine, 紡機 ʻfong-ki.
Spend, 使費 ʻshai-faiʼ, (a day) 過日 kwohʼ-yat.	Spinster, 老女 ʻlo-ʻnue.
Spend-thrift, 浪子 ʻlong-ʻtsze.	Spiral, 螺線 loh-sinʼ, 螺紋 loh-*mun.
Sphere, 球 kʻau.	Spire, 塔 tʻaapʼ, 鐘樓 chuung-*lau.
Sphex, 螺蠃 ʻkwoh-ʻloh.	Spirit, 神 shan, (drink) 燒酒 shiu-tsau, (animal spirits) 精神 tsing-shan.
Spice, 香料 heung-*liuʼ.	Spiritual, 靈 ling, 神 shan.
Spider, 蟢蟧 kʻum-*lo, 蜘蛛 chi-chue, 壁虎 pikʼ-ʻfoo.	Spit, 吐 tʻoʼ, 唾 tʻohʼ, ʻlŏʼ, (a) 炙肉乂 chekʼ-yuukʼ-chʻa.
Spiderʼs web, 蜘蛛網 chi-chue-ʻmong.	
Spike, 刺 tsʻzeʼ, 錐 chui, (wooden) 木丁 muuk-teng.	Spite, 怨恨 uenʼ-hanʼ, 怨毒 uenʼ-tuukʼ.
Spikenard, 甘松香 kom-tsʻuung-ʻheung.	
Spill, 流出 lau-chʻuutʼ, 漏瀉 lauʼ-seʼ.	

注 釋

【睇见之人】旁观者。
【追想】猜测。
【切音】拼写。
【使费】花费。

Spittle, 口水 ʻhau-ʻshui, (ejected) 口水花 ʻhau-ʻshui-fa.	Spoon, 匙羹 shi-ʻkang, 羹 ʻkang.
Spittoon, 痰罐 tʻaam-koonʼ, 痰盂 tʻaam-*ue.	Sport, 頑耍 waan-ʻsha.
Splash, (to throw) 澆 kiu, (to rebound or splash up) 濺 tsaanʼ, tsaanʼ.	Spot, 點 ʻtim, 砧 timʼ, 疵 tsʻze, (place) 笪 taatʼ.
	Spotted, 一笪笪 yat-taatʼ-taatʼ.
Spleen, (the) 脾 pʻi, 臁貼 lim-tʻipʼ, (feeling) 鬱氣 wat-hiʼ.	Spout, (of a kettle) 嘴 ʻtsui, (on a roof) 水槽 ʻshui-tsʻo, (to) 浙 chit, 噴 pʻun.
Splendid, 光亮 kwong-leung, 華美 wa-ʻmi.	Sprain, 扭傷 ʻnau-sheung, 趨親 ʻchʻau-tsʻan.
Splice, 駁纜 pokʼ-laamʼ.	Spray, of water, 水花 ʻshui-fa.
Splinter, 片 pʻinʼ, 孿 ʻnin.	Spray } 枝 chi.
Split, 打裂 ʻta-lit, 破 pʻoh, 劈 pʻek.	Sprig
	Spread, out, 攤開 tʻaan-hoi, 散開 saanʼ-hoi, 鋪開 pʻo-hoi, (as ink) 淰開 numʼ-hoi.
Spoil, 整壞 ʻching-waaiʼ, 爛 laanʼ.	
Spokes, 輻 fuuk.	
Spoliation, 搶劫 ʻtsʻeung-kipʼ.	Sprightly, 英敏 ying-ʻmun.
	Spring, (season) 春天 chʻun-tʻin, (water-) 源泉 uen-tsʻuen, (of a machine) 機關 ki-kwaan, 連機 lin-ki, (main-) 發條 faatʼ-*tʻiu, (to) 跳 tʻiuʼ, 發 faatʼ.
Sponge, 水泡 ʻshui-pʻo.	
Sponge-cake, 雞蛋糕 kai-taanʼ-ko.	
Spongy, 吥 pauʼ.	
Spontaneous, 自自然然 tszeʼ-tszeʼ-in-in.	

Spring-water, 山水 shaan-ˊshui.
Sprinkle, 灑 ˊsha, 澆 kiu.
Sprout, 萌芽 mang-nga, 啉 ˊlum, 味 muuk, (bamboo-) 竹笋 chuuk-ˊsuun, (to) 出味 chˋuut-muuk.
Spur, 距 ˊkˋue, (to) 踢 tˋek.
Spurious, 僞 ngaiˋ, 假 ˊka.
Spurn, 擯棄 punˋ-hiˋ.
Spurt, 噴水 pˋunˋ-ˊshui.
Sputter, 噴口水花 pˋunˋ-ˊhau-ˊshui-fa.
Spy, (a) 線人 sinˋ-yan, 探子 tˋaamˋ-ˊtsze, (to) 打探 ˊta-tˋaamˋ, 訪事 fong-ˋsze, 覸 chong, hau.
Squabble, 嗌交 aaiˋ-ˊkaau.
Squad, (a) 一隊 yat-tuiˋ.
Squalid, 襤褸 laam-lueˋ.
Squall, (a) 一陣風雨 yat-chanˋ-fuung-ˊue.
Squall, (to) 啞啞聲 ˊnga-ˊnga-sheng.
Squander, 花散 fa-saanˋ.
Square, 方 fong, 四方形 szeˋ-fong-ying, (a tool) 曲尺 huuk-chˋek.

Squash, (a) 瓜 ˌkwa, hairy, 節瓜 tsitˋ-ˌkwa, bitter, 苦瓜 ˊfoo-ˌkwa, bottle, 江葡 kong-pˋoo, (to) 壓扁 aatˋ-ˊpin.
Squat, 踎 mau.
Squeak, 齾齾聲 ngit-ngit-sheng.
Squeamish, 懨飲 imˋ-ueˋ, 作悶 tsokˋ-moonˋ.
Squeeze, 榨住 chaˋ-chueˋ, 壓 aatˋ, 夾住 kaapˋ-chueˋ, (extort) 勒索 lak-sokˋ.
Squib, 起火仔 ˊhi-ˊfoh-ˊtsai.
Squint, 斜眼 tsˋe-ngaan, 到眼 toˋ-ˊngaan.
Squirrel, 果鼠 ˊkwoh-ˊshue.
Squirt, (a) 水浙筒 ˊshui-chit-*tˋuung, (to) 浙 chit.
Stab, 剖 kat, 攙 chˋaam, ˊchˋaam.
Stable, (a) 馬房 ˊma-fong, (firm) 安穩 ohn-ˊwan, 定實 tingˋ-shat.
Stack, (a) 禾堆 woh-ˊtui.
Staff, 柺杖 ˊkwaai-*cheungˋ.

注 釋

【啉】花蕾。
【嗌交】吵架。
【踎】蹲。
【齾齾声】吱吱声。
【起火仔】爆竹。
【水浙筒】喷水筒。

注 释

【行得啤啤吓】走路摇摇晃晃。
【遛口】口吃。
【撑眼睇】睁大眼睛盯着。

Stag, 鹿 *luuk, 鹿公 *luuk-kuung.
Stage, (a platform) 臺 t'oi, (scaffold) 棚 p'aang, (of a journey) 驛站 yik-chaam⸰.
Stagger, reel and, 行得啤啤吓 hang-tak-⸌p'e-⸌p'e-⸌ha.
Stagnant, 遲滯 ch'i-chai⸰, 不流 'm-lau.
Stain, (a) 印迹 yan⸰-tsik, (to) 染污 ⸌im-oo.
Stairs, 樓梯 lau-t'ai, (stone-) 石級 shek-k'up.
Stake, 杙 tak, 椿 chong, 棟 tuung⸰, (to risk) 拚 p'oon.
Stalactite, 鐘乳石 chuung-⸌ue-shek.
Stale, 陳 ch'an, 舊 kau⸰, 宿 suuk.
Stalk, 竿 kohn, 枝 chi, 秆 ⸌kohn.
Stall, (for goods) 賣貨攤 maai-foh⸰-⸌t'aan, (for cattle) 欄位 laan-wai⸰, (horse's) 馬槽 ⸌ma-ts'o.

Stamen, 花蕊 fa-⸌yui, 花粉蕊 fa-⸌fun-⸌yui.
Stammer, 遛口 lau⸰-⸌hau, 講得肋喀 ⸌kong-tak-lak-k'ak.
Stamp, 印 yan⸰, (the foot) 蹈腳 tum⸰-keuk⸰.
Stamp Office, 印捐局 yan⸰-kuen-kuuk.
Stanch, (to) 止 ⸌chi, (hearty) 堅心 kin-sum.
Stand, 企立 ⸌k'i-laap, 企到 ⸌k'i-to, (up) 起身 ⸌hi-shan, 企起 ⸌k'i-⸌hi, (aside) 企開 ⸌k'i-hoi, (endure) 抵住 ⸌tai-chue, 啌 k'um; (a) 架 ka⸰.
Standard, (flag) 旗 k'i, (rule) 度 to⸰.
Staple, (a) 鐵耳 t'it⸰-⸌i.
Star, 粒星 nup-⸌sing, ⸌seng.
Star-board, 船右 shuen-yau⸰.
Starch, 漿 tseung.
Stare, 撑眼睇 chang-⸌ngaan-⸌t'ai.

| STA | 244 | STE |

Start, (set out) 開行 hoi-hang, (by water) 開身 hoi-shan, (up) 跳起 t'iu-‘hi.
Startle, 振驚 chan’-king.
Starve, 制食 chai’-shik, (to death) 制死 chai’-‘sze, 餓死 ngoh’-‘sze.
State, (condition) 情勢 ts‘ing-shai’, (nation) 國 kwok; (to) 講實 ‘kong-shat, 話 wa’, 陳說 ch‘an-shuet, (to a superior) 禀告 ‘pun-ko’.
Statics, 重學 chuung’-hok.
Station, 身分 shan-fun’, 位 wai’, (on a road) 站頭 chaam’-t‘au, (guard's) 汛地 suun’-ti’, (position) 所在 ‘shoh-tsoi’, (police) 差館 ch‘aai-‘koon.
Stationary, 不郁 ’m-yuuk.
Stationer's shop, 紙筆舖 ‘chi-put-*p‘o, 紙料舖 ‘chi-liu’-*p‘o.
Statistics, 志 chi’.
Statue, 偶像 ‘ngau-tseung’.

Statute, 律例 luut’-lai’.
Stay, (to) 等吓 ‘tang-ha, 歇 hit’, 住 chue’.
Steady, 穩當 ‘wun-tong’, (stand) 企穩 ‘k‘i-‘wun.
Steak, (beef-) 牛肉耙 ngau-yuuk-*p‘a.
Steal, 偷 t‘au, 竊 sit’.
Steam, 滾水氣 ‘kwun-‘shui-hi’, (to) 蒸 ching.
Steamer, 火輪船 ‘foh-luun-shuen.
Steel, 鋼 kong’.
Steelyard, 把秤 ‘pa-ch‘ing’, (money-) 釐戥 li-*tang’.
Steep, 企斜 ‘k‘i-ts‘e’, 斜 ts‘e’.
Steep, (to) 浸 tsum’, (dip) 泔吓 ‘yum-‘ha.
Steeple, 鐘樓 chuung-*lau.
Steer, (to) 把舵 ‘pa-t‘oh, (COL.) 揸舦 cha-t‘aai.
Steersman, 梢公 shaau-kuung.
Stem, 竿 kohn, 枝 chi, 莖 ‘k‘waang, (to) 阻止 ‘choh-‘chi, 抵住 ‘tai-chue’.

注 释

【制食】餓死。
【重学】静力学，物理学的一个分支。
【志】统计资料。
【等吓】停下，停留。
【滾水气】蒸汽。

注 释

【一捧随】一股子气味（多用于贬义）。
【局死】扼杀，使窒息。
【驳脚棍】高跷。
【悭】小气。

Stench, 臭 ch'au', 一棒隨 yat-puung'-ts'ui, (a vile) 臭亨亨 ch'au'-hang-hang.
Step, 步 poo', (to) 進脚 tsuun'-keuk', 行 hang, (in a stair) 級 k'up, 階級 kaai-k'up.
Step-father, 繼爻 kai'-foo', (-mother) 繼母 kai'-'mo.
Stepping-stone, 踏脚石 taap-keuk'-shek.
Sterculia, 擷婆 p'an-*p'oh, 梧桐 'ng-t'uung.
Sterile soil, 瘠土 tsek'-'t'o.
Stern, 嚴肅 im-suuk, (the) 後邊 hau'-pin, 尾 'mi.
Stew, (to) 會 ooi'.
Steward, 管事人 'koon-sze'-yan, (comprador) 買辦 'maai-*paan'.
Stick, (a) 條棍 t'iu-kwun', (pierce) 刮 kat, (adhere) 黐緊 ch'i-'kan, (fail) 不能行 pat-nang-hang, (to paste) 貼 t'ip', (stick in) 插落 ch'aap'-lok.
Stickle, 拘執 k'ue-chup, 泥 ni'.

Stiff, 硬 ngaang', 骾 'kang.
Stiffnecked 拗頸 aau'-'keng.
Stifle, 局死 kuuk-'sze.
Stigma, 忝辱 'tim-yuuk.
Still, (ADV.) 仍然 ying-in, 重 chuung', 還 waan, (quiet) 寂靜 tsik-tsing', 靜靜 *tsing'-tsing', tsing'-*tsing'.
Still, (a) 酒甑 'tsau-tsang'.
Stilts, 駁脚棍 pok'-keuk'-kwun'.
Stimulate, 聳起 'suung-'hi.
Sting, 釘 'teng, 針 chum, (to) 刺 ts'ze'.
Stingy, 慳 haan, 刻薄 haak-pok.
Stink, 臭氣 ch'au'-hi', 齾臭 ngat'-ch'au'.
Stink-pot, 灰煲 fooi-'po.
Stint, (to) 限制 haan'-chai', (a) 工課 kuung-foh'.
Stipulate, 約定 yeuk'-ting'.

STO 246 STO

Stipulations, 條欵 t'iu-ˏfoon, 約條 yeuk`-t'iu.
Stir, (to) 攪 ˋkaau, (begin to move) 興起 hing-ˋhi, 動身 tuung`-ˏshan, (a) 鬧熱 naau`-it.
Stitch, (of a needle) 針步 chum-poo`, (to) 釘 teng, (fine) 鉤密 k'au`-mat, (pain) 刺痛 ts'ek`-t'uung`.
Stock, (of a tree) 木頭 muuk-t'au, 樹身 shue`-ˏshan, (of a musket) 牀 ch'ong, (in trade) 貨本 foh`-ˏpoon, (shares) 股分 ˋkoo-fun`.
Stockings, 襪 mat.
Stocks, 脚架 keuk`-ka`.
Stoical, 無情 ˏmo-ts'ing.
Stolid, 鈍 tuun`.
Stomach, 脾胃 p'i-wai`.
Stomach-pump, 入喉水浙 yup-hau-ˋshui-chit.
Stone, 石 shek, 石頭 shek-t'au, (of fruit) 核 wat, (to) 俾石打 ˋpi-shek-ˋta.
Stone-cutter, 打石人 ˋta-shek-yan.

Stool, 凳 tang`, (go to) 如厠 ue-ts'ze`, 出恭 ch'uut-ˏkuung.
Stoop, 攣腰 luen-iu, 噁低 oo`-tai.
Stop, 停吓 t'ing-ˋha, 歇息 hit`-sik, 止住 ˋchi-chue`, (with the hands) 拃住 cha`-chue`, (up) 塞住 sak-chue`.
Stopper, 枳 chat.
Store, (to) 積貯 tsik-ˋch'ue, 積埋 tsik-maai, (-house) 貨倉 foh`-ˏts'ong, 棧 *chaan`, 棧房 chaan`-*fong, (basement) 土庫 ˋt'o-foo`.
Stores, 積貨 tsik-foh`, (food) 伙食 ˋfoh-shik.
Stork, 白鶴 paak-*hok.
Storm, 風雨大作 ˏfuung-ˋue-taai`-tsok`, 風暴 ˏfuung-po`.
Story, (a) 一段古 yat-tuen`-ˋkoo, (of a house) 層 ts'ang.
Stout, 精壯 ˏtsing-chong`, (fat) 肥壯 fi-chong`.

注 释

【入喉水浙】胃唧筒（一种医疗器具）
【噁低】低下，弯低。
【枳】塞子，栓。
【一段古】一个故事。

注 释

【装埋】收藏，存放。
【丫开脚】叉开脚。
【蛇莓】一种药用植物，果子似草莓。
【行散】走失。

Stove, 火爐 ꞌfoh-lo, 局爐 kuuk-lo.
Stow away, 裝埋 chong-maai.
Straddle, 丫開脚 ngaꞌ-ꞏhoi-keukꞌ.
Straggle, 行散 hang-ꞌsaan.
Straight, 直 chik, 掂 timꞌ.
Straighten, 做直 tsoꞌ-chik, 整掂 ꞌching-timꞌ.
Straightway, 卽時 tsik-shi, 就正 tsauꞌ-ching.
Strain, 隔渣 kaakꞌ-cha, (tighten) 扭緊 ꞌnau-ꞌkan.
Strainer, 羅斗 loh-ꞌtau, (wine-) 酒漏 ꞌtsau-*lau.
Strait, 迫窄 pik-chaakꞌ, 淺窄 ꞌtsꞌin-chaakꞌ, 阨 akꞌ, (a) 陝 haap.
Stramonium, 鬧羊花 naauꞌ-yeung-fa.
Strange, 奇怪 kꞌi-kwaai, (not at home) 生外 shaang-*ngoiꞌ.
Stranger, 新客 san-haakꞌ, 生步 shaang-*poꞌ, (ꞌpo) 生面 shaang-*minꞌ.

Strangle, 縊死 aiꞌ-ꞌsze, 勒死 lak-ꞌsze, (with the hand) 揸死 cha-ꞌsze.
Strap, (a) 皮帶 pꞌi-*taaiꞌ.
Strata, 層隔 tsꞌang-kaakꞌ.
Stratagem, 謀畧 mau-leuk, 韜畧 tꞌoꞌ-leuk.
Straw, 禾稿 woh-ꞌko, 禾稈 woh-ꞌkohn.
Straw-hat, 草帽 ꞌtsꞌo-*mo.
Strawberry, 蛇莓 she-mooi.
Stray, 行散 hang-ꞌsaan, 行錯 hang-tsꞌohꞌ, (from the flock) 離開隊 li-hoi-*tuiꞌ.
Streaks, 虎班紋 ꞌfoo-paan-*mun.
Stream, 流水 lau-ꞌshui, (small) 溪澗 kꞌai-kaanꞌ, 條水 tꞌiu-ꞌshui.
Streamer, 旗帶 kꞌi-taaiꞌ.
Street, 街 ꞌkaai, (a) 條街 tꞌiu-ꞌkaai.
Strength, 力 lik.
Strengthening, 補力 ꞌpo-lik.
Strenuous, 慇懃 yan-kꞌan.

Stress, 重 chuung›, 重處 chuung›-ch‘ue›, (on) 重在 chuung›-tsoi›.
Stretch, 搤長 mang›-ch‘eung, (out) 伸 shan, (as clothes) 撐開 chaang-hoi.
Strew, 撒 saat›, ‹sum.
Strict, 嚴緊 im-‹kan.
Stride, 丫脚 nga›-keuk›, (long) 大步 taai›-po›.
Strike, 打 ‹ta, 泵 ‹tum, (stop) 罷 pa›, (a match) 畫 waak.
String, (a) 條繩 t‘iu-*shing, 帶 *taai›, (a string of) 一串 yat-ch‘uen›, (1,000 cash) 一吊 yat-tiu›, (to) 貫串 koon›-ch‘uen›, 穿埋 ch‘uen›-maai.
Strip, (a) 一條 yat-t‘iu, (to) 脫 t‘uet›, 捋 luet›, 戩 ‹chin.
Stripe, 班紋 paan-*mun, 柳條紋 ‹lau-t‘iu-*mun.
Strive, 爭 chaang, 相爭 seung-chaang, (endeavour) 出力 ch‘uut-lik.

Stroke, (line) 畫 waak, (a blow) 打一吓 ‹ta-yat-‹ha, (rub) 攊 lip.
Stroll, 逛 k‘waang›, liu›.
Strong, 有力 ‹yau-lik, ‹yau-lik-ke›, 壯健 chong›-kin›, 主固 ‹chue-koo›, (as tobacco) 掯 k‘ang›, (as tea, &c.) 濃 nuung, yuung.
Strop, (to) 喝利 hoht›-li›.
Struggle, 打武咁打 ‹ta-‹moo-kom›-‹ta, 勉強 ‹min-‹k‘eung, 苦爭 ‹foo-chang.
Strut, 岳頭行 ngok-t‘au-hang.
Strychnine, 馬前 ‹ma-ts‘in.
Stubborn, 硬頸 ngaang›-‹keng, 板頸 ‹paan-‹keng.
Stucco, 石膏 shek-‹ko.
Stud, (a button) 粒鈕 nup-‹nau, 雙粒鈕 sheung-nup-‹nau.
Study, (to) 習學 tsaap-hok, 讀書 tuuk-shue, (a) 讀書房 tuuk-shue-*fong.

| STY | 249 | SUB |

Stuff, (material) 材料 ts'oi-liu', (useless) 廢物 fai-mat, (nonsense) 諧話 ngaam'-wa', (to) 塞實 sak-shat.

Stuffing, 入材料 yup-ts'oi-liu'.

Stumble, 踢着脚 t'ek'-cheuk-keuk', 失脚 shat-keuk', (fall) 跌倒 tit'-'to.

Stumbling block, 窒碍 chat-ngoi', 碍石 ngoi'-shek.

Stump, (a) 榾頭 kwut-t'au.

Stun, 震瘟 chan'-wan, 驚迷 keng-mai.

Stunted, 屈短 wut-'tuen.

Stupid, 愚蠢 ue-'ch'uun, 笨呆 pun'-ngoi, (boy) 笨仔 pun'-'tsai.

Stupified, 失魂 shat-wan, 昏迷 fun-mai.

Sturdy, 大力 taai'-lik.

Sturgeon, 鱘龍魚 ts'um-luung-*ue.

Stuttering, 吃口 kat-'hau, 遛口 lau'-'hau.

Sty, 猪欄 ,chue-,laan.

Style, 文 mun, 文法 mun-faat', 樣 *yeung', (address) 稱呼 ch'ing-foo.

Suavity, 温柔 wan-yau.

Sub, 下 ha', 下屬 ha'-shuuk.

Subdue, 勝服 shing'-fuuk.

Subject, 臣下 shan-ha', (people) 民 mun, (of discourse) 所論 'shoh-luun', (of an essay) 章旨 cheung-'chi, 提目 t'ai-muuk.

Subject } 打服 'ta-fuuk.
Subjugate

Sublimate, 霜 seung.

Sublime, 崇大 shuung-taai'.

Submissive, 服屬 fuuk-shuuk.

Submit, 服 fuuk, 歸服 kwai-fuuk.

Subordinate, 屬下 shuuk-ha'.

Suborn, 買囑 'maai-chuuk.

Subscribe, 簽題 ts'im-t'ai.

Subserve, 供應 kuung-ying'.

Subside, 擎 k'ing, 平翻 p'ing-faan, 息 sik.

Subsidiary, 助 choh'.

注 释

【入材料】填充物。
【榾头】树桩。
【屈短】长得矮小的。
【遛口】大舌头，口吃。
【买嘱】唆使，收买。

| SUE | 250 | SUL |

Substance, 質體 chat-ʻt'ai, 材料 ts'oi-liu, 物 mat.
Substitute, (a) 代做 toiʻ-tso'.
Subtile, 靈活 ling-oot, (subtle) 巧 ʻhaau.
Subtract, 減 ʻkaam.
Subtraction, 減法 ʻkaam-faatʻ.
Suburbs, 城外 sheng-ngoiʻ.
Subvert, 傾倒 kʻing-ʻto.
Succeed, (get on) 得成 tak-shing, (follow) 繼 kaiʻ, 接做 tsipʻ-tsoʻ.
Successive, 陸續 luuk-tsuuk.
Succinct, 簡畧 ʻkaan-leuk.
Succumb, 服 fuuk.
Such, 噉 ʻkom, 如此 ue-ʻtsʻze.
Suck, 啐 tsuetʻ, 欶 shokʻ.
Suckle, 餒奶 waiʻ-naai.
Sudden, 忽然 fut-in, fut-in-keʻ.
Suddenly, 忽然間 fut-in-kaan.
Sudorific, 發汗藥 faatʻ-hohnʻ-yeuk.
Sue, 告 koʻ, (for) 求 kʻau.

Suet, 版油 ʻpaan-yau, 腰油 iu-yau.
Suffer, 抵受 ʻtai-shauʻ, 受 shauʻ, 抵捱 ʻtai-ngaaiʻ, (permit) 准 ʻchuun.
Suffering, 受苦 shauʻ-ʻfoo.
Sufficient, 彀 kauʻ, 足 tsuuk.
Suffocate, 局死 kuukʻ-ʻsze.
Sugar, 糖 t'ong.
Sugar-candy, 冰糖 ping-t'ong.
Sugar-cane, 蔗 cheʻ.
Suggest, 提起 t'ai-ʻhi.
Suicide, 自殺 tszeʻ-shaatʻ, 自盡 tszeʻ-tsuunʻ.
Suit, (to) 合 hop, 着 cheuk, (a, of clothes) 一脫 yat-t'uetʻ, (petition) 禀 ʻpun.
Suitable, 着使 cheukʻ-ʻshai, 啱 ngaam.
Suite, 跟班 ʻkan-ʻpaan.
Sulky } 嬲人嘅 nau-yan-
Sullen } keʻ, 古毒 ʻkoo-tuuk, 鼓氣 ʻkoo-hiʻ, 黑面 hak-min.
Sully, 玷污 timʻ-ov.

注 释

【啐】吸。
【餒奶】喂奶。
【着使】适当的，相配的。
【古毒】绷着脸，愠怒的。

注释

【暑暍】暑热。
【傳叫】召唤。
Sumptuous:奢侈的。与"破费"的词义有差别。
【海心石】暗礁。
【溺信古怪】迷信的。
【跳疾】灵活的。

SUN　　　251　　　SUP

Sulphur, 硫磺 lau-wong, (flowers of) 硫磺末 lau-wong-*moot.
Sultry, 暑暍 ꞌshue-ai.
Sum, 共計 kuungꞌ-kai, 攏總 ꞌluung-ꞌtsuung.
Summer, 夏天 haꞌ-tꞌin.
Summer-house, 涼亭 leung-*tꞌing.
Summit, 頂 ꞌting, ꞌteng.
Summon, 傳叫 chꞌuen-kiuꞌ.
Summons, 傳票 chꞌuen-pꞌiuꞌ.
Sumptuous, 破費 pꞌohꞌ-faiꞌ.
Sun, 日 yat, 熟頭 it-*tꞌan, 太陽 tꞌaaiꞌ-yeung, (to) 晒 shaaiꞌ.
Sunday, 禮拜日 ꞌlai-paaiꞌ-yat, ꞌlai-paaiꞌ.
Sundries, 什碎 sup-sui.
Sun-flower, 向日葵 heungꞌ-yat-kꞌwai.
Sunken-rocks, 海心石 ꞌhoi-sum-shek.
Sun-rise, 日出 yat-chꞌuut.
Sun-set, 日入 yat-yup, 日落 yat-lok.
Sunstroke, 中暑 chuungꞌ-ꞌshue.

Sup, 喫 yaakꞌ, 嗑啖 haapꞌ-taamꞌ.
Super-, 過 kwohꞌ, 上 sheungꞌ.
Supercargo, 班上 paan-sheungꞌ, 大班 taaiꞌ-paan.
Superficial, 淺 ꞌtsꞌin, (scholar) 充斯文 chꞌuung-sze-mun.
Superfluous, 太多無用 tꞌaaiꞌ-toh-mo-yuungꞌ, 無用 ꞌmo-yuung, 無為 ꞌmo-wai, 蛇足 she-tsuuk.
Superintend, 督理 tuuk-ꞌli, (work) 督工 tuuk-kuung.
Superintendent, 監督 kaam-tuuk.
Superior, 長 ꞌcheung, 上好 sheungꞌ-ꞌho, (better) 更好 kangꞌ-ꞌho, 好過 ꞌho-kwohꞌ.
Supernatural, 神異 shan-iꞌ.
Supersede, 廢去 faiꞌ-hueꞌ.
Superstitious, 溺信古怪 nik-suunꞌ-ꞌkoo-kwaaiꞌ.
Supervene, 自至 tszeꞌ-chiꞌ.
Supine, 袖手 tsauꞌ-ꞌshau.
Supper, 晚餐 ꞌmaan-ꞌtsꞌan.
Supplant, 迫甩 pik-lut.
Supple, 跳疾 tꞌiuꞌ-tsaatꞌ.
Supplement, 添補 tꞌim-ꞌpo.

Supply, 供給 kuung-k'up.
Support, 承住 shing-chue', (with the hand, or morally) 扶住 foo-chue', 扶持 foo-ch'i.
Suppose, 估量 'koo-leung', 估 'koo.
Supposing, 假使間 'ka-'sze-kaan.
Suppress, 鎮壓 chan'-aat', 彈壓 t'aan-aat'.
Supreme, 至上 chi'-sheung', 最上 tsui'-sheung'.
Supreme Being, 上帝 Sheung'-Tai'.
Supreme Court, 臬署 nip-'shue, nip-'ch'ue.
Sure, 確實 k'ok'-shat, 穩當 'wun-tong'.
Surety, (a) 担保 taam-'po.
Surface, 面 min', 上面 sheung'-min'.
Surfeit, 食到飫 shik-to'-ue'.
Surfeited, 饜飽 im'-'paau, 飽俗 'paau-nau'.
Surge, 浪如壁立 long'-ue-pik-laap.

Surgery, 外科 ngoi'-foh.
Surloin, 尾龍扒 'mi-luung-p'a.
Surly, 蠻 maan.
Surmise, 估 'koo.
Surmount, 勝 shing', 勝得過 shing'-tak-kwoh'.
Surname, 姓 sing'.
Surpass, 超卓過 ch'iu-ch'euk'-kwoh', 越過 uet-kwoh'.
Surplus, 餘剩 ue-shing'.
Surprise, 驚愕 king-ngok.
Surprised, 見怪 kin'-kwaai', (frightened) 失愕 shat-ngok.
Surprising, 出奇 ch'uut-k'i.
Surrender, 投降 t'au-hong, (to prison) 投監 t'au-kaam, (give up) 付交 foo'-kaau.
Surround, 圍埋 wai-maai, 圍住 wai-chue'.
Survey, 查察 ch'a-ch'aat'.
Surveyor, 量地官 leung-ti'-koon, General, 工務司 Kuung-moo'-sze.

注释

【布拂】擦拭。
【烂溅】沼泽。
【话埋凑】断言。
【起尾注】欺骗，行骗。

SWA 253 SWI

Survive, 尚活 sheung'-oot, 還在世 waan-tsoi'-shai'.
Susceptible, 易感 i'-ʻkom, i'-ʻkom-ke.
Suspect, 猜疑 ch'aai-i, 恐怕 ʻhuung-p'a'.
Suspend, 掛 kwa', (stop) 罷 pa', 停 t'ing.
Suspense, 掛望 kwa'-mong'.
Suspicion, 思疑 sze-i.
Sustain, (suffer) 抵受 ʻtai-shaa', (be fit for) 克當 hak-tong, (keep up) 扶住 foo-chue', 承住 shing-chue', (alive) 存 ts'uen, 養 ʻyeung.
Sustenance, 飲食 ʻyum-shik.
Swab, (a) 布拂 po'-fut.
Swagger, 誇大 k'wa-taai'.
Swallow, (a) 燕子 *in-ʻtsze; (to) 吞下 t'un-ʻha, 吞 t'un.
Swamp, 爛溅 laan'-paan'.
Swan, 鵠 kuuk, 天鵝 t'in-ngoh.
Swarm, (a) 一堆 yat-tui.
Sway, (power) 權柄 k'uen-ping'.

Swear, 發誓 faat'-shai'.
Sweat, 汗 hohn', (to) 出汗 ch'uut-hohn'.
Sweep, 掃 so', 打掃 ʻta-so', (at a) 一掃 yat-so', 一掃光 yat-so'-ʻkwong.
Sweeping assertion, 話埋湊 wa'-maai-ts'au'.
Sweet, 甜 t'im, 甘 kom.
Sweet-bread, 牛核 ngau-wat.
Sweet-potato, 番薯 faan-*shue.
Swell, (to) 腫起 ʻchuung-ʻhi, (a) 裝腔 chong-ʻhong, 大駕子 taai'-ka'-ʻtsze.
Swelling, 腫脹 ʻchuung-cheung'.
Swift, 快 faai', 速 ts'uuk, 疾速 tsaat-ts'uuk.
Swim, 泅水 yau-ʻshui, 游 yau.
Swimming, (dizziness) 頭暈 t'au-wan.
Swindle, 誆騙 hong-p'in', (and run) 起尾注 ʻhi-ʻmi-chue'.
Swine, 猪 ʻchue.

Swing, (a) 鞦韆 ₍ts'au-ts'in, (to) 搖 iu, 搖擺 iu-₍paai.
Switch, 鞭 pin.
Swivel, 轉楤 ₍chuen-suut.
Swoon, 失魂 shat-wan.
Swoop, (to) 一扑抓住 yat-p'ok'-₍chaau-chue'.
Sword, 把劍 ₍pa-kim'.
Sycee, 紋銀 mun-*ngan.
Sycophant, 白鴿眼 paak-kop'-₍ngaan.
Symbol, 表意之物 ₍piu-i'-chi-mat, ₍piu-i'-ke'-₍ye.
Symmetrical, 相稱 seung-ch'ing', 對得好 tui'-tak-₍ho.
Sympathy, 同情 t'uung-ts'ing, (with sorrow) 心酸 sum-suen, 相憐 seung-lin.
Symptom, 形迹 ying-tsik, (of disease) 病形 peng'-ying.
Synagogue, 會堂 ooi'-t'ong.
Synonymous, 同解 t'uung-₍kaai, 同意 t'uung-i'.
Syphilis, 生疔病 shang-teng-peng'.

Syphon, 角筒 kok'-t'uung.
Syringe, 水浙 ₍shui-chit.
System, 法式 faat'-shik, (a set of things) 一副應當 yat-foo'-ying'-tony'.

T

Table, 張檯 cheung-*t'oi, 棹子 cheuk'-₍tsze, (a spread) 席 tsik.
Tablet, 牌 p'aai, 碑 pi, (ancestral) 神主牌 shan-₍chue-*p'aai.
Taciturn, 不多出聲 'm-toh-ch'uut-sheng.
Tack, (nail) 釘仔 ₍teng-₍tsai, (on) 奶住 naai'-chue', 帶住 taai'-chue', (in sailing) 轉篷 ₍chuen-p'uung, 摳篷 k'au-p'uung.
Tackle, 器用 hi'-yuung'.
Tact, 智謀 chi'-mau.
Tactics, 韜畧 t'o-leuk.
Tadpole, 雷公魚 looi-₍kuung-*ue.
Tael, 兩 ₍leung.
Taffeta, 絹 kuen'.

【白鴿眼】諂媚者。
【水浙】針筒。
【雷公魚】又稱"胭脂魚",是中國特有的淡水珍稀物種,享有"亞洲美人魚"的美稱。

注释

【口疏】告密。
【手多】干涉，贿赂。
【临阵弦断】意为"干着急"。
【水口】水龙头。

Tail, 尾 ʿmi, 條尾 tʻiu-ʿmi, (cue) 辮 pin.
Tailor, 裁縫 tsʻoi-*fuung.
Tailor-bird, 巧婦鳥 ʿhaau-ʿfoo-ʿniu.
Taint, 染 ʿim, 沾染 chim-ʿim.
Take, 攞 ʿloh, 撩 ning, nim, 將 tseung, 取 ʿtsʻue, 把 ʿpa, 搣 kʻaai, kʻaaiʾ, (up) 執 chup, (an opportunity) 乘機 shing-ki.
Tale, 雲母石 wan-ʿmo-shek.
Tale, (a) 一段古 yat-tuenʾ-ʿkoo.
Tale-bearer, 口疏 ʿhau-shoh.
Talent, 才 tsʻoi.
Talk, 談 tʻaam, 講 ʿkong, 話 wa.
Talkative, 好講 hoʾ-ʿkong.
Tall, 高 ko, 身體高 shan-tʻai-ko.
Tallow, 脂油 chi-yau, (ox's) 牛油 ngau-yau, (sheep's) 羊油 yeung-yau.
Tallow-tree, 烏桕木 oo-ʿkʻau-muuk.

Tally, (a) 籌 chʻau, (to) 符合 foo-hop.
Talon, 爪 ʿchaau.
Tamarind, 酸子 suen-ʿtsze.
Tamarisk, 垂絲柳 shui-sze-ʿlau.
Tambourine, 單面鼓 taan-minʾ-ʿkoo.
Tame, 熟 shuuk, 養得熟 yeung-tak-shuuk, 純熟 shuun-shuuk.
Tampering, 手多 ʿshau-toh.
Tan, 硝皮 siu-pʻi, 醃皮 im-pʻi.
Tangible proof, 執據 chup-kueʾ, 把柄 ʿpa-pingʾ.
Tank, 石池 shek-chʻi.
Tanner, 皮匠 pʻi-tseungʾ.
Tantalizing, 臨陣弦斷 lum-chanʾ-in-tʻuen.
Tap, 拍 pʻaakʾ, (let out) 放 fongʾ.
Tap, (a water) 水口 ʿshui-ʿhau.
Tape, 棉紗帶 min-sha-taaiʾ.
Tape-worm, 蛔蟲 ooi-chʻuung.

Tapering, 尖 tsim.	Tax, 稅餉 shui²-‘heung, (to) 收餉 shau-‘heung, 收稅 shau-shui².
Tapioca, 西米 sai-‘mai.	
Tar, 吧碼油 ‘pa-‘ma-yau.	
Tardy, 遲 ch'i, 慢 maan².	
Tares, 稗 pai².	Tea, 茶 ch'a, (leaves) 茶葉 ch'a-ip.
Target, 靶子 ‘pa-‘tsze.	Teapoy, 茶几 ch'a-ki.
Tarnish, 失光 shat-kwong.	Tea-taster, 茶師 ch'a-‘sze.
Taro, 芋頭 oo²-*t'au.	Teach, 教 kaau².
Tart-fruit, 路菓 lo²-‘kwoh, 酸菓 suen-‘kwoh.	Teacher, 先生 sin-shang, 掌教 ‘cheung-kaau².
Tartan, 棋盤布 k'i-p'oon-po².	Teak, 油木 *yau-muuk.
Tartar, 滿洲 ‘Moon-‘chau, 蒙古 Muung-‘koo.	Teal, 水鴨 ‘shui-*aap, (mandarin duck) 鴛鴦 ‘uen-‘yeung.
Task, 工課 kuung-foh².	Tear, (to) 撕破 sze-p'oh², 擘裂 maak²-lit, (off) 戩 chin.
Tassel, 把繸 ‘pa-*sui².	
Taste, 味道 mi²-to², (to) 餂 ‘t'im, 嘗 sheung.	
Tasteless, 淡 ‘t'aam.	Tears, 淚 lui², 眼淚 ‘ngaan-lui².
Tattered, 藍褸 laam-lue².	Tease, 難爲 naan-wai, 嫐 nat-nau, (comb) 刷 shaat², (with a bow string) 彈 t'aan, (oakum) 撕蔴根 sze-ma-kan.
Tattle, (to) 吸 ngup.	
Tattooed, 文身 mun-shan.	
Taunt, 譏誚 ki-ts'iu².	
Tautology, 重覆話 ch'uung-fuuk-*wa².	
Tavern, 酒店 ‘tsau-tim².	Teasing, 囉唆 loh-soh.
Tawdry, 光面 kwong-*min².	Teat, 奶頭 ‘naai-t'au, 乳頭 ‘ue-t'au.
Tawny, 老黃 ‘lo-wong.	Tedious, 長氣 ch'eung-hi².

注释

【车歪】四方陀螺。
【讲古】讲故事。
【冷热分】温度。
【把实】紧握。

Teeth, 牙 nga, 齒牙 ʻchʻi-nga.
Teetotum, 車歪 chʻeˍ-ʻme.
Telegraph, (electric) 電報 tinʼ-poʼ.
Telephone, 德律風 tak-luut-fuung, 地里喚 tiˍ-ʻli-foonʼ.
Telescope, 千里鏡 tsʻin-ʻli-kengʼ.
Tell, 話─知 waʼ─chi, (stories) 講古 ʻkong-ʻkoo, (-tale) 口疏 ʻhau-shoh, (lies) 講大話 ʻkong-taaiʼ-waˍ.
Temerity, 冒險 moʼ-ʻhim.
Temper, 脾氣 pʻi-hiʼ, 品格 ʻpun-kaakʼ, (to temper steel) 見水 kinʼ-ʻshui.
Temperate, 節制 tsitʼ-chaiʼ, 節儉 tsitʼ-kimʼ, (weather) 溫和 wan-woh.
Temperature, 冷熱分 ʻlaang-it-funʼ.
Tempest, 暴風 poʼ-fuung, 風雨大作 fuung-ʻue-taaiʼ-tsokʼ.

Temple, 殿堂 tinʼ-tʻong, 廟堂 miuʼ-tʻong, (an idol-) 神廟 shˍu-miuʼ, *miuʼ.
Temporary, 暫時 tsaamʼ-shi, tsaamʼ-shi-keʼ.
Temporize, 隨時轉 tsʻui-shi-ʻchuen.
Tempt, 試惑 shiʼ-waak, 誘感 ʻyau-waak, 引誘 ʻyan-ʻyau.
Ten, 十 shap.
Tenacious, 把實 ʻpa-shatʼ, 韌皮 nganʼ-pʻi, 韌 nganʼ.
Tenant, 客 haakʼ, 鋪客 pʻoʼ-haakʼ.
Tench, 鯇魚 ʻwaan-*ue, 大頭魚 taaiʼ-tʻau-*ue.
Tend, (attend) 看住 hohn-chueʼ, (the sick) 服事 fuuk-szeˍ, (towards) 向 heungʼ, 致 chiʼ, 噲 ʻooi.
Tender, (soft) 腍軟 num-ʻuen, (brittle) 脃 tsʻui, up-up-tsʻui, (hearted) 軟心 ʻuen-sum, (young) 嫩 nuenʼ.
Tender, (a) 票投 piu-tʻau.

Tendon, 筋 kan.	Testimony, 指證 ʻchi-chingʼ.
Tenon, 榫頭 ʻsuun-taʻu.	Testy, 扭頸 ʻnau-keng.
Tendrils, 躝絲 laan-sze.	Text, (subject) 題目 tʻai-muuk, (classic) 正文 chingʼ-mun.
Tenor, 大意 taaiʼ-iʼ, 意向 iʼ-heung, 去向 hueʼ-heungʼ.	
	Texture, 織紋 chik-mun.
Tense, 緊 ʻkan.	Than, 過於 kwohʼ-ue, 於 ue.
Tent, (a) 帳房 cheungʼ-*fong.	Thank, 謝 tseʼ, (many thanks) 多謝 toh-tseʼ.
Tenth, 第十 taiʼ-shap, (part) 十分一 shap-funʼ-yat.	Thankful, 感恩 ʻkom-yan, 感謝 ʻkom-tseʼ.
Tepid, 煖 nuen.	Thankless, 忘恩 mong-yan.
Term, (time) 限期 haanʼ-kʻi, (word) 話頭 waʼ-tʻau.	That, 個個 ʻkoh-kohʼ (Put the proper classifier, when known, instead of kohʼ), 個 kohʼ, ʻkoh, (things not numbered, as water) 個的 kohʼ-ʻti.
Termination, 收尾 shau-ʻmi.	
Terrace, 天臺 tʻin-*tʻoi, 臺 tʻoi.	
Terrible, 好矣關 ʻho-kaau-kwaan.	Thatch, 蓋茅 kʻoiʼ-maau.
	The, 個 kohʼ, 其 kʻi.
Terror, 悚怯 ʻsuung-hipʼ, 畏懼 waiʼ-kueʼ, 觳觫 huukʼ-tsʻuuk.	Theatre, 戲場 hiʼ-*chʻeung, 戲園 hiʼ-*uen.
	Theatricals, 做戲 tsoʼ-hiʼ.
Test, 試驗 shiʼ-imʼ.	Thee, 你 ʻni, (Sir, Madam, &c. are used for the 2nd person in polite discourse).
Testament, 遺書 wai-shue, (Old and New) 新舊約書 San-kauʼ-yeukʼ-shue.	
	Theft, 偷野 tʻau-ʻye.
Testicles, 外腎 ngoiʼ-ʻshan, 卵子 ʻluun-ʻtsze.	Them, 佢地 ʻkʻue-tiʼ.

注释

【躝絲】卷须。
【好交关】很糟糕。
【扭颈】易怒的。
【偷野】偷东西。
【佢地】他们。

注释

【个阵时】那时候。
【自个时起】从那时候起。
【个处】那处。
【呢的】这些。
【颈渴】口渴。
【呢个】这个。
【到个处】到那里。
【艻】刺。

THI 259 THO

Theme, 題目 t'ai-muuk.
Then, 個陣時 ‵koh-chan⸴-shi⸴, (afterwards) 然後 in-hau⸴, 就 tsau⸴
Thenceforth, 自後 tsze-hau⸴, 自個時起 tsze⸴-‵koh-shi-‵hi.
There, 個處 ‵koh-shue⸴, (is or are) 有 ‵yau, (is no more) 無咯 ‵mo-lok⸴.
Thereabout, 個處左右 ‵koh-shue⸴-‵tsoh-*yau⸴, 左右 ‵tsoh-*yau⸴, 約模 yeuk⸴-*mok⸴.
Therefore, 所以 ‵shoh-‵i, 故此 koo⸴-ts‵ze.
Thermometer, 寒暑針 hohn-‵shue-‵chum.
These, 呢的 ni-‵ti.
They, 佢地 ‵k'ue-ti⸴.
Thick, 笨 ‵p'an, 厚 ‵hau, (as soup) 濃 nuung, 結 kit, (close) 密 mat, 稠密 ch'au-mat.
Thicket, 矮林 ‵ai-lum, 荆棘林 king-kik-lum.
Thief, 賊 *ts'aak, 賊佬 ts'aak-lo⸴.

Thigh, 大髀 taai⸴-‵pi.
Thills, 杠 kong⸴.
Thimble, 針頂 ‵chum-‵ting, (archer's) 披指 p'aan-‵chi.
Thin, 薄 pok, (rare, watery) 稀 hi, (lean) 瘦 shau⸴, 凹 nip, (-skinned) 薄皮 pok-*p'i.
Thing, 物件 mat-kin⸴, 野 ‵ye, 東西 tuung-sai, (affair) 件事 kin⸴-sze⸴.
Think, 思想 sze-‵seung, (guess) 估 ‵koo.
Thinly, 疏落 shoh-lok.
Third, 第三 tai⸴-saam, (a) 三分一 saam-fun⸴-yat⸴.
Thirst, 頸渴 ‵keng-hoht, 口渴 ‵hau-hoht, (after) 渴想 hoht⸴-‵seung.
This, 呢個 ni-koh⸴, (that or) 彼此 ‵pi-ts‵ze, (See That).
Thistle, 大薊 taai⸴-‵kai, 蒺藜 tsaat-lai.
Thither, 到個處 to⸴-‵koh-shue⸴.
Thorn, 艻 lak, 莿 ts‵ze, (bush) 艻林 lak-lum.

| THR | 260 | THU |

Thorough, 通 t'uung.
Thoroughfare, 通行 t'uung-hang, 通路 t'uung-lo'.
Thoroughly, 盡地 tsuun'-*ti', 嘥 saai'.
Those, 個的 koh'-,ti.
Thou, 你 'ni, (See Thee).
Though, 雖則 sui-tsak, 雖然 sui-in, 雖 sui.
Thought, 思念 sze-nim', 念頭 nim'-t'au, 意思 i-sze, 想頭 'seung-t'au.
Thousand, 千 ts'in.
Thread, 線 sin', (a) 條線 t'iu-sin', (to) 穿 ch'uen.
Threaten, 嚇 haak', 話 wa', (frighten) 恐嚇 'huung-haak'.
Three, 三 saam.
Thresh, 使棒打 'shai-p'aang-'ta, 打 'ta, (grain) 打禾 'ta-woh.
Threshing-floor, 禾塲 woh-ch'eung.
Threshold, 門根 moon-ch'aan ('ch'aam).
Thrifty, 慳儉 haan-kim'.

Thrill with pleasure, 歡喜到震 foon-'hi-to'-chan'.
Thrilling, (sound) 吵耳 'ch'aau-'i, 刮耳 kat-'i.
Thrive, 發達 faat'-taat.
Throat, 喉嚨 hau-luung.
Throne, 王位 wong-*wai', 御坐 ue'-tsoh'.
Throng, 擠擁 tsai-'yuung, 人迫 yan-pik'.
Through, 由 yau, 經過 king-kwoh', 透 t'au'.
Throw, 丟 tiu, 揼 wing, 擗 p'ek, (dice) 擲 chaak, (one's self) 投 t'au.
Thrush, (white eyed) 畫眉雀 wa'-*mi-tseuk', (black) 豬屎鴉 chue-'shi-*cha, (a disease) 口爛 'hau-laan'.
Thrust, 剽 piu, (in) 插 ch'aap'.
Thuja, 圓栢 uen-paak'.
Thumb, 手指公 'shau-'chi-kuung.
Thump, 捀 p'uung, 捀着 p'uung'-cheuk', 泵 'tum.

注 释

【嘥】完全。
【个的】那些。
【门棖】门槛。
【口烂】鹅口疮。
【手指公】大拇指。

注释

【噉样】这样。
【揩阻】阻碍。
Tide-waiter: 海关稽查员。
【食晏】吃午餐。
【兜起】跷起。

TID 261 TIM

Thunder, 雷轟 lui-kwang, (clap) 霹 p'ek, 霹靂 p'ik-lik.
Thunderer, the, 雷公 lui-ʿkuung.
Thunder-struck, 失驚 shat-king.
Thursday, 禮拜四 ʿlai-paai-ʿszeʾ.
Thus, 噉 ʿkom, 噉樣 ʿkom-*yeungʾ, (-much) 咁多 komʾ-ʿtoh.
Thwart, (to) 揩阻 k'angʿ-ʿchoh, 嚦 ngaak.
Tick, (to) 滴滴聲 tik-tik-sheng.
Ticket, 票 p'iuʾ, piu, ʿp'iu 帖 t'ipʾ, 紙 ʿchi.
Tickle, 整癢 ʿching-ʿyeung, 折 chitʾ.
Ticklish, 痠軟 suenʾ-ʿuen, (troublesome) 難料理 naan-liuʾ-ʿli.
Tide, 潮水 ch'iu-ʿshui.
Tide-waiter, 老太 ʿlo-ʿt'aai 簽字手 ts'im-tszeʾ-ʿshau.
Tidings, 消息 siu-sik.

Tidy, 齊整 ts'ai-ʿching, 雅潔 ʿnga-kitʾ.
Tie, (a) 帶 *taai, 條帶 t'iu-*taai, (to) 綁 ʿpong, (up, or on) 叻住 naai-chueʾ, (a knot) 打結 ʿta-kitʾ (litʾ).
Tiffin, 晏餐 aanʾ-ts'aan, (take) 食晏 shik-aanʾ.
Tier, 層 ts'ang.
Tiger, 老虎 ʿlo-ʿfoo.
Tiger-lily, 捲丹 ʿkuen-taan.
Tight, 緊 ʿkan, 行 hang.
Tile, 瓦 ʿnga, (round) 瓦筒 ʿnga-*t'uung, (flat) 瓦片 ʿnga-*p'in, (for floors) 堦磚 ʿkaai-ʿchuen.
Till, 到 toʾ, 及 k'ap.
Till, (to) 耕田 kang-t'in.
Tiller, (of a boat) 舦柄 ʿt'aai-pengʾ.
Tilt, 兜起 tau-ʿhi, 牕側吓 chaap-chak-ʿha.
Timber, 木料 muuk-liuʾ.
Time, 時 shi, 時候 shi-hauʾ, (set) 期 k'i, (at, or keep) 準 ʿchuun.

| TIN | 262 | TIT |

Times, (occasions) 回 ooi, 賬 cheung, 次 ts'ze, 變 pin, 勻 wan, (three times three are nine) 三三該九 saam-saam-koi-‘kau, 三三如九 saam-saam-ue‘kau.
Time-server, 隨風佞 ts‘ui-fuung-ning.
Timely, 着時候 cheuk-shi-hau, (early) 早 ‘tso.
Timid } 膽細 ‘taam-sai,
Timorous 無膽 ‘mo-‘taam, 膽怯 ‘taam-hip.
Tin, 錫 sek.
Tincture, 藥酒 yeuk-‘tsau, 酒開 ‘tsau-hoi, (See Tint).
Tinder, 火煤絨 ‘foh-mooi-yuung.
Tinder-case, 火鎌包 ‘foh-lim-paau, (-box) 火煤箱 ‘foh-mooi-‘seung.
Tinfoil, 錫薄 sek-*pok.
Tinge, 染的 ‘im-‘ti.
Tingle, 响 ‘heung.
Tinkle, 玎璫响 ‘ting-tong-‘heung.

Tin-plate, 馬口鐵 ‘ma-hau-t'it.
Tinsel, 金花彩紅 kum-fa-‘ts'oi-huung.
Tint of, (tinge of) 帶有的 taai-yau-‘ti.
Tiny, 牙 ngan, 牙細 ngan-sai, 細細 sai-sai.
Tip, 尖處 tsim-ch'ue.
Tipple, 飲慣 ‘yum-kwaan.
Tiptoe, 牙高脚 ngan-ko-keuk, (of expectation) 牙脚望 ngan-keuk-mong.
Tired, 見倦 kin-kuer, 見瘡 kin-kooi.
Tiresome, (tedious) 長氣 ch'eung-hi.
Tissue, 羅紋 loh-mun, 砌成 ts‘ai-shing, ts‘ai-shing-ke.
Title, 尊號 tsuen-ho, 官銜 koon-haam, (title to) 應得 ying-tak.
Title page, 書面 shue-min, 書名紙 shue-meng-‘chi, 書軌 shue-‘kwai.
Tittle-tattle, 贅話 chui-*wa, 支支咋咋 chi-chi-cha-cha.

注 释

【蠄蟝】蟾蜍。
【呫吓呫吓】东倒西歪的样子。
【装身枱】盥洗室。
【做得过】可以做的。
【听日】明天。
【黐脷】大舌头。

TOI   263   TON

To, 與 'ue, 過 kwoh², (up to) 至到 chi²-to², (in order to) 欲 yuuk.
To and fro, 來往 loi-'wong.
Toad, 蠄蟝 k'um-*k'ue, kop²-'kwaai.
Toast, (to) 炕 hong², 炕焦 hong²-tsiu, (bread) 炕麵包 hong²-min²-ₚpaau.
Tobacco, 烟葉 ᵢin-ip, 烟 ᵢin.
To-day, 今日 kum-yat.
Toddle, 呫吓呫吓 tut-'ha-tut-'ha.
Toe, 脚趾 keuk²-'chi, (of a shoe) 鞋頭 haai-t'au, (great-) 脚趾公 keuk²-'chi-kuung.
Together, 共埋 kuung²-maai, 同埋 t'uung-maai, ₙa-maai, (united) 孖埋 ₘa-maai, 共 kuung², 同一齊 t'uung-yat-*ts'ai.
Toil, 鹹苦 haam-'foo, 苦 lo-'foo, (to) 勤勞 k'an-lo, 勞碌 lo-luuk.
Toilet, 裝身枱 chong-shan-t'oi, (lady's) 妝奩 chong-lim.

Token, 記號 ki²-ho², 號 ho².
Tolerable, 做得過 tso²-tak-kwoh².
Tolerate, 任從 yum²-ts'uung, 容縱 yuung-tsuung².
Tomato, 金錢桔 kum-ts'in-kat, 番茄 faan-*k'e.
Tomb, 墳墓 fun-moo², (vaulted) 明塜 ming-'ch'uung.
Tomfoolery, 蠢蠢呆呆 事幹 'ch'uun-'ch'uun-ngoi-ngoi-sze²-kohn².
Tomorrow, 聽日 t'ing-yat, 明日 ming-yat.
Ton, 墩 ₜan, 十六担 shap-luuk-taam².
Tone, 聲音 sheng-yum.
Tongs, 火鉗 'foh-k'im.
Tongue, 條脷 t'iu-li², 舌頭 shit-t'au.
Tongue-tied, 黐脷 ch'i-li², 齟牙 nak-*nga.
Tonic, (med.) 補血 'po-huet².
To-night, 今晚 kum-'maan.
Tonsure, 落髮 lok-faat².

| TOR | 264 | TOT |

Too, 太 t'aai', 過頭 kwoh'-t'au, 得嚟 tak-tsai', (also) 都 ₍toc.

Tool, 傢伙 ka-₍foh, 器具 hi'-kue'.

Tooth, 牙 ᵘga, 牙齒 nga-₍ch'i, (a) 隻牙 chek'-nga.

Tooth-ache, 牙痛 nga-t'uung'.

Tooth-brush, 牙刷 nga-chaat', 牙擦 nga-*ts'aat'.

Tooth-pick, 牙簽 nga-ts'im.

Tooth-powder, 牙灰 nga-fooi.

Top, 頂頭 ₍teng-*t'au.

Topiary work, 屈古樹 wat-₍koo-shue'.

Topic, 題目 t'ai-muuk.

Topple over, 蹼轉 p'uuk-₍chuen.

Topsy-turvy, 顛倒 tin-₍to, 顛頭倒脚 tin-t'au-₍to-keuk'.

Torch, 火把 ₍foh-₍pa.

Torment, 磨難 moh-naan, 磨苦 moh-₍foo, (to) 難為 naan-wai.

Torn, 裂曉 lit-hiu, 爛曉 laan'-hiu.

Torpedo, (fish) 鯆哥魚 ₍p'o-koh-*ue, (in warfare) 水雷 ₍shui-lui.

Torpid, 不仁 pat-yan, 麻木 ma-muuk, (insects) 蟄蟲 chat-ch'uung.

Torrent, 急流水 kup-lau-₍shui, (mountain) 山灘 shaan-t'aan.

Torrid, 熱 it, (zone) 熱帶 it-taai'.

Tortoise, 龜 ₍kwai.

Tortoise-shell, 玳瑁 toi'-*mooi, to'-*mooi'.

Tortuous, 攣捐 luen-kuen.

Torture, 拷打 haau-₍ta, 行刑 hang-ying.

Toss, 拋 p'aau, 㧎 wing, (roll) 搣身 luuk-shan.

Total, 一總 yat-₍tsuung.

Totter, 嚀嚀吓 ning'-ning'-ha.

Tottery, 險險地 ₍him-₍him-*ti'.

注 释

【屈古树】灌木修剪。
【蹼转】推翻；覆盖。
【吟吟吓】蹒跚的样子。
【险险地】摇摇欲坠的样子。

注释

【火颈】易怒的。
【铺家】商人，店主。
【讲坏】中伤。
【次第随从】行列，队列。

Touch, 掂着 tim⁾-cheuk, 摩着 moh-cheuk, (meddle) 鬥 tau⁾.
Touchy, 火頸 ⸍foh-⸍keng.
Tough, 靭 ngan⸌.
Tour, 出外 ch'uut-ngoi⸌.
Tow, 粗蔴 ts'o-ma, (to) 使纜拖 ⸍shai-laam⸌-t'oh, 拉纜 laai-laam⸌, (at the stern) 奶住 naai⸌-chue.
Towards, 向 heung⸌.
Towel, 面巾 min⸌-⸍kan.
Tower, 塔 t'aap⸌, 高樓 ko-*lau, 土府 ⸌t'o-⸍foo.
Towering, 頂天高 ⸌ting t'in-ko.
Town, 邑 yup, (walled) 城 sheng.
Toys, 公仔 ⸍kuung-⸌tsai.
Trace, 踪跡 tsuung-tsik, 形跡 ying-tsik, (on paper) 印 yan⸌, 描 miu.
Track, (a boat) 拉纜 laai-laam⸌, (foot steps) 揾脚跡 ⸍wan-keuk⸌-tsik.
Tract (small book), 小書 ⸌siu-shue.

Tractable, 受教 shau⸌-kaau⸌, 聽話 t'eng-wa⸌.
Trade, 生意 shaang-i⸌, 貿易 mau⸌-yik.
Tradesman, 舖家 p'o⸌-⸍ka.
Tradition, 口傳 ⸍hau-ch'uen.
Traduce, 講壞 ⸌kong-waai⸌.
Tragedy, 報應戲文 po⸌-ying⸌-hi⸌-mun, 苦情戲 ⸍foo-ts'ing-hi⸌.
Trail, 拖 t'oh, (a) 拖痕 t'oh-han.
Train, (in a) 次第隨從 ts'ze⸌-tai⸌-ts'ui-ts'uung, (of followers) 從人 ts'uung-yan, (of powder) 火藥線 ⸍foh-yeuk-sin⸌, (of carriages, &c.) 一連 yat-lin, 一剌 yat-laat.
Train, (to) 教養 kaau⸌-⸍yeung.
Trait, 處 ch'ue⸌.
Traitor, 奸臣 kaan-shan, 賣主 maai⸌-⸍chue, maai⸌-⸍chue-ke⸌.
Tramp, (trample) 踐踏 ts'in-taap, 蹈踏 ch'aai-taap, 踐 ⸌ts'in.

Trance, (in a) 入定 yup-ting, 出神 ch'uut-shan.	Transpire, 露出來 lo-ch'uut-lai.
Tranquility, 安寧 ohn-ning, (general) 太平 t'aai-p'ing.	Transplant, (rice) 揷田 ch'aap-t'in, 蒔秧 shi-yeung, (a tree, &c.) 種過 chuung-kwoh.
Transact, 辦 paan.	
Transcend, 超卓過 ch'iu-ch'euk-kwoh.	Transport, 搬運 poon-wun, (convicts) 充軍 ch'uung-kwun.
Transcribe, 抄 ch'aau.	
Transfer, 挪移 noh-i, 移過 i-kwoh, 交過 kaau-kwoh.	Transpose, 調轉 tiu-chuen, 相換 seung-oon.
	Transverse, 橫 waang.
Transformation, 變化 pin-fa.	Trap, 笯 kaap, 籠 *luung.
Transgress, 犯 faan.	Trap-door, 樓口板 lau-hau-paan.
Transgression, 過犯 kwoh-faan.	Trash, 擸撞 laap-saap, 壞傢伙 waai-ka-foh.
Transient } Transitory } 暫時 tsaam-shi, 無耐 mo-noi.	Travail, 產痛 ch'aan-t'uung, 劬勞 k'ue-lo, (to) 分娩 fun-min.
Translate, 繙譯 faan-yik, 譯出來 yik-ch'uut-lai.	Travel, 出行 ch'uut-hang, 行遊 hang-yau.
Transmigration, 輪囘 luun-ooi.	Traverse, 橫過 waang-kwoh, (go about) 週遊 chau-yau.
Transmit, 傳 ch'uen, 交寄 kaau-ki, 傳遞 ch'uen-tai.	Travesty, 改作笑話 koi-tsok-siu-*wa.
Transparent, 透光 t'au-kwong, t'au-kwong-ke, 睇得過 t'ai-tak-kwoh.	Tray, 托盤 t'ok-*p'oon.

注 释

【踹亲】踹到，踩踏。
【榄核】有格子的，成格状的。
【真正交关】惊人的。

Treacherous, 詭譎 ʻkwai-kwut, 猾 waatʼ, 欺人 hi-yan.
Treacle, 糖水 tʻong-ʻshui, (thick) 糖膠 tʻong-kaau.
Tread, 行 hang, (on) 踏 taapʼ, 踹親 ʻchʻaai-tsʻan, ʻnaai-tsʻan.
Treason, 謀反 mau-ʻfaan.
Treasure, 銀兩 ngan-ʻleung, 錢銀 *tsʻin-*ngan, (wealth) 財帛 tsʻoi-paak, (a) 寶貝 ʻpo-pooiʼ.
Treasurer, 管庫人 ʻkoon-fooʼ-yan, (provincial) 布政司 poʼ-chingʻ-sze.
Treasury, 銀庫 ngan-fooʼ, 庫務署 fooʼ-mooʼ-shue.
Treat, 看待 hohn-toiʼ, 管待 ʻkoon-toiʼ, 待 toiʼ, (discuss) 講 ʻkong.
Treaty, 和約 woh-yeukʼ, 憑約 pʻang-yeukʼ.
Treble, 三倍 saam-ʻpʻooi.
Tree, 樹木 shueʼ-muuk, (a) 矞樹 pʻoh-shueʼ.

Trellised, 欖核 ʻlaam-wat.
Tremble, 打震 ʻta-chanʼ, 打戰 ʻta-chinʼ, 戰慄 chinʼ-luut.
Tremendous, 眞正交關 chan-chingʼ-kaau-kwaan.
Trench, 壕 ho, 坑 haang, 池 chʻi.
Trespass, 犯 faanʼ, (idle people are forbidden to) 閒人免進 haan-yan-ʻmin-tsuunʼ.
Triad-society, 三合會 saam-hopʼ-*ooiʼ.
Trial, 試 shiʼ, 試驗 shiʼ-imʼ, (to make) 探試 tʻaamʼ-shiʼ, 試吓 shiʼ-ʻha.
Triangle, 三角形 saam-kokʼ-ying.
Tribe, 族 tsuuk, 支派 chi-pʻaaiʼ.
Tribulation, 患難 waanʼ-naanʼ.
Tribulus, 蒺藜 tsaat-lai.
Tribunal, 公案 kuung-ohnʼ.
Tribute, 貢 kuungʼ, (to pay) 納貢 naap-kuungʼ, 納稅 naap-shuiʼ.

Trice, 頃刻之間 'k'ing-hak-chi-kaan.
Trick, 詭計 'kwai-kai, (to) 混 wun', 整頓 'ching-tan'.
Trickle, 滴滴落來 tik-tik-lok-lai.
Trident, (a) 一枝扒 yat-chi-p'a, 三叉 saam-ch'a.
Trifle, (a) 微物 mi-mat, (to) 弄 luung', (with things) 憖 'nun, (play) 頑耍 waan-'sha.
Trigger, 條制 t'iu-chai'.
Trim, 整齊 'ching-ts'ai.
Trimmer, (a) 隨風佞 ts'ui-fuung-ning'.
Trimming, (fancy braid) 欄杆 laan-kohn.
Trinity, 三一 saam-yat, 三合一 saam-hop-yat.
Trinket, 小件頭 'siu-kin-*t'au.
Trip, (the foot) 失腳 shat-keuk', (up) 撬馬 kiu-'ma, 鉤腳 kau-keuk', (a) 遊一回 yau-yat-ooi.
Tripang, 海參 'hoi-shum.

Tripe, 牛肚 ngau-t'o, 牛百葉 ngau-paak'-ip.
Triphasia, 山枮 shaan-nim.
Triple, 三倍 saam-p'ooi.
Tripod, 鼎 'ting.
Trippingly, 輕步 heng-po'.
Trite, 講到俗 'kong-to'-tsuuk.
Triumph, 凱歌 'hoi-koh.
Trivial, 小小 'siu-'siu.
Trocar, 放水針 fong'-'shui-chum.
Troop, 軍 kwun.
Tropic, (N.) 熱帶北限 it-taai'-pak-haan', (S.) 熱帶南限 it-taai'-naam-haan'.
Trot, 跑花蹄 'p'aau-fa-t'ai, 遛花 lau'-fa.
Trouble, 艱難 kaan-naan, (to) 煩擾 faan-'iu, 勞動 lo-tuung', (I will) 多煩 toh-faan.
Troublesome, 費事 fai'-sze', (person) 俺尖 im-tsim.
Trough, 槽 ts'o.
Trousers, 條褲 t'iu-foo', (short) 牛頭褲 ngau t'au-foo'.

注 释

【滴滴落来】滴，细流，淌。
【条制】引发，引起。
【小件头】小东西。
【撬马】绊倒。
【讲到俗】陈腐的。

注释

【灰匙】泥铲，批灰用具。
【骤吓】步履艰难地走。
【辘仔】小滑轮。
Tuber:指块茎，译成"一个种"不太准确。
【只髻】一支簪。在某些注释中，词典编者将量词和名词直接放在一起作注，不加数词。
【一执】一簇。

Trowel, 灰匙 fooi-shi (*ch'i).
Truant, (to play) 逃學 t'o-hok.
Truce, 暫息干戈 tsaam'-sik-kohn-kwoh.
Trudge, 驟吓 'ch'au-'ha, chuung-'ha.
True, 眞 chan, 眞實 chan-shat.
Truly, 果然 'kwoh-in, 眞正 chan-ching'.
Trump up, 揘成 nip-shing.
Trumpet, 號筒 ho'-t'uung, (COL.) hö-tö.
Trundle, 轆 luuk, 轆仔 luuk-'tsai.
Trunk, (for) 箱 ,seung, (body) 身 shan, 大身 taai'-shan, (elephant's) 象拔 tseung'-pat.
Trunnions, 炮耳 p'aau'-'i.
Truss, (for hernia) 小腸氣夾 'siu-ch'eung-hi'-kaap', (frame) 金字架 kum-tsze'-ka'.
Trust, 信賴 suun'-laai', (on-) 賖 she, 過信 kwoh'-suun'.
Trustworthy, 老實 'lo-shat.
Truth, 眞理 chan-'li, 眞話 chan-*wa'.
Try, 試吓 shi'-,ha, 試一試 shi'-yat-shi', (before a court) 審問 'shum-mun'.
Tub, 木盤 muuk-p'oon.
Tube, 管 'koon, 筒 t'uung, *t'uung.
Tuber, (a) 一個種 yat-koh'-'chuung.
Tuberose, 玉簪花 yuuk-tsaam-,fa.
Tuck up, 歛起 'lim-'hi, 押起 yaap'-'hi.
Tuesday, 禮拜二 'lai-paai'-i'.
Tuft, 隻髻 chek'-*kai', (a) 一執 yat-tsap.
Tug, (to) 拖 t'oh, 拉 laai.
Tumble, 跌落 tit'-lok, 慣倒 kwaan'-'to, (roll) 擺倒 luuk-'to.
Tumbler, (on the stage) 六分 luuk-fun, (glass-) 玻璃杯 poh-,li-,pooi.
Tumour, 肉瘤 yuuk-*lau (lo), 粉瘤 ,fun-*lau (lo).

TUR　　　　　TWI

Tumult, (bustle) 鬧熱 naau²-it, (uproar) 嘈鬧 ts'o-naau².
Tune, (a) 一調 yat-tiu², (to) 較線 kaau²-sin², 較準 kaau²-˙chuun.
Tunnel, 山峒 shaan-tuung².
Turban, 纏頭巾 chin-t'au-kan.
Turbid, 濁 chuuk.
Turbot, 左口魚 ˙tsoh-˙hau-*ue.
Turbulent, 滋事 tsze-sze².
Tureen, 湯兜 t'ong-tau.
Turf, 草皮 ˙ts'o-p'i.
Turgid, 浮腫 fau-˙chuung, (bombastic) 張大 cheung-taai².
Turkey, (a) 火雞 ˙foh-˙kai.
Turmeric, 黃薑 wong-keung.
Turmoil, 勞碌 lo-luuk.
Turn, 轉 ˙chuen, 反轉 ˙faan-chuen², (as a wheel) 畓畓轉 t'um-t'um-chuen², (in a lathe) 車 ch'e.
Turner, 車匠 ch'e-tseung².

Turns, by, 輪流 luun-lau.
Turning-lathe, 車牀 ch'e-ch'ong.
Turnip, 蘿蔔 loh-paak.
Turpentine, 松節油 ts'uung-tsit²-yau.
Turtle, 玳瑁 toi²-*mooi², 鼈 pit, 腳魚 keuk²-*ue.
Turtle-dove, 斑鳩 paan-˙kau.
Tush, 咪聲 ˙mai-sheng.
Tusk, 長牙 ch'eung-nga.
Tutenag, (zinc) 白鉛 paak-uen, (white copper) 白銅 paak-t'uung.
Tutor, 掌教 ˙cheung-kaau².
Twang, 迸聲 k'wang-sheng.
Tweezers, 鋏仔 kaap²-˙tsai, 小鑷 ˙siu-nip.
Twelfth, 第十二 tai²-shap-i².
Twelve, 十二 shap-i².
Twenty, 二十 i²-shap.
Twice, 兩回 ˙leung-ooi, (See Times).
Twigs, 蔑 mit, 枝莖 chi-hang (˙k'waang).

注 释

【一调】和谐，使一致。
【左口鱼】大比目鱼。
【汤兜】汤盘。
【咪声】呸（表示轻蔑的声音）。
【迸声】"砰"的一声。

注释

【瘹】阵痛，悔恨。
【疮瘺】溃烂。
【佛青】青蓝色。
【把遮】一把伞。
【断事中人】裁判，仲裁人。

TYA　　　271　　　UNA

Twilight, (eve) 黄昏 wong-fun, (morn) 昧爽 mooi-ʿshong.
Twilled, 斜纹 tsʻe-*mun.
Twine, 繩仔 shing-ʿtsai, (to) 絞 ʿkaau.
Twinge, 瘹 tsʻekʾ, (to) 扭 ʿnau.
Twinkle, 閃 ʿshim.
Twinkling, (a) 轉眼 ʿchuen ʿngaan.
Twins, 孖生仔 ma-shang-ʿtsai, 雙生 sheung-shang.
Twist, 扭 ʿnau, 絞 ʿkaau.
Twitching, 扭 ʿnau, (of the muscles) 筋轉 kan-ʿchuen, tsaatʾ-ʿha.
Twitter, 嘶嘶聲 si-si-sheng, 吱吱喞喞 chi-chi-ʿchaau-ʿchaau.
Two, 二 iʾ, 兩 ʿleung.
Type, 活板字 ootʾ-ʿpaan-tszeʾ, a (sign) 預表 ueʾ-ʿpiu.
Typhoon, 風颶 fuung-kauʾ.
Typhus, 身虛熱症 shan-hue-it-chingʾ.
Tyrannical, 暴虐 poʾ-yeuk.
Tyranny, 霸道 paʾ-toʾ.
Tyrant, 霸王 paʾ-wong.
Tyro, 初學 chʻoh-hok, 亞初 aʾ-chʻoh.

U

Ubiquity, 無處不有 mo-chʻueʾ-patʾ-ʿyau.
Ugly, 醜 ʿchʻau, 不好睇 ʾm-ʿho-ʿtʻai.
Ulcer, 瘡瘺 ʿchʻong-*lauʾ.
Ultimately, 到底 toʾ-tai, 到頭 toʾ-tʻau.
Ultramarine, 佛青 futʾ-tsʻeng.
Umbra, 陰 yum, 影 ʿying.
Umbrage, 狐疑 oo-i.
Umbrella, 把遮 ʿpa-ʿche, 雨遮 ʿue-ʿche.
Umpire, 斷事中人 tuenʾ-szeʾ-chuung-*yau.
Unable, 不能 ʾm-nang, 不會 ʾm-ʿooi.
Unaccommodating, 不相讓 ʾm-seung-yeungʾ.
Unaccountable, 解不得 ʿkaai-ʾm-tak, 欠解 himʾ-ʿkaai.

Unaccustomed, 不慣 'm-kwaan'.
Unacquainted, 不識 'm-shik.
Unadorned, 樸素 p'ok'-so'.
Unadvisable, 不合勢色 'm-hop-shai'-shik, 不好 'm-'ho.
Unadulterated, 精純 tsing-shuun,
Unaffected, 無感動 'mo-'kom-tuung', (real) 眞 chan.
Unalienable, 不俾得人 'm-'pi-tak-yan-ke'.
Unalloyed, 足色 tsuuk-shik, 正色 ching'-shik.
Unalterable, 無可更改 mo-'hoh-kang-'koi.
Unanimous, 一心 yat-sum, 無不中意 mo-pat-chuung-i'.
Unanswerable, 辭無可駁 ts'ze-mo-'hoh-pok'.
Unanticipated, 不曾想到 'm-ts'ang-'seung-to'.
Unapt, dull, 蠢拙 'ch'uun-chuet'.
Unassisted, 無人幫 'mo-yan-pong.

Unassuming, 謙遜 him-suun'.
Unavoidable, 無奈何 'mo-noi'-hoh, 無可避 mo-'hoh-pi', 不免 pat-'min.
Unaware, 不估 'm-'koo.
Unbend, 放鬆 fong'-suung.
Unbiassed, 無偏 'mo-p'in.
Unbind, 解甩 'kaai-lut.
Unblamable, 無責處 'mo-chaak'-ch'ue'.
Unblemished, 無瑕疵 'mo-ha-ts'ze.
Unblushing, 無臉 'mo-'lim, 無廉恥 'mo-lim-'ch'i.
Unboiled, 未煲 mi'-po.
Unbounded, 無限 mo-haan'.
Unbridled, 放肆 fong'-sze'.
Unbusiness-like, 不合事例 'm-hop-sze'-lai'.
Unceasing, 不止 pat-'chi, 不息 pat-sik, 不歇 pat-hit'.
Uncertain, 不得定 'm-tak-ting', 不定 pat-ting'.
Unchangeable, 無改變 'mo-'koi-pin'.

注 释

【揿开】掀开。
【私吓】欺诈的，阴险的。
【打地窿】暗中破坏。
【包承】承担，保证。

Uncharitable, 無人情 'mo-yan-ts'ing.	Undefiled, 潔淨 kit'-tsing.
Unchaste, 不正經 'm-ching'-king.	Under, 下 ha', 下底 ha'-tai, (to be) 在下 tsoi'-ha'.
Uncivil, 無禮 mo-'lai, 傲慢 ngo'-maan'.	Undergo, 受 shau'.
Uncle, 伯叔 paak'-shuuk, (maternal) 舅父 'k'au *foo'.	Underhand, 私吓 sze-*ha', 暗中 om'-chuung, 陰手 yum-'shau.
Unclean, 不潔淨 'm-kit'-tsing'.	Undermine, 打地窿 'ta-ti'-luung.
Uncomfortable, 不爽快 'm-'shong-faai'.	Understand, 曉 'hiu, 明白 ming-paak, 會 'ooi.
Uncommon, 非常 fi-sheung.	Undertake, 包承 paau-shing.
Unconcerned, 不上心 'm-'sheung-sum.	Undertaker's shop, 壽板舖 shau'-'paan-*p'o'.
Unconscious, 不知不覺 pat-chi-pat-kok'.	Undervalue, 看低 hohn'-tai, 睇輕 't'ai-heng.
Unconstrained, 自然 tsze'-in.	Undeserved, 不應受 'm-ying-shau'.
Uncouth, 粗俗 ts'o-tsuuk.	Undesigned, 不故意 'm-koo'-i'.
Uncover, 揿開 'k'in-hoi.	Undignified, 下賤 ha'-tsin'.
Undaunted, 不喪膽 'm-song'-'taam, 無畏懼 'mo-wai'-kue'.	Undisguised, 顯然 'hin-in.
Undecided, 無定 mo-ting', 無定準 mo-ting'-'chuun.	Undivided attention, 專一 chuen-yat, 專心 chuen-sum.

| UNF | 274 | UNI |

Undo, (loose) 解開 ʻkaai-hoi, (ruin) 破敗 pʻohˋ-paaiˋ.
Undoubted, 定然 tingˋ-in.
Undoubting, 無疑 ʻmo-i.
Undress, 除衫 chʻue-ʻshaam.
Undulating, 波紋 poh-*mun, 波浪樣 poh-longˋ-*yeungˋ.
Uneasy, 欠安 himˋ-ohn, 唔安樂 ʼm-ohn-lok.
Unemployed, 無事業 ʻmo-szeˋ-ip.
Unequal, 不等 pat-ʻtang, 不相等 ʼm-seung-ʻtang, 不同 ʼm-tʻuung.
Unequalled, 無雙 ʻmo-sheung.
Uneven, 不平 ʼm-pʻing, 不齊 pat-tsʻai.
Unexpected, 再不估 tsoiˋ-pat-ʻkoo, 意外 iˋ-ngoiˋ.
Unfair, 不公道 ʼm-kuung-toˋ.
Unfavourable, 不遂 pat-suiˋ, 逆 ngaak, 不順 ʼm-shuunˋ.

Unfeeling, 薄情 pok-tsʻing.
Unfilial, 不孝 pat-haauˋ.
Unfinished, 未成 miˋ-shing.
Unfit, 不合 ʼm-hop, 不着 ʼm-cheuk.
Unfold, 解開 ʻkaai-hoi, 展開 ʻchin-hoi, 舒 shue.
Unforeseen, 不料 pat-liuˋ, 料不到 liuˋ-ʼm-toˋ, 偶然 ngau-in.
Unforgiving, 爭啖氣 chaang-taamˋ-hiˋ.
Unfortunate, 無彩 ʻmo-ʻtsʻoi.
Unfounded, 無根無本 mo-kan-mo-ʻpoon.
Ungenerous, 小器 ʻsiu-hiˋ.
Ungovernable, 制不得 chaiˋ-pat-tak, chaiˋ-ʼm-tak.
Ungrateful, 忘恩 mong-yan.
Unhappy, 無福 mo-fuuk.
Unhealthy, 不爽 ʼm-ʻshong.
Uniform, 通都一樣 tʻuung-too-yat-yeungˋ, 同式 tʻuung-shik, (dress) 號衣 hoˋ-i.

注 釋

【除衫】脱衣服。
【逆】不利的,反对的。
【争啖气】争口气。
【无彩】倒霉,不幸。
【制不得】无法控制的,难以抑制的。
【不爽】不健康的。

注释

【合埋】联合,团结。
【纯一】一致,团结,联合。
【若唔系】若不是。
【尽地】全然的,纯粹的;未改的。
【逆性】不自然的,不正常的。

Unimportant, 無緊要 ῾mo-῾kan-iu῾, 無相干 ῾mo-seung-kohn.
Unintentionally, 無意中 ῾mo-i῾-chuung.
Uninterrupted, 流連不斷 lau-lin-pat-῾t'uen.
Union, 合會 hop-ooi῾, (heart and soul) 同心協力 t'uung-sum-hip῾-lik, (sexual) 交媾 kaau-kau῾.
Unison, 同音 t'uung-yum.
Unite, 合埋 hop-maai, 連埋 lin-maai.
United States, 合眾國 Hop-chuung῾-kwok῾, 花旗國 ῾Fa-k'i-kwok῾, 美國 ῾Mi-kwok῾.
Unity, 一 yat, 純一 shuun-yat.
Universal, 普遍 ῾p'oo-p'in῾, (peace) 太平 t'aai῾-p'ing.
Universe, 宇宙 ῾ne-chau῾, 宇內 ῾ue-noi῾, 天地萬物 t'in-ti῾-maan῾-mat.

Unjust, 不公道 ῾m-kuung-to῾.
Unkind 無人情 ῾mo-yan-ts'ing.
Unlawful, 不合法 ῾m-hop-faat῾.
Unless, 若唔係 yeuk-῾m-hai῾.
Unlike, 不似 ῾m-῾ts'ze.
Unlimited, 無限 ῾mo-haan῾.
Unload, 出貨 ch'uut-foh῾, 卸貨 se῾-foh῾.
Unloose, 解甩 ῾kaai-lut.
Unlucky, 凶 huung, 不好彩 ῾m-῾ho-ts'oi῾.
Unmanly, 非大丈夫 fi-taai῾-cheung῾-foo, ῾m-hai῾-taai῾-cheung῾-foo, 小人哉 ῾siu-yan-tsoi.
Unmerciful, 殘忍 ts'aan-῾yan.
Unmitigated
Unmixed } , 盡地 tsuun῾-*ti῾.
Unmodified
Unnatural, 逆性 yik-sing῾, 反常 ῾faan-sheung.

Unnecessary, 不使 'm-ʿshai, 不使亦得 'm-ʿshai-y'-tak, 不必 pat-pit.	Unremitting, 不歇 pat-hit'.
	Unrepining, 不懷怨 pat-waai-uen'.
Unnoticed / Unobserved } 睇不出 ʿtai-'m-chʻuut.	Unreserved, 直白 chik-paak, 坦易 ʿtʻaan-i'.
Unofficial, 民間 mun-kaan.	Unrestrained / Unrestricted } 無限 ʿmo-haan'.
Unpardonable, 不赦得用 'm-sheʼ-tak-lut.	Unrighteous, 不義 pat-i'.
Unpleasant, 不合情 'm-hop-tsʻing.	Unripe, 未熟 mi'-shuuk.
Unpolluted, 不沾污 pat-chim-oo.	Unroll, 展開 ʿchin-hoi.
Unpopular, 不得人心 'm-tak-yan-sum.	Unruly, 不守法 pat-ʿshau-faat', 放肆 fong'-sze'.
Unprecedented, 從來無 tsʻuung-loi-ʿmo.	Unsafe, 不穩 'm-ʿwan, 險 ʿhim.
Unprejudiced, 無偏 ʿmo-pʻin.	Unsatisfactory, 不如意 'm-ue-i'.
Unprepared, 無準備 ʿmo-ʿchuun-pi'.	Unsay, 反口 ʿfaan-ʿhau, 反轉話 ʿfaan-chuen'-wa.
Unprincipled, 無道理 ʿmo-to'-ʿli.	Unseasonable, 不着時 'm-cheuk-shi.
Unprofitable, 無益 ʿmo-yik.	Unseemly, 不合式 'm-hop-shik, 不好意思 'm-ʿho-i'-sze', 醜 ʿchʻau.
Unreasonable. 無情理 ʿmo-tsʻing-ʿli.	Unselfish, 無私心 ʿmo-sze-sum.
Unrelenting, 無可憐 ʿmo-ʿhoh-lin.	Unsettle, 搖動 iu-tuung'.

【不使】不必。
【睇不出】未被注意的；被忽视的。
【不赦得用】不可原谅的，不可宽恕的。
【反口】收回说出去的话。

注释

【不好手势】技术不好。
【不着】不适合。
【拗颈】倔强的。
【僭分】不能保证的。
【不喜接】不受欢迎的，不被接受的。

| UNT | 277 | UPH |

Unsightly, 貌醜 maau²-ʻchʻau, 不好睇 ʼm-ʻho-tʻai.
Unskilful, 不好手勢 ʼm-ʻho-shau-shai².
Unsociable, 無和氣 ʻmo-woh-hi², 冷 ʻlaang.
Unsophisticated, 不乖巧 ʼm-kwai-ʻhaau.
Unsound, 不堅實 ʼm-kin-shat.
Unspeakable, 言不能盡 in-pat-nang-tsuun².
Unspotted } 無瑕疵 ʻmo-ha-tsʻze.
Unstained
Unsteady, 無定向 ʻmo-ting²-heung², 不穩 ʼm-ʻwun.
Unsuitable, 不着 ʼm-cheuk.
Unsurpassed, 未有勝過 mi²-yau-shing²-kwoh².
Unteachable, 不受教 ʼm-shau²-kaau².
Unthankful, 忘恩 mong-yan.
Untidy, 不齊整 ʼm-tsʻai-ʻching.

Until, 至到 chi²-to², 等到 ʻtang-to².
Untoward } 拗頸 aau²-ʻkeng.
Untractable
Untrue, 不眞 ʼm-chan.
Unusual, 非常 fi-sheung, 非俗 fi-tsuuk, 深 shum.
Unwarrantable, 僭分 tsʻim²-fuu².
Unwearied, 無倦 ʻmo-kuen², 無瘁 ʻmo-kooi².
Unwelcome, 不喜接 ʼm-ʻhi-tsip².
Unwell, 不受用 ʼm-shau²-yuung².
Unwilling, 不肯 ʼm-ʻhang, 不願 ʼm-uen², 不中意 ʼm-chuung-i².
Unworthy, 不堪 pat-hom.
Up, upon, 在 — 上 tsoi² — sheung², (to go) 上 ʻsheung, (get) 起 ʻhi, (raise) 舉 ʻkue.
Upbraid, 罵 ma², 鬧 naau², 譏誚 ki-tsʻiu².
Uphold, 扶持 foo-chʻi.

Upper, 上 sheung⸒, (of a shoe) 面 *min⸒.	Urine, 尿 niu⸒.
Upright, 企 ⸌k'i, 直立 chik-laap, (just) 正直 ching⸒-chik.	Urn, 礛 t'aap⸒, 缸 kong.
	Ursa major, 北斗 pak-⸌tau.
	Urticaria, 寒粒 hohn-nup.
Uproar, 吧嗍 pa-pai, 嘈亂 ts'o-luen⸒, 拉亂 la-luen⸒.	Us, 我地 ⸌ngoh-ti⸒.
	Use, (to) 使 ⸌shai, 用 yuung⸒, (treat) 待 toi⸒.
Upset, (to) 打倒 ⸌ta-⸌to, (price) 至平 chi⸒-p'eng, 開價 hoi-ka⸒.	Useful, 便用 pin⸒-yuung⸒.
	Useless, 無中用 ⸌mo-chuung-yuung⸒.
Upshot, 結果 kit⸒-⸌kwoh.	Usual, 平常 p'ing-sheung. 尋常 ts'um-sheung.
Upside down, 顛倒 tin-⸌to.	
Upstairs, 樓上 lau-sheung⸒, (go) 土樓 sheung-*lau.	Usurp, 霸佔 pa⸒-chim⸒, 搶奪 ⸌tseung-tuet.
	Usury, 利息重 li⸒-sik-⸌ch'uung.
Upwards, 向上高 heung⸒-sheung⸒-ko, (of) ——零 ——ling, ——幾 ——⸌ki, ——把 ——⸌pa, ——以上 ——i-sheung⸒.	Utensil, 器皿 hi⸒-ming.
	Uterine, 同胞 t'uung-paau.
	Utmost, 至極 chi⸒-kik, 十分 shap-fun.
	Utter, (to) 講出 ⸌kong-ch'uut.
Urbanity, 禮貌 ⸌lai-maau⸒.	Utterance, 口角 ⸌hau-kok⸒, 口鉗 ⸌hau-k'im.
Urge, 催逼 ts'ui-pik, 嗁 ngai.	
Urgent, 急 kup, 着緊 cheuk-⸌kan.	Utterly, 清楚 ts'ing-⸌ch'oh. 盡地 tsuun⸒-*ti⸒.
Urinate, 屙溺 oh-niu⸒, 小便 ⸌siu-pin.	Uvula, 吊鐘 tiu⸒-chuung.

注 释

【企】站。
【吧嗍】吵闹。
【至平】最便宜。
【寒粒】荨麻疹。
【吊钟】悬雍垂（俗称"小舌"）。

> 注 释

【娇奢温】自高自大的，爱虚荣的。
【幅衽】帷幔。
【定风旗】风向标。

V

Vacancy, (office) 缺 k'uet›.
Vacant, 空虛 huung-hue.
Vacate, 搬空 poon-huung, (an office) 卸 se›.
Vacation, 空閒 huung-haan, 假 ka›, 散班 saan›-paan.
Vaccinate, 閹痘 im-*tau›, 種洋痘 chuung›-yeung-*tau›.
Vacillate, 反覆 ‹faan-fuuk, 朝三暮四 chiu-saam-moo›-sze›.
Vagabond, 浪蕩 long› (‹long) tong›.
Vagina, 陰戶 yum-oo›, 產門 ‹ch'aan-moon.
Vagrant, 遊手 yau-‹shau, 流離 lau-li.
Vague, 舒闊 shue-foot›, 恍惚 ‹fong-fut, 泛 faan›.
Vain, 裝腔 chong-,hong, 虛浮 hue-fau, (proud) 嬌奢溫 kiu-ch'e-wun, (in) 虛徒 hue-t'o.

Valance, 幅衽 fuuk-*yum.
Valerian, 孩兒菊 hoi-i-kuuk.
Valetudinary, 養病 ‹yeung-peng›.
Valiant, 勇敢 ‹yuung-‹kom.
Valid, 妥當 ‹t'oh-tong›.
Valise, 皮箱 p'i-‹seung.
Valley, 山谷 shaan-kuuk, 谷 kuuk.
Valour, 勇氣 ‹yuung-hi›.
Valuable, 貴重 kwai›-chuung›.
Value, 價 ka›, (of) 值錢 chik-*ts'in, (to prize) 貴重 kwai›-chuung›, (to) 估價 ‹koo-ka›.
Valve, 弇 ‹im, 蓋 koi›.
Vampire, (蝙蝠 p'in-fuuk), 蝠鼠 fuuk-‹shue.
Van, 先鋒 sin-,fuung, 前隊 ts'in-tui›.
Vane, 風信旗 ,fuung-suun›-k‘i, 定風旗 ting›-,fuung-k‘i.
Vanish, 銷滅 siu-mit, (disappear) 絕迹 tsuet-tsik, 無曉 ›mo-hiu.

| VEI | 280 | VEN |

Vanity, 虛幻 *hue-waan'*.
Vapour, 氣 *hi'*, (rising) 烟蓬蓬 *in-puung'-puung'*, (of water) 水氣 *'shui-hi'*.
Vapouring, 虛誇 *hue-k'wa*.
Variance, 爭 *chaang*.
Variegated, 斑色 *paan-shik*.
Various, 各樣 *kok'-yeung'*, 不定 *pat-ting'*.
Varnish, 明油 *ming-*yau*, (lacquer) 漆 *ts'at*.
Vary, 變轉 *pin'-'chuen*, 參差 *ts'aam-ts'ze*.
Vase, 花罇 *fa-'tsuun*, 花瓶 *fa-*p'ing*.
Vast, 甚大 *shum'-taai'*.
Vault, (cellar) 地牢 *ti'-lo*.
Vaunt, 誇大 *k'wa-taai'*.
Veer, 轉 *chuen'*, 轉彎 *'chuen'-waan*.
Vegetable, 菜 *ts'oi'*, (kingdom) 草木 *'ts'o-muuk*.
Vehement, 猛 *'mang*.
Vehicle, 載車 *tsoi'-ch'e*.
Veil, (to) 遮護 *che-oo'*, (a) 蓋面紗 *koi'-min'-'sha*.

Vein, 回血管 *ooi-huet-'koon*, (streak) 紋 *mun*.
Velocity, (relative) 快慢 *faai'-maan'*.
Velvet, 剪絨 *'tsin-*yuung*, 多羅絨 *toh-loh-*yuung*.
Venal, 買得 *'maai-tak*, *'maai-tak-ke'*, 買囑得 *'maai-chuuk-tak*.
Venerable, 老成 *'lo-shing*, 老 *'lo*.
Venerate, 尊重 *tsuen-chuung'*.
Venerial, 春情 *ch'uun-ts'ing*, *ch'uun-ts'ing-ke'*, 交合 *kaau-hop*, 花柳 *fa-'lau*.
Venetians, 百葉窗 *paak'-ip-'ch'eung*.
Vengeance, (to take) 報仇 *po'-ch'au*.
Venial, 恕得過 *shue'-tak-kwoh'*.
Venison, 鹿肉 **luuk-yuuk*.
Venom, 毒 *tuuk*.
Vent, (escape) 去路 *hue'-lo'*, 通籠 *t'uung-'luung*.

注 释

【买得】用金钱买来的。
【恕得过】可宽恕的。
【通籠】通风口。

注释

Verb: 现译为"动词"，"生字、活字"是旧时的译法。
【呡门】边缘。
【系天顶处】在头顶。
【胞仔】泡儿。

VER　281　VES

Ventilate, 通風 t'uung-fuung.
Ventricle, 竅 k'iu', 寵 ¸luung, 房 fong.
Venture, 敢 ¸kom, (hazard) 拚 p'oon'.
Venus, (planet) 金星 ¸Kum-¸sing.
Veracity, 老實 ¸lo-shat.
Verandah, 騎樓 k'e-*lau, 天臺 t'in-*t'oi.
Verb, 活字 oot-tsze', 生字 shang-tsze'.
Verbal, (spoken) 口話 ¸hau-wa'.
Verbatim, 句句相同 kue'-kue'-seung-t'uung, 逐字 chuuk-tsze'.
Verbose, 贅累 chui'-lui'.
Verdant, 青活 ts'ing-oot, 秀茂 sau'-mau'.
Verdict, 批判 p'ai-p'oon'.
Verdigris, 銅綠 t'uung-luuk.
Verge, (on the) 呡門 mun'-moon.
Verify, 證驗 ching'-im'.

Vermicelli, 粉絲 ¸fun-¸sze, 粉仔 ¸fun-¸tsai.
Vermilion, 銀硃粉 ngan-chue-¸fun.
Vermin, 蟲 ch'uung.
Vernal, 春 ch'uun.
Verse, (poetry) 詩 ¸shi, (a) 節 tsit'.
Versed in, 熟 shuuk.
Version, (a) 翻譯書 fuan-yik-shue, (more than one) 重譯 ch'uung-yik.
Vertex, 頂 ¸teng.
Vertical, (to be) 喺天頂處 ¸hai-t'in-¸teng-shue', 頂天 ¸ting-t'in.
Vertigo, 頭暈 t'au-wan, (wun).
Very, 實首 shat-¸shau, 實在 shat-tsoi', 十分 shap-fun, 好 ¸ho, 甚 shum', 太 t'aai', 極 kik.
Vesicle, 胞仔 p'aau-¸tsai, 泡仔 p'aau'-¸tsai, ¸p'o ¸tsai.
Vessel, 器皿 hi'-¸ming, (ship) 船 shuen.

Vest, (a) 背心 pooi'-sum.
Vested estate, 實業 shat-ip.
Vestige, 蘚痕 'sin-han, 痕迹 han-tsik.
Veteran, 老手 'lo-'shau, 老主固 'lo-'chue-*koo'.
Vex, 撓 'naau, 煩擾 faan-'iu, 難爲 naan-wai, (irritate) 激 kik.
Vexed, 煩悶 faan-moon', 煩惱 faan-'no, 淹悶 im-moon'.
Vial, 小玻璃罇 'siu-'poh-'li-'tsuun.
Viands, 肴饌 ngaau-chaan'.
Vibrate, 搖郁 iu-yuuk, 擺動 'paai-tuung', (quiver) 震 chan'.
Vice, 惡端 ok'-tuen, 弊病 pai'-peng'.
Vice, (a tool) 老鼠鋏 'lo-'shue-*kaap'.
Viceroy, 總督 'tsuung-tuuk, 制臺 chi'-t'oi.
Vicinity, 近處 kan'-ch'ue'.
Vicissitude, 更變 kang-pin'.

Victimize, 當牛使 tong'-ngau-'shai.
Victory, 獲勝 wok-shing', 得勝 tak-shing', (a) 贏一陣 yeng-yat-chan'.
Victuals, 飯食 faan'-shik, 飯 faan', 食 shik.
Vie, 鬥 tau', 爭先 chaang-sin.
View, (to) 睇見 't'ai-kin', 看見 hohn'-kin', (a) 光景 kwong-'king.
Vigorous, 壯健 chong'-kin'.
Vigour, 力量 lik-leung', 精神 tsing-shan.
Vile, 醜 'ch'au, 惡 ok', (mean) 下賤 ha'-tsin'.
Vilify, 譭謗 'wai-p'ong'.
Village, 鄉村 heung-ts'uen, 鄉下 heung-*ha', (a) 條村 t'iu-ts'uen.
Villain, 光棍 kwong-kwun'.
Villainous, 黑心 hak-sum, 奸狡 kaan-'kaau, (ugly) 醜 'ch'au.

注释

Violin: 现译为"小提琴"，"四弦乐器"为当时的译法。
【元神】男子气，元气。
【有形色】看得见的。
【甕想】幻想。
【人客】访问者，参观者。

Vindicate, 保護 ʻpo-oo’, 表白 ʻpiu-paak, (avenge) 報仇 po’-chʻau.
Vine, 菩提樹 pʻo-tʻai-shue’, (葡萄 pʻo-tʻo).
Vinegar, 醋 tsʻo’.
Violate, 犯 faan’, (defile) 汚辱 oo-yuuk.
Violence, 強 kʻeung, (to use) 強 ʻkʻeung.
Violent, 猛烈 ʻmang-lit.
Violet, 紫羅蘭 ʻtsze-loh-laan, 菫菜 ʻkan-tsʻoi.
Violin, 四弦樂器 sze-in-ngok-hi’.
Viper, 毒蛇 tuuk-she, 飯匙頭 faan’-shi-tʻau.
Virago, 惡婆 okʻ-*pʻoh.
Virgin, 童女 tʻuung-ʻnue, 處女 ʻchʻue-ʻnue.
Virility, 元神 uen-shan.
Virtue, 德 tak.
Virulent, 鴆毒 shum-tuuk.
Viscera, the five, 五臟 ʻng-tsong’.
Visible, 有形色 ʻyau-ying-shik.

Vision, (faculty) 眼官 ʻngaan-koon, (a) 異像 i’-tseung’.
Visionary, 甕想 uung’-ʻseung.
Visit, 探見 tʻaam’-kin’, 見 kin’.
Visiting-card, 名帖 ming-*tʻip’.
Visitor, 人客 yan-haak’, (a lady) 堂客 tʻong-*haak’.
Vital, 關性命 kwaan-sing’-ming’, 要關 iu-kwaan.
Vitals, 命門 ming’-moon.
Vitiate, 整壞 ʻching-waai’.
Vitriol, (blue) 膽礬 ʻtaam-faan.
Vivacious } 活潑 oot-pʻoot’.
Vivid }
Viviparous, 胎生 tʻoi-shang.
Vocal, 口音 ʻhau-ʻyam.
Vocation, 事業 sze’-ip.
Vociferate, 喧嘩 huen-wa, 嘈吵 tsʻo-ʻchʻaau.

Vogue, 時欵 shi-ʻfoon.
Voice, 聲 sheng, 聲氣 sheng-hi.
Void, 空 huung.
Volatile, 曾飛散 ʻooi-fi-ʻsaan.
Volcano, 火山 ʻfoh-shaan.
Voluble, 油嘴 yau-ʻtsui.
Volume, 本 ʻpoon, 部 poʼ.
Voluntarily, 甘心 kom-sum.
Voluntary, 情願 tsʻing-uenʼ, tsʻing-uenʼ-keʼ.
Volunteers, 民牡 mun-chong, 義兵 iʼ-ping, (to raise rebel-) 起義 ʻhi-iʼ.
Voluptuary, 膏粱子弟 ko-leung-ʻtsze-taiʼ.
Vomit, 嘔 ʻau.
Voracious, 大食 taaiʼ-shik, taaiʼ-shik-keʼ, 貪食 tʻaam-shik, 爲食 waiʼ-shik.
Vortex, 漩水心 suen-ʻshui-sum.
Vote for, 舉 ʻkue, 願舉 uenʼ-ʻkue.
Voucher, 憑據 pʻang-kueʼ.
Vow, 許願 ʻhue-uenʼ, 誓願 shaiʼ-uenʼ.

Voyage, 水路 ʻshui-loʼ, 水程 ʻshui-chʻing.
Vulgar, 俗 tsuuk, (low) 市井 ʻshi-ʻtseng.
Vulture, 鸇 chin.

W

Wabble, 轉得鬆 ʻchuen-tak-suung.
Wadded, 綿納 min-naap.
Waddle, 咄吓咄吓 tut-ʻha-tut-ʻha, ʻleung-pin-chaap.
Wade, 涇水 kaangʼ-ʻshui.
Wafer, 火漆片 foh-tsʻat-pʻinʼ.
Waffles, 夾餅 kaapʼ-ʻpeng.
Waft, 飄流 pʻiu-lau.
Wag, (a) 好趣人 ʻho-tsʻueʼ-yan, (to) 擺 ʻpaai, 搖 iu.
Wager, 賭賽 ʻto-tsʻoiʼ.
Wages, 工錢 kuung-*tsʻin, 工銀 kuung-*ngan, 人工 yan-kuung.
Waggle, 調調侒 tiuʼ-tiu-fingʼ.

【时欵】时尚的款式。
【油嘴】健谈的。
【棉纳】棉絮，棉袄。
【好趣人】爱说笑打趣的人。
【调调侒】来回摇动。

| WAL | 285 | WAR |

Waggon, 載貨車 tsoi³-foh³-c‘he.
Wagtail, 鶺鴒 tsek³-ling.
Wail, 哀哭 oi-huuk.
Waist, 腰 iu.
Waistcoat, 背心 pooi³-ˌsum.
Wait, 等候 ˈtang-hau³, 等下 ˈtang-*ha³.
Wait on, (serve) 服事 fuuk-sze³.
Waiter, 事仔 sze³-ˌtsai.
Waive, 由得 yau-tak.
Wake, 醒 ˈseng, (from sleep) 瞓醒 fun³-ˈseng.
Waken, 打醒 ˈta-ˈseng, 叫醒 kiu³-ˈseng.
Walk, (to) 行 hang, 行路 hang-lo³, (take a) 去逛 hue³-k‘waang³, (path) 小路 ˈsiu-lo³.
Wall, 牆 ts‘eung, 壁 pik, (a) 幅牆 fuuk-ts‘eung.
Wallow, 攣 luen, 展轉 ˈchin-ˈchuen, (like a beast in the mud) 陷溦 aam³-paan³ (paam³), (in the water) 陷水 aam³-shui.

Walnut, 核桃 hop-t‘o.
Wampee, 黃皮 wong-*p‘i.
Wan, 白白地 paak-paak-*ti³.
Wand, 枝鞭杆 chi-ˌpin-ˌkohn.
Wander, 流離 lau-li, 週遊 chau-yau, (miss the way) 蕩失路 tong³-shai-lo³.
Wane, 衰 shui, 虧 fai, (of the moon) 月缺 uet-k‘uet³.
Want, 要 iu³, (defect) 缺乏 k‘uet³-fat, (destitution) 窮飢 k‘uung-ki, 坳翳 aau-ai.
Wanton, 好色 ho³-shik, 好嫖 ho³-p‘iu, 放蕩 fong³-tong³.
War, 打仗 ˈta-cheung³, 戰事 chin³-sze³, 交兵 kaau-ping, 干戈 kohn-kwoh.
War-vessel, 兵船 ping-shuen.
Ward, (division) 街坊 ˌkaai-ˌfong, (apartment) 房 *fong, (to) 防守 fong-ˈshau.

注 释

【事仔】服务生。
【陷水】沉溺。
【枝鞭杆】枝干。
【荡失路】迷路。

Wardrobe, 衣服櫃 i-fuuk-kwai'.
Warehouse, 棧房 chaan'-*fong, 貨倉 foh'-ts'ong.
Wares, 貨 foh'.
Warlike, 武 ‘moo, (man) 武夫 ‘moo-foo, (arms) 干戈 kohn-kwoh.
Warm, 煖 ‘nuen. 熱 it.
Warming-pan, 煖鍋 ‘nuen-‘woh.
Warn, 儆 ‘king, 警戒 ‘king-kaai', 提醒 t'ai-‘sing, 預先話知 ue'-sin-wa'-chi.
Warp, 經線 king-sin', kaang.
Warp, (to) 攣 luen, 屈攣 wat-luen.
Warped, 攣 luen, 拗 ‘aau.
Warrant, (a) 票 p'iu', (police) 差票 ch'aai-p'iu', (to) 包保 paau-'po.
Warren, (苑囿 ‘uen-yau'), 圍 *wai.
Warrior, 勇士 ‘yuung-sze'.
Wart, 瘊子 hau-‘tsze, 飯蕊瘡 faan'-‘yui-ch'ong.
Wary, (be) 睇真 ‘t'ai-chan.
Wash, 洗 ‘sai.

Washer-man, 洗衣人 ‘sai-i-yan, ('s itch) 油蟄 yau-tsze.
Wash-stand, 面盤架 min'-*p'oon-*ka'.
Wasp, 黃蜂 wong-fuung.
Waste, (to) 費 fai', 浪費 long'-fai', 嘥 saai, saai-t'aat'.
Watch, (to) 看 hohn, (at night) 看更 hohn-kaang, 睇更 ‘t'ai-kaang, (a time-piece) 時辰鏢 shi-shan-‘piu.
Watches, (the five) 五更 ‘ng-kaang.
Watchful, 謹慎 ‘kan-shan', 醒定 ‘sing-ting'.
Watchman, 更夫 kaang-foo.
Watch-tower, 更樓 kaang-*lau.
Watch-word, 暗號 om'-*ho'.
Water, 水 ‘shui, (to) 淋 lum, 瀨 laai'.
Water-caltrops, 菱角 ling-kok', 荄 ki'.
Water-chestnut, 水栗 ‘shui-luut, 馬蹄 ‘ma-*t'ai.

注释

【龙上水】海上龙卷风。
【路客】旅人。
【蒌】外套。
【着坏】穿破，用坏。

WAX　287　WEA

Water-closet, 厕所 ts'ze-‛shoh.
Water-course, 水沟 ‛shui-kau.
Water-cresses, 水芹菜 ‛shui-k'an-ts'oi, 西洋菜 sai-yeung-ts'oi.
Water-fall, 瀑布水 puuk-po'-‛shui.
Watering-pot, 花洒 fa-‛sha.
Water-lily, 莲花 lin-‛fa.
Water-melon, 西瓜 sai-kwa.
Water-mill, 水磨 ‛shui-*moh.
Water-spout, 龙上水 luung-‛sheung-‛shui.
Watery, 淡 ‛t'aam, 生水 shang-‛shui, (thin) 稀 hi.
Wave, (of the sea) 浪 long', 波浪 poh-long', (to) 摇摆 iu-‛paai.
Waver, 反覆 ‛fuan-fuuk, 思疑 sze-i.
Waving, 浪纹 long'-*mun; 水波纹 ‛shui-poh-*mun.
Wax, 蜡 laap, (white) 虫白蜡 ch'uung-paak-laap.

Wax, (to) 长 ‛cheung, shaang, 成 shing.
Wax-candle, 蜡烛 laap-chuuk.
Way, 条路 t'iu-lo', 道路 to'-lo', (method) 方法 fong-faat.
Way-farer, 路客 lo'-haak.
Wayward, 拗颈 aau'-‛keng.
We, 我哋 ‛ngoh-ti, (our, or my) 我的 ‛ngoh-‛ti, ‛ngoh-‛ti-ke'.
Weak, 软弱 ‛uen-yeuk, (watery) 淡 ‛t'aam.
Wealth, 财帛 ts'oi-paak, (man of) 财主 ts'oi-‛chue.
Wean, 断奶 ‛tuen-‛naai.
Weapons, 利器 li'-hi', 器械 hi'-haai'.
Wear, (clothes) 穿着 ch'uen-cheuk', (a hat) 戴帽 taai'-*mo', (a shawl) 蒌 lau, (out) 着坏 cheuk'-waai', (well) 噙 k'um.
Wearisome, 劳神 lo-shan.
Weary, 疲倦 p'i-kuen', 疲倦 kau'-kuen', kooi'.

Weasel, 鼬鼠 yau-ʽshue.
Weather, 天氣 tʻin-hi', 天時 tʻin-shi, (good) 好天 ʽho-tʻin, (hot) 天時熱 tʻin-shi-it.
Weather-cock, 順風魚 shuunʼ-fuung-*ue.
Weave, 織 chik.
Web, 一機布 yat-ki-poʼ.
Web-footed, 脚指間有膜 keuk'-ʽchi-kaan-yau-*mok, 鵝掌 ngoh-ʽcheung.
Wed, 娶親 tsʻueʽ-tsʻan.
Wedding, 婚姻 fun-yan.
Wedding sedan, 花轎 fa-*kiuʼ.
Wedge, 尖橕 tsim-chaangʼ, (to) 搹 sipʼ.
Wednesday, 禮拜三 ʽlai-paaiʼ-saam.
Weed, 野草 ʽye-ʽtsʻo, (to) 搣草 mangʼ-ʽtsʻo.
Week, 禮拜 ʽlai-paaiʼ.
Weep, 流淚 lau-luiʼ, 哭泣 huuk-yup, (aloud) 喊 haamʼ.
Weeping-willow, 垂楊柳 shui-yeung-ʽlau.

Weevils, 米牛 ʽmai-*ngau.
Weigh, 稱 chʻing', 兌 tui'.
Weighing-machine, 千斤秤車 tsʻin-kan-chʻing-chʻe, 磅 pongʼ.
Weights, 法碼 faatʼ-ʽma.
Weighty, 重 chʻuung.
Welcome, (to) 喜接 ʽhi-tsipʼ, 歡迎 foon-ying.
Weld, 鎔埋 yuung-maai.
Welfare, 平安 pʻing-ohn, 福 fuuk.
Well, (a) 井 ʽtseng, 眼井 ʽngaan-ʽtseng.
Well, 好 ʽho, (in health) 自在 tszeʼ-tsoiʼ, 好 ʽho, (get) 好翻 ʽho-faan.
Well done, 做得好 tsoʼ-tak-ʽho, (meat) 好熟 ʽho-shuuk, (bravo!) 好 ʽho!
West, 西 sai, (the) 西邊 sai-pin, 西方 sai-fong.
Wet, 濕 shup.
Wether, 閹羊 im-yeung.
Wet-nurse, 奶媽 ʽnaai-ʽma, 濕媽 shup-ʽma.
Whale, 海鰍魚 ʽhoi-tsʻau-*ue, 鯨魚 kʻing-ue.

注 释

【順風魚】风向标。
【尖橕/搹】楔入。
【米牛】象鼻虫。
【鎔埋】焊接。

注 释

【乜野】什么东西。
【瘕声】喘息声。
【由边处】从哪里。
【系边处来】从哪里来。
【边吓】哪里。
【边个】哪一个。
【㖭气】抽噎。
【反拗】古怪的。
【㖭声】嘎嘎声。

Wharf, 馬頭 ꞈma-t'au, 步頭 po'-t'au.
What? 乜野 mat-ꞈye? (that which) 所 ꞈshoh.
Whatever }
Whatsoever } 乜野 mat-ꞈye, 不論乜野 'm-luun-mat-ꞈye.
Wheat, 麥 mak.
Wheedle, 挪搌 noh-ꞈnun.
Wheel, 輪 luun, 車輪 ch'e-*luun, (turn the) 轉車 ꞈchuen-ch'e, (round) 輪轉 luun-ꞈchuen.
Wheel-barrow, 手車 ꞈshau-ch'e.
Wheezing, 瘕聲 ha-sheng.
When? 幾時 ꞈki-shi?
When, —个時 — koh'-shi.
Whence? 由邊處 yau-pin-ch'ue'? 係邊處來 ꞈhai-pin-ch'ue'-lai?
Whenever, 隨時 ts'ui-shi, 每逢 ꞈmooi-fuung.
Where? 邊處 pin-ch'ue'? 邊吓 pin-ꞈha? 邊位 pin-*wai'?

Where, — 个處 — koh'-ch'ue' (shue').
Whereabout, 近邊處 kan'-pin-ch'ue'.
Wherefore, 所以 ꞈshoh-ꞈi.
Whereupon, 就 tsau'.
Whet, 磨利 moh-li'.
Whether or not, — 係唔係 — hai'-'m-hai', — 是不是 — shi'-pat-shi'.
Which? 邊個 pin-koh'? 邊的 pin-ꞈti? (that which) 所 ꞈshoh, (that by which) 所以 ꞈshoh-ꞈi.
While, (a) 一時間 yat-shi-kaan.
Whilst, 當—個時 tong —koh'-shi.
Whimper, 㖭氣 shok'-hi'.
Whimsical, 反拗 ꞈfaan-aau'.
Whine, 㖭聲 nge-sheng.
Whip, (horse-) 馬鞭 ꞈma-pin, (to) 鞭打 pin-ꞈta.
Whirl, 窗窗轉 ꞈt'um-ꞈt'um-chuen'.

Whirlpool, 漩水心 suen-ʿshui-sum, 倒槽水 ʿto-tsʿo-ʿshui.	Who, ——個個—— ʿkoh-koh'.
Whirlwind, 旋風 suen-fuung.	Whole, 完全 uen-tsʿuen, 一概 yat-kʿoi', 成 shing, (the) 隴總 ʿluung-ʿtsuung, hamʿ-pang-langʾ.
Whisk, 拂 faak'.	
Whiskers, 鬍 im, 鬍鬚 oo-lim-so.	Wholesale, 發行 faatʾ-hong.
	Wholesome, 爽 ʿshong.
Whisper, 陰聲講 yum-sheng-ʿkong.	Wholly, 嘥 saai', 盡地 tsuunʾ-*tiʾ.
Whistle, (to) 吹音 chʿui-yum, 嘯 siuʾ, (a) 啤啤 pi-pi.	Whore, 娼妓 chʿeung-ki', 老舉 ʿlo-ʿkue.
	Whose? 乜誰嘅 mat-*shui-ke'?
Whit, 絲毫 sze-ho, 一的 yat-tik.	Why? 爲乜事幹 wai'-mat-szeʾ-kohn? 因何 yan-hoh? 做乜 tsoʾ-mat?
White, 白色 paak-shik, 白 paak.	
Whitebait, 銀魚仔 ngan-ue-ʿtsai, 白飯魚 paak-faanʾ-*ue.	Wick, (lamp-) 燈心 tang-sum.
	Wicked, 惡 okʾ, 惡僻 okʾ-pʿik.
Whites, 白帶 paak-taai'.	Wickerwork, 用籐編做 yuungʾ-tʿang-pin-tsoʾ.
White-wash, 灑灰水 ʿsha-fooi-ʿshui, 掃白 soʾ-paak.	Wicket gate, 篳門 patʾ-moon.
Whiting, 長魚 chʿeung-ue.	Wide, 廣闊 ʿkwong-footʾ.
Whitlow, 指甲疽 ʿchi-kaapʾ-tsue.	Widgeon, 鷖 i.
Who? 乜誰 mat-shui(*shui)? 邊個 pin-koh'?	Widow, 寡婦 ʿkwa-foo, 寡母婆 ʿkwa-ʿmoo-*pʿoh.

注释

【揸】拿，挥。
【固意】故意的，任性的。
【矯埋】绕在一起。
【清数】(账户)收支平衡，没有欠款。

Widower, 寡佬 ʿkwa-ʿlo, 鰥夫 kwaan-foo.
Wield, 揸 cha.
Wife, 老婆 ʿlo-pʻoh, (respectfully) 妻室 tsʻai-shat, 妻 tsʻai, (your) 夫人 foo-yan, 令正 lingʾ-ching.
Wig, (for women) 網巾 ʿmong-ʿkan, (false hair) 頭髮 tʻau-piʾ, (for the cue) 辮排 pin-*pʻaai.
Wild, 野 ʿye, (mad) 狂 kʻwong, (roving) 放蕩 fongʾ-tongʾ.
Wilderness, 曠野 fongʾ-ʿye, 野外 ʿye-ngoiʾ.
Wile, 詭計 ʿkwai-kaiʾ.
Will, (a) 囑書 chuuk-shue, 遺書 wai-shue, (wish) 主意 ʿchue-iʾ, 志意 chiʾ-iʾ, (future tense) 將 tseungʾ, 要 iuʾ.
Wilful, 固意 kooʾ-iʾ, 固執 kooʾ-chup.
Willing, 肯 ʿhang, 中意 chuungʾ-iʾ.
Willingly, 甘心 kom-sum.

Willow, 柳樹 ʿlau-shueʾ.
Wily, 乖巧 kwaai-ʿhaau.
Win, 贏 yeng.
Wince, (to) 畏縮 waiʾ-shuuk.
Wind, (to) 纏埋 chinʾ-maai, 矯埋 ʿkʻiu-maai, (up) 摺埋 chipʾ-maai, (a watch) 上鏈 ʿsheung-*lin, (an account) 清數 tsʻing-shoʾ, (an affair) 了事 ʿliu-szeʾ.
Wind, (the) 風 fuung.
Winding, 彎曲 waan-huuk.
Windpipe, 硬喉 ngaangʾ-hau, 氣管 hiʾ-ʿkoon.
Windlass, 轆轤 luuk-lo, luut-ʿloh.
Window, 窗 ʿchʻeung, 窗門 ʿchʻeung-*moon.
Window-bars, 窗遏 ʿchʻeung-aatʾ.
Windward, 風邊 fuung-pin (pinʾ).
Wine, 酒 ʿtsau, (port) 黑酒 hak-ʿtsau, (sherry) 白酒 paak-ʿtsau, (claret) 紅酒 huung-ʿtsau.

Wine-strainer, 酒漏 ʻtsau-*lau?.

Wing, 翼 yik.

Wink, 眨眼 chaap? (yap)-ʻngaan, 打眼色 ʻta-ʻngaan-shik, (at) 詐不見 cha?-ʻm-kin?, 姑縱 koo-tsuung?.

Winnow, 吹穅 chʻui-hong, 簸穀 poh?-kuuk.

Winnowing-machine, 風櫃 fuung-kwai?.

Winter, 冬天 tuung-tʻin, 冬令 tuung-ling?, (hold the winter festival) 做冬 tso?-tuung.

Wipe, 抹 moot?, maat?, 搇 ʻkiu.

Wire,——線——sin?.

Wisdom, 智 chi?, 智識 chi?-shik, 智慧 chi?-wai?.

Wish, 願欲 uen?-yuuk, 願 uen?, 想 ʻseung, 愛 oi?, 宜得 i-tak, 情願 tsʻing-uen?, (what is wished) 所願 ʻshoh-uen?.

Wistaria, 紫籐花 ʻtsze-tʻang-.fa.

Wit, 詼諧 fooi-haai, 講笑 ʻkong-siu?, 笑話 siu-*wa?, (ready) 快口 faai-ʻhau, (lost wits) 喪心 song?-sum.

Witch, 覡婆 ʻsheng-pʻoh.

With, 共 kuung?, 同埋 tʻuung-maai, 湊 tsʻau?, (by) 使 ʻshai, 俾 ʻpi, 用 yuung.

Withdraw, (go) 退 tʻui?, 離開 li-hoi, (take) 收翻 shau-fnan.

Wither, 乾萎 kohn-ʻwai, 焦乾 tsiu-kohn, 凋謝 tiu-tse?, 殘 tsʻaan.

Withhold, 不俾 ʼm-ʻpi.

Within, 裏頭 ʻlue-tʻau, ʻlue-ʻtai, 在內 tsoi?-noi?, 內中 noi?-ɡhuung.

Without, 外頭 ngoi?-tʻau, (wanting) 無 ʻmo, mo.

Withstand, 擋住 ʻtong-chue?, 拒住 ʻkʻue-chue?, 抵住 ʻtai-chue?, 敵住 tik-chue?.

注释

【觋公】巫师。
【肥蛛】木虱。
【好手势】好手艺。
【菘蓝】板蓝根。

Witness, (a) 証人 ching'-yan, 千証 kohn-ching', 見証 kin'-ching', (to) 親見 ts'an-kin', (bear) 質証 chat-ching', 作證 tsok'-ching', 做見証 tso'-kin'-ching'.
Wizard, 觋公 ʻsheng-kuung.
Woad, 菘藍 suung-laam.
Woe, 禍 woh', 禍哉 woh'-tsoi!
Woful, 凄涼 ts'ai-leung.
Wolf, 豺狼 ch'aai-long.
Wolf's bane, 蔦頭 oo-t'au.
Woman, 女人 ʻnue-ʻyan, 婦女 ʻfoo-ʻnue, 婦人 ʻfoo-yan.
Womankind, (disrespectfully) 女流 ʻnue-lau, (the attraction of) 女色 ʻnue-shik.
Womanly, 女德 ʻnue-tak.
Womb, 胎 t'oi.
Wonder, (to) 見奇 kin'-k'i, (a) 奇事 k'i-sze', (not to know) 不知得 ʻm-chi-tak.

Wonderful, 出奇 ch'uut-k'i, 奇怪 k'i-kwaai'.
Wont, (accustomed) 慣 kwaan'.
Woo, 乞憐 hat-lin, 求愛 k'au-oi', 求配 k'au-p'ooi'.
Wood, 木 muuk, (forest) 樹林 shue'-lum.
Wood-louse, 肥蛛 fi-chue, 鼠婦 ʻshue-ʻfoo, 硬殼蟲 ngaang'-hok'-ch'nung.
Wood-pecker, 啄木鳥 teuk'-muuk-ʻniu.
Woof, 緯線 ʻwai-sin'.
Wool, 羊毛 yeung-mo.
Woollens, 絨 °ynung, 氈 ʻchin.
Word, (written) 字 tsze', (spoken) 音 yum, 話 wa', 個字眼 koh'-tsze'-ʻngaan, (news) 音 yum, (the Word) 道 To'.
Work, 工夫 kuung-foo, (to) 做工夫 tso'-kuung-foo, 打工 ʻta-ʻkuung.
Workman, 工人 kuung-yan, (good) 好手勢 ʻho-ʻshau-shai'.

World, 世 shai⁻, 世界 shai⁻-kaai⁻, (the whole) 普天下 ꞌpʻo-tʻin-ha⁻, (the present) 今世 kum-shai, (the future) 來世 loi-shai⁻.

Worldly custom, 世俗 shai⁻-tsuuk.

Worm, (earth-) 黃犬 wong-ꞌhuen.

Worms, 蟲 chʻuung, 蚯蚓 yauꞌ-yan, (internal) 蛔蟲 ooi-chʻuung.

Wormwood, 茵陳蒿 yan-chʻan-ho.

Worried, 淹悶 im-moon⁻.

Worry, (bite) 咬壞 ꞌngaau-waai⁻ (tease) 難爲 naan-wai, 撈亂 lo-luen⁻, 混賬 wan⁻-cheung⁻.

Worse, 更不好 kang⁻-pat-ꞌho, kang⁻-ꞌm-ꞌho, 重弊 chuung⁻-pai⁻, 惡過 okʻ-kwoh⁻.

Worship, 崇拜 shuung-paai⁻, 拜 paai⁻.

Worst, 至惡 chiꞌ-okꞌ.

Worsted, 絨線 yuung-sin⁻.

Worth, 值 chik, 抵 ꞌtai, 抵得 ꞌtai-tak, (virtue) 德 tak.

Worthy, 堪 hom, (man) 賢人 in-yan.

Would, 欲 yuuk, 願 uen⁻, 想 ꞌseung, (-that) 恨不得 han⁻-pat-tak, 巴不得 pa-ꞌm-tak.

Wound, 傷 sheung, (to) 傷親 sheung-tsʻan.

Wrangle, 嗌交 aai⁻-ꞌkaau.

Wrap, 打包 ꞌta-paau, 包裹 paau-ꞌkwoh, 包好 paau-ꞌho.

Wrapper, 包袱 paau-fauk.

Wrath, 震怒 chan⁻-no⁻, 忿怒 ꞌfun-no⁻.

Wreck, (a ship) 破船 pʻohꞌ-shuen, 破爛隻船 pʻohꞌ-laan⁻-chekꞌ-shuen.

Wren, 鷦鷯 tsiu-liu.

Wrestle, 角力 kokꞌ-lik, 較勝 kaau⁻-shing⁻, 鬥力 tau⁻-lik.

Wretched, 凄涼 tsʻai-leung, 凄慘 tsʻai-tsʻaam.

注释

【挛捐】蠕动
【咪咪吓】扭动的样子。
【打喊露】打呵欠。
【系咯】就是。

Wriggle, 挛捐 *luen-kuen*, 嫋娜 'niu-'noh, (as a worm) 咪咪吓 'miu-'miu-ha.
Wring, (dry) 扭乾 'nau-kohn, (out) 扭出 'nau-ch'uut, 撚 'nin.
Wrinkle, 绉纹 tsau²-*mun, (to) 绉埋 tsau²-maai, ch'aau-maai.
Wrist, 手腕 'shau-'oon, 手眼骨 'shau-'ngaan-kwut.
Write, 写 'se, 写字 'se-tsze² (*tsze²), (down) 写落 'se-lok, (an essay, &c.) 作 tsok².
Writhe, 抽搐 ch'au-ch'uuk.
Wrong, 错 ts'oh², 不着 'm-cheuk, (all) 错晒 ts'oh²-saai², (to) 损害 'suen-hoi².
Wry, 歪 waai, 'me, 斜 ts'e, (to make a, face) 扯歪面 'ch'e-'me-min².

Y

Yak, 犛牛 li-ngau.
Yam, 大薯 taai²-shue.
Yama, 阎罗 Im-loh.
Yard, (of a ship) 杠 kong², (measure) 码尺 'ma-ch'ek².
Yarn, 纱 sha, 线 sin².
Yawn, 打喊露 'ta-haam²-lo².
Year, 年 nin, 岁 sui².
Yearn, 痛想 t'uung²-seung.
Yeast, 酵母 kaau²-mo, 酒饼 'tsau-peng.
Yell, 大喊 taai²-haam².
Yellow, 黄 wong, 黄色 wong-shik.
Yes, 系咯 hai²-lok, 是 shi².
Yesterday, 昨日 tsok-yat, 寻日 ts'um-mat, k'um-yat, (the day before) 前日 ts'in-yat, (the day before that) 大前日 taai²-ts'in-yat.
Yesternight, 昨晚 tsok-'maan.
Yet, 尚 sheung², 重 chuung², (not) 未曾 mi²-ts'ang.

Yew-tree, 榯樹 ˈfi-shue².
Yield, (submit) 歸服 kwai-fuuk, (bend) 屈 wut, (produce) 產 ˈchʻaan, (concede) 許准 ˈhue-ˈchuun, (up) 讓 yeung².
Yoke, 軛 aak, (of oxen) 對牛 tui²-ngau.
Yolk, 蛋黃 taan²-*wong.
Yonder, 個處地方 koh²-ˈshue²-ti²-ˌfong.
You, 你 ˈni, (PLUR.) 你地 ˈni-ti², 你等 ˈni-ˌtang, (See Thee).
Young, 少年 shiu²-nin, 少嫩 shiu²-nuen², 年輕仔 nin-hing, (of animals) 仔 ˈtsai.
Young gentleman, 少爺 shiu²-ye.
Young lady, 姑娘 koo-neung.
Your, 你嘅 ˈni-ke², 你地 ˈni-ti².
Youth, (time of) 年輕時 nin-hing-shi, (a) 後生 hau²-ˌshaang.

Z

Zeal, 烈熱之意 lit-it-chi-i².
Zealous, 發憤 faat²-fun, 憤烈 fun-lit.
Zebra, 虎斑馬 ˈfoo-paan-ˌma.
Zedoary, 高良薑 ko-leung-keung.
Zenith, 天頂 tʻin-ˈteng.
Zest, 滋味 tsze-mi².
Zigzag, 之字 chi-tsze².
Zinc, 白鉛 paak-uen, 窩擇 woh-chaak.
Zizyphus, 棗 ˈtso.
Zodiac, 黃道 wong-to², 日道 yat-to², (signs of, Chinese) 二十八宿 i²-shap-paat²-suuk.
Zone, 帶道 taai²-to².